# Inside the Film Factory

Soviet Cinema

General editors: Richard Taylor and Ian Christie

**The Film Factory**
Russian and Soviet cinema in documents 1896–1939
*ed. Richard Taylor and Ian Christie*

**Inside the Film Factory**
New approaches to Russian and Soviet cinema
*ed. Richard Taylor and Ian Christie*

**Eisenstein Rediscovered**
*ed. Ian Christie and Richard Taylor*

**Stalinism and Soviet Cinema**
*ed. Richard Taylor and Derek Spring*

**Early Cinema in Russia and its Cultural Reception**
*Yuri Tsivian*

# Inside the Film Factory

New approaches to
Russian and Soviet cinema

Edited by
Richard Taylor and Ian Christie

London and New York

First published in 1991 by Routledge

First published in paperback in 1994
by Routledge
11 New Fetter Lane, London EC4P 4EE

Simultaneously published in the USA and Canada
by Routledge
29 West 35th Street, New York, NY 10001

The collection as a whole © 1991, 1994 Routledge; individual chapters
© 1991, 1994 the respective contributors

Typeset in 10/12 pt Linotron Times by
Rowland Phototypesetting Ltd, Bury St Edmunds, Suffolk
Printed in Great Britain by
T.J. Press (Padstow) Ltd, Padstow, Cornwall

*British Library Cataloguing in Publication Data*
Inside the film factory: new approaches to Russian and Soviet cinema.
 1. Soviet cinema films, history
 I. Taylor, Richard   II. Christie, Ian
 791.430947

*Library of Congress Cataloging-in-Publication Data*
Inside the film factory: new approaches to Russian and Soviet cinema / edited by
  Ian Christie and Richard Taylor.
    p.    cm. – (Soviet cinema series)
  Includes bibliographical references and index.
    1. Motion pictures – Soviet Union.   2. Motion pictures – Political aspects –
Soviet Union.   I. Christie, Ian.   II. Taylor, Richard.   III. Series.
PN1993.5.R9157   1991
791.43'0947 – dc20                                                    90-40795

ISBN 0–415–11595–7

for
Naum Kleiman
without whom no tour
*Inside the Film Factory*
would be complete

At work shooting a film; photograph of an unidentified production from Yevgeni Petrov's book, *What the Cinema Actor Needs to Know* (Moscow: 1926).

# Contents

*Illustrations*                                                      ix
*Notes on contributors*                                             xi
*Notes on contributions*                                           xiii
*General editors' preface*                                          xv
*Acknowledgements*                                                 xvii
*Note on transliteration and translation*                          xix

**Introduction: Entering the film factory**
*Richard Taylor and Ian Christie*                                    1

1 **Early Russian cinema: some observations**
   *Yuri Tsivian*                                                    7

2 **Kuleshov's experiments and the new anthropology of the actor**
   *Mikhail Yampolsky*                                              31

3 *Intolerance* **and the Soviets: a historical investigation**
   *Vance Kepley, Jr*                                               51

4 **The origins of Soviet cinema: a study in industry development**
   *Vance Kepley, Jr*                                               60

5 **Down to earth: *Aelita* relocated**
   *Ian Christie*                                                   80

6 **The return of the native: Yakov Protazanov and Soviet cinema**
   *Denise J. Youngblood*                                          103

7 **A face to the *shtetl*: Soviet Yiddish cinema, 1924–36**
   *J. Hoberman*                                                   124

8 **A fickle man, or portrait of Boris Barnet as a Soviet director**
   *Bernard Eisenschitz*                                          151

9 **Interview with Alexander Medvedkin**                           165

10 **Making sense of early Soviet sound**
    *Ian Christie*                                                 176

**11  Ideology as mass entertainment: Boris Shumyatsky and Soviet cinema in the 1930s**
  *Richard Taylor*                                                                    193

  *Notes*                                                                             217
  *Index*                                                                             248

# Illustrations

Frontispiece: Shooting a film

1 Poster for *Stenka Razin*      14
2 *Boris Godunov*      22
3 'Action score' for a Kuleshov Workshop étude      34
4 Kuleshov Workshop performance      43
5 *Intolerance*      55
6 *The Bear's Wedding*      71
7 'Koloss' cinema foyer      78
8 *Aelita*      83
9 *Aelita*      88
10 *Aelita*      95
11 *Satan Triumphant*      108
12 *His Call*      115
13 *The Tailor from Torzhok*      115
14 *Without a Dowry*      121
15 *Jewish Luck*      126
16 *Through Tears*      133
17 *The Return of Nathan Becker*      141
18 *The Girl With the Hat-Box*      154
19 *The Old Jockey*      157
20 *Happiness*      172
21 *Komsomol – Patron of Electrification*      185
22 *The Deserter*      189
23 Soundproofing the first Soviet sound studio      199
24 *The Happy Guys*      209
25 *Chapayev*      212

# Notes on contributors

Richard Taylor is Senior Lecturer in Politics and Russian Studies at the University College of Swansea. His books include *The Politics of the Soviet Cinema, 1917–1929*, *Film Propaganda: Soviet Russia and Nazi Germany*, *The Poetics of Cinema* (editor and part translator) and, with Ian Christie, *The Film Factory: Russian and Soviet Cinema in Documents 1896–1939*. He is currently working on *A Cinema for the Millions: Socialist Realism and Soviet Cinema, 1929–38*.

Ian Christie is Head of Distribution at the British Film Institute where he has helped to foster a renewed interest in both classic and contemporary Soviet cinema. His books include *FEKS, Formalism, Futurism: 'Eccentrism' and Soviet Cinema 1918–36* (co-editor, with John Gillett), *Powell, Pressburger and Others* (editor), *Arrows of Desire: The Films of Michael Powell and Emeric Pressburger* and, with Richard Taylor, *The Film Factory: Russian and Soviet Cinema in Documents 1896–1939*.

Yuri Tsivian is a Senior Research Fellow of the Institute of Language and Literature of the Latvian Academy of Sciences in Riga and headed the team of scholars in charge of the programme to restore the prints of pre-Revolutionary Russian films held in the Gosfilmofond archives. He has published widely on cinema in the Soviet Union and edited *Silent Witnesses: Russian Films, 1908–1919*.

Mikhail Yampolsky is a Senior Research Fellow of the All-Union Research Institute for the History of Cinema in Moscow. He has published widely on film theory, with special reference to France and Russia.

Vance Kepley, Jr is Associate Professor of Film at the University of Wisconsin-Madison. He has published *In the Service of the State: The Cinema of Alexander Dovzhenko* and a number of articles on Soviet cinema, and is currently working on a book on Eisenstein.

Denise J. Youngblood is Assistant Professor of History at the University of Vermont. Author of *Soviet Cinema in the Silent Era, 1918–1935* and a number of articles on early Soviet film, she is currently working on a book on popular cinema and Soviet society in the 1920s.

J. Hoberman writes on film for *The Village Voice* and is an adjunct Professor in the Cinema Studies Department at New York University. He is author of a forthcoming history of Yiddish cinema, to be published by the New York Museum of Modern Art.

Bernard Eisenschitz is a writer, film critic and cinema historian, formerly a member of the editorial board of *Cahiers du cinéma*, who has written widely in French on various aspects of Soviet cinema.

Alexander Medvedkin (1900–89) was a Soviet film director best known in the West for his film *Happiness* released in 1935. He was also responsible for the film train that toured the Donbass region in the early 1930s.

# Notes on contributions

Ian Christie's 'Down to earth: *Aelita* relocated', Denise Youngblood's 'The return of the native: Yakov Protazanov and Soviet cinema', and J. Hoberman's 'A face to the *shtetl*: Soviet Yiddish cinema, 1924–36' were written specially for this volume.

Yuri Tsivian's piece on 'Early Russian cinema: some observations' was written specially for this collection and is a considerably expanded version of 'Some Preparatory Remarks on Russian Cinema', in Yuri Tsivian *et al.* (eds), *Silent Witnesses. Russian Films, 1908–1919* (London and Pordenone: 1989), pp. 24–43. It was translated from the Russian by Richard Taylor.

Mikhail Yampolsky's 'Kuleshov's experiments and the new anthropology of the actor' has been slightly expanded from 'Les expériences de Kuleshov et la nouvelle anthropologie de l'acteur', which first appeared in *Iris*, vol. 4, no. 1 (1986), pp. 25–47. It was translated from the Russian by Richard Taylor.

Vance Kepley's '*Intolerance* and the Soviets: a historical investigation' is a slightly revised version of the article that appeared in *Wide Angle*, vol. 3, no. 1 (1979), pp. 22–7. The Russian prologue to *Intolerance* was first published by Viktor Listov in *Iz istorii kino*, no. 9 (Moscow: 1974), pp. 188–91, and is here translated from the Russian by Richard Taylor from a draft by Betty and Vance Kepley. 'The origins of Soviet cinema: a study in industry development' first appeared in *Quarterly Review of Film Studies*, vol. 10, no. 1 (Winter 1985), pp. 22–38, and is published here with minor revisions.

Bernard Eisenschitz's 'A fickle man, or portrait of Boris Barnet as a Soviet director' is a revised version of 'Un homme léger, ou Boris Barnet en metteur-en-scène soviétique', which appeared in: F. Albera and R. Cosandey (eds), *Boris Barnet. Ecrits. Documents. Etudes. Filmographie* (Locarno: 1985), pp. 174–93, and is here translated from the French by Ian Christie.

Alexander Medvedkin was interviewed by the late Martin Walsh and the Swedish researcher Kate Betz at the FIAF Congress in Varna, Bulgaria, in June 1977 and again by Richard Taylor at Dom kino, Moscow, in March 1985. Richard Taylor has translated, condensed and annotated both interviews from the Russian.

Ian Christie's 'Making sense of early Soviet sound' is a revised version of the article which first appeared as 'Soviet Cinema: Making Sense of Sound' in *Screen*, vol. 23, no. 2 (July/August 1982), pp. 34–49.

Richard Taylor's 'Ideology as mass entertainment: Boris Shumyatsky and Soviet cinema in the 1930s' is a slightly revised version of the article which first appeared in *Historical Journal of Film, Radio and Television*, vol. 6, no. 1 (1986), pp. 43–64.

The editors and contributors are grateful to the above-mentioned for the necessary copyright permissions.

# General editors' preface

Cinema has been the predominant popular art form of the first half of the twentieth century, at least in Europe and North America. Nowhere has this been more apparent than in the Soviet Union, where Lenin's remark that 'of all the arts for us cinema is the most important' has become a cliché and where cinema attendances today are still amongst the highest in the world. In the age of mass politics Soviet cinema has developed from a fragile but effective tool to gain support among the overwhelmingly illiterate peasant masses in the Civil War that followed the October 1917 Revolution, through a welter of experimentation into a mass weapon of propaganda through entertainment that shaped the public image of the Soviet Union – both at home and abroad and for both elite and mass audiences – and latterly into an instrument to expose the weaknesses of the past and present in the twin processes of *glasnost* and *perestroika*.

Cinema's central position in Soviet cultural history and its unique combination of mass medium, art form and entertainment industry, have made it a continuing battleground for conflicts of broader ideological and artistic significance, not only for the Soviet Union but also for the world outside. The debates that raged in the 1920s about the relative revolutionary merits of documentary as opposed to fiction film, of cinema as opposed to theatre or painting, or of the proper role of cinema in the forging of post-Revolutionary Soviet culture and the shaping of the new Soviet man, have their echoes in current discussions about the role of cinema *vis-à-vis* other art forms in effecting the cultural and psychological revolution necessitated by the process of the economic and political transformation of the Soviet Union into a modern democratic and industrial society and a state governed by the rule of law. Cinema's central position has also made it a vital instrument for scrutinising the blank pages of Soviet history and enabling the present generation to come to terms with its own past.

This series of books will examine Soviet films in the context of Soviet cinema, and Soviet cinema in the context of the political and cultural history of both the Soviet Union and the world at large. Within that framework the series, drawing its authors from both East and West, will cover a wide variety of topics and employ a broad range of methodological approaches and presentational formats. Inevitably this will involve ploughing once again over familiar ground in order to re-examine received opinions but it will principally mean increasing the breadth and depth of our knowledge, finding new answers to old questions and, above all, raising new questions for further enquiry and new areas for further research.

The continuing aim of the series will be to situate Soviet cinema in its proper historical and aesthetic context, both as a major cultural force in Soviet politics and as a crucible for experimentation that is of central significance to the development of world cinema culture. Books in the series will strive to combine the best of scholarship, past, present and future, with a style of writing that is accessible to a broad readership, whether that readership's primary interest lies in cinema or in Soviet political history.

Richard Taylor and Ian Christie

# Acknowledgements

Richard Taylor would like to thank the British Academy, the Kennan Institute (Washington, DC), the British Film Institute and the University College of Swansea for the financial assistance that made possible the original contacts from which this project has emerged. He would also like to express his heartfelt gratitude to Professor George Boyce for arranging the leave that made completion of the project possible, to Phyllis Roberts for unfailingly protecting him at vital moments from the trials and tribulations of reality, to Andrew Braddel for his assistance in overcoming obstacles to international communications, and Roger Davies for technical help. Lastly, he would like to thank most warmly of all his family and friends, especially Melva Taylor, Jeffrey Richards and Peter Matthews, for their generous support and encouragement, and Richard Shannon for a veritable montage of attractions.

Ian Christie would like to express his gratitude to present and former colleagues at the British Film Institute, notably Jayne Pilling, John Gillett and Clare Kitson, for many kinds of assistance. Acknowledgement is also due to Patsy Nightingale, for her unstinting tolerance and support, and to Melanie Tebb, for invaluable help throughout the editorial process.

We should both like to acknowledge the enormous debt we owe to our friends and colleagues among Soviet film historians, especially to Naum Kleiman, to whom this volume is dedicated with affection, to Yuri Tsivian and Mikhail Yampolsky, who have contributed essays, and to Rashit Yangirov, who has contributed in other ways with generous guidance, hospitality and support. We hope that this volume will be adequate recompense.

Richard Taylor
Ian Christie
London, January 1990

## PHOTO CREDITS

E. Petrov, *Chto dolzhen znat' kino-akter*, Moscow 1926 (frontispiece); Paolo Cherchi Usai/Gosfilmofond/Le Giornate del Cinema Muto, Pordenone (1, 2, 11); BFI Stills, Posters and Designs (9, 10, 14, 19, 20, 24); USSR Central State Archive of Literature and Art (TsGALI)/Ekaterina Khokhlova, *Lev Kuleshov: Fifty Years in Films*, Leningrad, 1987 (3, 4); BFI Distribution (5, 6, 22); *Teatralno-dekoratsionnoe iskusstva v USSR 1917–1927*, Leningrad 1927 (7); Ian Christie (8, 12, 13, 18, 21); Museum of Modern Art Film Stills Archive (15); J. Hoberman (16, 17); Contemporary Films (25); Nikolai Anoshchenko (23). Thanks are also due to the staffs of the Pacific Film Archive, Berkeley, and of BFI Stills, Posters and Designs for their kind co-operation, and to Erich Sargeant of BFI Distribution for technical assistance.

# Note on transliteration and translation

Transliteration from the Cyrillic to the Latin alphabet is a perennial problem for writers on Russian subjects. We have opted for a dual system: in the text we have transliterated in a way that will, we hope, render Russian names and terms more accessible to the non-specialist while in the scholarly apparatus we have adhered to a more accurate system for the specialist. Accepted English spellings of Russian names have been used wherever possible and Russian names of Germanic origin have been returned to their roots.

The translation of film titles poses problems as Russian does not have either an indefinite or a definite article. We have preferred to insert an article: hence *The Battleship Potemkin*, *The Arsenal*, etc. The convention by which Soviet films are known by bald titles like *Earth*, *Mother*, *Strike* is itself arbitrary: consider, for example, how Chekhov's plays have become known in English as *The Seagull* and *The Cherry Orchard*, but *Three Sisters*.

# Introduction
## Entering the film factory

*Richard Taylor and Ian Christie*

*Inside the Film Factory*, as its title suggests, begins where our previous collaboration *The Film Factory* left off. Whereas that anthology of documents aimed to provide the reader with a tool-kit with which to reopen the set questions of Russian and Soviet cinema history, this collection of essays is intended to point towards some of the ways in which those questions might be approached and answered in different ways, to indicate some of the new questions that might profitably be posed and to suggest some of the neglected areas that require further investigation.

It was the underlying premiss of *The Film Factory*, as expressed in Ian Christie's introductory essay, 'Soviet cinema: a heritage and its history', that Western – and indeed Soviet – views of the history of Soviet cinema had become overloaded with the canons of the past to the point where over-determined categorisation and periodisation had left the subject stranded in a whole series of blind alleys:

> The history of the early Soviet cinema has become a prisoner of its own mythology. When western historians and critics speak of 'Soviet revol-utionary cinema', they are invoking a very specific construct which, together with German Expressionism and Italian Neo-Realism, consti-tutes a cornerstone of the art-cinema tradition. . . . [The] continuing western preoccupation with a small group of 'masters' and their early work in the silent period, together with what seems like a wilful ignorance of their less famous contemporaries and of the furious debates that raged around Soviet cinema's policy direction throughout the decade before 1935 – these suggest that the actual history of Russian and early Soviet cinema has long been the victim of a self-confirming diagnosis, now enshrined in a persuasive mythology.[1]

It is our intention that *Inside the Film Factory* should broaden and deepen the challenge to that hitherto so persuasive mythology, taking advantage both of some of the questions raised by *The Film Factory* and of the major changes taking place in the Soviet historiography of Soviet cinema now that previously unaskable questions can be, and increasingly are being, asked.

If both history and historiography are seen as processes, then it stands to reason that no single historical event can be seen in isolation and no single historical period cut off from the preceding and succeeding periods by the historical equivalent of a scholarly iron curtain. We have after all argued elsewhere against the rigid periodisation of the subject itself. It follows therefore that the re-evaluation of the history of Soviet cinema is not something that has appeared out of the blue, any more than have the processes of *glasnost* and *perestroika* that have accelerated that re-evaluation. It is for this reason that we have chosen to include in the volume a number of reprinted articles that share a common questioning of the old shibboleths, by pursuing new approaches, by investigating new areas, by uncovering new evidence, or by a combination of these techniques. The inclusion of two pieces by Vance Kepley is an intentional tribute to his pioneering work: taken together, and with the addition of the translation of the Russian prologue to *Intolerance*, they exemplify these three basic methods of reappraisal. Similarly, Ian Christie's essay on 'Making sense of early Soviet sound' argues for a more complex reading of the conjunctions that 'divided' the 1920s from the 1930s than the oversimplistic good/bad normative judgement that has hitherto prevailed. Richard Taylor's piece on Boris Shumyatsky, previously merely reviled as the man who stopped Eisenstein's *Bezhin Meadow*, examines the role of the administrator/ bureaucrat during the period of what to current reformist orthodoxy is known as 'administrative command socialism' and argues for a more subtly shaded interpretation of his place in the development of Soviet cinema. Both this and Kepley's essay on 'The origins of Soviet cinema' presuppose a consideration of cinema not merely as an aesthetic phenomenon, an art form, but also as an administrative and industrial complex, with all the additional perspectives that this implies.

Part of the re-examination of the subject must also involve an attempt to bring the English-speaking reader up to date with ground-breaking articles published in other languages. For this reason we have included Bernard Eisenschitz's essay on the relatively little-known director, Boris Barnet, one of 'the less famous contemporaries' referred to above, but nevertheless a director whose career spanned a longer period than did those of the 'small group of "masters"' in the established canon. For the same reason we have also translated Mikhail Yampolsky's article on the context of Lev Kuleshov's theory of acting, which originally appeared in French. But another, and even more compelling, reason for including this is that it represents the very best of the wide-ranging research now being pursued by Soviet scholars, especially those of the younger generation. There is a similar justification for the inclusion of the opening essay by Yuri Tsivian, although the implications of his piece and the issues that he raises provide their own more than adequate justification. Apart from Leyda's pioneering sketch in *Kino* and the project supervised by Tsivian himself and only recently published, the pre-Revolutionary period is virtually a blank page in the history of Russian and Soviet cinema.[2] Tsivian's essay opens up numerous fields for further investigation, undermines another prevailing periodisation of Russian and Soviet cinema history, that between the pre- and post-Revolutionary epochs, and raises some absolutely fundamental questions.

What was the real relationship between theatre and cinema, and between theatre and cinema workers, in the early period? How widespread was the audience for film before the Revolution; what kind of audience was it; what kind of films did it want to see, and what kind of films did it actually see? How far has the founding ideology of the Revolution and its legitimising mythology obscured the achievements of this early period of Russian film-making? How far has this distorted our subsequent view of the ways in which the immediate post-Revolutionary generation reacted against the tenets of its predecessors, or indeed the ways in which the second generation in the 1930s might have been restoring, consciously or unconsciously, some kind of continuity with the pre-Revolutionary traditions?

To a certain extent the answers to at least some of these questions can be approached through direct contact with the surviving veterans of generations of Soviet film-makers, although memoir materials always have to be treated with a certain degree of caution. In the case of Soviet history the frailties of human memory have been exacerbated by the perceived need to justify past acquiescences, to settle old scores, to 'set the record straight' in what can all too often be a very particular and subjective sense. Nevertheless, as the *Cinema in Revolution* collection amply demonstrated,[3] the direct contact afforded by interviews with those who actively participated in the drama more often than not outweighs the difficulties encountered and provides us with a unique insight into the motivations of past film-makers and the conflicting pressures under which they worked. Too often these are obscured by the 'benefit' of our own historical hindsight! We have therefore included hitherto unpublished interview material with another 'less famous contemporary', Alexander Medvedkin, which clearly demonstrates both the strengths and weaknesses of this particular method of investigation.

Last, but most certainly not least, *Inside the Film Factory* includes essays written specifically for this collection which cover new ground in various ways. Two of them, by Ian Christie and Denise J. Youngblood, address complementary aspects of the career of Yakov Protazanov, one of the most popular of Russian and Soviet film directors with mass audiences, a film-maker whose first script was filmed in 1909, whose works encompassed the whole gamut of genres and whose last film was completed in 1943, a pre-Revolutionary figure who went into emigration and came back at a time when others were still leaving – in other words, a man whose career invalidates the conventional stereotypes even more than does the career of Boris Barnet. That we have devoted two contributions out of eleven to his reappraisal is a sign of the importance we attach to the task in hand and to the new perspectives that his re-evaluation opens up. Hoberman's essay on Soviet Yiddish cinema investigates one of the most important blank pages in

Soviet cinema history and illustrates the way in which cinema history is itself caught up in the tide of broader historical patterns. It resonates also upon our conventional overall view of the period that he discusses.

The purpose of *Inside the Film Factory* is then to open new doors, not to close existing ones. It is no part of our intention to set up a new orthodoxy in place of the one that we find desperately wanting. That is why this volume encompasses a *variety* of approaches, a *variety* of materials and a *variety* of authors, as we hope will the Routledge Soviet Cinema Series as a whole. It nevertheless behoves reformers, in cinema history as elsewhere, to offer at least some indication of the areas towards which they think future efforts should be directed.

One of the most important gaps in the literature on Soviet cinema, or indeed any cinema, in any language is the absence of a thoroughly re-searched economic history of the industry. In the Soviet instance, this would throw valuable light on the day-to-day workings of the administrative machine and on the constraints that helped to shape policy towards pro-duction, distribution and exhibition. It would also illuminate the nature of the relationship between commercial and ideological considerations – including the international dimensions – in the policy-making process and clarify the impact of organisational changes on the kind of films made. Finally, it would help us to understand more precisely the role of the studio and its own administrative hierarchy in the actual process of film production and the ways in which that role has changed from the 1920s to the present day.

There is also a place for a series of monographs examining the roles of particular individuals in the history of Soviet cinema. Readers may wonder why there is scarcely a mention of Eisenstein or his films in the present volume. They may rest assured that it is no part of our intention to devalue his contribution; on the contrary, a volume based on papers given at the 1988 Oxford Eisenstein Conference is in hand under the working title *Eisenstein Rediscovered*, which explores fresh perspectives on this crucial figure. There is indeed also a need for re-examination of other key figures in the canon – Pudovkin, Vertov and Kuleshov – and an even more pressing need for an investigation of those film-makers outside the established canon, such as Barnet, Protazanov and Medvedkin, or the FEKS group [Fabrika ekstsen-tricheskogo aktëra (Factory of the Eccentric Actor)], where our own paths first crossed. But the greatest need is simply to broaden the agenda – and not just in the Soviet context – so that we come to consider the history of cinema not just as the history of film directors but as the interactive history of all the individuals involved: directors, scriptwriters, cameramen, actors, designers, studio administrators, politicians – and of individuals who at various times performed more than one of these functions.

There is, for instance, no full study in any language of the role played in Soviet cinema by the man who supervised its first decade, Anatoli Lunacharsky, the People's Commissar for Enlightenment, whose wife,

Nataliya Rozenel, was a popular film actress in the 1920s and who himself scripted a number of films, including the horror hit *The Bear's Wedding* in 1925. Even a close examination of his scripts and of the films made from them might well provide us with a valuable new perspective on what was expected officially from Soviet cinema in the early period, and that in turn might throw up new continuities for us to consider. Similarly very little is known of the role played by such 'enabling' figures from the studios as Adrian Piotrovsky or Moisei Aleinikov, or by a historian and teacher like Venyamin Vishnevsky.

But cinema history cannot, of course, be merely the history of individuals: it must also be the history of the context within which those individuals were active. This has to include a consideration of the changing audience, its expectations and its reactions, and that leads us on to examine the role played by film critics and historians in the development of Soviet cinema. It also involves an examination of the relationship between that cinema and its audience and, more specifically, the reception of the films that were actually produced. Lastly, it must also include a study of the studio system and its implications and of the overall political context within which Soviet cinema has developed.

*Inside the Film Factory* is therefore only one step along the road, although we naturally hope that it will be a significant one. The need now is for a more concerted effort to extract more information and to make more sophisticated use of it. As the Soviet Union rejoins the world community, contact between Soviet and Western scholars proliferates. This provides us with an unparalleled opportunity to combine the methodologies that have been developed over the decades by Western scholars and critics – many originally deriving from Soviet sources – with the information that is more easily accessible to Soviet scholars in their archives and libraries. As more blank pages are filled, so others will appear: such is the nature of historical research, but collaboration in the future will bring us closer to the elusive goal of historical truth than have confrontation and all-too-frequently wilful misrepresentation – on both sides – in the past. If *Inside the Film Factory* and the series that it inaugurates help to promote that collaboration, they will have served their purpose.

We enter the film factory with trepidation, but not entirely without hope.

# 1 Early Russian cinema: some observations

*Yuri Tsivian*

A first encounter with early Russian cinema usually raises several puzzling questions. More often than not these questions are of the same kind: they concern the distinguishing features of the Russian film style that set it apart from the generally accepted practice of the 1910s. There is some sense in dwelling on these features, both to disperse doubt in the audience's mind and to understand the link between 'Russian style' in cinema and certain characteristics of Russian culture.

## RUSSIAN ENDINGS

In 1918 two cinema publications, one Russian and one American, made an identical observation independently of one another. *The Moving Picture World*, after viewing a batch of Russian pictures that had just arrived in the USA, confirmed the view of its own correspondent:

> As was pointed out in the first and favourable review of these films in *The Moving Picture World*, the tragic note is frequently sounded; this is in marked contrast to prevailing American methods. The Russian films, in other words, incline to what has been termed 'the inevitable ending' rather than an idealized or happy ending. That was the thing that gave the reviewers some slight shivers of apprehension as to the reception that might be accorded these films by our public.[1]

At the same time the Moscow *Kino-gazeta* was informing its readers:

> 'All's well that ends well!' This is the guiding principle of foreign cinema. But Russian cinema stubbornly refuses to accept this and goes its own way. Here it's 'All's well that ends badly' – we need tragic endings.[2]

The Russian audience's need for tragic endings was so insistent that in 1914 when Yakov Protazanov made *Drama by Telephone* [Drama u telefona], a Russian remake of Griffith's *The Lonely Villa* [USA, 1909], he had to change the ending: the husband was not in time to rescue his wife and came home to find her dead body – she had been killed by burglars. In 1918 Protazanov none the less tried to make a sentimental melodrama which ended with a wedding – *Jenny the Maid* [Gornichnaya Dzhenni] – but it is significant that he set the film abroad. In a Russian setting such a turn of events would have seemed forced.

There is nothing strange in the fact that Russian film factories, which were working to two markets – the domestic and the international – produced two different versions of the same subject. The idea undoubtedly originated with Pathé, whose Moscow office had had the international market in mind from the very beginning. When Sofya Goslavskaya, who played the leading role in André Maître's film, *The Bride of Fire* [Nevesta ognya, 1911?], wanted to watch her own film, it transpired that the film in distribution in Russia had employed other actors:

> Whereas in our first version the story was treated like a *lubok* with a happy ending – scenes of a peasant wedding with traditional ceremonies – which was made specially 'for export', in the second version, made by Kai Hansen, it was a drama which, if I'm not mistaken, ended with the deaths of the main characters.[3]

Another actress, Sofiya Giatsintova, has recalled how the firm of Thiemann & Reinhardt solved the export problem. The film *By Her Mother's Hand* [Rukoyu materi, 1913] had two endings, both made by Yakov Protazanov and both using the same actors and sets:

> One ending, the happy ending, was 'for export': Lidochka recovers. The other, more dramatic, was 'for Russia': Lidochka in her coffin.[4]

On the day after the February Revolution twenty boxes of films were hurriedly exported and so a batch of films with Russian rather than export 'tails' arrived in America. It is scarcely surprising that American reviewers were inclined to attribute their special quality to 'terrific Slavic emotions'.[5] However, one has to forewarn audiences of our time: like any generalisation about national psychology, the notion of the gloomy Russian soul was naive. 'Russian endings' came into cinema from nineteenth-century Russian theatrical melodrama, which always ended badly. Unlike the Western theatrical melodrama, the Russian version derives from classical tragedy adapted to the level of mass consciousness. Hence the only conclusion that we can draw about 'Russian endings' in cinema is one that relates to Russian mass culture as a whole: the peculiarity of Russian cinema and of Russian mass culture is its constant attempt to emulate the forms of high art. As we shall see, this attempt is conditioned by several other features of the 'Russian style' in cinema.

## THE FIRST RUSSIAN FILM

The desire in Russian cinema to compete with 'high art' was present from the very beginning. The story of how the first Russian feature film, Alexander Drankov's *Boris Godunov*, was made is indicative of this.

Traditionally *Stenka Razin*, shot by Drankov in 1908, has been accepted as the first Russian film. Drankov himself called it the 'first', conscious of the advertising value of such a description. Nevertheless *Boris Godunov*, a screen version of the tragedy by Pushkin, had already been made and shown in 1907 but Drankov preferred to forget all about it.

The history of *Boris Godunov* can be reconstructed from the texts of two unpublished memoirs, one by Moisei Aleinikov, the well-known film journalist and entrepreneur, the other by the stage actor Nikolai Orlov.[6] The events that led to the making of this film may be depicted as a chain of accidents and misunderstandings. What is more, they are entirely characteristic of the psychology of Russian cinema.

According to Aleinikov, it all began with a lottery ticket. In 1907 Aleinikov had as yet no connection with cinema but was a student at the Imperial Technical School. One day he won a lottery prize of a ticket for the Moscow Art Theatre production of Pushkin's *Boris Godunov*.

Traditionally *Boris Godunov* is regarded as difficult to stage. Pushkin preferred a minute series of fragmented excerpts to the gradual intensification of the conflict that is usual in tragedy. This particular quality, which had frightened other theatres off, was what attracted the Moscow Art Theatre. As early as 1899 Stanislavsky was nurturing the idea of a new stage form that he jokingly called the 'cinematograph' [sinematograf].[7] In the vocabulary of the Moscow Art Theatre the word 'cinematograph' developed as the designation for a show that presented the audience with a sequence of fragmented excerpts instead of a single action. In a letter to Anton Chekhov in October 1899 Vladimir Nemirovich-Danchenko explained Stanislavsky's concept:

> One could string together a large number of short pieces written by you, by Turgenev, Shchedrin and Grigorovich, or Pushkin's *The Feast in Plague-Time*. The scenes would change at the speed they change in cinema.[8]

Like *The Feast in Plague-Time*, Pushkin's tragedy *Boris Godunov* was entirely suited to this kind of stage experiment.

Let us return to Moisei Aleinikov's memoirs. At the Moscow Art Theatre performance of *Boris Godunov* he had a conversation that stuck in his memory:

> Scene followed scene. . . . There were twenty-two scenes in the play. . . . Eventually the curtain fell. . . . In the silence I heard the woman next to me remark: 'It's just like the cinema!'
>
> I thought this remark referred to the fact that we never saw the curtain but none the less, my very best feelings having been offended and prepared to deliver a rebuff, I enquired: 'In what sense?' . . .
>
> 'In cinema they also change the scenes all the time: first you're in one room, then another, and then you're on the street.'[9]

After the performance Aleinikov returned home and there he had another noteworthy conversation:

> In the hostel my neighbour in the next room held out a copy of *Cine-Phono*.
>
> 'My uncle has started publishing a cinema paper. I told him that you write for *Utro Rossii* [Morning Russia] and he wants you to write something about cinema!'
>
> I leafed through the pages and thought of the perceptive girl against whom I had taken up arms in vain. Then I remembered the arguments of Valeri Bryusov,[10] whose lecture to the Literary-Artistic Circle I had heard the day before. He had warned artists of the dangers of naturalism. . . .
>
> Mixing all these impressions together, I wrote a muddled little article, 'The Art Theatre's Production and the Cinematograph'. To liven things up I began with a report that I had made up about some discussions between the Moscow Art Theatre and a certain film company. I didactically reminded Stanislavsky that naturalism, the mere copying of life, was not art. . . . However, the author remarked that cinema would be taking a great step forward if it were to show the achievements of the Moscow Art Theatre on its screens.[11]

The lead story that Aleinikov devised 'to liven things up' (so that he had some pretext for abstract arguments) went as follows:

> According to rumours a large firm is proposing to film twenty-two scenes from *Boris Godunov* on the stage of the Moscow Art Theatre. (Based on interviews)[12]

This newspaper canard had an unexpected consequence. It excited Alexander Drankov, then a St Petersburg photographer (he and his brother Lev were the Russian photographic correspondents for the London *Times* and the Paris *Illustration*), who prepared the Russian titles for French films. Drankov was obsessed with the idea of being first to release a Russian film. The other memoir source, the actor Nikolai Orlov, recalls how Drankov, suspecting a flirtation between the Moscow Art Theatre and Khanzhonkov or the Moscow office of Pathé,[13] resolved to forestall them and produce his own Petersburg *Godunov*:

> When the idea came to him, Drankov was influenced by the newspaper rumours that a Moscow firm was intending to film twenty-two scenes of the Moscow Art Theatre production of *Boris Godunov*. Wanting to forestall this announcement, Drankov searched desperately for a theatre with *Boris Godunov* in its repertoire. That theatre turned out to be the Eden open-air theatre, where I was working as an actor at that time.[14]

As Orlov relates, the first conflict between Drankov and the actors arose over cuts. The Moscow Art Theatre took pride in the fact that, true to the structural principle of the 'cinematograph' discovered by Stanislavsky, it made practically no cuts in Pushkin's *Godunov*. As to the Eden open-air theatre production, the reviewers reproached the director, I. E. Shuvalov, for the significant cuts that he had made in the text of the tragedy.[15] None the less the conditions proposed by Drankov seemed quite absurd to the Eden actors:

> Most of the actors were opposed to this ridiculous undertaking: acting at nine o'clock in the morning in the open rather than on stage, but still using the sets. And when Drankov insisted on cutting Pushkin's tragedy, suggesting that we confine ourselves to four or five scenes, we reached an impasse.[16]

That would have been only a fifth of the whole play.

The second conflict arose over the sets. The actor G. F. Martini, who was playing the role of Grishka Otrepev,

> went on strike when he realised that the scene by the fountain would be shot without the sets but next to a real fountain that was situated between the theatre and a café-chantant. However, it was not long before Marina Mnishek (played by K. Loranskaya) and Drankov were able to convince him that everything would turn out even better by the real fountain. So they decided to start with this scene by the fountain. But it transpired that there were no trees around the fountain, and it was the view of both Martini and Loranskaya that the whole sense of the scene derived from precisely the point that Marina Mnishek suddenly appears from out of the bushes. After endless arguments Drankov decided to pay for some trees to be felled, brought along and re-erected as artificial shrubbery. . . . Next day, early in the morning, a lot of tall felled trees were brought along and laboriously erected round the fountain. They produced quite a picturesque landscape, but it was spoiled by the fact that, through the trees, you could see quite clearly and distinctly various buildings that were remote in style from the sixteenth century. . . . Martini, seeing the whole set that had been prepared for shooting, absolutely refused to start filming. He even began to take off his costume and his make-up. Once again it was Loranskaya who talked him round – she even cried, but she talked him round. We started to rehearse many times but we made no progress. The rehearsal degenerated into arguments and altercations.[17]

We must not forget that, while Drankov was an experienced photographer, *Boris Godunov* was his first excursion into shooting film for cinema. Previously he had merely shot Russian titles for V. I. Vasilieva, who owned several Petersburg cinemas. For this purpose Vasilieva had imported a second-hand Pathé camera for him from Paris.

When he took up 'moving photography', Drankov had to confront some unfamiliar problems. The first was that of changing light.

> When at last everyone had stopped arguing and agreed to 'rush' the scenes in front of the camera, it turned out that we had to move the trees. Since nine o'clock, when the trees had been erected round the fountain, the sun had moved and the shrubs were beginning to produce shadows that we didn't want. This meant that we had to change the whole *mise-en-scène* and that meant changing the set as well. Once again we began to argue: what should we change? The *mise-en-scène* or the set? Then the workmen came and began 're-making the scenery'.[18]

Drankov resolved this problem, just as Thomas Alva Edison had had to fifteen years earlier. But, whereas Edison had built a 'Black Maria' – a studio on a turntable base – Drankov's sets had to be moved each time the sun changed its position:

> We had to move the sets all the time to follow the movement of the sun. The camera, which Drankov was in charge of, moved with the sets.[19]

The second problem involved framing. In his photographic studio Drankov kept a reflex camera that he had brought from London in 1905. The owner of a camera like that naturally had no problem with framing. But the Pathé camera was another matter. It needed a certain amount of experience to capture within the frame, without a viewfinder, the precise scene that you wanted. The height and width of the sets did not allow Drankov to get far enough away. Orlov recalls:

> Drankov was disturbed more than anything else by the absence of a ceiling in the set for the Granite Palace. As he could not work out how to film a long shot of the Granite Palace from a distance, nothing came of it. Generally speaking, the whole picture had to be filmed only in medium shot. Even the boyars' procession could not be shot full-length.[20]

A year later, when Drankov was filming *Stenka Razin*, he remembered this lesson from *Boris Godunov* and declined to use sets at all. *Stenka Razin* was filmed in long and very long shot but even this was not accomplished without some errors in framing. In the 'forest revelry' scene the main characters, Stenka and the princess, are, according to tradition, placed to the left of the mass and slightly in front, but Drankov 'cut them off' almost completely on the left side of the frame. At the right side, however, a man in a bowler hat – probably Vasili Goncharov, the film's scriptwriter – jumps out of the right-hand frame for a moment and, gesticulating, shouts something to the actors.

The story of *Boris Godunov* came to an inglorious end. The lead actor, E. A. Alashevsky, who played Boris, categorically refused to be filmed. *Boris Godunov* was released without Boris Godunov. At one time the film was shown under the title *Scenes from Boyar Life* [Stseny iz boyarskoi zhizni] and later, from 1909 onwards, as *The False Dmitri* [Dmitrii samozvanets]. Later still the scene by the fountain was shown as a film recitation (see below, pp. 19–24). The film has not survived to the present day.

The example of the first Russian film is a good illustration of the dynamics of Russian culture. Russian culture was dynamic in the 'vertical' sense. When he staged *Boris Godunov* at the Moscow Art Theatre, Stanislavsky tried to get away from the canons of high tragedy. The twenty-two scenes in the production were supposed to produce the impression of the 'cinematograph'. Russian cinema, in contrast, imitated elevated models. Even though he did not know how to 'frame a shot', Drankov was already encroaching on *Boris Godunov*. When in the spring of 1908 at the international cinematographic exhibition in Hamburg the representative of a French firm heard about this, he exclaimed in astonishment, 'Fancy the Russians starting with that!'[21] In constructing the edifice of their own cinema, the Russians, as usual, had begun with the roof.

## THE SPEED OF THE ACTION

The most paradoxical of the many strange features of Russian cinema in the 1910s is the immobility of its figures. The static Russian *mise-en-scène*, which to the uninitiated might appear to be a sign of hopeless direction, in actual fact bore all the characteristics of a conscious aesthetic programme. At the centre of this programme lay the polemical formula 'film story, not film drama' which was the motto of Russian film style during the First World War.

There is preserved in Fyodor Otsep's archive the outline of a book that he was planning to write in 1913–14. He intended to have a chapter in the book on 'The Three Schools of Cinematography: 1. Movements: the American School; 2. Forms: the European School; 3. The Psychological: the Russian School'.[22] The 'psychologism' of the Russian style was defined as a denial of the external signs of 'cinema specificity' [kinematografichnost']: the dynamics of action and the dramatic quality of events. Later, in 1916, the champions of Russian style began to call American and French cinema 'film drama', a genre that in their view was superficial. 'Film drama' was contrasted with 'film story', the preferred genre of Russian cinema:

> The film story breaks decisively with all the established views on the essence of the cinematographic picture: it repudiates *movement*.[23]

But it was not only the Russian films made as 'film stories' that were judged from the standpoint of this paradoxical aesthetic doctrine. In 1916 we find a typical critical formulation in a review of the film *His Eyes* [Ego glaza], which was consistent with the Russian style:

> The scenes that are devoid of traditional cinematic movement produce a great impression.[24]

*Figure 1* Contemporary poster for Drankov's *Stenka Razin* [1908].

Sometimes even foreign films, which had apparently fallen behind Russian cinema, were treated in the same way. Hence the condescending review in *Proektor* in 1916 devoted to the American film which was released in Russia as *The Slave of Profit* [Raba nazhivy]:

> As far as the whole pace of the action is concerned, neither the director nor the cast have managed to capture that slow tempo that is so common in the Russian feature-film play. The actors are still too fidgety, as the Americans are wont to be; their acting still derives largely from the superficial, from objects and facts rather than from experiences and emotions.[25]

What in practice were the ideas behind the 'Russian style'? Genetically speaking, the aesthetics of immobility can be traced back to two sources: the psychological pauses of the Moscow Art Theatre and the acting style of Danish and Italian cinema. When they met in Russian cinema these sources transformed one another: the operatic posturing of the Italian *diva* acquired psychological motivation, while the acoustic and intonational pauses of the Moscow Art Theatre – the so-called 'Chekhov' style, which was far from presupposing a slow tempo on stage – found its plastic equivalent on the screen. That gave rise to the minimalist technique of the Russian film actor, which was dictated *inter alia* by the style of film direction. As one of the manifestos of the 'Russian style' stated:

> In the world of the screen, where everything is counted in metres, the actor's struggle for the freedom to act has led to a battle for long (in terms of metres) scenes or, more accurately, for 'full' scenes, to use Olga Gzovskaya's marvellous expression. A 'full' scene is one in which the actor is given the opportunity to depict in stage terms a specific spiritual experience, no matter how many metres it takes. The 'full' scene involves a complete rejection of the usual hurried tempo of the film drama. Instead of a rapidly changing kaleidoscope of images, it aspires to *rivet* the attention of the audience on to a single image. . . . This may sound like a paradox for the art of cinema (which derives its name from the Greek word for 'movement') but the involvement of our best actors in cinema will lead to the slowest possible tempo. . . . Each and every one of our best film actors has his or her own *style* of mime: Mosjoukine has his steely hypnotised look; Gzovskaya has a gentle, endlessly varying lyrical 'face'; Maximov has his nervous tension and Polonsky his refined grace. But with all of them, given their unusual economy of gesture, their entire acting process is subjugated to a rhythm that rises and falls particularly *slowly*. . . . It is true that this kind of portrayal is conventional, but convention is the sign of any true art.[26]

The best directors were, to a greater or lesser extent, followers of the Russian style: Chardynin, Bauer, Viskovsky, Protazanov. One of the ideologists of the style, Vladimir Gardin, called the school the 'braking school' and he had a clear claim to be its leader. Subsequently Gardin recalled:

> Protazanov developed and defined this school more by intuition than calculation. My peremptory shouts while we were filming *The Keys to Happiness* [Klyuchi schast'ya, 1913] – 'Pause!' 'The eyes!' – did not go unnoticed. He took up this method and developed it in his own direction. On more than one occasion while he was shooting, Yakov Alexandrovich would lift his conductor's baton and utter the magic word 'Pause!', sometimes holding his hand up for a long time and not letting it drop.[27]

Vladimir Gaidarov has given more details of Protazanov's method in his reminiscences about *Jenny the Maid*:

> There we were, face to face, and . . . pause, pause, pause . . . Jenny lowers her eyes . . . pause . . . she gets up quickly, turns and goes to leave. . . . Georges calls to her. . . . She lingers in the doorway without turning round . . . pause, pause . . . and then she turns and says, 'I must get your medicine. It's time for you to take it!' Pause . . . she turns and leaves . . . Georges is left alone. He looks after her . . . again pause, pause, pause. . . . Then we see his elbow resting on the arm of the chair, his head bowed towards his hand, and Georges thinking to himself, 'What a strange girl she is!' Pause, pause . . . and . . . iris.[28]

Lenny Borger, who has studied the problem of shooting speed in silent cinema, told me, after watching the films that Bauer and Protazanov made in 1916, that in his view Russian cameramen shot at a higher speed than was generally accepted, creating on screen a permanent slow-motion effect. It is possible that this was a means of insuring the film against deformation by projectionists, especially those in the provinces who were in the habit of 'driving the picture' faster than it had been shot. In 1915 Ivan Mosjoukine [Mozzhukhin], worried about the fate of the slow 'Russian style' in the hands of these projectionists, published an open letter in *Teatral'naya gazeta* calling on audiences who noticed discrepancies in speeds to 'make their protest known by banging their sticks and stamping their feet, etc.':

> The poor innocent actors jump and jerk about like cardboard clowns and the audience, which is unfamiliar with the secrets of the projection booth, stigmatises them for their lack of talent and experience. I cannot convey the feeling you experience when you watch your own scene transformed at the whim of a mere boy from normal movements into a wild dance. You feel as if you were being slandered in front of everyone and you have no way of proving your innocence.[29]

The 'Russian style' did not, of course, meet with universal approval. Its champions were grouped round the journal *Proektor*, while its opponents featured in the pages of that more 'cultured' journal *Teatral'naya gazeta*. Bauer's *Silent Witnesses* [Nemye svideteli, 1914], the paper remarked ironically, moved at about three miles an hour,[30] while his *Boris and Gleb* [Boris i Gleb, 1915] was spoilt by the rhythm it had almost found:

> The whole film is imbued with an irritating and unnecessary slowness. Unnecessary because the psychological climax emerges on screen in opposition to the drama, not through delays and pauses but, on the contrary, through accelerations. . . . The long drawn-out 'psychological' scenes allow the audience to start guessing and they have no difficulty in working out the subsequent course of events and the final denouement.[31]

Despite the paradoxical postulates of the 'Russian style', all this contributed to the fact that in the five years from 1914 to 1919, culminating in 1916, the films that were released in Russia were substantially different from the mainstream international production of the period. It was the ballet critic André Levinson who rather tellingly characterised this aesthetic system, writing in the Russian émigré paper *Poslednie novosti* in Paris in 1925 (by which time the system had already ceased to exist). Levinson recalled that pre-Revolutionary cinema

> created a style that was completely divorced from European and American experiments but enthusiastically supported by our own audiences. The scripts were full of static poetic moods, of melancholy and of the exultation or eroticism of a gypsy romance. There was no external action whatsoever. There was just enough movement to link the long drawn-out pauses, which were weighed down with languorous day-dreaming. The dramaturgy of Chekhov, which had had its day on stage, triumphed on the screen. The action of these intimate emotions was not played out against the expanse of the steppes or the steep slopes of the Caucasus, even though the steppes were as worthy as the pampas and the Caucasus as majestic as the Rocky Mountains! Russian characters dreamed 'by the hearth'. At that time the sentimental heroes of the American Vitagraph film were doing the same, abandoned by their brides, making out figures from the past through a light haze of smoke. Vera Kholodnaya and Polonsky came back from the ball in a car, facing the audience in close-up, each immersed in their own private pain; they did not look at one another and they never moved. It was in this immobility that their fate was decided. This was the drama. Nobody chased after their car. It did not gather speed. Nothing beyond its windows existed. It did not roll down a slope because the denouement did not need chance as its accomplice. However, in those years Tom Mix was already jumping from a bridge on to the roof of an express train. The 'adventure' script had triumphed. But the Russian product was preoccupied with feeling, with the vibration of the atmosphere surrounding motionless figures. The relationship between patches of black and white, the concepts of

chiaroscuro were more expressive than an occasional gesture by the characters. . . . Sometimes the banality of the attitudes and ideas was striking, but only to the Russian eye. To a Western audience this banality was something inscrutably and irrationally exotic. It is for this reason, rather than technical backwardness, that the style remained a localised phenomenon – and soon afterwards war broke out.[32]

## THE INTERTITLE

From the antithesis 'film drama'/'film story' the ideologues of the 'Russian style' derived yet another postulate: the regimen for the perception of film was rethought from scratch. 'The time has gone when we just looked at the screen: the time has come to *read* it.'[33] Films like *Tanya Skvortsova the Student* [Kursistka Tanya Skvortsova] and *His Eyes* (both 1916) openly imitated a book. In *Tanya Skvortsova* the reels were called 'chapters' rather than 'acts'. *His Eyes* began and ended with a shot of a girl leafing through the novel by Fyodorov on which the film was based; the pages of the novel also appeared during the course of the action and in the opening scene, the 'players' introduction', the characters were made to look like illustrations brought to life. When Fyodor Sologub suggested a screen version of *Lady Liza* [Baryshnya Liza] to Alexander Sanin in 1918 he absolutely insisted that the source for the screen version should be the short story rather than the play:

> I do not so much want pictures from real life, but rather as if you were turning the pages of an old, slightly naive, forgotten and touching book. What we want somehow is to look as though we are showing the pages of a book: the engravings, the vignettes, the head-pieces – all, of course, with great tact.[34]

Matters were not confined to the ornamental side. A serious reform of narrative syntax was announced. Equality between image and intertitle was proposed:

> The film story consists of two equally important elements: mimic scenes performed by artistes and literary excerpts; in other words, of picture proper and intertitles. . . . In a screen reading the 'pages' of words alternate with the 'pages' of images: both have an equal right to life.[35]

At first sight paradoxical, this did in fact correspond to the literary essence [literaturnost'] of Russian cultural consciousness. The Russian audience in the 1910s was glad to read the titles and even became anxious when a title did not appear for a long time. There is a curious case relating to the film based on a script by Hugo von Hofmannsthal, *Das fremde Mädchen* [The Strange Girl, 1913], which was shown in Russia under the title *A Mysterious Woman* [Nevedomaya zhenshchina]. The film was made as a mime and it was first distributed in the original version without titles. But this proved too disturbing, as one reviewer noted:

> This film – half fantasy, half real – did not have a single title throughout its entire length (about 1,000 metres), while the action developed so intelligibly, so freely that the fear arose almost instinctively that suddenly a title would appear and the effect would be ruined. . . . But later it was featured in one of the smaller cinemas with a large number of commonplace titles: obviously this was essential to the success of the film with the cinema-going public.[36]

In 1914 Alexander Voznesensky (who, like Hugo von Hofmannsthal, was a follower of the aesthetics of 'silence' enunciated in the famous article by Maurice Maeterlinck) decided to have another go and wrote *Tears* [Slezy], the first Russian script without words. The film was made later that year, but at the preliminary screening it was rejected by the author himself. Later Voznesensky explained:

> The shots with all their plot diversions were tiring to the eyes. Some kind of intervals were necessary. Then it became clear that in silent cinema the title does not play a purely explanatory role: rather it plays the role of a visual *entr'acte*. I suggested making a few literary inserts which would have no direct relation to the action but would provide a lyrical accompaniment to it and supplement it psychologically. This turned out to be what was needed: there were no explanations, but the visual *entr'actes* were preserved.[37]

A similar view prevailed among many who wrote about cinema in the 1910s: while titles were not really necessary, if you did not have them the loss would be that much more tangible. Lecturing on cinema in 1918, Vsevolod Meyerhold linked this effect to a longing for the word, to the logocentrism of our perception:

> Titles should be inserted not merely for clarification . . . but so that the word, which in art is so enchanting, should begin to resound. The title, which allows one to rest from the picture, should lend enchantment to the sense of the phrase.[38]

## FILM RECITATION

The logocentrism of Russian culture in the first decade of the twentieth century was not only reflected in the particular attention paid to film titles. The following episode is characteristic. In 1910 Russian papers reported the meeting in Yasnaya Polyana between two celebrities, Leonid Andreyev and Lev Tolstoy. Andreyev, who had just come back from a trip abroad, told Tolstoy about the progress of cinema in Western Europe. Tolstoy was interested and he returned to the subject the following day:

'You know,' said Lev Nikolayevich when he met me in the morning, 'I've been thinking about cinema the whole time. Even during the night I woke up and thought about it. I have decided to write something for cinema. There would of course have to be someone to read it out, like there was in Amsterdam, someone to communicate the text. Without a text it would be impossible.'[39]

By 'text' he meant the spoken commentary that, as we know, accompanied the showing of films in many cinemas right up until 1913. However, alongside the habit of film shows with a commentary from a 'lecturer' (which is what barkers were called in Russia; their performances were surrounded with the appropriate 'academic' paraphernalia: a small lectern or a table with a lamp in front of the screen), there existed in Russian cinema a peculiar genre, that of the 'film recitation' [kinodeklamatsiya] or 'speaking picture' [kinogovoryashchaya kartinag].[40] This genre emerged in 1909 and enjoyed unfailing success until 1917.

Strictly speaking, the idea of making the characters in a film 'speak' through a real-life actor seems to have originated in European cinema. We should recall that, according to the Star-Film catalogue, Méliès created a comic dialogue between the King of England (speaking French but with an accent) and the President of France for his film *Le Tunnel sous la Manche, ou le cauchemar franco-anglais* [Tunneling under the English Channel, or the Anglo-French Nightmare, France, 1907]. Lumière's earlier domestic experiment is well known. But, of course, none of these experiments reached Russia. There the 'film recitation' genre was conceived independently and the initiative came, not from the entrepreneurs, but from the actors. In the Central Film Museum Archive in Moscow there are two manuscript memoirs by 'film reciters': one by Yakov Zhdanov, a provincial actor, and the other by K. Novitskaya, who acted for, and was the first wife of, Pyotr Chardynin. Zhdanov relates in detail how he got the idea for 'talking pictures':

At that time I already knew what cinema was because I had seen several ordinary performances in Moscow at the Gryozy [Day-dreams] Cinema on Strastnoi Boulevard. The film show made such a stunning impression on me that, after the sequence with the train, I got up off the bench and went up to the screen so that I could look behind the canvas. . . . It was only after seeing these first films that I was seized with the obsession that you could add sound to a picture, so that the heroes would speak and crockery and furniture would be smashed realistically. I began to propagate this idea among my colleagues on stage and when at last the 'cinematograph pictures' appeared in our town, Ivanovo, we sat continually – even to the detriment of our work – through the performances, watching the pictures and studying the possibilities of making them 'sound'. We wanted to add sound to the pictures that might have been filmed from our own repertoire, only the more interesting ones that were suited to the conditions of cinema. . . . The actual technique of adding sound did not worry us and we thought it would all be easy and straightforward. Only time would prove how wrong we were: mastering the art of accompanying speaking pictures turned out to be a difficult matter, requiring a great deal of strenuous work. . . . I went to see Khanzhonkov but I was not allowed to meet the great man himself. The audience I was granted with his associates, Theodossiadis and Chardynin, made me realise that there was no hope for me there. They both said that I would need permission to be present at the filming and Chardynin added unambiguously that they would scarcely give me permission because cinema was a new art form 'and it should not be sullied by any kind of nonsense like stories and couplets'.[41]

If Zhdanov's account is reliable, Chardynin's behaviour was quite in character with the cinematic mores of the day: 'outliving' Zhdanov, he borrowed his idea. In any case, Novitskaya's reminiscences also deal with this notion:

When Chardynin was working for Khanzhonkov he had the idea of filming talking pictures. He did a lot of work to that end. From the outset he filmed himself, that is, he appeared in the picture and the cameraman [Boris] Zavelev filmed him. He made two pictures: *The Madman* [Sumas-shedshii], based on verses by Apukhtin, and *The Barge Haulers* [Burlaki]. He scarcely looked at them. He had very little time to travel from town to town. He decided to involve me, his wife – Novitskaya is my stage name. My first film was *The Breath of Death* [Dykhanie smerti]. He wrote the verses, it was shot in a very beautiful outdoor setting and it had a greater public success than all the others: *Don Juan Punished* [Nakazannyi Don-Zhuan], *Scenes Like This Are Unfamiliar* [Vam takie stseny nezna-komy], *Dreams, Dreams, Where is Your Fascination* [Mechty, mechty, gde vasha prelest'] and *Love Beyond the Grave* [Lyubov' za grobom].[42]

Thus it was due to Chardynin's efforts that in 1909 the genre of 'film recitation' – monologues in prose and verse, filmed and with sound added by a single actor – emerged. Meanwhile Zhdanov and his acting friends were still looking for someone who could help them realise a somewhat different project: a film involving several people speaking with different voices. This genre of film show was called 'speaking pictures'.

Zhdanov turned to Drankov 'and was pleasantly surprised at the simple reception I received, which was so different from the ceremonies at Khanzhonkov's'.[43] Drankov put his Moscow studio, where some dramatic miniatures based on Chekhov had been filmed, at Zhdanov's disposal.

The filming of 'speaking pictures' presented particular difficulties for both the actors and the cameramen. Louis Forestier has recalled how the big scene from a remake of *Boris Godunov* in 1911 was filmed:

*Figure 2* 'Speaking pictures': the cell scene from Pushkin's *Boris Godunov* filmed at the Khanzhonkov studio in 1911, to be widely toured by actors in the following year.

> The entire scene had to be filmed in one 320-metre shot but the camera only held 120 metres of negative. When the film was getting to the end we had to shout 'Stop!' to the actors. According to our prearranged plan, they had to remain rooted to the spot while I reloaded the camera. At the order 'Start' they continued acting until the end of the new reel, then stopped again and stood motionless, and so on until the end of the shot.[44]

So that they did not deviate from the text the actors had to have a prompter with them during the shooting.

But the most complicated part was the process of adding the sound. Zhdanov recalls:

> It was even worse when the picture was ready and Drankov wanted to check up on how we were getting on with the recitation. It was terribly embarrassing. We were unable to say a single word so that it matched the image and simply gabbled something hastily. The same thing happened the second time round. Another few tries produced almost exactly the same result. We were overcome with such confusion and despair that we

simply did not know where to hide our faces in shame. But Drankov tried to cheer us up, saying that perhaps after a few days of constant rehearsal we would manage something. But where and how were we to rehearse? We started searching and soon found a suitable cinema on Yelokhovskaya Street. We came to an agreement with the owner that we would have the building, light, equipment and a projectionist at our disposal and in return we were to appear for him free for as many days as we rehearsed. After four or five days we were so well prepared that we were able to start appearing before an audience.[45]

Novitskaya recalled yet another problem, which forced the reciters to rehearse all over again in each new town: the synchronisation of the speed of the projection with the rate of delivery of the monologue, because these rehearsals were more for the projectionist than for the actor:

The projectionist might project so fast that it would be difficult to catch the movement of the mouth and projecting slowly also would not work. The film had to be shown at medium-speed.[46]

'Film recitals' and 'speaking pictures' were very successful, mainly in the provinces. They gave rise to a number of touring groups: V. Niglov, D. Vaida-Sukhovy, A. Filgaber, S. Kramskoy, the Ukrainian troupe of A. Alexeyenko, the acting duo Nadezhda and Alexander Arbo, and others. In the Jewish Pale of Settlement Smolensky's 'singing' troupe was particularly successful. In 1913 *Cine-Phono* reported this event in Minsk:

Since 19 September the film reciter and vocalist, A. M. Smolensky, has been appearing at the Modern electric theatre for an extended season. He performs in Yiddish to special films, in which he plays the leading role, illustrating comic and dramatic scenes from Jewish life.[47]

The film *A Mother's Letter* [A Brivele der Mamen, 1912] was shown. In 1940 this event surfaced unexpectedly in a story by M. Daniel, the author of literary sketches of the Jewish past:

In the cinema they are showing the Yiddish picture *A Mother's Letter*. A real-life artist has come from Warsaw. He is behind the screen all the time while living people walk across it. He sings but you cannot see him.[48]

The film reciter's repertoire was rarely renewed. When the copies they owned had worn out the artistes preferred to film a new version of the same subject: the negative apparently remained at the disposal of the manufacturer. The opposite also happened: a film would pass to new performers. Sometimes the travelling troupes of 'film reciters' would buy an ordinary silent film and manage to 'add sound' to it. Hence Zhdanov's troupe appeared with Chardynin's *Dead Souls* [Mertvye dushi, 1909], in which, to the reciters' astonishment, the screen actors apparently spoke Gogol's actual lines. There were rumours that a gypsy camp had hired the film *Gypsy*

*Romances* [Tsyganskie romansy, 1914], featuring the celebrated singer M. Vavich, and were organising fake concerts.

In 1913, when Edison's 'Kinetophone' and Gaumont's 'Film Parlant' were being shown in Moscow and Petersburg to the accompaniment of a big advertising campaign, the film reciters, who were in control of the provinces, exploited the general interest in this new invention:

> Apart from textual accompaniment to the pictures in our repertoire, we have often, at the request of cinema owners and for a special fee, illustrated other pictures in the programme with sounds and noises, depicting the roar of a fire, dogs barking, cocks crowing, motor car horns, and so on. Many owners, who advertise our performances as some kind of miracle, have asked us to enter behind screens and leave unnoticed by the audience, so as to enhance the 'miracle' and the mystery of the effect.[49]

Some reciters, on the other hand, tried to exploit the effect of their presence. Novitskaya recalls:

> The audience was bewildered. What was happening? Was someone speaking or was there some equipment behind the screen? Even though on the hoardings it said that the actress Novitskaya was performing. Then I left Moscow for the provinces and there the confusion was even greater. You can't imagine it. They often asked the director to bring me out from behind the screen and put me on display. Only then were they convinced that it was an actress, and not a machine, speaking. I received invitations from all four corners of Russia and travelled across almost the entire country. I was in both large and small towns; I was in Kharkov, Kiev, Riga, Odessa. I was in remote places like Kutais. I travelled for almost three years with the pictures. I had my own manager who signed the contracts.[50]

## STAGE-SCREEN HYBRIDS

We need to mention another unusual genre in Russian cinema: stage-screen hybrids.

As was the case with the first experiments in film recitation, the combination of screen action with action on stage was not a Russian invention. However, as in the other case, Russian cinema went one stage further in the realisation of the project. This happened as a result of the efforts of the eminent theatre actor Pavel Nikolayevich Orlenev.

For the invention of the stage-screen performance we are apparently indebted to Méliès. According to Madeleine Malthête-Méliès it was in about 1905 that Méliès first realised the project that he later reproduced at the request of the organisers of the Méliès Gala anniversary retrospective in 1929:

Lost in the streets of Paris, he looked everywhere for the Salle Pleyel. . . . On a wall he saw an enormous poster for the Gala bearing a large portrait of himself. . . . He butted the poster with his head. Suddenly the lights went up in the hall. A screen was raised, revealing in the middle of the stage a frame to which the poster that we have just been was affixed. Suddenly the paper was ripped open by Méliès, appearing in the flesh.[51]

This stunt reached Russia in 1913: Max Linder repeated it in his own way when he visited Moscow and Petersburg. Here is a fragment of a newspaper report of Linder's appearance in the Zon Theatre in Petersburg:

The painful moments after the third bell passed slowly and the curtain had still not been raised. The audience hooted, stamped their feet and demanded a start – all apparently to no purpose. Eventually the director informed the audience that Max Linder was late and would probably not be coming. Those who wanted could have their money back. But no one left their seat. . . . The lights went out unexpectedly and on the screen that had appeared we watched Max Linder's journey to the Zon Theatre in a racing car along an endless road, then an accident (with no injuries whatsoever), a gallop on horseback, a swim across a river and, finally . . . a flight in a hot-air balloon, with Max Linder appearing over St Petersburg and above the roof of the Zon Theatre, where he intended to descend from the balloon by guide-rope, crashing through the ceiling straight on to the stage. . . . The screen suddenly gave way to a stage and there was Max Linder descending on a guide-rope, surrounded by plaster-work, wearing a grey sports coat and a battered and torn version of his famous top hat.[52]

In the 1920s Eisenstein realised something similar to Max Linder's stunt when he combined the performance of *The Wise Man* in the Proletkult Theatre with a screen on which the audience watched things that were happening on the roof of the same theatre. The Dadaistic ending to René Clair's *Entr'acte* [France, 1924] also resembled Méliès's exploit.

But even in the 1910s theatre remembered from time to time the opportunities that cinema had to offer. The first notion was to bring the stage sets alive. In 1911 P. Konradi wrote:

Take a set like a 'waterfall' or a 'river', which are quite common on the stage. However skilfully the canvas is painted, however 'realistically' you make it 'move', this kind of spectacle pales, in terms of its vividness and the power of the impression that it makes, in comparison with any cinematographic image of the same river and waterfall. The Maly Theatre was the first of the major Petersburg theatres to appreciate this advantage of cinema and in their production of V. P. Burenin's play *The King of Liberty* [Korol' svobody], they employed 'living photography' to depict the waterfall. The experiment was a complete success. On stage there was what looked like a real waterfall, sparkling in a cloud of spray and foam in the beams of a theatrical moon. Equally successful was the use of cinema at the People's House for a production of *20,000 Leagues Under the Sea*. In this the underwater world – a superb sequence of the actual marine depths and their various inhabitants – came to life before the audience's eyes in the window of the 'Nautilus'.[53]

In September 1911 the new Mozaika [Mosaic] Theatre opened in St Petersburg. This theatre, founded on the initiative of the well-known actor G. G. Ge, was conceived as a new type of theatre. The aim of the Mozaika was to compete with cinema. The productions were organised on the principle of the variety show, which was unfamiliar to the Russian audience. The newspaper *Artist i stsena* wrote as early as June 1911:

> Every production will include miniature operas, playlets, ballet scenes . . . and, to crown it all, a few pictures from cinema itself.[54]

In the Mozaika Theatre the film part of the production was interwoven with the stage part even more closely than in the Petersburg Maly Theatre. Here cinema did not merely perform the role of 'moving background'. In any event that was the case with the production (which caused a sensation) of *Submarine Shipwreck*, in which the screen alternated with the stage according to whether the setting for the action was an interior or an exterior. The critic B. Bentovin described the show in this way:

> To begin with, cinema shows you this submarine riding the waves in the midst of the other ships in the squadron; then catastrophe strikes: the boat sinks helplessly to the bottom. The next scene, inside the submarine hold, is played by live actors: you can hear them groaning, swearing and praying for salvation. When the sailors are suffocating to death, cinema once more shows the surface of the sea, where the squadron's ships are making all sorts of attempts to save the dying.[55]

My account of Drankov's *Boris Godunov* has already referred to the role of the 'cinematograph' in the reformist plans of the Moscow Art Theatre, although of course the theatre never lowered itself to a mechanical realisation of the idea of stage 'cinema', of experiments with stage-screen hybrids. For Stanislavsky the word 'cinematograph', when applied to theatre, signified a structural principle: fragmented dramaturgical construction, instantaneous changes of scene, portable sets. Hence the Art Theatre's love of works that were ill-suited to, or entirely unintended for, the stage: *Boris Godunov*, or Chekhov's short stories, which were staged in 1904. Later the 'cinematograph' method was used for a stage version of Dostoyevsky's novel *The Brothers Karamazov* in 1910.

The novel was broken down into short fragments. These fragments of action were linked to one another by the author's text, narrated by a special character, 'the reader'. The reader reminded the audience of the 'lecturer' in cinemas, while the actual scenic structure, alternating sections of action with sections of text, recalled the narrative regime of silent cinema: title, shot, title, shot. The critic Emmanuil Beskin, a fierce opponent of the Moscow Art Theatre, published a review in the Moscow newspaper *Rannee utro* [Early Morning] in which he used this comparison to compromise the theatre:

> The greatest page, not just in Russian, but in world literature has been crumpled. Rendered colourless. Bloodless. Mindless.
>
> Transformed into cinema. Into a film show.
>
> Scene after scene. Only instead of titles on the screen: a reader to one side.
>
> – Alyosha leaves the monastery . . .
>
> And Alyosha enters from the right slips.
>
> – Alyosha tells what has happened to him.
>
> And Alyosha remains silent, while the reader speaks. The reader finishes, and Alyosha walks on. . . .
>
> What is more, Dostoyevsky has been stylised. He is played without sets on the flat grey surface of the backdrop. . . .
>
> A series of five-minute cinematograph pictures.[56]

Vladimir Nemirovich-Danchenko, who staged *The Brothers Karamazov*, wrote to Stanislavsky about this production in October 1910:

> Something enormous has happened: there has been a colossal bloodless revolution. During the first performances there were a few who felt, but did not yet realise, that *Karamazov* marked the end of some vast process that had been maturing for ten years. What was it? It was this. Whereas with Chekhov theatre shifted the limits of convention, with *Karamazov* those limits are entirely destroyed.[57]

Developing the underlying concept of the production, he went further:

> We staged *Karamazov* against a single backdrop. This is too dogmatic. We must stage some scenes against a backdrop, others naturalistically with a proscenium arch, a third lot with almost straightforward live scenes, a fourth group like cinema, and a fifth like a ballet.[58]

As we can see, the principle of the stage 'cinematograph' as it evolved came close to the principle of variety as realised a year later on the Russian stage by the Mozaika Theatre of Miniatures. Yet neither Stanislavsky nor Nemirovich-Danchenko would have dreamed of combining theatre and cinema in the way that it was done in *Submarine Shipwreck*. I repeat: they had in mind not a stage mutant, but an implicit internal structural reorientation of stage action.

At the same time there were those in the Russian theatre world who, having grasped this idea, tried to take it to its logical conclusion. The critic B. Bentovin, who had written such an enthusiastic review of *Submarine Shipwreck* at the Mozaika, lost no time in suggesting to the Moscow Art Theatre that the same device should be transferred to a 'serious' production:

> I can imagine how successful this combination would be in an unwieldy play in which the performer has frequently and at length to relate what has happened to him in the interval between two acts. Cinema could show all this in a series of vivid pictures and, instead of a dry and boring story in the play, there would be the bonus, as it were, of more movement. . . . Of course, the most interesting part of the dialogue should be communicated by live actors, and the narrative part on the cinema screen. How beneficial this would be, for instance, to the staging of *Crime and Punishment* – cinema could reproduce Raskolnikov's wanderings before the murder – or to *The Brothers Karamazov* – cinema could depict the episodes that Mr Zvantsev reports so tediously from the rostrum.[59]

(In the Moscow Art Theatre production an actor called Zvantsev played the reader.)

The project did not remain a paper one. Pavel Orlenev, a star of the Russian dramatic stage, was attracted to the idea of hybrid performances. In December 1913 the newspaper *Teatral'naya gazeta* reported with astonishment that Orlenev and his troupe, on a guest visit to the 'Art Theatre of Miniatures', were performing

> the second and third act of *Woe and Misfortune* on stage, while the remaining three acts are shown on a screen. Mr Orlenev makes the same compromise in his performance of *Crime and Punishment*: only the scenes between Sonya Marmeladova and her father are performed on the theatre stage, while the rest are shown to the audience on a screen.[60]

Orlenev used the same method to play five of his most famous roles, in addition to those already mentioned for 1913, including Ibsen's *Ghosts* and *Brand* and Alexei Tolstoi's *Tsar Fyodor Ioannovich*, all in 1914. It is easy to understand why Orlenev preferred stage-screen performances to 'pure' cinema, from the memoirs of Vladimir Gardin, who produced the film episodes for Orlenev's *Ghosts*:

> I could never make Pavel Nikolayevich understand that there was no point in speaking the lines in front of the camera: they would have to be replaced by titles. He was disarmingly stubborn.
>
> 'If you deprive me of the words, I am no longer Orlenev,' he shouted in a touchingly childish manner. 'My whole life, all my emotions, have been given over to speaking . . .'

And he spoke . . . and spoke. . . . We enjoyed listening to him but we did not film. For us he only became a subject for the camera when his brilliant monologues had ceased. How unrepeatably fine he was then! We had to put a cover over the camera so that he did not see when we were cranking it and to signal imperceptibly to the cameraman when he should start and stop shooting.[61]

The relationship between Orlenev and cinema is symptomatic of Russian culture as a whole. Orlenev resorted to all sorts of devices so as not to deprive film of words and the sound of speech. He even filmed one scene in *Crime and Punishment* for so-called 'gramophone exhibition': the shooting and sound recording of films was undertaken by the Russian division of Edison Kinetophone. Like the film recitation genre, Orlenev's stage-screen hybrids were the fruit of the deep-seated logocentrism of the Russian stage. Pantomime did not exist in Russia. Russian audiences, and Russian directors, did not like films without titles. Had cinema been invented in Russia, it would probably not have been 'Lumière's cinematograph' that would have triumphed, but 'Edison's Kinetophone'.

What was the reaction to Orlenev's theatre and cinema shows? Judging by the critics, it was fairly cool. Emmanuil Beskin (who had savaged *The Brothers Karamazov* at the Moscow Art Theatre) quite neatly called the undertaking a 'chimera' and added:

> I am sorry for Orlenev, who is sincere in his enthusiasm, but I think this project is doomed to fail: you cannot paste living and dead material together; you cannot join a psycho-organic quiver to the soulless frigidity of the screen. Whatever the technical perfection of such a combination, there will never be a living cohesion between the picture and the transition to the plasticity of real movement.[62]

Orlenev himself recalled his Odessa tour with *Brand*, incorporating film, in his memoirs written at the end of the 1920s:

> The combination of cinema and stage was not properly prepared and was a failure. But I never trust my first steps in any undertaking and I always go on trying stubbornly to get what I want. After Odessa we toured with the same *Brand* for about three months. We made good money.[63]

The newspaper *Teatr* nevertheless remained dissatisfied:

> Orlenev is right to say that the Russian actor is heavy, bad at mime, and not vivid enough in his plastic movements. Even Orlenev is now playing Brand in a strange fashion: half the scenes are played as usual, but the other half appear only on the screen as a cinematographic performance. But the second half, printed on soulless film, is as pale as the first half, the spoken part, is vivid.[64]

On this basis it came to this conclusion, so common in the pages of the Russian theatre press:

The word is theatre's soul. Take away the word and you will destroy its soul.[65]

Were Orlenev's experiments unique? No: in the 1910s we come across references to Vladimir Maximov's stage-screen hybrids, for instance, in Lolo-Munshtein's *Dance Among the Swords*, to Baliev's sketches in *Die Fledermaus* and two or three cases of a similar kind. Leonid Trauberg relates that at the beginning of the 1920s in the FEKS show *The Wedding* there was someone on stage imitating Chaplin while they showed extracts from Chaplin's films on the screen. Nevertheless, unlike film recitations, experiments in the field of a symbiosis between stage and screen remained experiments, a peripheral, although not a secondary, offshoot of the history of Russian cinema.

A peripheral offshoot of the mainstream of world cinema history might be the best way to describe all the other features of Russian cinema that I have dealt with in this essay. In fact, on a map of the world Russian endings, the immobility of the figures, the predilection of Russian cinema for titles and film recitations would all appear as an anomaly. But, just as a magnetic anomaly leads the geologist to deposits of ore, so the anomalies of Russian cinema allow us to evaluate deep-rooted layers in the psychology of Russian culture.

# 2 Kuleshov's experiments and the new anthropology of the actor

*Mikhail Yampolsky*

Kuleshov's theoretical legacy is usually divided into two parts: one is devoted to the problems of montage and is rightly considered to be the more valuable and original, the second is concerned with the elaboration of the problem of the cinema actor and, in particular, of the theory of the *naturshchik* [model actor] and of rehearsal method. The books that Kuleshov wrote are organised along these lines. Both *The Art of Cinema* [Iskusstvo kino, 1929] and *The Practice of Film Direction* [Praktika kinorezhissury, 1935] begin with a statement of montage theory and then move on to an exposition of the problematic of the actor. This model has been adopted in most histories of cinema that contain an account of Kuleshov's theoretical views. Because of this, the correlation between montage theory and the anthropology of acting appears, as a rule, to be highly ephemeral. However, there is every reason to believe that the theory of montage derives genetically from the new conception of the anthropology of the actor and is based completely on it. The expositional structure adopted by Kuleshov and his popularisers masks to a considerable extent not just the profound unity of Kuleshov's film theory but also its true sense.

## I

Kuleshov's conception of the actor is not distinguished by any great originality, but is borrowed almost entirely from theatre theory of the 1910s and the beginning of the 1920s. There was at that time in Russia an active reaction against the method of Stanislavsky's Moscow Art Theatre. The principle of the transformation and embodiment of the actor in the character was being criticised from all sides. At the same time a new anthropology of acting was being actively elaborated at the beginning of the 1910s: the major influences on it were the views of two theorists, the Frenchman F. A. Delsarte and the Swiss J. Dalcroze. The teaching of Delsarte figures among the teachings of physiognomy, which were very popular in the nineteenth century and which owed much, for instance, to the old works of G. G. Engel. He had elaborated a highly pedantic lexicon of gestures, each of which, according to the author, had a direct correlation with the psycholo-gical state of man. The originality of Delsarte's teaching consisted to a large extent in the accentuation of the rhythmic side of mime and gesture that is predictable in a system created by a professional musician. Dalcroze created a system of rhythmic gymnastics which was extremely popular in the 1910s and on which he based an original aesthetic theory. Delsarte's ideas began to penetrate Russia at the very beginning of the twentieth century. Yuri A. Ozarovsky lectured on his teaching as early as 1903[1] but it achieved real popularity around 1910–13 when the former director of the Imperial Theatres, Prince Sergei Volkonsky, became its propagandist. He published a series of articles on Delsarte and Dalcroze in the periodical *Apollon* and then published, under that periodical's imprint, several books giving a detailed exposition of the new acting system. Since the Volkonsky–Delsarte–Dalcroze system had a fundamental significance for film theory at the beginning of the 1920s, and in particular for Kuleshov, we must familiar-ise ourselves briefly with at least those elements that were later used by film-makers.

The Volkonsky system can conventionally be divided into two parts: the theoretical system of Dalcroze and the technological system of Delsarte, synthesised into a single whole. In 1912 Volkonsky published his translation of the book by Dalcroze's disciple, Jean d'Udine, that had gone into his system organically and represented a kind of philosophical reworking of the teaching of the Geneva rhythmologist (d'Udine relied mainly on Le Dantec, Bergson *et al.*). D'Udine was an ardent propagandist of the idea of synaes-thesia and he compared man to a dynamo (in one of the first manifestations of the machine ethic in aesthetics) through which the rhythmic synaesthetic inductive impulses pass. Human emotion is expressed in external movement and, what is more, that movement can 'inductively' provoke in man the emotion that gave rise to the movement. He maintained that 'for every emotion, of whatever kind, there is a corresponding body movement of some sort: it is through that movement that the complex synaesthetic transfer that accompanies any work of art is accomplished'.[2] To ensure its artistic effectivity every movement has to be rhythmicised and music is the synaesthetic equivalent of body movement: 'the ability to express feelings through musical combinations consists in nothing other than finding sound movements whose subtle rhythm corresponds to the body movement of someone experiencing enjoyment or suffering.'[3] It is from this that d'Udine derives the idea of the mimetic character of music, 'imitating' the internal rhythms that accompany the phenomena that exist in life. Rhythmicised body movements must, according to d'Udine, be 'segmentary' – that is, they must be fixed in certain poses: 'The manifestation of real artistic quality . . . requires that the rhythms, whether felt or imagined, be crystallised in an immutable form',[4] he declared, making an analogy between human express-ive movement and the musical notation that records a melody. D'Udine promoted music to the position of the metalanguage of art: 'This would allow us', he wrote, 'to apply my plastic definition of melody, which is that all melody is a series of consecutive propositions, to the whole field of aesthetics and in the end that would allow us to say in more general terms: *every work of art is a series of consecutive propositions.*'[5] D'Udine concluded his work with this characteristic definition of art: art is '*the transmission of an emotion by means of stylised natural rhythm*'.[6]

In his articles 'Man as Material for Art. Music. Body. Dance' and 'Man and Rhythm. The System and School of Jacque-Dalcroze' (1912), Volkonsky refines some of the theses of the Swiss theorist: 'the first condition for creation in art is the adoption of a different rhythm, whether in the voice, in the movements of the body or in the soul's emotions.'[7] Furthermore, this different rhythm must be assimilated by the actor to the point where it becomes an unconscious automatism: 'Consciousness only plays its proper role when it is transformed into unconsciousness, that is when everything that has been acquired through consciousness is transformed into the mechanical impossibility of doing otherwise.'[8] Volkonsky's actor is distinguished from Gordon Craig's 'supermarionette' precisely because his rhythmicised movements are driven to unconsciousness by inner, conscious impulses and not by simple mechanical submission to the director's will.

The Delsartian, 'technological' part of the system is essentially orientated towards the search for a precise record of gesture, its segmentation like musical notation, and the exposure of the psychological content of each gesture. Delsarte, with his mania for the classification of the lexicography of mime, was even more categorical than d'Udine in his insistence on the extreme segmentation of gestures: 'Delsarte considered the independence of the limbs from one another to be the essential condition for expressiveness: any interference by another limb weakens the impression.'[9] To achieve a geometrically precise record of gestures Delsarte proposed to describe and produce them in three directions – width, height and depth: 'Each man is like the centre of his own universe. His "centrality" can develop dynamically in three principal directions, which correspond to the three "independent" directions in which the space of the universe is measured.'[10] Furthermore man can, as it were, stretch out from the centre and enter an eccentric state which expresses the manifestation of will, or gather himself in towards the centre (a concentric state), expressing the dominant of thought, of reason. Tranquillity, according to Delsarte, relates to the sphere of feeling. Volkonsky, following his teacher, describes all human movements according to the categories 'normal', 'eccentric' and 'concentric'. In *Expressive Man* Volkonsky provides a very detailed analysis of the sense of all sorts of 'segmentary' human movements in three directions (he calls this section of his system 'semiotics'), but the main content of his work is the elaboration of the 'laws of combination' of individual movements. He proclaims four principles of combination: 1. simultaneity; 2. succession; 3. opposition (total and partial); and 4. parallelism. Gesture acquires significance only in relation to its starting-point, the centre, but a combination of gestures

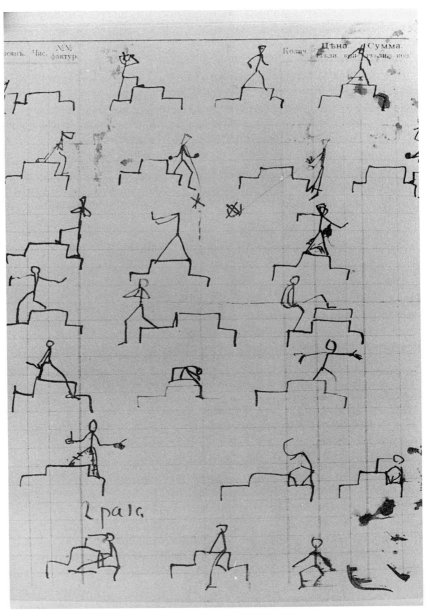

*Figure 3* 'Action score' by Kuleshov for a 1921 'film without film'.

acquires meaning only through the radial directions of movement (which is why Delsarte's three 'axes' are so important to him). Their opposition in radial directions is the fundamental expressive principle of the organisation of a 'phrase' chain. Volkonsky provides a long list of examples of these oppositions, for example, 'between the head, radiating along a perpendicular either away from or towards the body, and the hands, radiating from the elbows in the direction of breadth', and so on.[11] Volkonsky proposes that actors' movements should be constructed according to the principle of the succession of different combinations of gestures and asserts that 'only such a strict observation of the law of succession, stripped of the confusion that inevitably accompanies simultaneity, is a real organic *development* of movement'[12] constructed according to natural laws, the laws of mechanics: 'Just as the law of gravity is indisputable, so too are the laws of body movement and, consequently, also the laws of expressiveness; but, once laws are indisputable, their non-observance produces a lie. Study, master, observe the *law*, if you want your art to be true.'[13] It was on this basis that the original ethic of the new anthropology of the actor was constructed. The laws of movement were equated to the laws of nature (mechanics) and contrasted to the voluntarism of traditional artistic creation, in the same way as truth was contrasted to lie and nature to art. The following declaration by Volkonsky had a major significance for the aesthetics of the 1920s:

> Man is a machine; yes, this machine is set in motion by feeling and 'oiled' by feeling but, since it is a machine, it obeys the general laws of mechanics. But you must remember this: if you make something mechanical without feeling (or sense), you will produce a caricature of life; whereas, if you produce a feeling with false mechanics, nothing will happen – you will achieve the absence of life.[14]

This combination, which seems strange to us now, of mechanics and 'feeling' differentiates Volkonsky's ideas sharply from later Constructivism. We see before us the fruit of a meandering movement of thought that derived from the old physiognomy of pantomime and ballet but already anticipated the next step towards the machine ethic of the 1920s.

## II

The new anthropology of the actor spread through Russia with unusual speed. A large number of centres for Dalcrozian rhythmic gymnastics [eurhythmics] were set up and Volkonsky even started to publish a specialised periodical *Rhythmic Gymnastics Courses* [Listki kursov ritmicheskoi gimnastiki] (1913–14). In St Petersburg D. M. Musina-Ozarovskaya set up a 'School for Stage Expressiveness' and then the 'One Art' society, which set itself the aim of promoting a future synthesis of the arts on the basis of Delsarte's system. Representatives of the Petersburg artistic elite joined the society. Yuri A. Ozarovsky published a Delsartian journal called *Voice and Speech* [Golos i rech']. But the principal propagandist was Volkonsky, who

gave hundreds of lectures about his system. The spread of the new anthropology was facilitated by the flowering of the Russian ballet, the tours of
Isadora Duncan, etc. The ballet seemed for some time to be the principal
expression of the new anthropological model of the actor and, more broadly,
of man.

It was through theatre that the ideas of Volkonsky and his associates
penetrated film circles. The first traces of their influence can be found
around 1916. By 1918–19 among film-makers there was already an entire
group of followers of Delsarte and Dalcroze. By coincidence there were
among them a number of film-makers who actively supported Soviet power
and, as a result, occupied key posts in cinema immediately after the October
Revolution. Among them we should name first of all the famous director and
actor of pre-Revolutionary cinema, Vladimir Gardin, who in 1918 was head
of the fiction film section of the All-Russian Photographic and Cinematographic Section (VFKO) of the Russian Soviet Federated Socialist Republic
(RSFSR) People's Commissariat of Enlightenment (Narkompros). His
associate was his old friend Vasili Ilyin, a painter, an actor and likewise a
supporter of Volkonsky's system. Gardin had been interested in the training
of the new actor in 1916 and had at that time planned with Ilyin the
establishment of a 'Studio of Cinema Art'. In his diary entry for 15
December 1916 Gardin noted, 'Today Vasili Sergeyevich Ilyin is coming
again to continue our never-ending discussion about the studio, the new
army of film-makers who will conquer the world.'[15] He characterised his
attitude towards cinema at that time in the following way: 'I have not
withdrawn from cinema, but I have been dreaming of a studio and not of
productions . . . I am interested above all in research into working
methods.'[16]

Because of the war the studio never started work. After the Revolution
and after holding the leading position in VFKO, Gardin achieved the
improbable, the opening of the First State Cinema School, which he headed.
Initially Gardin's plan had a Cyclopean character: it was his intention to
open ten schools, each with a thousand students, and to create on the basis of
these a new 'army' of film-makers[17] and, although this was not made clear,
perhaps also a new anthropological type of man. There is little doubt that the
existence of the school owed much to Gardin's enthusiasm for Volkonsky's
new anthropology. It is enough to look at the complement of teachers. First
Sergei Volkonsky was invited to teach there and take charge of the courses
on the 'system of expressive man'. Many years later Gardin recalled
Volkonsky's courses from 1919–20: 'The students had their hands and feet
entangled in concentric, normal-eccentric and concentro-concentric
positions.'[18] Then there was Ilyin, of whom Kuleshov wrote in his memoirs,
'Ilyin was an enthusiastic admirer of the Delsarte school and applied its
teachings to our work at every opportunity. In addition, he developed and
perfected it himself. We were extremely pleased with Ilyin's research.'[19]
Elsewhere Kuleshov affirmed that it was in fact Ilyin who introduced him to

the Delsarte system.[20] One of the other teachers was Nikolai Foregger, creator of the machine dances which were to become famous in the 1920s and were so obviously linked to the 'new anthropology'. At one time the school was headed by Valentin Turkin who shared the general interest in Volkonsky's system. The school maintained particularly close contacts with the Experimental Heroic Theatre directed by Boris Ferdinandov, who had created the Dalcrozian theory of 'metro-rhythm'. For a while Kuleshov's Workshop even took shelter in the building of this theatre. The appearance within the film school's walls of Kuleshov, who had been Gardin's protégé since 1918 (when Gardin had invited him to take charge of the newsreel and re-editing section of VFKO), was to be expected. Kuleshov professed a Delsartism that was even more orthodox than that of the other teachers.

The foundations of future Soviet film theory were being laid around the film school and in its midst. We might apparently even be justified in talking about a specific GTK-GIK film theory.[21] Before we define the main body of ideas of this collective theory, we must answer the question: why has the history of film thought ignored this important theoretical complex? We can cite a whole range of reasons. There is no written record of the ideas expressed by many of the participants in the collective. Gardin, for example, never published his theoretical findings which became known only in 1949 after their detailed exposition in his *Memoirs*. We know practically nothing about Ilyin's ideas. By 1922–3 there was in addition a noticeable distance emerging between Kuleshov, who had adopted the positions of LEF [*Levyi front iskusstv* (Left Front of the Arts)], and his former associates (above all Gardin), who had maintained closer links with the pre-Revolutionary artistic tradition. And we must not forget personal quarrels. At the beginning of the 1920s there was a break between Kuleshov and Ilyin, which in Kuleshov's later memoirs was attributed to Ilyin's scholastic Delsartism,[22] although in this conflict we must obviously not exclude personal motives. The break with Turkin followed in 1925 after the publication of his book *The Cinema Actor* [Kino-akter], which contained scarcely veiled attacks on Kuleshov. Thus, at the very moment when Kuleshov's theory was beginning to achieve widespread popularity – 1925 – the collective of the film school was disintegrating and the traces of its former unity were being lost in later polemics and personal conflicts.

Gardin was the central figure in the history of the film school in its first stage. He had come to the notion of the need to create a new type of actor for cinema as early as 1913 while working on the film *The Keys to Happiness*. He invited the non-professional Alexander Volkov to play one of the leading roles and Volkov astonished him with the veracity of his acting. Gardin was later to call Volkov 'the first model actor [naturshchik] in cinema'.[23] It was then that he came to the idea of the prime importance for cinema of physiognomy and physiognomic characterology and he divided actors into three groups: the emotional type, the rational-technical type and the technical type. Simultaneously he began to use his rudimentary knowledge of physiology and reflexology in his work with actors. By 1916, as is evident from his diary, Gardin's film theory had been fully formed. His orientation towards the model actor was already evident: indeed in 1916 Gardin was already using the term widely (possibly for the first time in the history of Russian film theory). Gardin divided each action into four 'physiological' stages and based the actor's work on the transitions from one 'segmentary phase' to another. On 18 May 1916 he wrote in his diary:

> Today the shooting was difficult. In the schemata that I definitively adopted for absolutely every draft *close-up montage combination* (and also for the temporal calculations of the mechanics of spiritual life), I am beginning to assemble the individual signs that characterise each element in the four-part formula that I took as the basis for all schemata:
> 1. Sensation (impression) is the external or internal stimulant.
> 2. Perception is the orientation.
> 3. Comprehension is the brake.
> 4. Appellation is the (sound) reaction – the word.[24]

The desire to divide action into such minute physiological phases (and the enormous role that he attributed to the eye in this process of movement) led Gardin towards the widespread use of close-ups, that is, the cutting off of the actor by the frame of the shot, which was partly analogous to Delsarte's 'independence of the limbs from one another'. The desire to set out the elements of action according to a precise four-part formula created the necessity for properly thought-out 'close-up montage combinations'. Hence the requirements of the new anthropology of the actor encouraged in Gardin's mind the idea of montage. Gardin himself recognised perfectly the significance of these theoretical studies: 'That is how my first thoughts arose on the possibilities of montage combinations and on the conversion of acting to the expressive movement of the parts of the actor's body and to the condition of objects symbolising the actions of man', he wrote.[25] This formulation is interesting because we can still detect in it an indissoluble link between the idea of montage and the body of the actor: the 'possibilities of montage combinations' are directly linked to the 'conversion of acting to the expressive movement of the parts of the actor's body'. Montage was thus understood as a cinematographic form of organisation of the actor's behaviour.

Gardin was simultaneously taken by the idea of founding a film school where he intended to conduct a 'basic course' on 'man's behaviour in front of the camera lens'. He declared: 'One day a new man, unspoiled by theatre, will appear in cinema. He is the one with whom and on whom it will be possible to experiment.'[26] Thus by 1916 Gardin had already worked out an approach to the cinema actor as 'model actor' and as material for montage treatment. By 1919 Gardin's ideas had acquired a more and more openly expressed Delsartian character. Parallel with this came a further elaboration of montage category. Even before Kuleshov arrived at the film school,

Gardin was giving a special lecture on montage and at that time he defined cinema as 'a rhythmic alternation of film fragments whose composition . . . was united into a film on the basis of a montage calculation, which was one of the most important calculations in the direction of a film'.[27] Gardin wrote:

> Starting from this definition, I tried to establish the creative tasks in directing a work, above all to teach a sense of the rhythm of the film being made. . . . Rhythm is an endless theme. Movement and the endlessly varying alternation of acceleration and slow motion in accordance with certain calculations are the form of rhythm and the recording of them will be the technique and the sense included in the word 'cinematography'.[28]

Hence montage was also understood as the rhythmological key, given that the film was, in the spirit of Dalcroze and Volkonsky, proclaimed to be a 'recording' of rhythm.

In practice Gardin's promised experiments with the model actor took the form of a series of exercises with 'velvet screens'. With the aid of these screens he formed a window whose shape recalled the frame of a film shot. Into the window he put the face of the actor who had to work out precise mimic reflex reactions to stimuli. In this process most attention was devoted to the movement of the eyes, which were recorded in complex schemata. As a result Gardin elaborated '1,245 compositions which could be used to arrange the head of the person being filmed in the frame'.[29] These compositions were partly copied from Delsarte's schemata. These experiments with frames transferred the whole emphasis on to close-up and the miming of the actor. The rhythmic montage aspect was here almost absent, remaining principally in the field of theory. The methodology of the velvet screens was later vehemently criticised by Kuleshov. But it is obvious that this very methodology is the direct consequence of the path taken by Gardin, a return to the sources of his film theory, the close-ups of 1916 with the most scrupulous recording of the 'reactive phases'. But to a certain extent it is also Volkonsky's 'montage'; at any rate it is very reminiscent of the experiments that the latter conducted in his lectures. Thus, one account of his lectures reported as early as 1913 (the year when Gardin made his first film):

> S. M. Volkonsky showed nine faces on the screen with corresponding expressions, from the normal-normal (serene calm) to the eccentric-eccentric (ecstasy). These nine typical expressions incorporated nine typical glances. . . . Combined with the nine expressions that depended on the brows and eyelids, these nine glances produced 81 typical expressions for the eyes.[30]

The similarity to Gardin's experiments with the screens is striking: 1,245 compositions are of course the product of a gigantic detailed study of Volkonsky's 81 eye expressions. Let us note in passing that Volkonsky's faces were demonstrated on the screen and that Gardin's velvet screens corresponded to this pseudocinema.

After Gardin the film school was headed for a short time by F. Shipulinsky and his place was then taken by Valentin Turkin. His positions in the field of theory had a more radical character. Turkin's theoretical evolution is more difficult to reconstruct than Gardin's but it is similar in part. In 1918 Turkin was one of the leading figures on the Moscow newspaper *Kino-gazeta*. There he published an article which was fundamental for that time, 'Simulators and Models', in which he used Gardin's term in extremely declarative form:

> The first truth that I should like to proclaim is that on the screen the actor is equal to the model actor and valuable because he can, when he has thrown off the rags of stage theatricality, condescend, descend to the level of that picturesque theatricality of life that is characteristic of the beggar at the church door [etc., etc.].[31]

The pages of *Kino-gazeta* carried two other articles that were to have considerable significance later: the article 'The Screen and Rhythm' by Anna Lee (the pen-name of Anna Zaitseva-Selivanova, the future wife of Pudovkin) and Kuleshov's article 'The Art of Cinema', which contained Kuleshov's first reflections on montage. Turkin, as the 'leader' of the newspaper, was the 'godfather' of both. The two articles are almost the first Dalcrozian declarations in film theory. Anna Lee begins her piece with an almost word-for-word repetition of Volkonsky:

> It is necessary for our intuition, our taste, our heart, our intellect – for everything, everything to merge, to vibrate and to blend harmoniously with the tasks of the artist. This is only possible when the symbols, the signs through which he wants us to read his artistic intentions are rhythmically realised. . . . It is only when he is armed with a knowledge of rhythm, especially screen rhythm, that the actor, like a singer who has mastered the musical sol-fa, will be able to do battle with any element of chance, 'for no two things are more hostile to one another than art and chance' (Volkonsky).[32]

Anna Lee sensed the need to find a cinematographic equivalent to the rhythm of the actor but she did not contemplate montage. Her solution looked extremely naive:

> The actor performs and simultaneously the camera (cameraman) operates, like a metronome establishing a certain tempo. The unit of speed of the performing actor does not correspond to the unit of speed of the camera in operation and this causes arrhythmia. . . . But, if we add to this a third rhythm, that of the projector and the theatre, the result will be rhythmic inarticulacy.[33]

Anna Lee proposes to find a 'coefficient of movement', a 'general constant', an 'amalgamating unit' that would help to synchronise the three rhythms. Anna Lee's line of thought is very interesting: the new anthropology of the actor urgently requires the discovery of a rhythmic law of cinema and it is to be found in the natural 'metronome' of cinema, the cranking of the camera, the potential 'rhythmiciser' of the choreography of cinema. It is no accident that the article states: 'The grotesque results of dancing [on the screen], even when performed by professionals, confirm and underline the absence of rhythm from the screen.'[34]

Kuleshov's article was written before Anna Lee's piece. But it contains a direct response to 'The Screen and Rhythm'. In this article the problem of montage and rhythm was still in the background. It is evident that they did not completely preoccupy Kuleshov because the major part of the article (like his 1917 articles in *Vestnik kinematografii*) was devoted to the problems of the art of set decoration. There was none the less a passage that appeared to be extremely close to Gardin's views at that time:

> Each individual work of art has its own basic method to express the idea of art. Very few film-makers (apart from the Americans) have realised that in cinema this method of expressing an artistic idea is provided by the rhythmical succession of individual still frames or short sequences conveying movement – that is what is technically known as montage.[35]

This first definition of montage in Kuleshov's work is still pure Gardin and imbued with the spirit of Dalcroze–Volkonsky. The basis of cinema is rhythm (as in Anna Lee) but its realisation is in montage. Lee's article apparently had a powerful effect on Kuleshov and played a particular role in his theoretical evolution. In 1920 in his theoretical 'summing up', 'The Banner of Cinema', he openly argued against 'The Screen and Rhythm', beginning the exposition of his own theory with precisely the question of dance. Without naming Anna Lee, he sets out, with some misrepresentation, her position on the discrepancy between the camera and the choreography of cinema and then argues:

> Let us suppose that dance turned out on screen as well as when it was performed during the shooting, what would we have achieved by this? We should have achieved a situation in which the art of dance could be precisely reproduced on a strip of film. But in that case cinema would have been no more than living photography of dance and on screen we should have achieved the reproduction of the art of *ballet* but there would be no cinema art in it at all.[36]

This polemic explains the origin of one of Kuleshov's experiments, 'the dance'. But it is equally evident that it also follows the broad outlines of film theory at that time, from the rhythmic anthropology of man to rhythmic montage as its cinematographic quintessence. In this sense Kuleshov was not very original. Gardin was thinking along the same lines and Turkin was evolving in the same direction. In 1918 he was fighting for the model actor. And there is nothing more natural than that in 1922 he should be one of the principal propagandists of rhythmic montage.

We shall cite a lengthy quotation from Turkin which expresses his 1922 views:

> The basic element in the form of cinema art is montage. . . . Experience [perezhivanie], mood, the expression of movements of the soul are false means for the actor to make an impression on the audience. The principal means of making an impression in cinema is montage. Montage is the combination of separate moments of action according to the principle of the strongest impression. Action unfolds in space and lasts in time. Art consists in the construction of space and the composition of movement (action) in time. The composition of movement (action) in time is its distribution in a definite rhythmic schema. Action on screen is composed of the alternation of fragments and the movement of a man, a horse, a car, an aeroplane in individual fragments. Each movement of the fragments (between and within the fragments) must be constructed rhythmically (or metro-rhythmically, if we accept the new phraseology). The rhythmic construction of cinema action is montage.[37]

Everything in this statement is very characteristic of the type of thinking associated with the film school group. Everything begins with the actor, then passes to rhythm and concludes with the assertion that the rhythmic construction of a film is montage.

Turkin's position is of course close to Kuleshov's position in 1918. But we should not assume that this is the result of a straightforward borrowing. In 1918 Kuleshov was saying the same thing as Gardin. In 1922 Turkin is repeating both of them. What we have here is not so much the product of the individual creativity of each one of them as the fundamental principle of what we have already called 'the "film school" film theory'.

## III

Gardin had met Kuleshov in Moscow in 1918. 'In the space of ten minutes he managed to utter the word "montage" twenty times',[38] Gardin recalled. Kuleshov's enthusiasm for montage probably predetermined his assignment to the newsreel section and to his later work on re-editing films. In the process of re-editing Kuleshov discovered his famous 'effect' with Mosjoukine's face. In the summer of 1919 he set out with Eduard Tisse, later Eisenstein's cameraman, for the Eastern Front where he filmed a newsreel. He returned from the front in October 1919. Gardin's film school had begun work in September 1919. The work of the film school interested Kuleshov a great deal and he was always visiting it 'as a guest'. In 1920 he got what he had no doubt wanted very badly: he was appointed to the staff of the school as a teacher. This happened approximately at the end of March or the beginning of April 1920 and Kuleshov immediately joined in as one of the most active members of the collective. For the whole of April he worked with Gardin and his wife Olga Preobrazhenskaya on a 'sketch of film

*Figure 4* 'Every emotion . . . is accompanied by a specific sign in the body and face,' Vladimir Inkizhinov (*left*), Leonid Obolensky and Alexandra Khokhlova in a 1923 rooftop 'étude' by the Kuleshov Workshop.

rehearsals on an agitational theme in three reels and 86 scenes with an apotheosis'.[39] The sketch was based on Gardin's velvet screens and was shown on 1 May. At that moment Kuleshov was a long way from opposition to Gardin and was actively assimilating the new anthropology of the actor. At that time he was apparently mastering Volkonsky's teaching, with which he had come into contact at the school, and studying Delsarte and Dalcroze.

Kuleshov arrived at the school as a 'specialist in montage' with a whole series of relatively vague notions about it which gradually took shape into a system with an active orientation towards the new anthropology. The year 1920 was marked by a strengthening of his theoretical work. It was then that he wrote his programmatic text, 'The Banner of Cinema'. But the differences in principle between his theoretical position and Gardin's soon became apparent. They are recorded in the article 'What Must Be Done in Film Schools'. The starting-point for Kuleshov's argument here was Delsarte's system:

> nature has made man so that every emotion he experiences is accompanied by a specific sign in his body and face. . . . Consequently the teacher must show the pupil the law of nature that corresponds to the

particular task. . . . For theatre actors these laws have been discovered by Delsarte. It would not be a bad idea to re-examine them and extract from them anything that might prove useful to the film-maker.[40]

Kuleshov did not incline towards Delsartian semiotics, unlike Gardin, who had stuck with the search for a mimic alphabet of signs, but towards Volkonsky's 'laws of combination' in which the sense derived from oppositions, contrasts, parallelisms, etc. It was in this context that he subjected the system of velvet frames to a critique, but with one reservation: 'Basically, of course, this idea is fine but the significance of close-up for the film-maker lies solely in montage and it can have no independent value for him.'[41] He went on to set out his own methodology, demonstrating the error of Gardin's ways:

1. An incorrect exercise. In the first frame you show a man with a look of hatred: in the second another man whose look answers the first – triumph, etc.
2. A correct exercise, which has to be performed several times. The first frame is as in the previous instance, for the second time you see the man's look of hatred in the frame, and in the following frame a hand holding a letter. The content of the scene has changed.[42]

It is not difficult to see that Kuleshov was proposing to reconstruct his own experiment with Mosjoukine in the velvet frames. But the most interesting thing in the article was the fact that the Mosjoukine experiment, which was not directly mentioned, was inextricably linked to the body of the actor understood as the universal model for montage: 'If we mask the actor and force him to strike a sad pose, the mask will express sadness: but if the actor strikes a joyful pose, it will look to us as if the mask is joyful too.'[43] Kuleshov was already re-thinking the Delsarte–Volkonsky system as a source of pure montage: segments of the human body are like signs opposed to one another and they make sense in precisely that opposition. The description of the man in the mask is a direct transposition on to the actor's body of the 'Kuleshov effect', in which Mosjoukine's mask-like face changed its expression within various montage juxtapositions.

Thus, Kuleshov had fully mastered the main complex of ideas of the 'film school theory' but was fighting to reorientate it in principle towards montage, towards the cinematographisation of Delsarte on the basis of the principles of montage. The conclusion to the article left no doubt whatsoever on this score:

all kinds of art have one essence and we must look for that essence in rhythm. But *rhythm* in art is expressed and achieved in various ways: in theatre through the actor's gesture and voice, in cinema through montage. Consequently the arts differ from one another in their specific methods of mastering their material, their means of achieving rhythm. . . . In using the arguments that have just been set out, we want to remind you once again of the importance of Delsarte in the model actor's *pose*. For now it is more obvious that the working methods of other arts can also be applied to cinema but that this *must* be done in a cinematographic way: that is, we take the law of an idea that is common to all the arts and look for means that are *characteristic of cinema* to exploit that idea.[44]

An eloquent argument: for Kuleshov montage was a specifically cinemato-graphic analogue of the Delsartian pose. They had a common aim: rhythm.

By 1921 there was an urgent need to subject Kuleshov's ideas to ex-perimental verification (cf. Gardin's tendency to experiment with the model actor). In March 1921, after receiving 90 metres of film, Kuleshov shot six montage experiments. Here is a list of them taken from Kuleshov's appli-cation to the Photographic and Cinematographic Section of the Artistic Sector of the Moscow Regional Political Education Committee:

1. a dance, filmed from one place – 10 metres
2. a dance, filmed using montage – 10 metres
3. the dependence of the model actor's experience on the causes of that experience:
   (a) 14 metres
   (b) 20 metres
4. the arbitrary combination of various scenes of action into a single composition – 13 metres [the 'creative geography' experiment]
5. the arbitrary combination of the parts of different people's bodies and the creation through montage of the desired model actor – 12 metres [the 'created man' experiment]
6. the uniform movement of the eyes of a model actor – 2 metres.[45]

Of these six experiments the history of cinema has preserved the memory of only two: the 'created man' and 'creative geography' – the others are practically never mentioned. But, if we look at the whole programme of experiments in its entirety, we can easily see that the sixth experiment fell within the Dalcroze–Volkonsky orbit. The third experiment recalled the Mosjoukine experiment but was partly reformulated in the categories of reflexology. The first, second, fourth and fifth experiments are closely linked to one another. First we have the non-montage image of a dance (not specifically cinematographic), then we are offered three different types of the dismemberment and combination of objects. The dance is composed of fragments that have been filmed with a single model, while the fourth and fifth experiments assemble the body of a man or the 'body' of the world from fragments of various objects. The Delsartian idea of dismemberment and combination is here clearly evident.

Judging by the frequency of the references in the texts and its place in the list, the 'dance' experiment was the most important to Kuleshov, although in later analyses it has been completely overshadowed. The significance of this experiment does not depend merely on the retrospective polemic with the article by Anna Lee, to which we have referred. The dance was essentially the only subject which clearly raised the problem of rhythm. Rhythm had been postulated as the principal aim of montage, but neither the Mosjoukine experiment nor the 'created man' were complete responses to this aim.

It is also essential to remember that in the 1920s, even more than in the 1910s, the tendency to transform choreography into a metamodel for the performing arts was being reinforced. It was Tairov who made a significant contribution to choreographic rhythmology and Meyerhold's biomechanics is genetically linked to it. But for Kuleshov it was the theory and practice of Boris Ferdinandov's Experimental Heroic Theatre, with which he maintained very close links, that were of major importance. It is of course no accident that, after the break with the film school, the 'Kuleshov collective' moved into the building occupied by the Experimental Heroic Theatre. In his memoirs Kuleshov wrote enthusiastically about Ferdinandov, clearly counting him among his 'teachers'.[46]

Among Moscow theatres at the beginning of the 1920s there was none that was as clearly orientated towards choreography as the Experimental Heroic Theatre. V. Tikhonovich, who took Ferdinandov's ideas to the verge of absurdity, wrote:

> the 'anarchy' that reigned in the drama theatre was linked to the fact that in drama people do not dance, but walk, stand, sit, lie, etc., they do not sing, but speak, shout, cry, laugh, are silent, etc. . . . It has to be said that the dramatic theatre has simply *fallen behind* opera and ballet in its own artistic development. . . . But, say the Old Believers, we shall more or less eradicate the clear boundaries between drama, ballet and opera. Even better, this is a *compliment* to the Ferdinandov system: it seems to lead us towards a *synthetic* theatre, a theatre of gesture and dance merged into a single whole, of merged speech and song, a theatre which provides obvious opportunities for the future.[47]

Ferdinandov created the system of metro-rhythm that was popular in the 1920s. His starting-point was the fact that theatre was a wholly dynamic art. The organisation of the dynamics of artistic form had to take on a metro-rhythmic form that was subject to the basic laws of mechanics. Ferdinandov tried to reduce all stage movements to metres that were close to those of music and poetry. He distinguished two-beat and three-beat measures of movement. The metric organisation of stage movement set Ferdinandov the problem of recording movement: 'The resolution of the bases of theatrical recording', he wrote, 'is a problem for regular theatre: we are also working on it in our theatrical laboratory.'[48] He also paid a considerable tribute to reflexology. But it is particularly interesting for us that Ferdinandov spoke systematically of montage:

Theatre is the art of the human body, consisting of three basic elements: the acoustic (sound-voice), the mimic (movement proper) and the psychological (sensation, reflex, deed, feeling – in a word, emotion) – plus montage which surrounds the man-actor in his main work.[49]

Although for Ferdinandov montage was in many ways an external element, it was also subject to his metro-rhythm: 'The same laws of metro-rhythm, tempo, accord, theatrical harmony and counterpoint also guide the construction of theatrical montage . . . and its combination with the actor's basic work.'[50] Thus a kind of choreography was promoted to the position of an organisational principle in relation to montage as well. Furthermore the montage principle was also introduced into the actual work of the actor. Ferdinandov's theatre was called 'normative' or 'analytical' theatre precisely because it postulated the necessity for the montage segmentation of movements: 'you can construct a stage work on a succession of elementary movements, using the movement of only one organ of the body at each moment in time',[51] wrote the theatre enthusiast Nikolai Lvov. This 'successive' and analytical plastic art was described by Ferdinandov's opponent Ippolit Sokolov as a collection of 'typically Jewish artificial little gestures bordering on caricature . . . an insupportable uniformity of conventional and schematic movements'.[52] In many ways theatre was being constructed as an analogue of the system of 'notation' of rhythmicised movements.

Kuleshov's move away from Gardin's methodology was clearly stimulated by the influence of Ferdinandov's metro-rhythm, based essentially on Volkonsky's system which it had significantly modernised. 'In normative theatre people work unconsciously with primitive cinematographic technique',[53] Kuleshov wrote in 1922. But in the 'Work Plan for the Experimental Cinema Laboratory', compiled in 1923, we find: 'Work in time. The preparatory concept of metre and rhythm. Exercises. Notes and notation. Exercises.'[54] These are already Ferdinandov's themes. As early as 1914 S. Volkonsky had called for the use of cinema for the purpose of quasi-choreographic teaching, in conservatoires for instance, 'as the most powerful teaching instrument; it will be a mirror reflecting the way in which we should and should not move'.[55] By the 1920s cinema was already beginning to prove equal to choreographic notation. At that time the press put forward the idea of using cinema to record dance: 'It is very probable that a precise record of dance is not possible. . . . The failures that have characterised research in this field compel us to abandon the notion of developing a system to record dance and turn all our hopes to cinema.'[56]

Turkin fully shared the idea of cinema as transfigured choreography and the inclination towards Ferdinandov's system. In his 1925 book *The Cinema Actor* this problem is given prominence:

The developed technique of montage has enriched the transmission of dance on the screen. Dance has begun to be composed of dismembered moments of movement, filmed from various distances and various angles and alternating in a proper and measured order. Its compositional element has become the movement-fragment (i.e. a fragment of cinema film on which the dancer's movement has been recorded: because dance on screen is as much the 'dance' of man in individual fragments of film as the alternation, the 'dance' of the actual fragments of film).[57]

Cinema, as we shall see, was to be simultaneously an analytical record of dance and rhythmicised montage choreography. Turkin went on:

> The question of dance has a special significance for contemporary cinema and, in particular, for the mastery of film acting. The search for strict artistic form in cinema is moving towards the measured construction of the actor's movement on the screen and of the rhythmic montage of the film, i.e. towards the creation from the movement on the screen of a kind of 'dance'. . . . Film drama is trying to immerse itself in the culture of dance, in rhythm, so that it actually becomes 'dance', a sort of contemporary, realistic or, if you prefer, analytical or biomechanical ballet.[58]

(This is comparable to the ideas expressed in Fernand Léger's *Le Ballet mécanique* [France, 1924].)

That is why on 8 March 1921 Kuleshov filmed a dance by the ballerina Zinaida Tarkhovskaya in the first and most important of his series of projected montage experiments. Later, in Alexander Belenson's book *Cinema Today* [Kino segodnya, 1925] Kuleshov quite unambiguously indicated the link between montage and choreographic notation:

> Each gesture has its duration and that duration can be recorded by a sign that can be studied and reproduced. The alternation of accented and unaccented notes will create a temporal metre, which determines the metric system and the temporal character (just as in montage).[59]

Thus even in 1925 the 'dance' experiment preserved the importance of a 'symbol of faith' as the supreme expression of the link between montage and the new anthropology. Montage was now the expression of the new conception of man and derived literally from the human body, as a record of its movement, as the mechanical expression of its natural rhythm, as the embodiment of the concept of the body analytically dismembered. Montage was now induced by body rhythm, by the body's new being, in the broadest sense of the word. Man's body was the raw material for theatre. The 'body' of the world, transformed into the 'body' of the film stock, was the raw material for cinema. The analogies now were almost absolute and immutable.

The later development of cinema revealed the repetitive character of the metro-rhythmic element in montage. In Kuleshov's later analyses metro-rhythm passes into the shadows and the semantics of montage is promoted to the forefront. By 1929 Kuleshov was already concentrating exclusively on his experiments with 'creative geography' and 'created man' and furthermore he traced these experiments back to *Engineer Prite's Project* [Proekt inzhenera Praita, 1918].[60] The link with the anthropology of the 1910s was also camouflaged by Kuleshov's move closer to Constructivism. In 1922 he was one of the leading theorists of *Kino-Fot*, the journal headed by Alexei Gan, the theorist of Constructivism. This *rapprochement* was based on the machine cult. Volkonsky had already made the connection between the regularity of the movements of the human body, its automation and the machine. But in the 1920s these ideas were developed in a much more radical way. In this respect the polemic conducted by Ippolit Sokolov against the Dalcrozians was particularly characteristic:

> The actor on the stage must first of all become an automaton, a mechanism, a machine. . . . Henceforth painters, doctors, artists, engineers must study the human body, not from the point of view of anatomy or physiology, but *from the point of view of the study of machines.* The new Taylorised man has his own new physiology. Classical man, with his Hellenic gait and gesticulation, is a beast and savage in comparison with the new Taylorised man.[61]

This was a clear attack on Dalcroze–Volkonsky and their cult of antiquity. Sokolov went on to the heart of the matter: 'The training for the aesthetic gesture is the rhythmicisation of movement. The rhythmicised gesture must be constructed on psycho-physiological and technical rhythm and not on purely musical rhythm.'[62] The machine cult attempted to disavow its sources, to renounce the musical-choreographic model. Henceforth the model actor was to be understood in a purely mechanical sense. Oskar Bir set American film actors up as an ideal when he said, 'They are not actors at all but organs of movement.'[63] Cinema was once again described as an organism with, in its structure, the same constitution as the actor: 'Cinema is first of all a machine. . . . What it shows on the screen is the definitive mechanisation of life.'[64] Alexei Gan applied these ideas to the Kuleshov Workshop:

> Why? Because, as an element of cinema's raw material, disorganised nature, whether static or in motion, lies on the screen and produces absolutely unnatural images.[65]

As we can see, Gan's ethic repeated Volkonsky's almost word for word although it is true that he only repeated what corresponded to the mechanistic laws of nature. But the sudden move towards the declarative machine cult concealed the continuity of ideas. Kuleshov responded actively to Constructivist slogans. In an unsigned article, 'The History of the State Institute of Cinematography', published in *Kino-Fot* and probably written by Kuleshov, Gardin was given a 'dressing-down' for distancing himself from the 'left-wing tendency', and the orientation towards the 'mechanisation of human movements' was proclaimed.[66] The short period of *rapprochement* with the Constructivists played an important role in the later evaluation of Kuleshov's work and in his break with preceding tradition. But Kuleshov was too closely linked to the ideas of the new anthropology which had their roots in the 1910s. It is precisely this that doubtless explains in part the unexpected move by Kuleshov and his entire collective (Pudovkin, Barnet, Komarov and others) to Mezhrabpomfilm, the most traditional film studio in the 1920s, which preserved the best traditions of the pre-Revolutionary Russian cinema. The names of Delsarte and Dalcroze can be found in Kuleshov texts over a period of many years and this has puzzled researchers. By the end of the 1920s they were already being perceived as strange anachronisms. It is symptomatic that as late as 1924 an orthodox figure like Alexander Voznesensky, who belonged entirely to the pre-Revolutionary Russian cinema, persistently recommended the methods of Dalcroze and Delsarte as a means of achieving the maximum 'incarnation' [vzhivanie] in the character,[67] prolonging in his own way the Gardin line of film theory.

In the later Kuleshov texts (after 1929), which have until recently served as the basis for the evaluation of this film theory, montage and the anthropological ideas of the 1910s diverge, giving the impression of a strange eclecticism. The metro-rhythmic approach and the new anthropology differed in their methods of teaching the actor and of rehearsal but their direct link with the montage experiments of 1921 was lost.

Nevertheless the idea of the actor moving along axes, which was subsequently to provoke such censure, is no more than a fusion of Volkonsky's concepts on the directions of the movement of the body and Ferdinandov's inclination towards recording the movements of the actor. They make complete sense only in the context of the principle of the identity between montage and the movement of the body, of their mutual rhythmic resonance. The methodology of the training of the model actor, which was experienced in Kuleshov as a period of intensive research in the field of the 'synthetic' theory of cinema, rudimentarily preserved within itself the anthropological principle of montage.

The history of Kuleshov's theoretical research reminds us once again of the fact that for thousands of years the human body has served as a model for the universe, from the theory of macrocosm and microcosm to the physiognomic teachings of the eighteenth and nineteenth centuries. This traditional metamodel has evolved from the intact body of the Middle Ages to the dismembered corpse of the nineteenth century. The idea of montage as the specific basis of a new art, cinema, is an important link in the long history of this evolution.

# 3  *Intolerance* and the Soviets: a historical investigation

*Vance Kepley, Jr*

Tracing lines of influence in film history is one of the most popular en-deavours among film scholars; it is also one of the most treacherous. The appearance of similar styles or conventions among different schools of film often invites premature conclusions about direct lines of descent. The historian, therefore, must penetrate below such surface observations to identify the complexities and contradictions of historical continuity if we are truly to understand the links between one cinematic movement and another.

Historians agree that the most influential early film-maker was D. W. Griffith and that among his most precocious students were the Soviet directors of the 1920s. Furthermore, *Intolerance* is singled out as the most conspicuous link between Griffith and the Soviets, with the explanation that the radical editing style of Griffith's 1916 feature was instrumental in shaping the montage school of film which culminated in the USSR in the middle and late 1920s. *Intolerance* was admired in the Soviet Union. It was reputedly studied in the Moscow Film Institute for the possibilities of montage and 'agitational' cinema [agitfil'm], and leading Soviet directors, including Eisenstein, Pudovkin and Kuleshov, acknowledged a debt to Griffith in their writings.[1]

Such evidence would seem to support the assumption that Griffith and *Intolerance* were of paramount importance to the Soviets. Griffith's most loyal partisans attribute many of the salient characteristics of Soviet cinema to Griffith's legacy.[2] But more balanced studies argue that *Intolerance* was actually one of several sources for the Soviets and that the Soviet montage aesthetic originated in Russian avant-garde art, theatre and literature.[3] An examination of the circumstances and ramifications of the distribution of *Intolerance* in the USSR will considerably qualify our assumptions about Griffith's supposed hold over the Soviets.

## I

The Soviet directors of the early post-Revolutionary period were excited primarily by American films. These young artists dismissed the Russian cinema of the tsarist period, with its preponderance of love triangles and uneven literary adaptations, as hopelessly decadent. American adventure and mystery films – to which the Soviets attached the single genre label *detektiv* – captured the fancy of the Soviets. They admired the vitality and frenetic activity of these 'naive' films. Kuleshov noted of the *detektiv* that 'the fundamental element of the plot is an intensity in the development of action, the dynamic of construction'.[4] The Soviets hoped to adapt this energetic style into an aggressive, revolutionary cinema.

The Americans offered no more impressive example of dynamic cinema than *Intolerance*, and various incidents attest to its impact in the USSR; Pudovkin abandoned a scientific career for the cinema after watching the film;[5] *Intolerance* was so popular that in 1921 the Petrograd Cinema Committee organised an extremely successful two-week run of the film to raise funds for victims of the Civil War famine;[6] Soviet representatives reportedly even extended Griffith an invitation to work in the USSR.[7]

Nevertheless, other evidence indicates that we should not overestimate the film's importance – particularly as a stylistic inspiration. It would be incorrect to assume that the idea of film montage for the Soviets originated with *Intolerance*. Rather, it seems that when the film was shown in the Soviet Union in 1919, it merely popularised a style already evolving in the hands of Soviet artists. Kuleshov claims he began to forge his seminal theories well before *Intolerance* appeared in the Soviet Union. His experiments which defined the 'Kuleshov effect' apparently began as early as 1917–18. In March 1918, several months before the Russian première of *Intolerance*, Kuleshov published his theoretical essay 'The Art of Cinema', in which he argued that editing constituted the fundamental feature of film art.[8] Vertov writes that he worked out a rapid montage style in his early film *The Battle of Tsaritsyn* [Boi pod Tsaritsynom, 1919–20]. *Intolerance* played in Russia while he was still at work on the film, and the American picture helped acquaint audiences with the mode he sought to perfect: 'After a short time there came Griffith's film *Intolerance*. After that it was easier to speak.'[9] *Intolerance* may have been less a source than a vindication for these innovators.

Russia's familiarity with Griffith actually predated the Revolution. A number of Griffith's early Biograph shorts circulated in tsarist Russia, and at least one served as the source for a Russian film. Yakov Protazanov used the story of Griffith's *The Lonely Villa* for his *Drama by Telephone* [1914]. Protazanov's tale concerns a young wife who discovers that bandits are trying to break into her home. She immediately telephones her absent husband for help but, as he desperately rushes home, the bandits break in and overpower the wife. Whereas Griffith specialised in the successful rescue, in the Russian version the husband arrives too late and discovers that his wife has been murdered. This is not the only change Protazanov makes. Anyone searching for an early link between Griffith's cross-cutting device and Soviet montage must look elsewhere. Protazanov is not concerned with the rhythm or tension of the attempted rescue, and he does not exploit parallel editing. Rather he examines the psychological states of the characters during the crisis, the terror of the woman and the panic of the husband, and he employs an elaborate split-screen system which permits the audience simultaneously to compare the emotions of the husband, wife and culprits.[10] The Russian artist, in borrowing Griffith's tale, specifically rejects Griffith's most famous stylistic contribution to the genre.

## II

The familiar story that *Intolerance* first reached the USSR after it somehow slipped through an anti-Soviet blockade is apocryphal.[11] In fact the film was imported well before the Revolution. When the Italian spectacle *Cabiria* scored a success in Russia in 1915, it was assumed that a potential audience for spectacles existed there, and the Italian Jacques Cibrario, who headed the Transatlantic film distribution firm, brought *Intolerance* into Russia in 1916.[12] But, although *Intolerance* overshadowed *Cabiria* in size and splendour, it was quickly labelled too avant-garde for Russian movie audiences. No Russian exhibitor would agree to handle the film for fear that audiences would be confused by the four-part structure. Consequently, the film gathered dust on a shelf somewhere in Russia until after the Revolution. Not until 1918 did a special government decision clear the way for *Intolerance* to be shown commercially in the RSFSR.[13]

The première of *Intolerance* in Petrograd was a major cinema event for the Soviets. On 17 November 1918 the Petrograd Cinema Committee sponsored a special showing for an audience composed largely of government officials, including the Commissar for Enlightenment, Anatoli Lunacharsky.[14] The 25 May 1919 Moscow première was part of an official celebration. The occasion was the first anniversary of so-called 'Universal Military Training', the government's Civil War programme of training Red Army conscripts. *Intolerance* warranted a special closed showing at the prestigious Moscow movie theatre, the Artistic [Khudozhestvennyi].[15]

The Moscow première inspired an illuminating review in *Izvestiya*. The critic was impressed by the American film's scope and technical virtues, and he noted that it might serve as a model for future Soviet productions. But he dismissed the content as 'bourgeois': the theme of reconciliation and 'notorious tolerance' failed to resolve the issues of class conflict in the modern story. He suggested that *Intolerance* might be reconstructed into a thoroughly 'agitational' film by 'turning scenes around and changing titles'.[16] His remarks identify the ideological reservations that Soviet cinephiles had about the film. The Soviets recognised that *Intolerance* was a humanist, even a somewhat leftist film. But it certainly was not a revolutionary film. For Soviet artists anxious to find a cinematic model which combined the dynamic style of the *detektiv* with the political content of the *agitfil'm*, *Intolerance* was close yet still very far. *Intolerance* had its militant moments –

most notably the strike sequence – but its vague sentimental humanism left Griffith's Soviet admirers cold.

The *Izvestiya* critic advocated the re-editing of the film for commercial release to give it a proper slant. It is difficult to determine the extent to which that was done. At least one account indicates that the Christ section was abridged in the public versions of the film.[17] But there is reason to believe that the film was not completely altered by Soviet censors. The Soviet Union was entering the most eclectic years in all Russian intellectual history. Soviet artists were borrowing from numerous cultures and political systems, and as yet there was no Stalin or Zhdanov to enforce rigid conformity.[18]

More important, the Soviets employed a method of dealing with the ideological shortcomings of *Intolerance* that was far more ingenious and exciting than censorship. *Intolerance* was selected for presentation at the Congress of the Comintern in Petrograd in the summer of 1921. The Petrograd Cinema Committee undoubtedly hoped to impress the delegates with the potential of agitational cinema, but they were painfully aware of the film's ideological deficiencies. They decided the occasion required them to 'sharpen the class theme' of the film while at the same time respecting the author's original intentions.[19] Their method was not to censor or cut parts of the film but rather to add to it. Nikolai Glebov-Putilovsky of the Petrograd Cinema Committee prepared a live, dramatised prologue which would 'amplify the anti-exploitation theme of the film'. The practice of adding Soviet propaganda to pre-Revolutionary works of art was common in the young socialist country. Soviet writer Demyan Bedny's satirical poem at the base of a tsarist monument is another example of this method of 'finishing' a work of art.[20] This operation transcends censorship. It respects the integrity of the original work while at the same time allowing the Soviets to make ideological improvements. Indeed, it rather resembles Meyerhold's theatrical practice of staging classic and pre-Revolutionary plays in modern, Constructivist styles which were rich with propaganda.

It speaks well for Griffith that five years after *Intolerance* was made and almost two years after the nationalisation of the Soviet industry, the Soviets singled out this American film of dubious service to the Revolution for presentation at the Comintern Congress. Despite the shortage of celluloid, the Soviets did manage to prepare for the congress a series of documentary films on the work of the socialist government throughout the Soviet Union.[21] But these apparently were rather pedestrian educational films. For an impressive example of *agitfil'm*, *Intolerance* may still have seemed the most palatable choice available. Also, the American epic undoubtedly had a more cosmopolitan appeal to the international audience than a strict diet of Soviet films would have had.[22] In any event, the Cinema Committee was willing to sacrifice ideological purity to entertain and edify the socialist audience. The prologue would give the evening the proper dose of revolutionary spirit, and the movie would take care of itself.

The prologue allowed the Soviets to comment on the film and to add their

*Figure 5  Intolerance* [1916]: in honouring Griffith, the Soviets were compelled to criticise him.

own interpretations to certain scenes. The most glaring problem for the Soviets was the film's insistent theme that history is cyclical. *Intolerance* advances the argument that the same cycles of intolerance and injustice simply recur in different historical dress. Basic impulses and human emotions, the fundamental forces in all human endeavours, are as consistent as the hand that rocks the cradle. Not surprisingly, the same dilemmas appear in epoch after epoch. This is hardly compatible with a Marxist, economic-determinist philosophy which considers history progressive and dialectical.

The prologue goes about uniting Marx and Griffith with considerable finesse. Generally, the prologue seizes on certain vivid images of suffering and injustice in the film and casts these in a Marxist framework. The prologue opens with a call to those assembled:

> Hear ye, hear ye, O people! . . . Hear, ye who have come hither: men and women, young and old – and behold! Beyond your life in the distant depths of history you will see a broad road that the human race has been following for thousands of years.[23]

Already it is clear that the delegates are in for a history class. The prologue emphatically proclaims that the lessons of *Intolerance* are the lessons of the past. The road is the central metaphor of the first half of the prologue, and on it can be seen the bitter teachings of history. A look down the road reveals countless examples of hardship in the lot of the common people. For example, the Girl is 'tossed by the evil hand of life into the mud and dust'.[24]

The road reveals something of a dialectic and a clear class conflict in the constant presence of opposites. The powerful and the weak, the exploiter and the exploited, are always present: 'The ancient patrician and the plebeian, the king and his serf, Babylon and a simple settlement, love and hate, light and darkness'.[25]

The road metaphor disappears in the second half of the prologue and new imagery emerges. Now ancient mountains represent history. Out of these mountains of the past flow four small streams, the four tales of the film. The streams run in separate but parallel paths, suggesting the flux and turmoil of history – a counterpoint to the static, awesome mountains. We again see images of exploitation with the stories of *Intolerance*.

> Millions and billions of riches, created by slave labour and legally accumulated by those who have seized control of the law: the factory owners, the governors, the public prosecutors, the emperors and their fine retinue of concubines and lackeys. . . .
>
> The French Court with its overdressed dolls and a gallows demanding a sacrifice. A smoke-filled episode of religious baseness from the stately priests and St Bartholomew's Eve; a humble carpenter from Galilee; clean-handed Pilate and the wild instincts of the crowd, shouting, 'Crucify Him! Crucify Him!'[26]

The prologue concludes with a promise of ultimate salvation from this history of cruelty. The four currents flow down the mountains unto a gentle plain where they merge into one stream. This is, in a sense, the synthesis, and it leads to the Soviet utopia 'In the beautiful valley of life'. The film shows the ugly lessons of the past, but for the future there is the promise of the Soviet system: from 'the mire and slime and rottenness, from which we emerged with pain and torment towards the radiant Soviets: towards our temples of labour and liberty, through which we shall resurrect everything.'[27] The prologue then ends with an affirmation and a rallying cry reminiscent of a varsity cheer:

The Soviets! The Soviets! – the earth hums.
The road of the Soviets – the Soviets are our salvation!!![28]

By insisting that the stories of *Intolerance* represent some dreadful past, the Soviets could fit the film into a Marxist schema which promises a glorious future. The utopian vision in the prologue is no less naive than the film's coda which calls for an era of brotherhood when prison walls will dissolve. Griffith invests his faith in an amorphous notion of brotherly love, and the Soviets celebrate an equally dubious confidence in the ability of socialism to eradicate all strife. The reconciliation between Marx and Griffith proved an ingenious, albeit tenuous one.

The prologue's metaphor of the parallel streams originated in a playbill which accompanied the New York première of *Intolerance*:

Our theme is told in four little stories.

These stories begin like four currents, looked at from a hilltop. As they flow they grow nearer and nearer together, and faster and faster, 'until in the end, in the last act, they mingle in one mighty river of expressed emotion'.

Then you see that, though they seem unlike, through all of them runs one thought, one theme.[29]

The metaphor here is restricted to describing the structure of the film itself. The four stories merge in the last reel of *Intolerance* through cross-cutting to create an emotional climax, 'one mighty river of expressed emotion'. The Soviet prologue expands the metaphor into a historical one. Significantly, Eisenstein's celebrated analysis of *Intolerance* in 'Dickens, Griffith, and the Film Today', specifically cites the American playbill's stream metaphor to analyse Griffith's montage. He argues that Griffith's film, contrary to the claim set out in the playbill, fails to achieve a true synthesis of tales. For him, Griffith's montage is not truly dialectical, and he claims *Intolerance* remains a drama of comparisons – 'a combination of *four different stories*, rather than a *fusion of four phenomena* into *a single imagist generalisation*'.[30] The Soviet prologue subtly apologises for the ideological faults of *Intolerance*, and Eisenstein, who borrows the same metaphor from the same source, exposes what he considers the film's formal problems. In honouring Griffith, the Soviets were compelled to criticise him.

This investigation of the early history of *Intolerance* in Russia reveals some of the hazards of too-easy assumptions of historical continuity. The evidence on the Soviet reception of *Intolerance* raises questions about the actual extent of the Soviet debt to Griffith that can only be resolved through meticulous stylistic comparisons of the work of the early Soviets and that of Griffith – not to mention such Griffith contemporaries as Ince, King, Feuillade and Gance. As present it seems clear that for all the attention the Soviets lavished on *Intolerance*, it was as important to them for its flaws as for its virtues.[31]

## PROLOGUE TO *INTOLERANCE*[32]

Hear ye, hear ye, O people! . . . Hear, ye who have come hither: men and women, young and old – and behold! Beyond your life in the distant depths of history you will see a broad road that the human race has been following for thousands of years. Behold! . . . There is plump Virtue: she feeds on nothing but human blood and her soul accepts nothing else. There are the Scribes and the Pharisees: those great lackeys, who make great show of their worship, who preen themselves on their merits and their morality even before God Himself, and everywhere there exist even today the agents of that great sacrificial Golgotha. You will see the Girl: a little slip of a girl, a dream, a flower tossed by the evil hand of life into the mud and dust, beneath the filthy carts of the bazaar where souls are bought and sold. Who has not trodden this road before you? The ancient patrician and the plebeian, the king and his serf, Babylon and a simple settlement, love and hate, light and darkness, the factory owner and the worker, sincerity and vile cunning, the height of civilisation and the depth of ignorance, grief and joy, war and peace, life itself and death, and, as a symbol of this great path, from the depths of history to the present day, the eternally rocking cradle over which the golden head of the mother is bent low.

What goes through your mind?

Four streams run down from the high old mountain of history: a picture of everyday life; medieval Jerusalem;[33] France; and Babylon the magnificent.

Nightmarish wealth! Millions and billions of riches, created by slave labour and legally accumulated by those who have seized control of the law: the factory owners, the governors, the public prosecutors, the emperors and their fine retinue of concubines and lackeys. Those fleet-footed helmsmen . . . so obediently ready to oblige, devour with their masters the living human body and quench their thirst by drinking warm human blood.

The French Court with its overdressed dolls and a gallows demanding a sacrifice. A smoke-filled episode of religious baseness from the stately priests and St Bartholomew's Eve; a humble carpenter from Galilee;

clean-handed Pilate and the wild instincts of the crowd, shouting, 'Crucify Him! Crucify Him!'

From the great old mountain that we call life the familiar flows before you and, merging into the rapid change of days, leads unexpectedly to the Soviets.

The 'Soviets' – that is our word.

What does it mean?

In the beautiful valley of life. At the foot of the mountain of history, creating nobody knows what. With passionate faith and the iron strength of conviction. Spread by the magic cauldron of the Revolution – the Soviets!

And, looking back across the threshold, remembering the road that mankind has taken, you record in a book and relate to others this last tale of our long enslavement. A tale of basest flattery and the trading of souls. Of the mire and slime and rottenness, from which we emerged with pain and torment towards the radiant Soviets: towards our temples of labour and liberty, through which we shall resurrect everything.

The Soviets! The Soviets! – the earth hums.

The road of the Soviets – the Soviets are our salvation!!!

# 4 The origins of Soviet cinema: a study in industry development

*Vance Kepley, Jr*

In August 1919 Lenin affixed his signature to a sheet of paper and thereby assigned principal responsibility for the management of Soviet cinema to the government's Commissariat of Enlightenment and to that agency's head, Anatoli Lunacharsky. The new charge must have seemed anything but promising. The film industry was in chaos: resources remained in short supply; experienced personnel either fled the country or refused to co-operate with government authorities; and numerous theatres had closed or fallen into disrepair. The regime could manage only a handful of feature productions during this initial period of nationalisation, and it lacked the necessary distribution and exhibition apparatus to find any sizeable audience for the few films it did produce.[1]

Nevertheless, by the end of 1925 Soviet cinema had emerged as a vital public institution. Production levels had increased tenfold and continued to rise annually through the decade; and distribution and exhibition policies assured that even remote areas of Soviet Russia could expect at least some exposure to cinema. By any standard of industry development, this represented an impressive record, all the more so since it was effected despite such adverse conditions as civil war and political isolation.[2]

How might we account for this growth? What measures transformed a national problem into a national resource in little more than six years? The answers lie in a developmental history of the Soviet film industry from the late 1910s through the middle 1920s, one that takes into account the crucial policies of financial management, investment and resource allocation that nurtured the fledgeling cinema through this critical period.

Historians have paid surprisingly little attention to the Soviet film industry's economic development. General histories of film usually make passing reference to the sorry state of the industry in the late 1910s, mention Lenin's nationalisation decree, then concentrate on the Soviet cinema's mature period of the middle and late 1920s, an elliptical narrative that tempts one to conclude simply that Lenin's decree eradicated financial problems and led directly to the achievements of Eisenstein and his colleagues.[3] Even special-ised histories, valuable as they often are for their information on the industry, provide no systematic developmental record. In his widely read

*Kino*, Jay Leyda acknowledged that his interest remained with the careers of individual film-makers rather than impersonal economic forces.[4] Paul Babitsky, John Rimberg and Richard Taylor provide fuller chronicles of the industry's evolution, but their work concentrates far less on industry growth patterns than on the official measures taken to bring the cinema under the Party's ideological control.[5]

A genuine developmental history of the early Soviet film industry must represent a macro-economic study. It should take into account the large-scale trends of the entire Soviet economy during the period in question, including the efforts of Soviet leaders to encourage overall industrial growth. And by extension, such a history should draw on the discipline of developmental economics, some principles of which merit review.[6]

A developing nation, especially one which hopes to move rapidly from an agricultural to an industrial economy, as was the case with the Soviet Union, is likely at some point to undergo a period of so-called *capital accumulation*. This entails the rapid accumulation of the resources of production – factories, machines, tools, and the like – which can serve for future manufacturing. A national economy might effect such capital accumulation through forced savings by reducing the level of consumption for a time and investing instead in the machines and materials necessary for future production; consumer demand might be temporarily held in check on the promise of more and better consumer goods after capital goods industries had emerged. In some economies forced savings might be achieved by encouraging private savings through the manipulation of taxes and credit, and these funds would be used for investment in new capital. Reliance on forced savings might prove difficult, however, in a severely underdeveloped nation where a substantial part of the population lives at the subsistence level and thus generates no margin for investment; forced savings in such circumstances would represent a hardship political leaders might not wish to inflict on the population. To avoid the potential privations of forced savings, a developing nation might look to foreign investment and foreign credit to accumulate capital. These avenues can prove politically expedient, although they also involve concessions; revenues would be extracted from the affected industries by foreign investors and extensive foreign debts might compromise the developing nation in international affairs. Foreign trade, however, can provide concession-free capital as long as the developing nation establishes favourable terms of trade; typically, the developing nation must export what it can to offset the purchase of industrial machinery from abroad, and that usually means trading away raw materials and agricultural goods.

A condition to be avoided by any national economy, developing or otherwise, is an extended period of *net capital consumption*. This results from using up the resources of production faster than they can be replenished. Factory equipment must be replaced, for example, and raw materials secured. If such replacements are not provided regularly, industries will gradually grind to a halt. In such a crisis, industry planners must ration resources until such time as the economy can begin new capital accumulation.

Early Soviet planners confronted decisions on all these matters, and their choices were complicated by the particular position in which the USSR found itself. By virtue of climate, landscape, and cultural tradition, Russia represented a comparatively inefficient producer of industrial goods and a comparatively efficient producer of agricultural goods. In the late tsarist period, for example, Russia was a leading exporter of grain. The new Bolshevik regime, however, determined to defy the apparent dictates of nature and geography by transforming an age-old agricultural system into a world industrial leader. They undertook this formidable task despite external political threats from hostile capitalist nations and internal disorder culminating in the Russian Civil War.

The first phase of the Bolshevik economic system encompassed the period of War Communism (1918–21) in which the government effected a series of emergency measures to cope with the economic damage wrought by the Civil War and foreign blockade. With the eventual passing of these political crises, the regime initiated its New Economic Policy (NEP, 1921–9) to encourage economic recovery. This 'transitional mixed economy', as Lenin described it, involved returning much of the economy to a market system while leaving in place a large measure of government control in the hope that recovery could be facilitated by the forces of private initiative. The NEP period fell into two phases, an early interval of rapid capitalisation (1921–5) followed by successful production (1925–9). These trends and the previously discussed developmental principles define a clear periodisation: War Communism represented an interval of net capital consumption deriving from political and social dislocation while the first half of NEP was characterised by capital accumulation as industries geared up for the productivity that was eventually realised in the late 1920s. The first tactic of capital accumulation, forced savings, proved rather infeasible in the early Soviet economy given the limited private surpluses of the population; it would only be fully effected under Stalin's rapid industrialisation plans of the 1930s, and then at great cost to the population. Instead, various combinations of credit, investment, foreign concessions, and overseas trade were used to accumulate capital under NEP.

The film industry's pattern of early development conforms to that of the larger economy. The industry's shift from net capital consumption to capital accumulation conforms to the transition from War Communism to NEP, and the industry's new capital derived from foreign trade, foreign and domestic investment, and, to a lesser extent, credit. The early history of the Soviet film industry entails a record of hard-headed management of scarce resources and judicious use of various sources of capital. Whatever Lenin's nationalisation decree represented, it did not render the Soviet film industry productive. It only helped set in motion a complex developmental process, the details of which are the subject of this study.

## WAR COMMUNISM AND THE PERIOD OF NET
## CAPITAL CONSUMPTION

The combined effects of civil war, foreign intervention and international trade embargoes resulted in a near collapse of the Russian economy in the late 1910s. The British Royal Navy severed the major sea routes to Russia, precluding the importation of new industrial items and requiring Russia to survive on its economic inheritance from the pre-Revolutionary era. Although some industrialisation had taken place under the last tsars, many vital factories and railways suffered damage during the Civil War and production dropped to less than half the levels before the First World War. The only course available to the new government was to ration resources during the crisis and to postpone any sustained rebuilding effort until such time as the political situation stabilised. But even rationing efforts suffered from the government's limited authority. Many regions remained under the control of the White Guards and even areas under Red Army occupation answered more to local Party and military units than to the Kremlin. During the period of political chaos, most working decisions were made at the local level by the various Soviets of Workers', Soldiers' and Peasants' Deputies, the local governing bodies which derived from the Party's old cellular organisation and which often operated without orders from Moscow.[7]

These conditions prevented Lenin from establishing any integrated, national economic plan. He resorted to pragmatic emergency measures grouped under the umbrella term 'nationalisation', although, as practised, this term represented something of a misnomer. The term applied to any public takeover of private assets, whether at the national or local level. Usually, in fact, the initiatives were taken by local officials, often the local Soviets of Deputies, and Moscow only ratified the expropriations after the fact. Nationalisation often resulted from accusations of sabotage, from the refusal of particular capitalists to co-operate with the local Soviet of Deputies, or from a desire to let public authorities manage limited resources as a means of preventing hoarding and waste. The policy remained one of reaction rather than systematic action and betrayed the regime's lack of power.[8]

Such pragmatism obtained in early efforts to manage the film industry. Bolshevik leaders agreed that cinema could prove a useful propaganda and educational tool, a conviction that Lenin, for example, developed during his exile in the West. But the Party established no clear, long-range agenda on how to develop the film industry; nor was the integration of cinema into the national education system sufficiently outlined. The film industry that had been inherited from the tsarist period showed little promise of renewal as a national institution. Its production activity was centred almost entirely in Moscow, and distribution and exhibition facilities extended barely beyond the urban centres of European Russia. Lenin hoped that cinema would have its greatest utility in remote rural areas where literacy levels were lowest, but few villages contained exhibition facilities or any tradition of cinema. More ominous was the fact that no factories survived for the manufacture of cameras, projectors, printers, or film stock. Pre-Revolutionary film companies had simply relied on importation of materials through Western Europe, and heavy French and German investment in tsarist Russia encouraged such dependency. But the severing of trade routes, first by the World War and then by the anti-Soviet blockade, cut off the supply. As the Russian movie industry operated through the world war, it ate into a finite quantity of resources and left the post-Revolutionary industry with diminished reserves.[9]

Efforts by the Bolsheviks to use cinema in some official way began within months of the October Revolution, but they followed no grand design. In the *ad hoc* nature of War Communism, most steps were taken at the local level by different agencies acting unilaterally, and the measures were often limited in their effect to Moscow and Petrograd, the only sites of genuine Bolshevik authority. In January 1918 the Bolsheviks established a Division of Photography and Cinema which was attached to the Commissariat of Enlightenment. Although the measure seemed to clear the way for the making and showing of educational films on a national scale, in those early uncertain days of Revolution, the Commissariat's influence barely extended beyond the Petrograd city limits, and its Photo-Cinema Division remained largely a paper institution. Its first significant action was the expropriation of the assets of the Skobelev Committee, an organisation surviving from the World War which had done some film work at the behest of the tsarist and provisional governments. This provided the Commissariat with the assets to begin producing a few short newsreels. Such low-budget films seemed the most appropriate use of scarce resources during this period of privation.[10]

Meanwhile the local Soviets of Deputies in both Moscow and Petrograd made independent moves into cinema activity in the spring of 1918. The Moscow Soviet of Deputies took its initiative in response to reports of sabotage by the heads of the private production companies centred in that city. It encouraged film workers to monitor the activities of their bosses with particular attention to the hoarding of materials, and it followed with orders for a full inventory of the assets of Moscow companies and for an end to the transfer of assets. The measures came in response to reports that private producers would remove their headquarters to areas outside Bolshevik control since Moscow cinema entrepreneurs openly acknowledged their opposition to the Bolshevik regime and spoke of defying official directives. The Petrograd Soviet of Deputies, by contrast, inherited a much smaller capitalist cinema establishment within its jurisdiction and, hence, much less resistance to its initiatives. It established its own Photo-Cinema Committee and used such public funds as it could spare to make short newsreels and to maintain a few exhibition facilities in and around the city.[11]

In the haphazard manner of early War Communism, then, three separate public institutions, acting without mutual consent, established whatever control they could in the private sector. Only retroactively, in late 1918 and early 1919, did they make any effort at co-ordination; that effort remained limited to the Moscow-Petrograd axis. The film-related activities of the Moscow Soviet of Deputies, which consisted mostly of monitoring private production, reverted to the Commissariat of Enlightenment when the national government moved the capital to Moscow in 1918, and the Commissariat assigned agents to oversee local film companies.[12]

The shortage of resources became the primary concern of the Commissariat when it expanded its responsibilities, and it set about locating new stocks for both the private firms and the public agencies involved in cinema. The Commissariat undertook inventories which revealed every form of supply problem. Most working cameras were European imports whose vintage preceded the First World War, and the dearth of spare parts meant that their working days were numbered. Commercial theatres were left to re-run *ad nauseam* old, scratched and worn prints of pre-Revolutionary features. Although the sea lanes to Russia remained closed, land routes proved harder to seal, and some material, including film stock, was smuggled in through Latvia. But such contraband hardly proved sufficient to supply either the private or public film organisations in Moscow and Petrograd.[13]

The Commissariat responded to this situation by initiating several ill-fated ventures calculated to acquire new resources:

(1) A contract with a Moscow laboratory to produce raw film eventually fell through; the laboratory lacked the technical sophistication to produce film of a usable quality.

(2) A Russian chemist devised a scheme to coat exposed film with new emulsion as a way of exploiting used footage, but the recycled film lacked adequate resolution to generate decent imagery.

(3) In a plan that betrayed considerable naivety about the nature of technological research and development, a Russian technician was sent to Berlin to make notes about state-of-the-art film technology with the expectation that he would then pattern new Soviet-made equipment on the Berlin models; the technician received an expenses-paid round trip to Berlin, but the Commissariat received no workable designs in return.

(4) This comedy of errors culminated in the notorious Cibrario affair, when a cagey foreign entrepreneur promised to tour the West to purchase new equipment and film stock for the USSR but then proceeded to bilk the Commissariat out of more than one million dollars' worth of hard currency.[14]

Such desperate measures, though not unparalleled in other economic sectors during War Communism, demonstrated the necessity for greater centralisation of authority. Lenin's August 1919 nationalisation decree was designed to serve that end. The action, in fact, was taken as something of a last resort to bring some order to the activities of local governments and to minimise the squandering of precious film resources. The measure presented no agenda for future development; instead, it merely delineated certain forms of authority that the Commissariat of Enlightenment could exercise should it choose to do so. It transferred the authority to set film policy to the Commissariat and gave that agency the power to nationalise existing private firms to supervise future productions, and to issue more detailed directives. Far from instantly transferring all private assets to government ownership, the decree simply had the net effect of assigning the Commissariat the power to manage and ration the industry's supplies and to nationalise individual industry institutions on a case-by-case basis.[15] Similar to countless such measures which passed under Lenin's busy pen, it was a stop-gap device to help an industry through an inevitable period of capital consumption.

To facilitate the administrative responsibilities deriving from the decree, the Commissariat created a new bureaucratic layer, the All-Russian Photographic and Cinematographic Section (VFKO) which was to help co-ordinate local cinema activities, especially the haphazard process of nationalising individual film institutions. VFKO was to be the national agency linking the efforts of various localities, especially the Moscow and Petrograd Cinema Committees. In its first effort at general planning, VFKO collected an inventory of all prints that might be available for exhibition. The chronic shortage of films to supply commercial theatres encouraged VFKO to register for exhibition old tsarist films and pre-Revolutionary imports.[16]

Yet the weaknesses of the regime and the catch-as-catch-can nature of War Communism were manifested in the implementation of the Commissariat's nationalisation authority. Lenin's decree merely conferred on the Commissariat the power to nationalise on an individual basis, and, in practice, nationalisation of particular commercial institutions resulted from that institution's failure. Most of the nationalised institutions in cinema were movie theatres which had closed because of lack of product. The net effect of the practice was that the government took over closed theatres while working establishments remained in private hands. By the late autumn of 1919, approximately one-third of cinema assets in Bolshevik-controlled regions were nationalised: yet much of that represented dead weight.[17]

The lack of Bolshevik authority in most regions of the country further compromised the nationalisation policy. Far from preventing the hoarding or transfer of materials – the decree's announced goal – the threat of expropriation posed by the decree actually encouraged private entrepreneurs to seek friendlier political climes; this generally meant relocating to White-controlled areas in the south. Indeed, cinema would not seem to be an industrial form readily subject to nationalisation in times of emergency. Nationalisation worked best in heavy industries, such as steel and mining, where the assets could not be packed in a trunk and carried away. Film company owners simply carted off their inherently portable equipment and inventories to the Crimea, leaving Bolshevik officials to seize empty office buildings, barren shooting stages and darkened theatres.[18]

During the entire period of War Communism, private cinema out-produced government-affiliated producers in Moscow and Petrograd. The renegade firms in the south derived from strong pre-Revolutionary film companies and could draw on the expertise of experienced personnel. Lunacharsky and his colleagues in the Commissariat may have noted with envy the level of activity of private companies. From 1918 to 1921 private firms produced 296 fiction films, the lion's share of which – 209 – were feature-length. Government-registered productions during the same period amounted to just 104 fiction films, only 13 of which were features.[19]

There were also problems in the exhibition phase of the industry. According to one Soviet estimate, only 1,000 permanent commercial theatres operated in Russia in 1917, and many of those failed to survive the Civil War. Construction of new permanent installations was out of the question for the time being; the economy had no construction industry to speak of and little funding for expensive construction projects. Low-cost portable cinemas provided the answer. The agit-train, that ingenious Bolshevik institution for taking cinema and revolutionary culture into the countryside, owed much to economic necessity. The strategy of equipping trains with portable projectors and generators pre-dated the October Revolution, but it was also consistent with the War Communism practice of making maximum use of inherited resources. The Russian rail system had been considerably expanded by the last tsars and proved central to the Bolshevik exercise of power. Lenin put high priority on maintaining the rail system, partly out of military necessity (since the Red Army used trains to move troops to strategic locations). The same rail system also allowed the government to take propaganda into areas where popular support was deemed crucial. Trains equipped with old projectors carried Soviet-made documentaries and Bolshevik spokesmen into such regions and served the regime's propaganda needs without requiring substantial new capital.[20]

The strategy adhered to throughout War Communism – if one could call such hasty, reactive measures a strategy – was to locate and gain control over whatever assets were available and to use them as efficiently as possible. The liquidity of the film industry and the limitations of Bolshevik power complicated such efforts. As with many other industries, sustained expansion would have to wait until the Red Army had finished its work.

## NEP AND CAPITAL ACCUMULATION

With the end of the Civil War and the subsequent consolidation of Bolshevik power, the pragmatic tactics of War Communism gave way to the systematic recovery efforts of the early NEP period. Sometimes mistakenly characterised as a retreat from socialism, NEP's market economy was recognised by

Party officials as a necessary transitional phase of economic development, one that would lead to considerable capital accumulation.

NEP returned many previously nationalised enterprises to the private sector and encouraged competition. The government retained crucial industries such as transportation and mining and leased other concerns back to private entrepreneurs; in fact, many of those nationalised facilities had remained idle or operated below capacity and thus represented a drain on public funds. The government counted on private enterprise to revive such operations; by 1923 it had permitted 75 per cent of the nation's trade to revert to private hands.[21]

One method the government developed to retain some influence in this expanded private sector was the industry 'trust' system. One or more government trusts, large semi-private companies, were organised in each industry in such a way that they tended to dominate without monopolising the industry's market. They were designed to wield sufficient financial power to set standards of production, wages and prices that other firms would follow. The trusts represented a compromise between public and private commerce: the government oversaw their operation, but the trusts had to operate on a self-sustaining basis, generating sufficient income to cover their working expenses and, in theory at least, their expansion.[22]

The film industry adapted to NEP by following this model. The relative prosperity of private film firms during the Civil War indicated that the Soviet market harboured sufficient demand to sustain considerable commercial cinema activity. NEP permitted the old renegade firms to operate above board. Many of the ones that had not fled the country entirely relocated in Moscow, making it once again the nation's centre of private film activity. By early 1922 at least five major firms were involved in production and/or distribution activity in the Moscow area. The single strongest film company at the beginning of NEP, however, was Sevzapkino of Petrograd, which had evolved from the old Cinema Committee of the Petrograd Soviet of Deputies and had changed from a public to a private concern with the advent of NEP. The absence of significant competition from private film entrepreneurs in the Petrograd region permitted Sevzapkino to dominate its market and fund quick expansion. It soon integrated production, distribution and exhibition functions and gained control of Russia's north-west region, hence its new name Sevzapkino, or 'North-Western Cinema'.[23]

The central government in Moscow, meanwhile, placed its administrative chips on a film trust called Goskino, which it created in 1922 to supplant the old, unwieldy bureaucratic apparatus VFKO. But bureaucratic duplication survived, in that Goskino was to answer to the Soviet government in the form of three separate official agencies: the Commissariat of Enlightenment, under Lunacharsky, continued to hold sway over most policy decisions; the Supreme Economic Council [Vesenkha], the state's chief economic planning board, had control over the allocation of raw materials and producers' goods, and could, where cinema was concerned, ration such resources as film stock; and the Commissariat of Foreign Trade took over the management of film-related imports when serious film trading began in 1922. Initial assets of the trust, appraised at just 3.5 million roubles, consisted largely of the production facilities in the Moscow area which VFKO had controlled and a few movie theatres, though most previously nationalised theatres had been leased back to private management.[24]

Goskino remained woefully undercapitalised considering that it was designated the government trust for cinema and expected to take the lead in industry development. The government proved willing to capitalise other enterprises in crucial sectors of the economy such as agriculture and construction with direct investments and credits, but cinema did not initially merit such support. For all the talk of cinema being the most important of the arts, the government quite simply had more pressing responsibilities than subsidising movies – like feeding, clothing and housing a population recently visited by the scourges of war and famine. Lunacharsky's frequent requests in 1922 and 1923 for direct government support of Goskino went unheeded. Goskino, and by extension the rest of the film industry, went on notice that, for the time being at least, they would have to accumulate capital through their own initiatives rather than government subvention.[25]

Lunacharsky's first such initiative involved seeking foreign credits and investments for the film industry. This tactic took its source from Lenin's decision to grant foreign concessions in several industries beginning in 1921. Foreign capitalists received invitations to take over the operation of several moribund facilities in such areas as mining, oil and forestry. The Russians conceded a substantial amount of income from these facilities in return for the rehabilitation of the industrial units themselves. But while the foreign concession policy worked in these extraction industries, Russia received few foreign investments in manufacturing, apparently because foreign capitalists most wanted access to Russian raw materials and were leery of making investments in expensive production projects, especially since the Bolsheviks had cancelled foreign debts and confiscated foreign assets just a few years previously.[26]

Russian appeals to foreign investors in film went out in 1922 and ran into the problems related to those of non-extraction industries. The Russians petitioned German and American film companies to invest in Goskino, counting on the foreigners to supply the needed equipment, film stock and technical expertise to get dormant studios working at full capacity. But the film industry, unlike forestry, for example, had little to concede to foreigners as an investment incentive. Lenin and Lunacharsky could only promise foreign movie-makers that they might use Russian landscapes for location productions, a meagre incentive at best for film-makers who worked on artificial sets in well-appointed studios in Hollywood or Neubabelsberg; not surprisingly, studio moguls showed little interest in Russian ventures.[27]

Lunacharsky's effort did succeed in attracting one significant foreign investment for film: the investment came not from foreign capitalists but from an international socialist organisation with close pre-existing ties to the Soviet Union. In 1921 The Workers' International Relief (WIR) had been established on the Comintern's orders to provide aid to victims of the Russian famine. From its offices in Berlin, the organisation solicited relief funds from various leftist organisations in Europe and America. WIR promptly turned to film as a means of advancing relief efforts, sponsoring the production of documentaries about the famine which were exhibited in the West to raise donations. WIR's interest in cinema continued after the famine subsided, and the organisation turned its attention to Soviet economic recovery. In the course of supplying credits to several Soviet industries from 1922 to 1924, WIR supplied Goskino and other Russian film companies with celluloid and equipment valued at roughly 400,000 roubles; this advance was to be redeemed when WIR received foreign distribution rights for future Soviet feature productions.[28]

WIR's most ambitious venture, however, involved the capitalisation of a major Russian production company, Mezhrabpom. In 1924 WIR invested 53,000 roubles to acquire half-interest in a small Moscow film studio which survived from the pre-Revolutionary period. WIR increased its level of investment annually until it had acquired 100 per cent of the company's stock and had raised the firm's total capital to 1.2 million roubles. WIR managed Mezhrabpom effectively, consistently making profits that were reinvested in the company's expanded production schedule. Mezhrabpom concentrated on making big-budget entertainment films in such genres as comedy and science fiction, and it consistently outperformed other Russian companies at the box office. Typical of Mezhrabpom's commercial programming were the works of director Yakov Protazanov, such as the comedy *The Three Millions Trial* [Protsess o trekh millionakh, 1926], which starred the popular comedian Igor Ilyinsky, and the expensive science-fiction film *Aelita* [1924], with its elaborate, futuristic sets and costumes. And Mezhrabpom's horror melodrama *The Bear's Wedding* [Medvezh'ya svad'ba, 1926], to cite another example, emerged as one of the USSR's premier box-office successes of the 1920s. To advance the commercial performance of such films, Mezhrabpom became the first Soviet film organisation to establish a publicity department, which aggressively promoted Mezhrabpom productions. And the company made a move towards vertical integration as well, acquiring three of the USSR's largest commercial theatres, Koloss and Temp in Moscow and Gigant in Leningrad; these profitable first-run houses brought the company an average daily return of 8,900 roubles.[29]

Such aggressive commercialism led to occasional charges of 'NEPism', or profiteering under NEP. But Lunacharsky realised that profitable commercial activity was precisely what the whole industry needed to increase production, and Mezhrabpom's record became the envy of Goskino and other film companies. Mezhrabpom raised its annual production levels from four features and eight documentaries to sixteen features and twenty-three

*Figure 6* Konstantin Eggert, co-director (with Gardin) and star of *The Bear's Wedding* [1926], one of the most popular Soviet productions of the 1920s.

documentaries within five years. This impressive record owed much to the generous terms of the company's WIR investors who demanded no significant concessions from the USSR since they functioned precisely to assist Soviet development.[30]

Other Russian film companies had to accumulate capital without the aid of such benefactors. Ultimately foreign trade, not foreign investment, proved to be the most expeditious route for the rest of the industry, and in 1922 Lenin and Lunacharsky devised an ingenious trading scheme which significantly advanced the industry's growth. Lenin ordered the Commissariat of Foreign Trade to import large numbers of films into the USSR. The films were to provide Soviet commercial theatres with the product needed to begin generating revenues which could then be ploughed back into domestic production. All Soviet theatres were starving for product: the dearth of new feature-length productions meant that pre-Revolutionary Russian films and tattered prints of pre-blockade foreign films often were theatre managers' only feature attractions. New foreign imports, if marketed properly, could satisfy pent-up demand and provide income to be passed on to domestic producers.[31]

In issuing his importation directive, Lenin helped establish the developmental agenda that would last throughout the period of capital accumulation. His decree specified that imported films would be exploited as much for revenue as for popular diversion, and he mandated that imports were to be exhibited in conjunction with the educational and propaganda shorts that Russian studios were making on their limited means. Later celebrated as the 'Leninist film proportion', this second article of the importation decree not only assuaged official concern about the possible ideological damage of showing capitalist films to Soviet audiences, it helped to assure an audience for the Soviet-produced shorts. Lenin and Lunacharsky correctly anticipated that foreign, especially American, films would attract sizeable audiences, and they recommended that political speakers be placed on the programmes. Soviet propaganda would rise on the coattails of Hollywood entertainments. 'If you have a good newsreel, serious and educational pictures,' Lenin asserted, 'then it doesn't matter if, to attract the public, you have some kind of useless picture of the more or less usual type.'[32]

The decision to accumulate capital through overseas trade owed much to favourable market conditions. The foreign blockade finally ended in 1921, and the British began negotiating trade agreements with the USSR, a break that finally liberated the Soviet Union from almost three years of isolation. Russia used the opportunity to acquire crucial producers' goods for several industries, and it traded away raw materials and agricultural products in return. Ample supplies of grain, coal, timber and oil allowed the USSR to buy items ranging from Ford tractors to Paramount movies. The Soviet foreign trading system helped secure favourable terms. The government's Commissariat of Foreign Trade maintained a monopoly on overseas buying and selling, even during the most freewheeling phases of NEP. No individual firm could enter into negotiations with any foreign concern but instead had to apply to the commissariat, asking that body to acquire the needed foreign goods. The commissariat then purchased the items and delivered them to the firm in question in return for a credit which the firm paid off over a period of time. Since all sectors of the economy channelled their foreign trade requests through this one agency, the government could closely monitor the trade balance and arrange for surpluses in one sector to offset deficits in another. In an 'unprotected' economy, each individual firm would have to maintain its own trade balance or be prepared to pay for the imports in hard currency. In the Soviet system, however, weaker industries which had to import (e.g. film) could live off the surpluses of other, stronger industries. Fortunately, Soviet agriculture enjoyed good harvests beginning in 1922 and 1923 and running through much of the rest of the decade. These combined with high grain prices in several foreign markets to provide generally favourable terms of trade for the USSR. Industries such as film which could acquire their imports at a relatively low per unit cost (a movie costing less than a tractor, for example) were especially favoured by these circumstances. In net effect, good grain harvests bought the film industry its future.[33]

The Commissariat of Foreign Trade's status as the sole bargaining agent in international trade gave the Russians another edge in dealing with foreign film sellers. West European and American film companies, which had balked at investing in the USSR directly, proved eager to trade with Russia, recognising it as the largest untapped market in Europe. But they could not deal directly with various Russian distributors and exhibitors in competitive transactions. They had to abide by the 'take it or leave it' offers of the commissariat which enjoyed the power of a monopsonist, the sole buyer in a market. The commissariat could thus obtain foreign films at relatively low prices, thereby enhancing the USSR's trade advantage.[34]

When the importation plan went into effect, Goskino received a 2.3 million rouble credit from the Commissariat of Foreign Trade. The credit covered the anticipated worth of imports over a period of several years. Goskino would be given the opportunity to establish a distribution monopoly for all foreign films in the Russian market and these films were to erase the debt through income generated by Goskino's distributor's share. Any earnings above the credit could then be reinvested in new production activity. Film importation began in earnest in 1923 when at least 278 American, German and French films entered the USSR. It peaked in the mid-1920s when up to 85 per cent of films in the Soviet market came from abroad.[35]

The plan to exploit imports for capital formation ran into difficulty in its initial stages, however, due largely to problems in Goskino's organisation. The trust never managed to take advantage of its mandated distribution monopoly for imports. Goskino's distribution network existed largely on paper: while it managed to supply theatres in the Moscow region, it often failed to reach outlying areas. Theatre managers in the hinterlands had to acquire films from other sources, and competing distribution companies grew in strength relative to Goskino. Sevzapkino, for example, expanded its distribution activity well beyond its original Petrograd location, and it even established an exchange in Moscow to challenge Goskino's control of Russia's largest urban market. Smaller firms established regional distribution networks in outlying regions, acquiring prints (including imports) from Goskino and renting them to theatres at high prices because of the extra transaction. Rather than expanding its own distribution network, Goskino simply farmed out regional distribution to these middlemen.[36]

Goskino's failure to fulfil its mandate betrayed a flaw in the entire trust system that was just then becoming apparent to Soviet officials. The government wanted to encourage a competitive, free-market economy while exerting control over each industry through the government trusts. Yet the trusts were frequently undercapitalised and could not achieve sufficient size to effect genuine domination of their industries. When smaller competitors proliferated under NEP freedom, the trusts experienced difficulties supplying their product to private retailers in remote areas, an abiding problem given the USSR's geographical expanse and often uncertain transportation system. There promptly developed a layer of middlemen traders who bought goods from trust producers and supplied them to retailers not reached by trust deliveries, a practice that added to retail prices because of the traders' higher margins.[37]

Theatre managers (the retailers of cinema) in various regions fell prey to this expensive trading system when Goskino resorted to distributing through such middlemen. Some theatre managers were forced to pay a distributor's share of up to 70 per cent of gross receipts. This added to a set of circumstances which drove up ticket prices throughout 1923, causing a 'theatre crisis' which threatened to scuttle the industry's entire developmental agenda. All theatres showing foreign films were subject to a national tax of 25 per cent of gross receipts, a burden then passed along to consumers in the form of higher ticket prices. The taxes were earmarked for the Commissariat of Enlightenment, the agency which oversaw the film industry. But not all tax revenues went back into film-related work; much of the revenue was diverted to the Commissariat's non-income-generating responsibilities such as schools and libraries. Many local governments aggravated the problem by adding local taxes to ticket prices.[38]

This combination of uncertain distribution and quick inflation of ticket prices put the squeeze on commercial exhibitors, many of whom leased their theatres from the government under NEP leasing plans and so needed to realise sizeable profits to meet their annual lease payments. As a result scores of theatres closed during 1923 and early 1924. Moscow had only half as many theatres open in 1924 as 1917, and the drop was even greater in some outlying areas where middleman trading was in effect.[39]

This theatre crisis jeopardised the industry's entire development since plans hinged on the exhibition of foreign films in commercial theatres. The government responded by initiating an investigation which centred on Goskino's organisation and activity. A government commission originally recommended legislation to limit national and local taxes on movie tickets to 10 per cent. After further deliberation, the commission called for the dissolution of the Goskino trust and for its replacement by a stock company which would be sufficiently well capitalised to realise the distribution monopoly which had previously existed only as Goskino's ambition. Goskino was duly disbanded in 1924 and replaced by the stock company Sovkino. Goskino's 3.5 million roubles in assets were transferred to Sovkino and the new company was authorised to sell 1 million roubles' worth of stock to raise additional capital. The eventual buyers in this stock issue were not private citizens but the government agencies which had official links with cinema: the Commissariat of Enlightenment purchased 55 per cent of the stock, the Commissariat of Foreign Trade 30 per cent. The investments represented formalisation of the administrative authority these agencies had already assumed *vis-à-vis* the film industry, and since there were no private stockholders to demand dividends on their shares, the agencies could reinvest their gains in Sovkino's operation. Despite its earlier stated opposition to film industry subvention, the government had finally invested in cinema, and the windfall helped Sovkino assume its eventual position of industry dominance.[40]

The 1924 industry reorganisation also reduced the number of private firms with which Sovkino had to compete. Sovkino was ordered to buy out the smaller distribution firms which had operated simultaneously with Goskino and through such acquisition Sovkino established a genuine distribution monopoly which extended throughout Soviet Russia. Large, well-financed organisations such as Sevzapkino and Mezhrabpom continued to compete with Sovkino in the area of production, but Sovkino contracted to distribute their films. This consolidation of commercial cinema activity within Soviet Russia coincided with a major administrative reorganisation of the entire Soviet federal political system. Between 1922 and 1924 the empire was organised into first four and then six federal republics: Russia, Ukraine, Belorussia, Georgia, Armenia and Azerbaidzhan. By the time of the film industry's consolidation in 1924, the non-Russian republics had established film companies which were tied to the government of each republic. Each such studio became that republic's sanctioned national film company in 1924. Sovkino's distribution monopoly extended only to the borders of Soviet *Russia*; each national studio won a similar monopoly within its republic. These mutually exclusive monopolies proved beneficial to both Sovkino and the national studios. The national studios could, and constantly did, buy films from Sovkino for distribution to local theatres without having to compete directly with the larger, more powerful Sovkino, and Sovkino was spared the necessity of extending its distribution network beyond Soviet Russia.[41]

The 1924 industry reorganisation benefited development in several ways. It consolidated resources and ended the manipulations of middleman traders. This reduced inflationary pressures and provided incentives for theatres to reopen. The reorganisation also gave Sovkino a strong, vertical structure and status as the true industry leader. And finally, it opened the way for the implementation of Lunacharsky's long-range developmental strategy which was posited on the aggressive commercial exploitation of foreign films.

Major commercial theatres in large urban markets got first rights to imported films and to the industry's exhibition technology, mostly old Pathé and Ernemann projectors. Sovkino charged these favoured theatres high rental fees – usually 50 per cent of gross receipts – and reinvested its margin in increased production. The typical programme at major commercial theatres included a Russian-made documentary short or political speaker, a comedy short, and a feature production (the last two of which were usually imports). Ticket prices at these commercial theatres varied considerably, ranging anywhere from 25 kopeks to 1.50 roubles. These commercial theatres competed with cinema installations in urban workers' clubs which ran their theatres at cost and charged spectators only 12 to 15 kopeks. But union membership was often a requirement for patrons of workers' clubs, a condition which excluded wealthier classes and assured that they would attend commercial theatres. In addition the workers' clubs remained notorious for their poor facilities: patrons complained about the absence of heat, the poor musical accompaniment, and the uncomfortable seats. Hence the commercial theatres, with their comparatively attractive accommodation and constant supply of popular imports, attracted both bourgeois patrons who could afford higher ticket prices and workers who valued 'bourgeois' diversions. This made the commercial theatres the key revenue sources for the entire industry: although they constituted only 17 per cent of the total number of permanent exhibition outlets in the Russian market, they brought in 80 per cent of the industry's revenues.[42]

The following figures reporting total box-office grosses from the middle 1920s indicate how important foreign films were in initially attracting revenue and how quickly the Soviets converted their gains into domestic production.[43]

*1924–5*

4.66 million roubles total

| 992,000 roubles | (21%) | domestic films |
| 3.67 million roubles | (79%) | foreign films |

*1925–6*

12.56 million roubles total

| 4.36 million roubles | (35%) | domestic films |
| 8.2 million roubles | (65%) | foreign films |

*1926–7*

15.66 million roubles total

| 7.67 million roubles | (49%) | domestic films |
| 7.99 million roubles | (51%) | foreign films |

Both the total proceeds and the proportions derived from domestic versus foreign films deserve attention. As can be seen, total proceeds increased significantly each season during the mid-1920s. A huge increment (roughly 270 per cent) followed the 1924–5 season, testifying to the beneficial effects of the 1924 industry reorganisation. The figures also reveal that Soviet producers consistently narrowed the gap between revenues generated by their films and those deriving from imports. Since the annual number of imported films remained high during the mid-1920s, the sharply reduced gap is attributable not to a decrease in importation but to an increase in domestic production activity and to the greater prominence of Soviet films in commercial exhibition. Indeed, in 1928 Sovkino reported that Soviet films had finally surpassed imports as income earners.[44] Clearly, Russian producers wasted no time in converting their initial revenue source into domestic activity.

The Russians also used this income to expand their exhibition facilities. The USSR had inherited only about 1,000 commercial theatres from the pre-Revolutionary industry, a figure that was significantly reduced by the effects of the Civil War and the financial problems that culminated in the theatre crisis of 1923. By 1925, however, intensive investment had raised the number to 2,000 and the figure would approach 10,000 by the end of the decade.[45]

Meanwhile the extension of cinema into the countryside continued apace. The linking of cinema with the national rail system, which began as a marriage of necessity during the Civil War, was extended by the mid-1920s into a full-scale campaign to reach and inform previously isolated segments of the population. The Russians traded for foreign projectors which were then fitted with portable generators and transformed into itinerant cinema facilities. By 1925, 1,600 such units were touring the countryside by train. Within two years the figure had risen to 2,000; film industry officials boasted of approaching their goal of being able to reach literally every Soviet village with some form of cinema entertainment and enlightenment.[46]

The profitable activity of urban commercial theatres helped subsidise the daily operation of the itinerant units as well as the discount exhibition facilities in workers' clubs. While Sovkino was taking 50 per cent of gross receipts from commercial theatres, it charged only 5.50 roubles per programme in rentals to rural cinemas and 16 roubles per programme to the workers' clubs, figures that would have barely covered costs. Such generous rates permitted these institutions to offer their two programmes per week to patrons for nominal ticket prices: 5 to 8 kopeks in the villages and 12 to 15 kopeks in workers' clubs.[47]

Finally, a sustained level of growth in production levels attests to the wise reinvestment of industry surpluses. From a mere 13 features released in 1923, the beginning of the growth period, the number of feature releases jumped to 62 in just two years and continued to increase each subsequent year until it peaked in 1928 with 109. In the meantime Sovkino nearly tripled its total assets; from 4.5 million roubles in 1924, assets grew to 13.4 million roubles by the end of 1927. Sovkino was budgeting over 4 million roubles annually to new productions, a figure that approached its entire 1924 starting capital.[48]

The ultimate goal of industry planners was for Soviet cinema to reach full self-sufficiency, a goal which involved an end to the reliance on imported product and equipment and which began to become realised by the end of the decade. Under a mandate set down by the Fifteenth Party Congress in 1927, the Supreme Economic Council directed that film industry earnings be invested in the construction of facilities for the production of film stock and

*Figure 7* Interior of Mezhrabpom-Rus's cinema, the Koloss, in 1927 with advance advertising for Eggert's *The Lame Gentleman* [Khromoi barin, rel. 1928]. The Koloss occupied what was formerly and subsequently the Great Hall of the Conservatoire in Herzen Street, Moscow.

equipment. By the early 1930s two massive film laboratories and three equipment factories supplied most of the materials needed for domestic production and helped reduce reliance on the overseas purchase of production materials. In fact, terms of trade turned against the USSR in the late 1920s; wheat harvests dropped and the price of grain and raw material declined in foreign markets, thus compromising the key export items which had sustained Soviet foreign trade strategies through the decade. The Commissariat of Foreign Trade responded by curtailing imports in several non-essential industries, including the cinema. Foreign films finally began to disappear from Russian screens; Russian film-makers began to regularly purchase their resources from plants in Moscow, Leningrad or Samara rather than Berlin and Paris.[49]

The growth strategies which characterised the industry throughout the 1920s finally levelled off in the 1930s; and after the installation of tighter censorship measures under Stalin, the film industry reduced production levels.[50] It had achieved the status of a stable industry with sufficient capacity to satisfy the needs of its market once its resources were used efficiently. And that, after all, represents the goal of any developing industry.

The Soviet film industry's early developmental record owed its success to the stingy management of resources during the period of civil war scarcity and to the shrewd exploitation of market forces under NEP. No official decree, neither Lenin's 1919 nationalisation edict nor his 1922 importation order with its codicillary 'Leninist film proportion', fully accounts for the industry's eventual success. In fact, Lenin's two most celebrated interventions into film history should best be understood as ingredients of larger developmental formulas, the former representing a response to the exigencies of net capital consumption and the latter a part of capital accumulation efforts. The complex and imbricated histories of early Soviet borrowing, importation and investment explain the quick growth of the Soviet film industry. Perhaps the ultimate irony stems from the fact that the revolutionary cinema of Eisenstein, Vertov and Pudovkin owed its existence to the kind of shrewd trading and investment that would have been the envy of many a capitalist movie mogul.[51]

# 5 Down to earth: *Aelita* relocated

*Ian Christie*

Harmful literature is more useful than useful literature, for it is anti-entropic.

Yevgeni Zamyatin[1]

## 1 HAS ANYONE ACTUALLY *SEEN AELITA*?

*Aelita* undeniably has a bad reputation. As the first, and for long the only, Soviet 'spectacular', promoted and launched like its Western equivalents, it naturally attracted suspicion in many quarters, despite (or perhaps ultimately because of) its resounding box-office success. Today the film itself remains as little seen as ever in 'serious' circles, and shares with the likes of *High Treason* and *Things to Come* a reputation of amounting to rather less than the undeniable impact of its science-fiction décor, stills of which, however, enliven many general cinema histories.[2] These also appear in most surveys of science-fiction film and, especially, accounts of Russian avant-garde art, where their futuristic geometry provides an essential visual and plastic emblem of the era of heroic Soviet modernism.[3] Yet the accompanying commentary often belittles, when it does not directly condemn, the film itself – and usually on the basis of a misleading plot summary.

Thus a self-perpetuating tradition has developed which effectively substitutes the paradigmatic quality of the stills for the implied failure of the film. Its apparent subject – a Soviet expedition to Mars which incites revolution against the ruling despots – simultaneously evokes the utopian aspiration of much early Soviet art while sounding risible; and the obviously theatrical stills, although more impressive than those from most 'canonic' Soviet classics, also seem to justify the scorn which the film originally attracted from advocates of a revolutionary new approach to cinema.[4]

However, to screen *Aelita* is to discover something rather different from the *bête noire* of Soviet montage cinema's pioneers. Instead of the 'photographed muddle of curves and triangles' that so infuriated Kuleshov, we find an ambitious, multi-layered work which draws upon pre- as well as post-Revolutionary Russian sources and contemporary European influences to reflect the new Soviet life more fully than any other film of the time. Indeed, if we were not predisposed otherwise, Protazanov's juxtaposition of different registers and realities in *Aelita* might remind us, if not of Kuleshov's polemics, then of his own by no means straightforward realist practice, from *Mr West* to *The Great Consoler*.[5] But the fact that it was made by the 'wrong' director at a time when early Soviet production was being valued for quite different qualities, together with its 'inner space' project being persistently misconstrued, have all tended to erase the film's conjunctural specificity.

To grasp this involves sketching a number of contexts in order to explore the crucial significance of the film's drastic departure from the novel of which it is actually more a critique than an adaptation. What emerges is a work defined by multiple authorship *and* a product of the emergent 'cultural industry' of Soviet film-making – two perspectives rarely brought to bear on the cinema of an era so dominated by the mythology of protean artistic and ideological purpose. A 'polyphonic' text also, in Bakhtin's sense, which allows us to read some of the many discourses that defined the contested pluralism of the New Economic Policy (NEP), Lenin's contradictory legacy to the infant Soviet state.[6]

## 2  'ANTA . . . ODELI . . . UTA . . .'

Premièred at the end of September 1924, *Aelita* was undoubtedly *the* major event in Soviet cinema before the international breakthrough of *Potemkin* in 1926. Like the German *The Cabinet of Dr Caligari* [Das Kabinett des Dr Caligari, 1919], which reputedly served as inspiration, it proclaimed a major industrial thrust to produce cinema of 'international quality', which could both yield export earnings and compete effectively with imports in the domestic market. To aim at these ambitious goals amid the poverty and contradictory motives of Soviet production in 1923, its producers assembled a remarkable array of talent and scarce resources. They took advantage of the imminent return from exile of a well-known writer, Alexei Tolstoi, to base the film on his latest novel: a fantastic tale of adventure and romance set largely on Mars. Leading actors from the main theatres were engaged to make their film débuts, along with promising newcomers and a vast army of student extras.[7] To direct this prestigious subject, one of the most celebrated directors from pre-Revolutionary Russian cinema, Yakov Protazanov, also returned from exile.

Important as these coups must have been, a further vital ingredient was the stylistic novelty which had distinguished *Caligari*. In place of the German film's 'Expressionism', *Aelita* deployed the distinctive Russian modernism which was already becoming known abroad under the often inaccurately applied names of its various factions – Futurism, Cubo-Futurism, Suprematism and Constructivism – as these were rapidly assimilated into the design-conscious Russian theatre.[8] From Tairov's Kamerny Theatre came the distinguished painter Alexandra Exter as costume designer. Sets were commissioned from her former pupil Isaak Rabinovich, who had recently revolutionised the staid Moscow Art Theatre with his 'Constructivist' set for *Lysistrata*.[9] Finally, a German cinematographer was employed to work alongside the Russian cameraman, in recognition of the low level of technical expertise available in a Russian studio at this time.[10]

As the first Russian film to reflect the contemporary mixture of scientific and popular enthusiasm for astronautics, *Aelita* had massive potential appeal. After months of carefully nourished rumour about the resources involved in the production, its release was preceded by various publicity stunts, including novel 'teaser' advertising campaigns in *Pravda* and *Kino-gazeta*. In the former, a cryptic message appeared regularly from 19 September 1924: 'ANTA . . . ODELI . . . UTA . . .', while the latter explained:

> The signals that are being received constantly by radio stations around the world – Anta . . . Odeli . . . Uta . . . – have at last been deciphered! What do they mean? You will find out on 30 September at the Ars Cinema.[11]

On this occasion, the cinema façade was decorated with giant figures of Aelita and Tuskub, the princess and king of Mars, surrounded by illuminated columns and geometric shapes approximating to the film's 'Martian' décor, and animated by flashing lights. An accompanying orchestra played specially composed music by Valentin Kruchinin.[12] Demand for tickets was unprecedented, which kept the touts busy, and huge crowds apparently prevented Protazanov himself from attending the première!

The film, however, turned out to be an 'adaptation' which bracketed a drastically reduced version of Tolstoi's story within an entirely new narrative. This strategy puzzled and disconcerted many critics, but did not prevent the film becoming immensely popular with cinemagoers.[13] The next release to fare anything like as well would be Mezhrabpom-Rus's 1926 success (involving some of the same team) *The Bear's Wedding*, a shrewd exploitation of the vampire motif from a story by Mérimée, which witnesses recall generating a huge fan-mail.[14] We shall never know what the large audiences for these films – who were also the readers of Tolstoi's and other contemporary fantasy novels then abundantly available under the market conditions of NEP publishing – made of them, but we need to bear in mind the likelihood of responses other than the largely negative ones recorded, such as by 'B. G.' in *Pravda*:

> The theme of the picture and Tolstoi's novel, for all its ideological questionableness, has great literary worth. The authors of the scenario, Otsep and Faiko, wishing to correct the ideological side, describe the whole trip to Mars as a dream of the engineer Los. But it is unclear where he goes to sleep, or where and when he wakes up. It is as if he woke up after attempting to kill his wife, but then where do the scenes on Mars come from? And besides, to Tolstoi has been added the story of the engineer's life before his flight. . . . The rising of the Martian workers has

*Figure 8* The beginning of *Aelita* is set specifically in December 1921, amid the chaos bequeathed by the Civil War and the start of the NEP.

the stamp of the 'monumental' foreign films, striving to convey quantity rather than quality.[15]

*Izvestiya* ironically proclaimed 'the mountain has produced a mouse'; while Lunacharsky, writing in *Kino-gazeta*, hailed it as 'an extraordinary phenomenon', but felt that 'it would have been preferable not to depart from Tolstoi'.[16]

As actual familiarity with the novel and the film faded, criticism has largely recycled earlier opinions. Thus Thorold Dickinson, writing in 1948, could only speculate: 'It would be interesting to meet someone who can recall having seen *Aelita*. Perhaps the film failed to fuse so many divergent styles of acting.'[17] One of his sources was no doubt the pioneer English-language historian of Soviet cinema, Bryher, who had also been unable to see *Aelita* when preparing her *Film Problems of Soviet Russia* in 1928 but was aware of the eclectic composition of the film: 'It is reported that actors from opposite schools and pupils from the State School of Cinematography were used in the production, and that very interesting effects were achieved.'[18] Controversy raged from the outset, of course, over the stylised Martian décor, with *Pravda* describing it as 'like *Aida* at the Bolshoi'.[19] But, for serious Western critics, not opposed to stylisation in principle, the fundamental issue has probably been that first expressed by Rotha in his influential *The Film Till Now* in 1929.[20] Rotha, a passionate admirer of *The Cabinet of Dr Caligari*, insisted that the stylised 'Cubist' design of *Aelita* could not be compared with the earlier German film because it was 'designed fantastically in order to express an imaginary idea of the planet Mars, and *not*, as in *Caligari*, to emphasise the thoughts of a distorted mind'. For later art historians, the issue of Exter's Constructivist credentials has often loomed larger than any analysis of the film's plastic achievement.

## 3    THE MEZHRABPOM-RUS INITIATIVE

*Aelita* effectively inaugurated a new production force in Soviet cinema, Mezhrabpom-Rus: a strategic innovation that would do much to rescue film-making from the impoverishment it had suffered since nationalisation, but which would also earn the hostility of 'left' elements by its apparent compromises with the pre-Revolutionary past and the capitalist West – while also providing support for many of the same 'left' directors, including Pudovkin and, later, Kuleshov and Vertov, as well as such foreign leftists as Ivens and Piscator.[21] So ingrained has been the doctrine of Soviet cinema's 'invention' *ex nihilo* during the Civil War 'agit' period that the lines of continuity between pre- and post-Revolutionary production have only recently been recognised: yet these are vital to an understanding of the origins of *Aelita*.

Mezhrabpom-Rus was a quintessential creation of the New Economic Policy. It resulted from an injection of share capital into the existing Rus studio by the Berlin-based organisation Internationale Arbeiterhilfe, known in English as Workers' International Relief (WIR) and in Russian as *Mezhdunarodnaya Rabochaya Pomoshch'*, yielding the acronym 'Mezhrab-pom'. Rus itself had been re-formed as an experimental collective on the basis of Trofimov's pre-Revolutionary production company.[22] In the desperate situation that led to nationalisation of the Soviet cinema industry in August 1919, the commissar responsible, Lunacharsky, recognised the need to stimulate production that had some chance of meeting cultural and entertainment criteria, while being in some broad sense politically 'progressive'. He therefore supported and defended the group who formed the 'Artistic Collective of Rus' in early 1918 under the leadership of Moisei Aleinikov, for a long time the force behind *Cine-Phono*, a trade magazine largely financed by the producer Yermoliev. This collective included Fyodor Otsep, Aleinikov's former assistant and scriptwriter for such pre-Revolutionary films as Protazanov's *The Queen of Spades* [Pikovaya dama, 1916]; Yuri Zhelyabuzhsky, the cameraman and later director; Nikolai Efros, former head of the Moscow Art Theatre literary department, together with one of its assistant directors, Alexander Sanin, and a number of actors from the same theatre. Against all odds, the collective succeeded in producing a Lev Tolstoy adaptation, *Polikushka*, in 1919–20, which

Aleinikov was able to take to Germany and sell in order to raise funds for much-needed materials and equipment.[23]

But individual enterprise could not solve the problems of a whole industry and, despite formal nationalisation, foreign investment in Soviet production was actively sought in 1922 within the general strategy of NEP.[24] The search proved unsuccessful, except for WIR's subsidiary, Aufbau, offering a 50 per cent investment in a new joint venture, to be known as Mezhrabpom-Rus. WIR may have hoped to infuse the hitherto conservative Rus studio with 'ideological rigour', but it was also clearly relying on Rus's unique – in the Soviet context – capability to produce films which might make their way in domestic and foreign markets. An indication of Aleinikov's priorities and enterprise is provided by the terms of the script competition announced in September 1923 (with a jury headed by Lunacharsky in his capacity as chairman of the Artistic Council of Russfilm, as the company had now become):

> The theme may reflect the past and present of revolutionary and old-world Russia or contemporary life in either a realistic or a romantic treatment. But we do require fullness of content, clarity and entertainment in the plot, drawn in cheerful and wholesome tones, complexity of action unfolding within the framework of the beauties of nature, and a variety of experiences for the heroes.[25]

The list of suggested themes included in the advertisement offers a valuable insight into the generic possibilities and perceived needs as they appeared to Russfilm on the brink of its expansion:

1. the Russian folk epic
2. historical and epic tales with a heroic flavour
3. the everyday life of the workers and peasants past and present
4. contemporary everyday life (other than workers' and peasants')
5. modernised daily life
6. the everyday life of Nepmen
7. adventure films and films of everyday life 'on a USSR-wide scale'
8. wholesome revolutionary detective films
9. utopian films, such as a look into a happier future.

*Aelita*, as the new company's first prestige production, would actually combine no fewer than six of these themes in a novel imbrication, as if seeking to define the studio's whole field of operations and establish its distinctive approach to both conventional and controversial subjects.

But *Aelita* was not in fact the first production to emerge from the new enterprise. One week before its release, *Four and Five* [Chetyre i pyat', 1924] was reviewed in *Pravda* as a film 'coming from Rus, the organ of Mezhrabpom', in terms which established the pattern of response that would apply to many subsequent Mezhrabpom-Rus releases, while also revealing such rudimentary Party attitudes to cinema as existed at this time. *Four and Five* was described as showing

> the desperate struggle over a terrible death gas invented by aviator and chemist Dimitri with the intention of defending the Republic. The subject is not novel, but technically it is a great success and you watch it with unwavering attention. *Ideologically it is not our film.* . . . It is not shown clearly that the invention of the gas was only for the defence of the USSR and not for imperialist needs. For us there are other means of defence. Nothing is shown of our Soviet reality, only the millionaires and a statue of Pushkin. . . . The film could be shown successfully in a Parisian cinema of today and could have been a pre-war hit. . . . For a technically well-made film coming from Rus, the organ of Mezhrabpom, such ideological emptiness is both unexpected and unpleasant.[26]

The same review covered *Young Pioneers* [Yunye pionery], a short film by Alexei Gan, the editor of *Kino-Fot* and supporter of Vertov, which is described as 'a film attempting to have no scenario or director'. Significantly, this is judged mediocre and unsuccessful, but '*it is our film*'.

Here already is the polemical stance against compromised/escapist/ Westernised cinema more familiar from the writings of Vertov, Eisenstein and the LEF group, which amounts to a rejection of 'NEP culture' and a repudiation of Lunacharsky's declared strategy to counter the appeal of foreign cinema – then flooding Soviet screens – by competing in entertainment terms with 'relaxed' ideological requirements.[27] Mezhrabpom-Rus seems to have been condemned from the outset to incur both Party strictures and 'left' wrath, while in fact fulfilling state policy by achieving economic self-sufficiency and creating potential export products, as well as winning back the disenchanted mass audience for domestic production.

More research is required to reveal exactly what influence their German partners may have exerted on Rus. Did WIR perhaps take part in the negotiations for Protazanov, the most successful pre-Revolutionary Russian director still abroad, to come back and create a 'box-office hit'? Or, more likely, did Aleinikov's overall strategy to develop the studio coincide with Lunacharsky's interest in persuading famous artists to return? At any rate, Protazanov, who had directed in both France and Germany from 1920 to 1923, was not invited specifically to make *Aelita*, but for an historical project, variously reported as *Taras Bulba* or *Ivan the Terrible*.[28] That neither of these materialised and his Soviet début became *Aelita* was probably linked with the contemporaneous return of another distinguished émigré, Alexei Tolstoi. WIR may, however, have been involved in the struggle to keep *Aelita* going as the production costs rose far beyond Mezhrabpom-Rus's modest resources. But the offer of additional investment by a German company in return for monopoly distribution rights in Europe was apparently declined, presumably in anticipation of the film's potential to attract rival bids as a 'Soviet *Caligari*'.[29]

## 4 TOLSTOI – 'UNLUCKY IN CINEMA'

Alexei Tolstoi's involvement, however token this turned out to be, was clearly part of the original *Aelita* 'package' and a vital ingredient in the cultural politics of the project. Tolstoi, a minor aristocrat and distant relative of Lev Tolstoy from the south-east steppe, was already an established author of popular verse, novels and plays before 1917, when he joined the White Army and worked in the propaganda department of Denikin's staff. Moving to Paris after Denikin's defeat, he continued to write prolifically for the émigré Russian press and published the first volume of a *Bildungsroman* sequence, *The Road to Calvary*, tracing the fate of the Russian intelligentsia across the years of war and revolution.

He also began to modify his public attitude towards the Soviet state, joining the émigré group 'Changing Landmarks' [Smenovekhovtsy] and writing:

> [since] there is no other government in Russia . . . except the Bolshevik . . . we have to do everything to help the last phase of the Russian Revolution take a direction that would make our nation stronger, enrich Russian life, and obtain from the Revolution all its good and just elements.[30]

Tolstoi contributed a series of similarly conciliatory articles to the Berlin Russian paper *Nakanune* [On the Eve] in 1922; and in November of that year he joined Mayakovsky and others at a celebration of the fifth anniversary of the Revolution, where he read from his work in progress, *Aelita*. The full text then appeared in three consecutive issues of the Soviet journal *Krasnaya nov'* [Red Virgin Soil], by which time Tolstoi had made his peace with the Soviet regime and returned to live in Moscow. The NEP policy of encouraging 'repentant émigrés' to return was bearing fruit, although bitterly contested by such 'left' groups as 'On Guard' [Na postu] and LEF.

Science fiction had become perhaps the dominant genre of Soviet literature, finding a new popular audience in the market conditions of NEP publishing and serving a wide range of functions, from propaganda to escapist entertainment.[31] Tolstoi's first venture shrewdly combined material he knew well with a scattering of exotic inventions and ill-disguised borrowings. The novel tells of an expedition to Mars undertaken by a resourceful engineer Los, whose wife has recently died, and who is accompanied by a restless ex-soldier Gusev.[32] On Mars, or Tuma, they encounter a decaying society, which was first seeded by the invading Magatsitls, as they fled the destruction of Earth's Atlantis. While Los falls in love with Aelita, daughter of the Martian ruler Tuskub, his companion Gusev captivates her maid. But a rising by the oppressed Martian proletariat, under the leadership of an engineer, interrupts these idylls and leads to civil war in which Gusev takes command. The insurgents are eventually routed by Tuskub's forces and the Earthmen barely escape. On their return home (via a splashdown on Lake

*Figure 9* Engineer Los's day-dream transports him to the court of Princess Aelita (Nikolai Tsereteli and Yuliya Solntseva).

Michigan!) they are fêted as heroes, but Los pines for Aelita and is finally rewarded, yet tormented, by a radio message from Mars in which she calls for him.

Closer in spirit to Edgar Rice Burrough's Martian romances (already available in Russian translation) than the didactic Martian utopias of Bogdanov, Tolstoi's novel had undeniable popular appeal. Yevgeni Zamyatin, author of *We* [My] and a science-fiction authority, saw its strengths as well as the obvious weaknesses:

> In his latest novel, *Aelita*, Tolstoi attempted to transfer from the mail train to the airplane of the fantastic, but all he managed to do was jump up and plop back on the ground with awkwardly spread wings. . . . Tolstoi's Mars is no further than forty versts from Ryazan; there is even a shepherd there, in the standard red shirt; there is 'gold in the mouth' [fillings]. . . . The only figure in the novel that is alive, in the usual Tolstoian fashion, is the Red Army soldier Gusev. He alone speaks, all the others recite.[33]

Tolstoi was later to complain that he had been 'unlucky in cinema', and in the case of *Aelita* he had reasonable grounds for complaint.[34] For, whatever else it was, Protazanov's film could scarcely be considered an adaptation of Tolstoi's novel. Little, in fact, was retained beyond the title and the names of the main characters, while the additions amounted to a substantially new narrative embodying very different themes.

The film begins, in effect, with the novel's ending and a very different hero. This Los is a sensitive engineer, far from the 'Elk' his name evokes in Russian, whose fascination with space travel encourages him to day-dream about life on Mars. He interprets a cryptic message received at a Moscow radio station as coming from the beautiful Aelita, who he thinks has fallen in love with him. This interplanetary fantasy becomes increasingly real to Los when he believes his own wife, Natasha, to be attracted to a suave speculator, Erlich, who is lodged in their apartment. Natasha works at a reception centre for refugees (the film spans the period 1921–3) where, apart from Erlich and his scheming wife (soon to seduce Los's friend Spiridonov, a fellow space enthusiast), she meets a wounded Red Army soldier Gusev, who eventually marries his nurse Masha and becomes a helper.[35]

Aelita, meanwhile, is imagined by Los to be in rebellion against her father Tuskub, especially when he curbs her passion for viewing Earth (and Los) through a new apparatus. Natasha, increasingly neglected by Los, reluctantly accompanies Erlich to a decadent ball for anti-Soviet elements, while her husband seeks solace by going to work on a remote construction project. On his return, Los jumps to the conclusion that she has moved in with Erlich and in despair shoots at her. He flees to the railway station, but decides to remain in Moscow and disguise himself as Spiridonov, who has shortly before written to say he is emigrating. He succeeds in building the rocket ship they had long planned and sets off for Mars, accompanied by Gusev, now bored with civilian life, and a stowaway – the amateur detective – Kravtsev, who is investigating Erlich's swindles and Spiridonov's seeming disappearance. When they land, Aelita has arranged for her maid to bring the visitors to her and she satisfies her curiosity about Earth customs with a kiss from Los. Gusev charms the maid with his accordion playing, until Tuskub's militia arrest her for having murdered, on Aelita's orders, the astronomer who had predicted where the ship would land. Kravtsev is taken to the dungeons where the toiling Martian masses are kept, and are refrigerated when they are not needed. Momentarily, Los imagines that his wife is still alive and begs her forgiveness.

Meanwhile Gusev successfully appeals to the Martian workers to 'throw off their thousand-year hypnosis by the Elders' and Aelita offers to lead the uprising. But when the insurgents have overcome the Elders, she persuades them to lay down their arms, then orders the militia to open fire. Los pushes her off the dais – and finds that it is his wife he is pushing – before awakening from his dream in the station where he had gone after the shooting. The original 'Martian' message is revealed as part of an advertisement slogan for tyres! Gusev and his wife, waiting for a train to the east, follow as he returns to his apartment and discovers Natasha unharmed. Upstairs the militia are arresting Erlich on suspicion of Spiridonov's murder, while Los retrieves the rocket plans that Spiridonov had hidden and destroys them, telling Natasha that 'a different sort of work awaits us'.

The deeper cultural and ideological significance of both the novel and the film's new scenario will be considered further below, but at this point it is worth noting that Tolstoi's Martian tale can scarcely be regarded as innocent escapism. Its 'ideological questionableness', as we have seen, was noted as a matter of course in the *Pravda* review; and Zamyatin's contemporary article drew attention to Tolstoi's reliance on the Theosophist mystic Rudolph Steiner for his Atlantis myth. Even at a superficial level, the novel's rejection of Mars – whether construed either as the decadent West or the Imperial Russian past – seemed ambivalent.

*Aelita* was of course written while Tolstoi was still abroad. It may well be significant that one of his first works *after* returning to the Soviet Union, *Azure Cities*, has a remarkably similar theme to that of the *Aelita* film.[36] In it an idealistic young communist architect dreams of building 'azure cities', but when illness forces him to return to his provincial home town, he finds that little has changed since the Revolution, except for the worse, as opportunists take advantage of NEP. In despair, he sets fire to the town, hanging his utopian designs aloft on a pole, then turns himself over to the authorities with the bitter words: 'Life does not forgive rapt dreamers and visionaries who turn away from it.' Although Tolstoi would also pioneer the fully fledged Soviet science-fiction thriller in *The Garin Death Ray*, Protazanov's *Aelita* 'adaptation' anticipated the direction of the novelist's more serious and personal work, culminating in the third volume of *The Road to Calvary*.

## 5   PROTAZANOV – ON THE THRESHOLD OF A DREAM

The impetus to tamper seriously with Mezhrabpom-Rus's prestigious literary property, whatever the probable outcry, seems to have come from Protazanov, who was certainly no stranger to controversy. Indeed his early career had benefited greatly from the scandal created by the film he co-directed giving a lurid account of the circumstances that led to Lev Tolstoy's death, *The Great Man Passes On* [Ukhod velikogo startsa, 1912].[37] Later, within weeks of the October Revolution, his *Satan Triumphant* [Satana likuyushchii, 1917] became a byword for 'diabolism', with its Expressionistic portrayal of the havoc wrought on a pastor and his flock by the devil incarnate.[38] But, on the strength of his surviving pre-Revolutionary work, it would be a mistake to categorise Protazanov as a mere sensationalist or opportunist. He was already a complex and above all a versatile artist, placing his skills and stylistic daring at the service of the dramatic material chosen for each film – which choice would seemingly often be influenced by topicality and the potential for publicity.

One of his scenarists on *Aelita*, the young playwright Alexei Faiko, recalled:

> Protazanov was very keen to do something contemporary. Work on the script was neither fast nor smooth. Protazanov made all sorts of

demands . . . [he] was always searching and striving for something new and more interesting.[39]

That Protazanov should want to deal with the Soviet reality to which he had returned seems highly plausible, if only to ward off the inevitable suspicion attaching to returned émigrés and likely attacks from the vigorous young opponents of entertainment cinema who had increased their influence during his absence. The cost of a full-scale Martian spectacle was another practical reason for revision and, despite contemporary rumours of reckless extravagance (possibly encouraged by Aleinikov as a shrewd publicist), the original set designs for *Aelita* still proved too costly and had to be reduced in scale.[40]

The key to combining the exotic potential of Tolstoi's Martian romance with 'something contemporary' proved to be a device which Protazanov had used to great effect in his first production abroad, *The Agonising Adventure* [L'Angoissante aventure, France, 1920]. This was the 'uncued dream', whereby an apparently realist narrative moves into dream mode un-beknownst to the spectator until the unexpected dénouement of awakening – of which the best-known later example is probably Lang's *Woman in the Window* [USA, 1944]. But, whereas this device functions in *The Agonising Adventure* to enclose a typical tragic melodrama of the pre-Revolutionary Russian cinema within an acceptably sophisticated French 'frame', *Aelita* attempts an altogether more complex structure. Here dream and reality alternate from the outset, with a minor motivation in Tolstoi's novel – Los has thrown himself into invention after his young wife's tragic death – transposed into Los's neurotic jealousy of his living wife Natasha, which produces the 'Martian narrative' as a compensatory fantasy satisfying (or combining?) his erotic frustration and engineering ambition. This narrative hierarchy is then destabilised when Los appears to build the rocket which will take him to his imaginary Mars, until the resulting paradox is resolved by his awakening in the railway station. So effective was this device that Protazanov would use it again, for the British soldier's dream, in his first sound film *Tommy* [Tommi, 1931].[41]

Protazanov's Los thus becomes a recognisably Russian hero and, as such, one virtually unique in early Soviet cinema: a 'bourgeois specialist' osten-sibly committed to building communism, but still emotionally, perhaps unconsciously, unadjusted to the new order – a Soviet version of Russian literature's traditional 'superfluous man'. Protazanov had succeeded in getting from his scenarists a remarkably apt vehicle for entering the world of Soviet Russia, a time machine that deals with the contradictory present of the NEP in terms of a discredited past (flashbacks to the pre-Revolutionary privileges of Erlich's cronies) and an imagined future, still shaped by Symbolist culture. *Aelita* recapitulates the 'threshold' strategy of *The Agonising Adventure* by interleaving a Russian *film d'art* (moreover one more ambitious than anything attempted before the Revolution) with the portrayal of Soviet reality, as seen with the affectionate curiosity of the returning native.[42]

## 6  PARIS – MOSCOW – MARS

Although the Martian scenes occupy little more than a quarter of the film, they have constituted the film's main claim to fame. But the question posed by Rotha and others still stands: is their fantastic décor 'motivated'? Certainly Rotha's unfavourable comparison with *Caligari* can be rebutted: the stylisation of *Aelita* represents just as much 'the thoughts of a distorted mind' as does that of the German film. Indeed the relationship between the two films seems to have been quite explicit, at least for those involved. According to Huntly Carter, an early traveller to Soviet Russia and writer on its theatre and cinema, Alexandra Exter personally cited *Caligari* as her main inspiration.[43] This would be consistent with the assumption that *Caligari* pointed towards an explicitly cultural strategy for European national cinemas, faced with growing American trade hegemony and protectionism. Only by creating 'cultural difference' could they hope to compete with the efficiency and universal appeal of American entertainment cinema. So, in place of the 'Expressionism' of *Caligari*, *Aelita* deployed the latest fruits of the close relationship that linked avant-garde Russian artists with the theatre. But this 'motivation' scarcely does justice to the remarkable integration of architecture, décor, costume and indeed acting, which remained unequalled until Lang's *Metropolis* [Germany, 1926] – a film backed by much vaster resources and reputedly in part inspired by *Aelita*.[44]

Here again, the impetus may well have come from Protazanov, who had spent his French sojourn amid the Russian émigrés of the Ermolieff [Yermoliev] group who were close to the avant-garde *cinéastes* then pre-occupied with introducing modernist art and design into their productions.[45] In Paris Protazanov would certainly have been aware of the activities of Louis Delluc, prophet of *photogénie* and organiser of the first French screenings of *Caligari* in 1921, and of Ricciotto Canudo, promoter of Le Club des Amis du Septième Art (CASA), which brought together artists, architects, poets and musicians to contribute to raising the artistic level of cinema.[46] He might even have known of L'Herbier's production *L'Inhumaine*, started in September 1923, which combined the Art Deco architecture of Robert Mallet-Stevens with a kaleidoscope of striking décors, costumes and artefacts, including a laboratory set designed and built by the Cubist painter Fernand Léger.[47]

Léger was also one of the circle of French artists whom Alexandra Exter already knew from pre-war visits to Paris and, when she moved there permanently in the same year as *Aelita*, she soon began teaching at his Académie de l'Art Moderne.[48] We may never know the exact sequence of events that led to Exter's involvement in *Aelita*, but it is clear that, whether this was cause or effect, it brought to the production both a cosmopolitan awareness of design trends in Western Europe *and* a distinctive Russian tradition, namely that of the Moscow Kamerny Theatre. For it was at the Kamerny that Exter had played a leading part in realising Alexander Tairov's vision of an 'emancipated' theatre in the three landmark productions she designed: Annensky's *Thamyras Cythared* [Famira kifared] in 1916, Wilde's *Salomé* in 1917 and Shakespeare's *Romeo and Juliet* in 1921.[49]

Tairov had been inspired in large part by Edward Gordon Craig's 1911 Moscow production of *Hamlet*, with its novel combination of two- and three-dimensional décor aiming at a Symbolist synthesis.[50] The Wagnerian Adolphe Appia had challenged the dominant naturalistic theatre with a proposed integration of set, actors and plot within a mood created largely by music; and Georg Fuchs's *Theatre of the Future* encouraged not only Tairov but also Meyerhold to treat the stage as an entirely artificial self-sufficient 'world', with increased emphasis on non-verbal, plastic and phatic means of communication.[51] Tairov's first steps towards the realisation of this new ideal in 1914–15 involved collaboration with the painters Pavel Kuznetsov and Nataliya Goncharova, members, like Exter, of the explosive Russian avant-garde movement that began to distance itself from Symbolism with the 'Blue Rose' and 'Wreath' exhibitions of 1907. A contemporary critic prophetically dubbed them 'heralds of the new Primitivism to which our modern painting has come'; and indeed Primitivism was to be the *Leitmotif* of this factional movement until, from about 1913, Futurism introduced a utopian social and quasi-scientific rationale for its highly eclectic activity.[52]

Exter, almost alone among these artists, spent considerable time in Italy and France between 1908 and 1914, mixing in Futurist and Cubist circles, while exhibiting in all the main Russian avant-garde shows. By the time the outbreak of war confined her to Russia, her painting reflected these diverse influences in a highly chromatic abstract Cubo-Futurism. The war period brought the new outlet of theatre and, back in her native Kiev, led her to establish what was probably the first art school to teach the formal grammar of modern art and deliberately lead its students towards abstract work.[53] Significantly, many of the young Ukrainian artists who studied with her in Kiev and Odessa from 1916 to 1919 went on to become leading stage designers, including Bogomazov, Meller, Petritsky, Tchelitchew and her collaborator on *Aelita*, Rabinovich.[54] While their idioms would vary greatly, Exter had reached a degree of mastery at the very point where the Futurist quest was about to face its final challenge. The Kamerny *Salomé* opened less than a month before the October Revolution and its importance is attested by Andrei Nakov:

> This production provided a stylistic example which would nourish 'Constructivist' production until almost the end of the 1920s. In *Salomé*, skilful lighting made the geometric forms vibrate, giving an impression of floating, while moving on the vertical. The actors' costumes were the

result of an ordering of geometric forms and their acting was constrained by the limits of these forms. Like the scenery for *Victory Over the Sun* in 1913 (the real prototype of this formal sequence), the décor for *Salomé* produced a strange monumentalisation of dramatic tonality. The new pathos of the 'machine age' was born.[55]

Exter's theatre design from the start had aimed to give three-dimensional depth to the stage picture and to animate its immobile décor. Not only did *Aelita* continue this line of design experiment, but it made use of Kamerny actors, including Nikolai Tsereteli – the Kamerny's Romeo – making his screen début as Los/Spiridonov. But, whereas *Romeo and Juliet* was embellished with extraordinary 'frozen dynamics', echoing Boccioni's sculpture, *Aelita* received a more austere treatment and moreover one precisely conceived for the medium of cinema.[56]

As in cinema history, canonic considerations in art history seem to have told against Exter. It would certainly be wrong to classify her and Rabinovich's work as 'Constructivist' in the narrow sense defended by Christina Lodder, but equally the latter's critique seems to be based on doubtful premisses:

> aesthetic factors dominate [Exter's] creations for the School of Fashion . . . and her costume designs for the film *Aelita*. In both these branches of work considerations of strict utility played no role, and Exter's use of geometrical forms as decorative elements stressed the essentially painterly nature of her approach to clothes. Aelita's costume billowed out into extravagant vegetable protrusions more reminiscent of Art Nouveau than Constructivism, and her maid's trousers, constructed of rectangular metallic strips, seemed designed to impede rather than facilitate movement. It is significant that whereas Stepanova and Popova used the theatre to realise *prozodezhda* ['production' or work clothing] Exter produced these decorative fripperies.[57]

Another historian of Russian and Soviet art, John Bowlt, makes the important observation that, while the *Aelita* costumes may look 'unwieldy and rather absurd' on paper, 'in the movie they function perfectly'. This is because they rely upon and actually exploit the changing viewpoint of cinema and its artificial 'additive' space.[58]

> Knowing that in the black and white film, color in her designs would be superfluous, Exter restored to other systems of formal definition. This, together with her acute concern with space as a creative agent, prompted Exter to use a variety of unusual materials in the construction of the costumes and to rely on sharp contrasts between material textures – aluminium, perspex, metal-foil, glass.[59]

Many judgements on *Aelita* have been passed without doubt on the basis of drawings or stills alone, but viewing confirms how accurately the effects were calculated for this (literally) fantastic, yet flat and monochrome, world of Los's dream – a very different challenge from the theatre projects tackled by other artists during the short-lived moment of Constructivism, but one approached according to the same analytic principles:

> both in Exter's costumes and Rabinovich's sets, industrial materials served a definite objective: they defined form in the absence of color; in their transparency or reflectivity they joined with the space around them and created an eccentric montage of forms.[60]

The Martian dream in this *Aelita* was not after all intended as a vision of the future or an exercise in anti-aesthetic design efficiency. On the contrary, thematically it had to combine an impression of extreme technological refinement with the trappings of a feudal, hieratic society and an erotic motive. Hence the highly effective play of stasis and movement centring on the representation of light – petrified rays, dynamic translucent forms

*Figure 10* Los's dream companions, Kravtsev (Ilyinsky) and Gusev (Batalov), meet the Martian slave-labourers underground, when they are arrested with Aelita's maid, Ikushka (*left*).

echoing the perspex sculptures of Gabo – and the subtle evocation of an Atlantean-Egyptian autocracy largely through costume and make-up. By evoking a modified Kamerny style, Protazanov was acknowledging the power of the Symbolist tradition, yet also gaining distance from it through the film's cultural montage form.

In practice, it appears that both Rabinovich's 'Constructivist' cityscape and Simov's sets proved too expensive for Mezhrabpom-Rus and much of the actual design seen in the film was by Viktor Kozlovsky, an accomplished cinema art director from the pre-Revolutionary industry who had gained valuable experience on its lavish historical subjects and, especially, on the fantastic live-action films of Władysław Starewicz.[61] Kozlovsky seems to have occupied the same supervisory role at Mezhrabpom-Rus as the art-department heads of Hollywood studios, mediating between bold stylistic innovation and the demands of budget and timetable. And all that is not 'Martian' in *Aelita* was presumably designed by him.

For it is not Mars, but Moscow, that is the film's main setting. As befitted a film directed by a returning exile, it uncovers an extraordinary range of the early Soviet experience – from the crowded trains and stations as recovery begins after the Civil War, through relics of the *ancien régime* (climaxing in the decadent night-club which resembles nothing so much as a *bal des victimes*), to signs of the new culture – posters, an agit-performance at the evacuation centre, the orphanage where Masha goes to work – and industry (the radio station and bustling construction sites where Los works) and the streets and crowded apartments of Moscow at the peak of the New Economic Policy. More thoroughly than in any other Soviet film of the period, the precarious equilibrium of the NEP, with idealism and opportunism both rife, is exposed and indeed becomes the film's dramatic and ideological pivot.

## 7   DREAMERS AND DETECTIVES

What undoubtedly must have seemed most attractive about filming *Aelita* was the prospect of Soviet cinema's first science-fiction film, for the early 1920s had seen an extraordinary explosion of Soviet writing and publishing in a genre which had previously been the preserve of the intelligentsia. The Revolution had given fresh impetus to a long-standing Russian fascination with programmatic fantasy, itself already enshrined in the Bolshevik tradition. Lenin had titled his 1902 strategic pamphlet *What Is To Be Done?* explicitly after Chernyshevsky's 'underground' novel written in 1862, which included the dream of a future social order based on female emancipation and the rational division of labour. Another Bolshevik leader, Alexander Bogdanov, had responded to the defeat of the 1905 Revolution with a novel, *Red Star* [Krasnaya zvezda, 1908], in which a discouraged Russian activist is inspired by the discovery of a Communist utopia on Mars.[62] Now the creation of utopia was a state aim; and even H. G. Wells, one of the many foreign science-fiction writers already well known in translation, was surprised by Lenin's enthusiasm for technological and even interplanetary speculation amid the country's devastation in 1919.

Surveying the prodigious range of science-fiction publishing during NEP, from the experimental (a 'cinematic montage' novel by Bobrov and a 'factographic' collaboration by Shklovsky and Ivanov) to the ephemeral, Leonid Heller concludes simply that 'science-fiction accompanied Soviet literature from the moment of its birth'.[63] Indeed fantastic adventure and the characteristic Soviet genre of detection-cum-disaster novel, the 'Red Pinkertons', created a short-lived common culture, at least among urban workers and intellectuals. A good example was Marietta Shaginyan's *Miss Mend* [Mess-Mend, 1924], featuring an intrepid female detective and *Fantômas*-like situations, published under the pseudo-American *nom de plume* 'Jim Dollar' with cover designs by the Constructivist Rodchenko, and filmed for Mezhrabpom-Rus as a serial by a group consisting largely of Kuleshov alumni, though with Protazanov's 'discovery', Ilyinsky, playing the lead.[64] For, in the character of the comic detective Kravtsev, realised with manic precision by one of Meyerhold's young actors, Protazanov had unerringly caught the cultural pulse of the period – Eccentric, populist and fascinated by all things American.[65] He also succeeded in defusing the essentially reactionary thrust of Tolstoi's *Smenovekh* nationalism and anti-Semitism, by making the film in effect a critique of 'cosmism'.

It was the strident utopianism of the 'proletarian' writers promoted by Bogdanov's Proletkult organisation that gave rise to this tendency,[66] mocked by Trotsky:

> The idea here approximately is that one should feel the entire world as a unity and oneself as an active part of that unity, with the prospect of commanding in the future not only the earth, but the entire cosmos. All this, of course, is very splendid and terribly big. We came from Kursk and from Kaluga, we have conquered all Russia recently, and now we are going on towards world revolution. But are we to stop at the boundaries of 'planetism'?[67]

Beneath its derivative surface, Tolstoi's novel also remained faithful to a mystical tradition in Russian fantasy and science fiction. Probably the most pervasive source of this was the late nineteenth-century religious thinker Nikolai Fyodorov, who preached in his 'Philosophy of the Common Task' a mystical, yet literal millenarianism. The achievements of science, including travel to other planets, victory over death and the realisation of a heavenly utopia on earth were all linked goals in Fyodorov's influential doctrine and their imprint can be found across a remarkable range of Russian thought and art. Even Konstantin Tsiolkovsky, the rocket pioneer, was one of many inspired by Fyodorov and, significantly, he did not win final support for his scientific research until he too published a programmatic novel, *Beyond the Stars*, in 1920.[68] But there was also widespread interest in theosophy, in

Spengler's doctrine of the decline of the West and in the anti-Semitism of the *Protocols of the Elders of Zion*, traces of which can all be found within the nostalgic romanticism of Tolstoi's *Aelita*.[69] To this extent unreconstructed nationalists found common cause with the 'proletarian' poets in a shared conviction of Soviet Russia's destiny to conquer death, the world and the universe. Without some understanding of this context, the particular irony of Protazanov's revision is lost.

## 8   CREATING THE NEW MAN

Where might the ideological strategy for revising Tolstoi into a more topical tract for the times have originated? One possible answer is to be found in the career of the co-scenarist Alexei Faiko, a newcomer to cinema paired with the young though already experienced Fyodor Otsep. If Otsep brought his pre-Revolutionary experience of 'psychological' scripting to the project – including the notable *Queen of Spades* he had written for Protazanov in 1916 – we may suppose that Faiko contributed a sharper sense of contemporary ideology. Essentially a playwright, he had already scored a precocious success in 1923 with *Lake Lyul*, a detective story set in an imagined capitalist country, directed at Meyerhold's Theatre of the Revolution by the future film director Abram Room. Faiko's later successes of the 1920s would all satirise the careerism that flourished openly under NEP; and his most famous play, *The Man With the Briefcase*, dealt directly with the issue of the pre-Revolutionary intelligentsia's adjustment – or lack of it – to Soviet demands. Recasting Tolstoi's somewhat cardboard hero as a dreamer obsessed with an erotic Martian fantasy situates him in the Symbolist tradition, and perhaps links him with Wells's apocalyptic fantasy 'A Dream of Armageddon' (also a 'dream counterpoint' narrative); above all it makes him a more complex and, as suggested earlier, recognisable character in the Russian vein.

He has indeed a precursor in Dostoyevsky's late story 'The Dream of a Ridiculous Man'.[70] In this the narrator is overcome by a feeling of useless-ness and contingency in relation to the contemporary world and decides upon suicide, only to fall asleep and dream of his resurrection before being transported to a planet similar to Earth where the whole cycle of the Golden Age myth is in progress. The 'ridiculous man' believes he has corrupted this paradise and caused its Fall: he begs the now warring inhabitants to kill him, by crucifixion, but they refuse. He then wakes, convinced of the need to preach the 'old truth' – 'love your neighbour as yourself'. Here, before the vogue for Wellsian 'scientific romance' which would prove so influential upon later Russian utopian materialists, we find a curious fusion of Dostoyevsky's radical evangelism and his anticipation of the dystopic vein that would dominate Russian Symbolism. It has been suggested that the story marks a further refutation of *What Is To Be Done?* and in particular its vision of a future Crystal Palace, expounded in the 'fourth dream' of one of the characters, Vera Pavlovna.[71] Dostoyevsky had already attacked Chernyshevsky's novel in his *Notes from the Underground*; now he adopted its dream form to imagine a 'moral utopia' which could result from an apocalyptic conversion experience due to what Bakhtin identifies as a 'crisis dream'.[72]

The thrust of Otsep's and Faiko's scenario for Protazanov is towards a Soviet model of this conversion allegory. Although Los is shown first as a conscientious Soviet citizen married to an equally conscientious wife, both of them willing to put duty before domesticity, the arrival of Erlich triggers their latent dissatisfaction. Hitherto Los has been able to keep his rocket researches with Spiridonov and his Martian dream as a 'private' domain, a compensation for the dissatisfactions of everyday life and work. But, when Erlich is assigned to the apartment spare room he has used for research, the state implicitly invades such remaining pockets of 'bourgeois individualism': Los longingly traces Aelita's name on the dusty ornate window of his threatened sanctuary and summons her image immediately before the chairwoman of the Housing Committee announces the unwanted lodger. Los's unconscious response is to fantasise Erlich's seduction of his wife, as 'justification' for his sense of loss, while this erotic fantasy is acted out in the calculated seduction of Los's *alter ego* Spiridonov by Erlich's wife Elena. Indeed, as Leonid Pliushch notes in his acute reading of the film against the background of Tolstoi's reactionary *Smenovekh* sympathies, the film's 'doubling' of the novel's single character into a 'good' and a 'bad' engineer effectively echoes Tolstoi's identification of Mars with the decadent West and also with the 'paradise lost' of tsarist Russia.[73] Spiridonov actually emigrates under the influence of Elena – his note confesses 'the past turned out to be stronger' – and Los, symbolically, starts his dream flight to Mars still disguised as Spiridonov (the same actor plays both roles).

The interpretation of Los *twice* killing the image of his wife proposed by Pliushch identifies the first jealousy 'murder' with the petty-bourgeois world of NEP and the second, of Aelita, as a *political* act necessitated by her betrayal of the Revolution. This reading gains support from the crucial linking of Natasha and Aelita through 'transgressive' intercutting, first when Los embraces Aelita after arriving, then when he pushes her off the podium above the main Martian arena as she orders the capture of the disarmed workers. Indeed an early image of the exotic Aelita is ironically intercut with Natasha scrubbing at the sink. Killing the fantasy of Aelita, as well as his distorted image of Natasha (whose name, Pliushch notes, signifies 'she who is born'), is the necessary prelude to her 'rebirth' as a true Soviet woman and to Los's regeneration as a 'good' Soviet engineer. In terms of allegory, there is a distinct echo of Mayakovsky's *Mystery Bouffe*, which ends with representatives of the 'unclean' class killing Queen Chaos and declaring 'the door into the future is open'.

## 9    BACK THROUGH THE LOOKING-GLASS

*Aelita* clearly disconcerted its first critics through a failure to respect genre and narrative conventions; and the Soviet critical tradition has eventually categorised it as a kind of generic melting-pot, from which can be traced Protazanov's subsequent comedies with Ilyinsky and, in Batalov's Gusev, the early evolution of the obligatory 'positive hero'.[74] Such a view, however, though convenient, denies the film's integral structure and contemporaneity. One way to retain these, as suggested at the outset, is to adopt the methodology applied by Bakhtin in his 1929 study of Dostoyevsky and consider *Aelita* as a 'polyphonic' work. Thus we are free to consider how and why its different discourses coexist, and what kinds of dialogue they conducted with its original audience.

Bakhtin's book on Dostoyevsky also contains a highly relevant analysis of 'The Dream of a Ridiculous Man', treating this as a prime instance of the genre of 'Menippean satire', which may help to define more precisely the processes at work in *Aelita*. According to Bakhtin:

> The most important characteristic of the Menippea lies in the fact that the most daring and unfettered fantasies and adventures are internally motivated, justified and illuminated here by a purely ideological and philosophical end – to create *extraordinary situations* in which to provoke and test a philosophical idea. . . . A very important characteristic . . . is the organic combination within it of free fantasy, symbolism, and – on occasion – the mystical-religious element, with extreme . . . *underworld naturalism*. . . . The Menippea is a genre of 'ultimate questions'. [It] seeks to present a person's ultimate, decisive words and actions, each of which contains the whole person and his whole life. . . . [It] often includes elements of *social utopia* which are introduced in the form of dreams or journeys to unknown lands. . . . Finally, the Menippea's last characteristic – its topicality and publicistic quality. This was the 'journalistic' genre of antiquity, pointedly reacting to the issues of the day.[75]

In a fairly obvious sense, Protazanov's film amounts to a 'menippea' based on the would-be epic of Tolstoi's novel; and the process which achieves this is what Bakhtin termed 'carnivalisation'.[76] The crucial aspect of carnival, he argues, is the ambivalent ritual of crowning and discrowning, which embodies notions of change, relativity, parody, death, renewal, etc. Typically, the slave or jester is crowned and thus, temporarily, the world is turned upside down.

It is Bakhtin's powerful concept of carnival that may help illuminate the organic function of otherwise puzzling aspects of the film. Consider, for instance, the role of Kravtsev, the fool, jester, doggedly pursuing his investigation and eventually helping unmask Erlich; or the extraordinary pantomime of Gusev being forced to rush through the Moscow streets in women's clothing when his wife hides his own clothes to prevent him going to

Mars. What could be more 'carnivalesque', more subversive of Tolstoi's romanticism, than the start of the space flight, with Gusev cross-dressed, Los disguised and Kravtsev playing 'Pinkerton'? Bakhtin, both in his acute analysis of the Dostoyevsky story and his 'historical poetics', offers more insight into this much-maligned film than cinema history has yet produced.

In the historiographic tradition of belittling *Aelita* it has become customary to invoke the animated film *Interplanetary Revolution* [Mezhplanetnaya revolutsiya] released in the same year as a 'parody' of it.[77] In fact, viewing confirms that there is no discernable relationship between the two (although a script for an unrealised parody of *Aelita* by Nikolai Foregger apparently exists in the cinema archives) but the idea clearly remains attractive, since Protazanov's film represents an *anomalous* mingling of genres and ideologies.[78]

Much has been made of the fact that its subject and genre(s) were not repeated, as if to confirm an implicit verdict of misjudgement or failure: even the sympathetic Leyda describes it as Protazanov's 'least important' Soviet production.[79] This, however, is to apply too narrow and conventional criteria. For *Aelita* can surely lay claim to being *the* key film of the early NEP period, born of a unique moment in post-Revolutionary Soviet society, reflecting its realities as well as its aspirations in a complex and original form, and linking its hitherto isolated cinema with important currents in world cinema. Rather than serve as a model for future films, it chronicled the acute period of adjustment that followed the end of the Civil War – the film's time-span of 1921–3 is crucial – and probed the new contradictions of NEP.[80] *Aelita* may have earned the anathemas of Vertov and LEF, standard-bearers of the new 'factography', but it was by no means out of step with other, less dogmatic, currents of artistic innovation, like the young writers of the Serapion Brotherhood, or of such individualists as Zamyatin and Olesha.[81] With its bold juxtaposition of diegetic levels and complex reworking of both literary and visual sources, the film celebrates a heterogeneity and topicality that are, in their way, as impressive as the achievement of either Kuleshov or Eisenstein at this early stage in Soviet film-making. More than their first polemical, propagandistic sketches for a radically new cinema, *Aelita* appears truly, in Bakhtin's sense, a 'polyphonic' work, conducting a dialogue between past and present which is traversed by as many different discourses as indeed were their later works.

But did *Aelita* in fact have any successors? The film that comes closest to its carnivalesque spirit is probably Mezhrabpom-Rus's 1925 short *Chess Fever* [Shakmatnaya goryachka], which again combines fantasy, slapstick and street realism in a highly topical satire, with another eclectic cast – this time consisting largely of film-makers, including Protazanov himself.[82]

Beyond this immediate echo, *Aelita* looks forward to the elaborate 'making strange' of Soviet life attempted in Ermler's masterly *A Fragment of Empire* [Oblomok imperii, 1929] by means of an amnesic protagonist. The only other Soviet film before the 1960s which makes similar use of a fantastic dream counterpoint may well be Room's suppressed *A Severe Young Man* [Strogii yunosha, 1934].[83] But during the 1940s this form would flourish abroad in fables both Freudian (*Lady in the Dark, Spellbound, Dead of Night*) and philosophical (*A Matter of Life and Death, Orphée*).[84] *Aelita*, like its director, richly deserves rescuing from the periphery of a largely static, parochial view of early Soviet cinema.[85] To do so involves breaching the *cordon sanitaire* that has long protected the canon of Soviet 'left' modernism from its antecedents and competitors, and taking new bearings amid the cultural, economic and political cross-currents of the 1920s.

# 6  The return of the native: Yakov Protazanov and Soviet cinema

*Denise J. Youngblood*

Among the many film-makers who left Russia during the Civil War was Yakov Protazanov (1881–1945), one of the flourishing pre-Revolutionary film industry's most prominent directors. The more than eighty movies he had made since his directorial début in 1911 included the top-grossing film of Russian cinema, *The Keys to Happiness* [1913], and the most infamous product of its dying days, *Satan Triumphant* [1917]. From 1920 to 1923, Protazanov lived in Paris and Berlin, making a name for himself in both French and German cinemas.[1] In Berlin, in 1923, he received a visit from Moisei Aleinikov, one of the directors of the Rus studio (soon to become Mezhrabpom-Rus), who persuaded Protazanov that the time was right for him to return home.[2] Three weeks later he was back in Moscow, and shortly thereafter at work on his first Soviet film, *Aelita*. A recent Soviet reference book on film says that Protazanov was among the originators of the 'acting school' in Soviet cinema[3] but, to aspiring young directors, the return of the king of Russian silent cinema meant something quite different indeed.

Protazanov quickly re-established himself as a major, if not *the* pre-eminent, director of the Soviet screen. It is probably safe to assert that no other director in the first decade of Soviet cinema had as varied – and unpredictable – an oeuvre. Certainly no other Soviet director was as prolific and as consistently successful at the box office. The consummate professional, Protazanov was immune to the political and artistic controversies bedevilling his younger, more 'Soviet' colleagues, both due to his temperament and his record of commercial success.[4] He made ten silent films for the Mezhrabpom-Rus studio in six years, beginning with *Aelita* in 1924 and ending with *The Feast of St Jorgen* [Prazdnik svyatogo Iorgena] in 1930.

By way of comparison, the output of those young directors whose names are virtually synonymous with Soviet silent cinema (in the West, anyway) was dramatically lower. Sergei Eisenstein, Lev Kuleshov, Vsevolod Pudovkin, Dziga Vertov, Alexander Dovzhenko and the team of Grigori Kozintsev and Leonid Trauberg each made only four full-length features in the same period. These men made 'difficult' films not intended as light entertainment for mass audiences, but the figures are also comparable for those major directors from the younger generation who *did* make movies more easily accessible to general audiences. Boris Barnet made six films, Fridrikh [Friedrich] Ermler four, and Sergei Yutkevich, two.

In the context of the stormy cultural politics of the early Soviet film industry, these figures were significant, and not necessarily attributable to the younger directors' inexperience. The first point to be made is somewhat obvious, but none the less important: the more films he has on the market, the more potential influence a director has with audiences and studios. This was definitely the case with Protazanov, whose pictures were crowd-pleasers almost guaranteed to draw at the box office. The second point is that to the young cohort, Protazanov symbolised everything they perceived to be wrong with the Soviet film industry in the 1920s – its emphasis on profits, its lack of support for experimentation, its 'pandering' to the tastes of the masses. Why was 'Soviet power' banking on 'the little Moscow merchant' to create the new cinema?[5]

The social history of Soviet cinema and the history of early Soviet culture cannot be fully understood without reference to the most popular, really the *only* truly popular, native director of the 1920s – Yakov Protazanov. Most of the 'revolutionary' masterworks which made Eisenstein and Pudovkin and others 'household' names in avant-garde artistic circles in the 1920s were seen by few Soviet filmgoers – and liked by fewer still. As we shall see, Protazanov's Soviet films were widely distributed, enjoyed runs of several weeks in the largest theatres, and consistently earned profits for the studio. These by themselves serve as adequate indicators of popularity but, to cite additional evidence, Protazanov's movies were frequently named in the 'top ten' surveys conducted among audiences. Throughout his career he seemed to have an uncanny understanding of what viewers liked, whether those viewers were Russian, French, or Soviet.

Because Protazanov came to Soviet cinema as a mature artist, his career is a particularly interesting and significant one which has the potential to illuminate key issues in the development of Soviet society. By virtue of his family background, education, and professional experience, Protazanov was the quintessential 'bourgeois specialist' – so his story can shed light on the role of the 'former' middle classes in the formation of the new society. And because he lived and worked abroad both before and after the Revolution – and made films that were recognisably 'Western' in style – Protazanov and his movies can elucidate the extent to which nascent Soviet culture relied on Westernised pre-Revolutionary traditions. That this director, labelled in his time a 'reactionary', 'socially primitive' maker of 'shallow entertainment' pictures, not only survived but prospered as a Soviet film-maker is a testament to the tenacity of the old tradition and the adaptability of its leading practitioner. Protazanov, who served as a bridge between the Russian past and the Soviet present, is an outstanding example of the importance of 'transitional' figures in the evolution of Soviet popular culture.

When Protazanov made the crucial decision to return to Soviet Russia in 1923, the battle lines on the cultural front were only starting to be drawn. Because the director was a circumspect individual, writing virtually nothing and responding to interviews as laconically as possible,[6] we can only conjecture about his true reasons for coming back and his reactions once home. Even his Soviet biographers make no effort to claim a political awakening for him. Given the circumstances of his early life, however, it is reasonable to surmise that Protazanov might have been a little bemused to find himself at the centre of a controversy in which he was cast at the age of 42 as a representative of the 'old order'.[7]

Yakov Alexandrovich Protazanov was born in Moscow in 1881, on his mother's side the member of a well-to-do merchant family named Vinokurov.[8] His father, a somewhat shadowy figure of whom Protazanov's conservative grandfather disapproved, was from Kiev, and probably an accountant by profession. The Vinokurovs were not the prototypical, traditional merchant family, although they did have some patriarchal and authoritarian characteristics. Contrary to the stereotype, Protazanov's mother was reasonably well educated, preferred to speak French at home, and took her children to the theatre.

Protazanov early evinced an interest in the theatre and was especially attracted by the glamour of the actors who frequented the Vinokurov residence (where the Protazanovs lived) since several relatives were in the 'business'.[9] And yet, despite the somewhat eccentric cast to this merchant family, there seems to have been no question that Protazanov would attend any school other than the Moscow Commercial School, though his interests and inclinations lay in other areas. After graduating from the school in 1900, he apparently hoped to enter the Petersburg Technical Institute to study engineering, but some reversals in family fortunes forced him to work in an office instead.

This experience as a wage earner was so disagreeable that Protazanov noted in his own brief memoirs that he was looking for the first opportunity to escape from 'slavery'. The opportunity finally came in 1904 when he received a 5,000 rouble inheritance from his father's aunt. Protazanov left the country in June 1904 and did not return permanently until 1907. With his characteristic dry humour he observed that 'I didn't finish with slavery, but I did finish off my inheritance very quickly.'[10]

Protazanov travelled all over Europe, but it was his trip to Paris that altered the course of his life. While there, he added the Pathé studio, centre of pre-war European cinema, to the standard tourist itinerary. To the surprise (and even horror) of his family and friends, Protazanov fixed suddenly and irrevocably upon movie-making as his career of choice. Yet, given his background and character, cinema held obvious attractions.

Protazanov was something of a rebel, chafing at the strictures of the office job to which he had been assigned by family tradition. Given that he was apparently little interested in politics (as demonstrated by his European junkets during the Revolution of 1905–7), the revolutionary road that served so many of his generation did not attract him as an outlet for rebellion.[11] At the turn of the century movies were considered a bastard 'art' and film-making was an *outré* profession, if one even dared to call it a profession. It offered Protazanov the opportunity to thumb his nose at his respectable family, throw off the chains of his regimented job, and indulge in his interest in theatre. That cinema held out the promise of making a great deal of money while having a good time also attracted him to film but, given the course of his career, one should not overemphasise this point.[12]

Moscow's infant film industry was centred in the merchant district around Pyatnitskaya Street. Although it was dominated by foreigners, Russian entrepreneurs were involved as well, and in 1907 Protazanov went to work for the Russian-armed 'Gloria' film studio as an interpreter for a Spanish 'cameraman' who knew French (Protazanov's language of expertise) about as well as he knew how to operate a movie camera. 'Gloria' quickly failed, and Protazanov offered his services to the more established concern of Thiemann & Reinhardt.[13] He again worked as an interpreter for the cameraman, this time an Italian, who did not speak French but, unlike the Spaniard, did know his business. Protazanov quickly learned all aspects of movie-making as Thiemann & Reinhardt's jack-of-all-trades. In 1909, he began writing scripts and acting in small parts, and in 1911, when he married the sister of 'Gloria's' former owner, Thiemann raised his salary from fifty to eighty roubles a month. His 'break' came in 1911, when he dashed off a script called *A Convict's Song* [Pesn' katorzhanina], which he sold to Thiemann for twenty-five roubles.[14] The film, Protazanov's directional début, was a rousing success. As a result Protazanov found himself promoted to director and earning 400 roubles a month.

The production practices that Protazanov developed in his pre-Revolutionary career and continued in the Soviet period reflect early developments in the Russian industry. Perhaps most important was the close relationship that existed between Russian theatre and cinema. Many early Russian movie directors came to cinema from theatre – Vladimir Gardin (with whom Protazanov had frequently collaborated), Pyotr Chardynin and Yevgeni Bauer, to name only a few. Similarly, actors and set designers moved from theatre to film and back, depending on where the jobs were. Throughout his long career in the movies, Protazanov preferred to use actors with theatre training and to hire production personnel he had known in the pre-Revolutionary cinema. In the Soviet period, where breaking with the past in general and the theatre in particular was part of the radical credo, this proved an especially sore point.

Protazanov enjoyed an excellent working relationship with actors, was an astute judge of talent, and cast his pictures well. His ability to attract actors of the stature of Ivan Mosjoukine [Mozzhukhin], Nataliya Lisenko, Vera Kralli, Olga Gzovskaya and Vladimir Maximov doubtless contributed to the popularity of his pre-Revolutionary movies with a public which had heard of these stars but could not afford to attend the theatre.[15] He did not depend exclusively on established names, however, and gave Olga Preobrazhenskaya, then a little-known actress from the provincial stage deemed 'too old' for major roles, the chance that made her a star.[16]

Protazanov came to be known for his screen adaptations of famous literary works. The film industry has since its earliest days turned to print literature as a handy source for proven story-lines. In the Russian cinema, adapting 'great works' to the screen was especially popular, since the classics lent an aura of respectability to a form of entertainment that might otherwise have been a shade too vulgar for the bourgeois audiences the studios hoped to attract. (In Russia, as elsewhere at this time, the urban middle classes were the chief filmgoers.) Protazanov directed his share of these lavish costume dramas and screen adaptations, the best-known being his mammoth version of *War and Peace* [Voina i mir, 1915, with Gardin] and *The Queen of Spades* [Pikovaya dama, 1916].[17]

But the film that placed Protazanov at the forefront of Russian film directors did not bring a serious work of literature down to the lowly screen; it was instead an adaptation of one of the most popular works of Russian *boulevard* fiction, Anastasiya Verbitskaya's sensational novel of illicit miscegenistic love, *The Keys to Happiness*, made in 1913. Protazanov's instinct for the entertaining was an unerring as his instinct for the cinematic, and *The Keys to Happiness* was a legendary box-office success. It was sold out for days in advance and attracted an audience that had never before attended the movies. At ten reels, in two parts, this film was four to five times longer than the typical movie of the day and demonstrated to the Russian studio heads that lengthy movies could sustain audience attention. In direct response to the phenomenon of *The Keys to Happiness*, Thiemann & Reinhardt established its famous 'Golden Series' of full-length feature films, mainly directed by Protazanov.[18] Although Protazanov continued making movies based on the classics, his biggest hits were usually derived from popular fiction. It is not surprising that these enjoyed great success with audiences, which as mentioned above were drawn largely from the middle classes – especially from the petty bourgeoisie, which also formed the market for this fiction.[19]

The outbreak of the First World War scarcely affected the pace of his production: he completed nineteen pictures in 1914; twelve in 1915; and fifteen in 1916. As late as 1917, he managed eight, including the notorious *Satan Triumphant*, a film about demonism apparently so lurid that Soviet histories of the Russian film gloss over it.[20] The war did, however, affect his studio, as the 'German' firm of Thiemann & Reinhardt was attacked by mobs. In 1915, after making *War and Peace* for the 'Golden Series', Protazanov left Thiemann to join the Yermoliev studio; like Protazanov, Iosif Yermoliev was the scion of a Moscow merchant family but the princely 20,000-rouble salary that Yermoliev promised probably influenced Protazanov more than did class solidarity.[21] The fact that he was drafted at the end

*Figure 11  Satan Triumphant* [1917] gave Protazanov's regular stars Mosjoukine and Lisenko a rare opportunity for Expressionist acting in this account of Satan causing havoc in a devout Scandinavian community.

of September 1916 and remained in uniform at least until the end of February 1917 was of so little import that neither Protazanov nor his friend Aleinikov bother to mention it when discussing the director's work during this period.[22]

After the February Revolution, the Yermoliev studio adjusted to the new Revolutionary mentality and began producing works on Revolutionary themes. Protazanov adapted as well and in 1917 made two films on Revolution in quick succession: *Andrei Kozhukhov* and *We Don't Need Blood* [Ne nado krovi] (about Sofiya Perovskaya). More to his taste, certainly, was his adaptation of a story which he had wanted to film for some time, but which the pre-Revolutionary censors had suppressed as a movie script – Tolstoy's *Father Sergius* [Otets Sergii, 1918]. This picture, starring Ivan Mosjoukine as the tsarist officer who becomes a monk, was one of the most important movies to appear immediately after the October Revolution.[23]

In the winter of 1918–19, Yermoliev became alarmed at the direction the Revolution was taking and concerned for the health and safety of his company in cold and hungry Moscow. He persuaded the entire group, including Protazanov, to move with him to Yalta and set up shop there. The

Yermoliev studio's sojourn in Yalta was a short one, and at the beginning of February 1920 the troupe was again on the move, this time ending up in Paris.[24] That 1920 was a bad year for Protazanov is best demonstrated by noting that it was the first since 1909 that he did not add a single production to his filmography, though he had been working under less than ideal conditions for some years.

Professionally speaking, Protazanov effortlessly adjusted to émigré life. A Francophile since childhood, he spoke French fluently and, as previously mentioned, had lived in France as a young man. From 1921 to 1923 he made six movies, five in France and one in Germany. By the time Aleinikov contacted him in Berlin, Protazanov had joined the ranks of established European directors.[25] There can be no doubt that Protazanov, like so many of the other Russians from the Yermoliev and Khanzhonkov studios, could have had a successful career in exile in the West. It is not clear, therefore, why the maker of *The Keys to Happiness* and *Satan Triumphant* chose to return to Soviet Russia, abandoning a lucrative European career. This decision would seem to give the lie to his own assertion that money was one of cinema's chief attractions for him.

In any case, he skilfully charted an independent course once back, demonstrating yet again his tough-mindedness and adaptability in the face of adversity. A cursory glance at his ten Soviet silents reveals an oeuvre in keeping with the topical concerns of Soviet society in the 1920s (with the possible exceptions of *The Three Millions Trial* [Protsess o trekh millionakh] and *Ranks and People* [Chiny i lyudi]).

In 1924, he made *Aelita*, a science-fiction fantasy about a proletarian revolution on Mars, very loosely based on Alexei Tolstoi's novella; in 1925, *His Call* [Ego prizyv], an adventure melodrama incorporating the theme of the 'Leninist enrolment' in the Party, and *The Tailor from Torzhok* [Zakroishchik iz Torzhka], a comedy both about the housing shortage and the state lottery. In 1926, to be sure, he reverted to type with *The Three Millions Trial*, a crime caper set in Italy that was one of several film adaptations of Umberto Notari's play *The Three Thieves*. But he returned to more typically Soviet subjects in 1927 with *The Man from the Restaurant* [Chelovek iz restorana], an updating of Ivan Shmeliev's 1911 novella about a downtrodden waiter who saves his daughter's virtue; and especially with *The Forty-First* [Sorok pervyi], from Boris Lavrenev's popular novella about the Red Army sharpshooter who kills her 'White' lover.

In 1928, Protazanov released two pictures: *The White Eagle* [Belyi orel], a controversial adaptation of Leonid Andreyev's story about a provincial governor who orders his troops to fire on civilians during the 1905 Revolution, and *Don Diego and Pelageya* [Don Diego i Pelageya], a fresh and witty comedy attacking the excessive bureaucratism of Soviet society. His final silent productions were *Ranks and People* [1929], drawn from three of Chekhov's slightest short stories, and *The Feast of St Jorgen* [1930], an anti-religious comedy which, although adapted from the work of the Danish writer Harald Bergstedt, was commissioned as part of the campaign against religion taking place at the time. These ten films conformed to generally accepted standards of narrative realism; they featured clearly delineated and believable heroes and villains; and for the most part, they were fast-paced and entertaining. Protazanov worked quickly and efficiently; unlike many of his younger Soviet colleagues, he knew how to finish a film on time and within budget.[26] His movies made money and were popular with audiences, at least in the major cities, where movie theatres were concentrated.

And yet Protazanov and his films were frequently subjected to a barrage of criticism from reviewers and from other film-makers throughout the decade. This can be attributed in part to *perception*, to the fact that he symbolised the 'Golden Series'.[27] In order to understand Protazanov fully, we need to examine his films and their reception in more detail, to situate them in the context of the cultural politics of the era. Recognising the inevitable errors of oversimplification, the cultural politics of the film industry in the mid-1920s can be briefly summed up as a struggle between young and old; between avant-gardists (the 'montage school') and realists; between those who inclined toward permanent revolution and those who favoured 'socialism at a snail's pace'.[28] Fellow-travellers and bourgeois specialists like Protazanov charted a course that was truly between Scylla and Charybdis. The one issue that most politically conscious film activists could agree on was the need to create a totally new Soviet cinema, one which would end the influence of the 'pernicious' foreign films beloved of Soviet audiences.[29] How to go about creating this new Soviet cinema was quite another matter, and three broad approaches to the problem can be delineated.

Once again acknowledging the oversimplification of this division, we can none the less say that the avant-garde believed that their obligation to society was fulfilled by creating the art of the future; under the cultural and social transformation engendered by socialism, the masses would be uplifted and thereby able to enjoy and appreciate hitherto 'inaccessible' art.[30] The artistic right, on the other hand, may be characterised as narrative realists. This group was less diverse than the avant-garde, so it is possible to identify two subgroups splitting along political lines. The proletarian 'watchdogs' – especially critics connected with the All-Russian Association of Proletarian Writers [Vserossiikaya assotsiyatsiya proletarskikh pisatelei] (VAPP) and the staff of the film section of Glavpolitprosvet, the Main Committee on Political Education in the Commissariat of Enlightenment – favoured a tendentious kind of realism, either narrowly political fictional films or strictly educational *kulturfil'my*. In sharp contrast, the Commissar of Enlightenment Anatoli Lunacharsky – husband of a film actress and himself author of several entertaining film scripts as well as many articles and even a book on film – believed that there was nothing especially anti-Soviet about entertainment.[31] Lunacharsky felt that the goal of Soviet cinema should be to make Soviet films (focusing on melodramas, adventures and comedies) to entertain the Soviet people. This was the line vigorously pursued by the state film trust Sovkino and the semi-independent studio for which Protazanov worked, Mezhrabpom.[32] To the proletarians, this brand of cinema realism was tantamount to counter-revolution and was no less dangerous than the 'Formalist' heresies preached by Eisenstein, Vertov and many others.

These debates were taking shape as Protazanov set to work in February 1923 on his first Soviet film, the science-fiction fantasy *Aelita*, the tale of a Soviet engineer who dreams of building a spaceship, taking off for Mars, and falling in love with a Martian princess named Aelita. Because this dream includes a 'proletarian' revolution on Mars, Protazanov was able to exercise his talent for adventure and fantasy in a movie with a Soviet theme and, in its terrestrial part, a contemporary Soviet setting.

The production history of *Aelita* indicates that Protazanov prepared for his Soviet début with great care and forethought. Though schooled in the break-neck pace of pre-Revolutionary film-making, averaging more than ten films annually before the Revolution, he took over a year to complete *Aelita*. According to the handsome programme that was distributed at screenings of the picture, Protazanov shot 22,000 metres of film for the 2,841-metre movie (an unusually high rate of waste) and employed a cast and crew of thousands.[33]

This cast and crew was certainly one of the most impressive ever assembled in the 1920s for a single picture. Fyodor Otsep, the head scenarist, and Yuri Zhelyabuzhsky, the cameraman, had had considerable pre-Revolutionary film-making experience. Although Protazanov's Russian films had not been noted for their external decorativeness (that being the hallmark of Yevgeni Bauer, whose work Protazanov disliked), Protazanov paid tribute to new artistic trends by having Alexandra Exter and Isaak Rabinovich design for the Martian scenes the Constructivist costumes and sets for which the movie is famous. The casting was stellar and, according to Protazanov's custom in his Russian work, drawn almost exclusively from the ranks of theatre actors. The troupe included the director Konstantin Eggert, Vera Orlova, Valentina Kuindzhi, Olga Tretyakova and Nikolai Tsereteli, and introduced to the screen Igor Ilyinsky, Nikolai Batalov and Yuliya Solntseva. Ilyinsky and Batalov became the leading male stars of Soviet silent cinema, and Solntseva enjoyed a following as well.[34]

The promotional campaign was as lavish as the production itself: in the provincial city of Voronezh, for example, aeroplanes dropped thousands of leaflets advertising *Aelita*.[35] Protazanov intended to make his presence felt in his Soviet début: the director of *The Keys to Happiness* had returned! *Aelita* did cause a sensation but not quite the one that the Mezhrabpom studio and Protazanov had hoped for.

No other film of early Soviet cinema was attacked as consistently or over so long a period as *Aelita*. From 1924 to 1928, it was a regular target for film critics and for the many social activists who felt that the film industry was not supporting Soviet interests. This lively movie that the British critic Paul Rotha labelled 'extraordinary', though theatrical, was greeted quite differently in the pages of the Soviet film press. *Kino-gazeta*, a relatively moderate newspaper, was unrelenting in its opposition to *Aelita*, going so far as to label it 'ideologically unprincipled' and to warn that the potential danger of a 'rallié' like Protazanov might outweigh the benefits of his experience and professionalism.[36]

These criticisms were echoed elsewhere, especially (but not exclusively) in 'proletarian' circles. *Proletarskoe kino* claimed *Aelita* had cost too much; another newspaper with a proletarian orientation, *Kinonedelya*, attacked *Aelita*'s scriptwriters as individuals 'alien to the working class' and advised that the Party keep bourgeois specialists like Protazanov under close watch.[37] But the following examples, similar in tone, came from varying sources. Viewers in Nizhni Novgorod allegedly criticised its 'petty-bourgeois' [meshchanskii] ending and complained that the hardships of the Civil War years were absent from the film;[38] to the young director Lev Kuleshov, *Aelita* exemplified 'the blind alley of pre-Revolutionary cinema'. Prominent critic Ippolit Sokolov, a supporter of the entertainment film, deemed *Aelita* too complicated for viewers to understand: Soviet in content but not in form, and 'too Western'.[39] As late as 1928, *Aelita* was still brought forth as an object of scorn (admittedly, this was in the pages of Mayakovsky's journal *Novyi Lef* which resolutely opposed 'old-fashioned' entertainment pictures such as these).[40]

*Aelita*'s aftershocks jolted Protazanov. Except for his first movie (a 1909 short never released for which he served as scenarist, based on Pushkin's 'The Fountain of Bakhchisarai') every picture he had made had been a critical as well as a popular success. Protazanov learned his lesson well – from this point on, both the style of his films and their manner of production changed to conform to Soviet reality better. He eschewed special effects, expensive sets and fanciful scripts in favour of realistic contemporary films with modest productions (but he never abandoned his preference for seasoned crews and theatre actors, preferably with pre-Revolutionary experience).

Protazanov also reacted to the *Aelita* 'scandal' by resuming a low public profile (although he was once singled out in the press for enjoying a higher standard of living than did other film workers).[41] His absence from the debates then raging in the press about actors and acting, plots and scripts, montage, rationalisation of production, etc., while not unique, was noticeable because of his prominence. Perhaps the most amusing example of Protazanov's practice of keeping close counsel is a two-part series which appeared in *Na literaturnom postu*. Directors and others prominent in Soviet cinema were called upon to answer several questions about film and literature posed by the journal's editors. Sergei Eisenstein's response to the three questions was about 1,300 words; Protazanov's, exactly 84. Yet his attitude towards his critics was quite clear:

I like to read literary criticism because it doesn't criticise me. For that reason, I read film criticism with less pleasure.

Igor Ilyinsky relates another example of Protazanov's extreme reluctance to speak on the record. During the filming of *The Tailor from Torzhok*, a reporter attempted to interview Protazanov on film genres. The question 'Which genres do you prefer?' elicited from Protazanov: 'In my opinion, all genres are good except boring ones', but the reporter thought the director was joking. He pressed on, asking Protazanov 'Which comedies, in your opinion, are needed by the Soviet viewer?' When Protazanov replied, 'The Soviet viewer needs good and varied comedies', the reporter realised there would be no interview and left.[42]

Despite Protazanov's recognition that he was living in a new world and despite his ability to make good films in different genres on different subjects, content continued to pose problems for him (as it did for many other directors) because of rapidly changing cultural politics. From 1925 to 1929, his movies can be divided into two groups: the 'good' films: *His Call*, *The Forty-First*, and *Don Diego and Pelageya*; and the 'bad': *The Tailor from Torzhok*, *The Three Millions Trial*, *The Man from the Restaurant* and *The White Eagle*. (For reasons that will be discussed below, *The Feast of St Jorgen* and *Ranks and People* did not attract the unwelcome attention they might have earlier.) Whether knowingly or not, Protazanov alternated between making films which his critics found acceptable and those which they found unacceptable. Though the critical reception of his films might be unpredictable, their public reception was quite predictable, and Mezhrabpom was much more concerned with box-office success than with 'critical' acclaim.

*His Call* [1925], *The Forty-First* [1927] and *Don Diego and Pelageya* [1928] baffled Protazanov's opponents and help explain his survival during the Cultural Revolution. How could the director of *Aelita* have made 'truly Soviet' films such as these? *His Call* appealed immediately to Soviet audiences and appeared on a 'top ten' list in 1925.[43] In *His Call*, Protazanov succeeded where other Soviet directors had not – he had made an entertaining but indubitably 'correct' film about Soviet life.

The melodrama begins in the final days of the Revolution; a rich industrialist and his son Vladimir (Anatoli Ktorov, who was to become a favourite of Protazanov's) hide some of their fortune before fleeing abroad. Although Protazanov dwells with obvious pleasure on the scenes of their lavish life in Paris, he took care to contrast this 'decadence' with the suffering that Soviet citizens, especially children, were simultaneously undergoing. Several years after the Revolution, the pair has spent all their money, and so Vladimir returns to Soviet Russia to retrieve the cache, enlisting a *kulak* as his accomplice. Young Katya (Vera Popova, from the Vakhtangov Theatre) and her grandmother (Mariya Blumenthal-Tamarina, a famous stage actress) now occupy the room where the treasure was stashed. Katya, attractive but very naive, is easily seduced by the depraved Vladimir. Quick to resort to violence despite his successful seduction, Vladimir murders Katya's grandmother in his desperate efforts to retrieve the gold. He ends up, fittingly, with a bullet in the back. In the meantime, Lenin has died, and the Party has issued its 'call' for new members, dubbed the 'Leninist enrolment'. The 'fallen woman' Katya hears the call but, unworthy to join the Party's ranks, resists it. Eventually she is convinced that joining the Party will redeem her sins. *His Call* had everything social critics wanted – contemporary subject-matter and precise details of everyday life, and everything the public wanted – love, violence and a happy ending. The usually dour reviewers could find little about which to complain.[44]

Protazanov repeated this formula for success (Soviet subject + melo-drama + love interest) in *The Forty-First*. He transformed Boris Lavrenev's somewhat wooden novella into a memorable picture that, like *His Call*, was quite entertaining. The plot of *The Forty-First* is high melodrama: a Red Army sharpshooter, Maryutka (played by the engaging Ada Voitsik, then a student at GTK, the state film institute) and the White officer who is her prisoner (Ivan Koval-Samborsky from the Meyerhold Theatre) are stranded on a desert island after a storm. Once on the island, separated from the rest of her Red Army company, Maryutka falls in love with the young aristocrat, and the story becomes a kind of reverse 'Admirable Crichton' until the point of rescue. Maryutka, mindful of her duty as a Bolshevik, claims her lover as her forty-first victim. Is this her victory as a Bolshevik or her defeat as a person?

*The Forty-First* made the 'top ten' chart in 1928, listed as the third-most-popular film.[45] But in 1927 (the year of the film's release), critics were much more cautious than they had been two years earlier when *His Call* appeared. Although *The Forty-First* was generally quite well received,[46] there were some disquieting notes that portended problems soon to come. 'Arsen', one of the most censorious of the new breed of 'hard-line' critics, labelled it a 'socially primitive' and 'decadent' example of the 'Western adventure' picture, all the more 'dangerous' because it was so well done.[47] Fortunately for Protazanov, Arsen's view of *The Forty-First* was in the minority.

The final movie to be discussed among the triad of 'good' films, *Don Diego and Pelageya*, is arguably the finest Soviet comedy of the 1920s. Based on a *feuilleton* by Bella Zorich called 'The Letter of the Law' which appeared in *Pravda*,[48] *Don Diego and Pelageya* is the story of an old woman's unwitting attempts to circumvent Soviet power, personified by 'Don Diego', a foolish daydreamer who is the village station master. Don Diego (Anatoli Bykov) arrests Pelageya (Mariya Blumenthal-Tamarina) for illegally crossing the railroad tracks, despite the fact that she could not read the warning sign.

After a farcical trial, she is sentenced to three months in jail. Enter the Party; two members of Komsomol (the Communist Youth League) and the local Party secretary come to the rescue of Pelageya and her bewildered husband. Protazanov's depiction of provincial life is scathing and very funny

*Figures 12, 13* The 'good' and the 'bad': *His Call* (top) made a stirring melodrama out of émigrés scheming to recover their wealth at the expense of honest workers, while *The Tailor from Torzhok* starred Ilyinsky as an innocent provincial trying to recover a winning lottery ticket from his scheming landlady.

indeed, revealing much about the problems of Soviet society: peasants are more than a little mystified by the ideals and goals of the Revolution, and tsarist *chinovniki* have been replaced by rigid, lazy and insolent Soviet *apparatchiki*. This movie, which coincided with the campaign against the 'bureaucratic deviation', demonstrated that it was possible to make a topical movie that could transcend the concerns of the moment and entertain at the same time.

*Don Diego and Pelageya* enjoyed widespread praise as a fine example of what the film comedy (a notoriously weak genre in Soviet cinema) could and should be. But film critics, whatever their stripe, were nervous in 1928. Some felt compelled, therefore, to assert that the role of the Party in solving problems had been insufficiently developed, and that the great evil of bureaucratism had been too individualised in the unlikely person of Don Diego. Despite these reservations (and a fear that the film might be edited abroad in an unflattering fashion) *Don Diego and Pelageya* was justly hailed, most concurring with A. Aravsky's assessment that the film was a 'great event' in the development of Soviet comedy.[49]

The pictures that critics considered reasonably 'good' were well-made films, popular with viewers, which demonstrated Protazanov's increasing mastery over the medium. Among his 'bad' pictures – that is, those that came under heavy critical fire – *The Tailor from Torzhok* [1925] is the least interesting. Although it features the popular comic actor Igor Ilyinsky, *The Tailor* is a slight comedy. Petya (Ilyinsky) needs to retrieve his winning lottery ticket from his landlady, whom he was supposed to marry and with whom he has quarrelled. A poorly integrated subplot, inserted to inject some 'ideology' into the farce, concerns the maltreatment of Petya's true love, Katya (Vera Maretskaya), who is being exploited by her cruel relation, a minor Nepman who owns a shop.

Modest though it was, *The Tailor from Torzhok* obviously struck a responsive chord with Soviet audiences, since it recorded a healthy profit only two months into its run.[50] Critics like Khrisanf Khersonsky (an intelligent, generally moderate, critic who enjoyed movies), on the other hand, found the picture only sporadically funny and the character of the tailor 'alien'.[51] Nevertheless, *The Tailor* escaped any serious opprobrium until the Cultural Revolution: Protazanov was still reaping the benefits of *His Call*.

His next comedy, *The Three Millions Trial* [1926], was a different matter. More 'bourgeois' in setting and style than just about any other film of Soviet production, *The Three Millions Trial* is a sophisticated crime comedy-adventure that is virtually indistinguishable from Western productions of the era. Among the movies shown Mary Pickford and Douglas Fairbanks when they visited Moscow in 1926, *The Three Millions Trial* alone garnered no praise from the stars, the absence of which was noted in the press.[52]

Yet *The Three Millions Trial* does have a 'class-conscious' theme. It concerns a banker who has sold his house for three million so that he will have the capital necessary to speculate on food shortages. The famous 'gentleman thief' Cascarillia (played by the debonair Anatoli Ktorov), with the assistance of the banker's lascivious wife Nora (Olga Zhizneva) steals the money, only to have his glory stolen from *him* by the 'common thief' Tapioca (Igor Ilyinsky). Tapioca is arrested trying to rob the banker's house, and the police assume that he took the three million. Since no one can imagine where the fortune is, Tapioca becomes a folk hero for having outsmarted the police. Unable to stay out of the limelight, Cascarillia dramatically appears at Tapioca's trial and tosses the three million to the wildly cheering crowd.

Despite the didactic potential of the theme, this stylish film was played for entertainment value, so it is not surprising that 90 per cent of audiences surveyed liked it. (Fairbanks and Pickford, expecting to see 'revolutionary' Soviet films, naturally found it unremarkable.) The public embraced *The Three Millions Trial* wholeheartedly and, like *His Call* and *The Forty-First*, the picture made a 'top ten' list.[53] Since Soviet audiences preferred European and especially American movies, it was quickly recognised that *The Trial*'s popularity was largely due to its resemblance to Western films (namely its genre, 'Western-adventure', and its emphasis on sex and greed) – as well as to the phenomenal popularity of Ilyinsky (who was reprising the role he had created for the Kommissarzhevsky Theatre's adaptation of the same story).[54] Even Sergei Eisenstein, who did not much concern himself with Protazanov, singled out *The Three Millions Trial* as an exemplar of the 'Western-local' film that was in his opinion anathema to a revolutionary cinema.[55]

Though *The Tailor from Torzhok* and *The Three Millions Trial* were criticised fairly harshly, they had escaped lightly compared with *The Man from the Restaurant* [1927] and *The White Eagle* [1928]. Both pictures represented Protazanov's return to melodramas on revolutionary themes but, unlike *His Call* and *The Forty-First*, they lacked adventure and romance. Protazanov may nevertheless have expected that he could repeat the success he had enjoyed with *His Call* and *The Forty-First*.

*The Man from the Restaurant* takes place in 1916–17 and concerns the social awakening of a poor waiter (played by the Moscow Art Theatre actor Mikhail Chekhov). The waiter's musically gifted daughter (Vera Malinovskaya) must for financial reasons leave school to play the violin in the restaurant. There she attracts the unwelcome attention of a wealthy industrialist who hopes to make her his mistress. The contrasts between the *haute bourgeoisie* (greedy, profligate, immoral and cruel) and the proletariat (as depicted by the waiter and his daughter – hard-working, humble, and honest) are sharply drawn. Protazanov's efforts to evoke the waiter's growing sense of outrage were apparently sincere, but the film suffers from a number of shortcomings.

The plot and *mise-en-scène* are laboured and strongly reminiscent of F. W. Murnau's *The Last Laugh* [Der letzte Mann, 1924] which leads to an inevitable and unfortunate comparison. At a time when there was an ever-increasing clamour for a positive Soviet hero, the protagonist of *The Man from the Restaurant* is far from positive. The waiter is so tediously humble that the picture lacks dramatic focus, a problem intensified by Chekhov's mannered and theatrical performance. Moreover, the waiter's 'political' transformation seems to spring from purely personal sources: his desire to protect the virtue of his beloved daughter (and his grief over the death of his son at the front). It certainly did not help *The Man from the Restaurant*'s reception, considering the political climate in 1927, that the plot had been derived from a pre-Revolutionary story by Ivan Shmeliev. (Like Protazanov, Shmeliev was a member of the Moscow *kupechestvo* who had emigrated to the West; unlike Protazanov, he had not returned.)

In 1927, on the eve of the March 1928 Party Conference on Cinema Affairs which heralded the start of the Cultural Revolution in cinema, the two major studios – Sovkino and Mezhrabpom-Rus – found themselves under heavy fire. *The Man from the Restaurant*, along with *The Tailor from Torzhok* and *The Three Millions Trial*, became ammunition in the assault on Mezhrabpom.[56] *The Man* was specifically attacked, over and over, as too theatrical and 'reactionary'.[57]

When *The White Eagle* was released, the Cultural Revolution was definitely under way. While the film is flawed, it illustrates that Protazanov was *not* – as his critics often charged – a 'formula' film-maker; certainly he was not the 'epigone of *Khanzhonkovshchina*' that Sergei Tretyakov (an opponent on the artistic left) claimed.[58] *The White Eagle* is an adaptation of Leonid Andreyev's story about a provincial governor during the Revolution of 1905. The governor (V. Kachalov) orders troops to break up a street demonstration by firing on a crowd and three children are among those killed in the ensuing mêlée. Rewarded for his success at crowd control with the Order of the White Eagle, the governor is tormented by his bad conscience, and his struggle to come to terms with his deed is the crux of this psychological drama. The corollary to the governor's angst is that of the governess-cum-revolutionary (Anna Sten), who cannot bring herself to assassinate the governor, although she is convinced that it would be just retribution for the massacre.

The American critic Dwight MacDonald admired the film enormously, going so far as to call Kachalov's performance 'the high-water mark of movie acting',[59] but his opinion was assuredly not shared by his Soviet contemporaries, at least by those who went on record about the film. *The White Eagle* was castigated by critics from different points on the cultural-political spectrum for humanising the 'class enemy', for being only superficially revolutionary, for being boring ('like a prison sentence' to watch), and for making a direct appeal to the petty-bourgeois viewer.[60] It was regularly used as a stick with which to beat Mezhrabpom.[61]

And yet, despite all this, in the darkest days of the Cultural Revolution Protazanov not only avoided a sustained personal attack (a major achievement in itself ), but he continued to work. No doubt his resolute silence on the burning questions of the decade (regardless of his motivations) served him well. Since he had neither written nor said anything, nothing could be held against him except his movies. While, as we have seen, there was much that the new 'proletarian' critics (who eventually took over the cinema press)[62] found to dislike in these films, no one had ever charged Protazanov with the crime of technical innovation. It was the 'Formalists' – the code word for youthful avant-garde directors – who were the chief targets of the Cultural Revolution in cinema.[63]

Given the political climate, Protazanov's final two silent films, *Ranks and People* [1929] and *The Feast of St Jorgen* [1930], are understandably cautious. *Ranks and People*, based on three stories by Chekhov (the alternative title was *A Chekhovian Film Almanac*), represents Protazanov's return to Russian classics as a source for his films for the first time since *Father Sergius*. The vignettes stay very close to the stories on which they were based: 'The Order of St Anne' [Anna na shee], 'Death of a Bureaucrat' [Smert' chinovnika] and 'Chameleon' [Khameleon]. Apart from some fine acting – Ivan Moskvin as the hapless *chinovnik* whose sneeze leads to his death and Maria Strelkova as the unhappy young woman in a loveless marriage – nothing would indicate to the uninitiated viewer that this film was the work of a major director. Indeed, the *mise-en-scène* is so unimaginative that it seemed Protazanov had lost his zest for movie-making.

*The Feast of St Jorgen*, an anti-religious comedy, is much livelier, which is not surprising considering its stars, Anatoli Ktorov and the irrepressible Igor Ilyinsky, who play two escaped convicts masquerading as nuns on a pilgrimage. Ktorov, in a variation of his role as Cascarillia in *The Three Millions Trial*, is an 'international thief' by the name of Corcoran who seizes the unexpected opportunity to claim the pretty 'bride' (Mariya Strelkova) who each year is chosen for the saint on his feast day. Corcoran sheds his habit and 'appears' to the worshipful throng as the saint. *The Feast of St Jorgen* displays a lighter touch than many films that were part of the campaign against religion, but is only intermittently funny and does not demonstrate Protazanov's capabilities as well as some of his earlier work.

What distinguishes these 'neutral' movies from the 'bad' ones (*The Tailor from Torzhok*, *The Three Millions Trial*, *The Man from the Restaurant* and *The White Eagle*)? To the disinterested observer, *Ranks and People*'s portrayal of pre-Revolutionary life differs little from that of *The Man from the Restaurant*, and yet the former picture received only half-hearted criticism for its 'soft' portrayal of hard times. The mystery deepens when *The Feast of St Jorgen* is compared to *The Three Millions Trial*. The films are quite similar – satires set abroad featuring the type of thief-hero popular in folklore. Yet *The Trial* was much maligned while *The Feast* was termed 'valuable and well-made'.[64] How can this difference in critical reception be explained?

It is possible to answer this question by referring to the chaos of the times:

much was happening that was ambiguous, confusing and contradictory. But, even as the Cultural Revolution was playing itself out, carrying numerous directors, scenarists and critics into the maelstrom, the outlines of the second phase of post-Revolutionary culture were discernible. This new culture was based on the tenets of Socialist Realism, fulfilling at least in part the programme espoused by the proletarian radicals (simplicity, realism and optimism). But a component that increased in importance and was *not* part of the 'proletarian' platform in the 1920s was its traditionalism. This manifested itself in the arts by the call for a 'return to the classics', and by generally trying to re-establish Soviet ties to the Russian past. Protazanov's films fit these criteria quite well, laying the foundation for an eventual re-evaluation of his work.

In his person and through his art, Protazanov carried on the bourgeois tradition of Russian cinema. With varying success, Protazanov infused his Soviet films with a 'Westernised' version of Russian style. Exploring the differences in reception between Protazanov's films like *The Three Millions Trial* and *The Feast of St Jorgen* sheds some light on the Cultural Revolution's impact on cinema, but more revealing to the larger issues under consideration here are the differences between the movies that were well-received critically and those that were attacked.

All Protazanov's pictures are realistic. Story development was not an area of particular strength, but his plots are always easy to follow, with enough action to engage the viewer. He excelled in characterisation and casting, a key in understanding the popularity of his films with a public already in love with Western stars like Fairbanks and Pickford. Soviet audiences, not surprisingly, responded best to the movies that were lively and amusing: *His Call*, *The Forty-First*, *Don Diego and Pelageya*, *The Tailor from Torzhok* and *The Three Millions Trial*. As we have seen, critics liked the first three, but not the last two, claiming with considerable disingenuity that these judgements had to do with relative social and political impact. Protazanov was always willing to tell an ideologically acceptable story *if it were entertaining*; from watching these films, it is clear that what counted for him was the characters, not their ideology (or lack of it).

*The Tailor from Torzhok* and *The Three Millions Trial* are not anomalies in Protazanov's work any more than are *His Call*, *The Forty-First* and *Don Diego*. Given these parameters, how does one situate *The Man from the Restaurant* and *The White Eagle* in this oeuvre? By the late 1920s, due to the rapidly changing political climate, audience reactions to movies rarely appeared in the press, but both films are so relentlessly downbeat that it is hard to imagine lines at the box office.[65] Yet both these films, and certainly *The White Eagle*, demonstrate that, in his own unspectacular way, Protazanov was willing to take the risks that all true artists need to take to advance their art and grow creatively, despite the perception that he was a director who cared only for box-office success.

While there can be little doubt of Protazanov's popularity with the mass audience in the 1920s, he was held in very low repute by another audience that cannot be lightly dismissed: Soviet critics, especially those critics who rejected film as entertainment. Their point of view was summarised by B. Alpers in his review of *The Feast of St Jorgen*, which he, unlike others, disliked. Alpers attacked Protazanov as a master at making superficially Soviet films that enjoyed widespread appeal due to their 'social neutrality and external decorativeness'. He admitted that Protazanov knew how to craft films so well that they held one's attention, a talent Alpers found deplorable. Alpers charged the director with adhering to the 'traditional' path, a path which he awkwardly described as 'balancing on a thin and swaying tightrope of shallow entertainment'.[66] Yet, significantly, Alpers' opinion was echoed by critics much more talented than he. Viktor Shklovsky, who wrote the screenplays for *The Wings of a Serf* [Kryl'ya kholopa, 1926], *By the Law* [Po zakonu, 1926] and *Bed and Sofa* [Tret'ya Meshchanskaya, 1927] (among many others), called Protazanov a representative of 'the old cinematography of the European type, a little out-of-date'. Adrian Piotrovsky, artistic director of the Leningrad studio and friend of the avant-garde, saw Protazanov as the head of the reactionary 'right deviation'. Even a supporter and practitioner of the entertainment film like Commissar

*Figure 14* The classic Ostrovsky play *Without a Dowry* provided Protazanov with a safe yet ideal showcase for his talents in 1937.

of Enlightenment Anatoli Lunacharsky called Protazanov a good director, but 'not of our time'.[67] The times, however, were changing in a way that favoured Protazanov.

Yakov Protazanov made six more movies in the last fifteen years of his life and completed his final film in 1943, two years before his death in 1945 at the age of 64. The best known of these was his handsome 1937 adaptation of Ostrovsky's play *Without a Dowry* [Bespridannitsa]. While his absolute rate of production declined, the total of his films is comparable to the output of other directors at this time. The decline represents the slow recovery of cinema after the havoc wrought by the Cultural Revolution and the coming of sound.

Protazanov's legacy extends beyond his impressive body of work, the sum of which proved to be greater than any of the parts. First, he provided an element of historical continuity to the Soviet film industry; the importance of this link with the Russian past became more evident as revolutionary fervour subsided, and Stalin sought to emphasise stability and continuity. The cultural values and tastes of the educated, Westernised bourgeoisie remained a strong influence on early Soviet society through the works of Protazanov, Vladimir Gardin, Alexander Ivanovsky, and Cheslav Sabinsky and, of course, their very popularity attested to the vitality of this taste and culture.

Second, Protazanov kept alive the tradition of the narrative entertainment film, which in its dramatic and comedic forms enjoyed great public popularity. Even in the darkest days of the Stalinist era, this tradition was carried on, especially in the work of Grigori Alexandrov, who much admired Protazanov.[68]

Third, Protazanov was responsible – along with Fridrikh Ermler, a director of proletarian origin – for returning the actor to a place of importance in Soviet cinema; present-day Soviet cinema is known for its exceptional acting talent, not for its technical innovations. Unlike Ermler, whose pistol was his method of persuasion on the set, Protazanov was the complete professional, whose skills and tact have been attested to by a generation of Soviet actors.[69]

Fourth, Protazanov proved that well-made entertainment films did not require huge outlays of time and material. *Aelita* aside, Protazanov's movies were often held up to the younger generation as examples of how much an experienced director could accomplish with very little. *Don Diego and Pelageya* [1928] was completed in three months at a cost of only 40,000 roubles, whereas Vertov's documentary *A Sixth Part of the World* [Shestaya chast' mira, 1926] had taken nineteen months and 130,000 roubles.[70]

Protazanov's heirs have recognised what many of his contemporaries did not – that he was a director of the first magnitude. Protazanov has been honoured with two editions of Aleinikov's *Festschrift*, by Arlazorov's biography, and by favourable notices in all the standard film histories.[71] The attitude of this succeeding generation towards Protazanov is exemplified by N. M. Zorkaya, who has stated:

> Without institutes and surveys, he empathised with the viewer and unerringly knew what would work on the screen and what the public would like. . . .
>
> Then, they often complained about the level of his pictures. Oh, if it were possible to reach the Protazanovian level in all of today's screen productions![72]

Protazanov gave a great deal to Soviet cinema, but the influence was very much reciprocal. Speculation on what he might have accomplished if he had remained in the West is beside the point. Back home, Protazanov, though past his first youth, continued to mature as a director and enjoyed a long and fruitful career in the movies. Despite the fact that his work was not obviously influenced by the experiments of his younger contemporaries, I would suggest that the impact of the ferment of the 'Golden Age' of Soviet cinema *is* visible in his best films and that it is not coincidental that his outstanding pictures – *Don Diego and Pelageya*, *The Forty-First* and *The White Eagle* – happened to be those on subjects closely reflecting the issues and concerns of Soviet society in the 1920s.

# 7 A face to the *shtetl*: Soviet Yiddish cinema, 1924–36

*J. Hoberman*

> A directive to a propagandist lay next to the notebooks of a Jewish poet. The portraits of Lenin and Maimonides were neighbours – the gnarled iron of Lenin's skull and the dim silkiness of Maimonides' picture. A lock of woman's hair marked a page in a bound volume of the Resolutions of the Sixth Party Congress, and crooked lines of Hebrew verse were crowded into the margin of political pamphlets.
>
> Isaak Babel, 'The Rabbi's Son'[1]

Given the conflict that characterised its transitory existence, it is scarcely surprising that the Soviet Yiddish cinema has been largely forgotten, despite a number of impressive achievements.[2] This national cinema had no national base, it was founded on dislocation and ambivalence. Like the rucksack of the rabbi's son, those films that remain bespeak an impossible synthesis. For some Russian Jews, the Revolution meant the violent superimposition of one religion over another. For others, it represented the complete destruction of the past. For all, it precipitated a crisis of national identity. The cinema which arose from this crisis was a battlefield upon which a powerful desire for collective representation struggled with numerous proscriptions against it.

The pre-Revolutionary economy had restricted Russian Jews to the Pale of Settlement, forbidden them to own land, and compelled most to eke out a living as small traders, artisans and middlemen, exchanging goods with the neighbouring peasants in the Pale's hundreds of *shtetlekh* (market towns). Even before the Revolution, these activities were regarded by Jewish radicals as 'unproductive'. But, if the *shtetl* had been a subject of satire for pre-Revolutionary Yiddish writers, for post-Revolutionary Jewish Bolsheviks it was, as Zvi Gitelman has observed, something akin to 'a leper colony'. It was in these backward hamlets, which had been devastated by the First World War, the Civil War and the implementation of War Communism, 'that Jewish traditional life seemed to hang on most tenaciously and where the least desirable social elements – traders, *luftmenshn* (literally 'air men'), clerics – seemed to dominate'.[3]

In April 1923, the Twelfth Party Congress created a Council of Nationalities and proposed legislation that would implement the use of indigenous languages by those state agencies serving the national minorities. The next few years saw the creation of numerous such cultural and political institutions. In the Ukraine and Belorussia, the two republics which encompassed the former Pale, Yiddish-language schools, courts, and theatres were established – as well as a number of Jewish municipal Soviets. In 1923, as well, in a conciliatory attempt to 'productivise' the tens of thousands of 'declassed' Jews and persuade surviving petty-bourgeois elements to participate more fully in socialist construction, the party's Yevsektsiya (Jewish section) announced its own version of the New Economic Policy (NEP) – a 'face to the *shtetl*'.

Like the Yevsektsiya, the new Soviet Yiddish culture laboured under a double burden. 'That Yiddish literature has always been a literature of the poor, the untutored, the lowly, inclines the Communists to be respectful to the earliest Jewish authors,' Avraham Yarmolinsky wrote in the late 1920s. 'But although the past is reverenced, there is a strong feeling that literature, together with the other arts, stands on the threshold of a new era.'[4] But where Soviet Russian literature might simply direct Russian workers and peasants across the threshold of the new era, a Soviet Yiddish literature or cinema would have first to transform the Jewish masses into workers and peasants.

When, in 1924, Alexander Granovsky – founder and director of Moscow's State Yiddish Theatre (GOSET) – wrote to a New York-based colleague that he hoped to make 'a grandiose Jewish film', he was hardly the only Soviet theatrical director who was drawn to the new medium.[5] Les Kurbas, head of the Ukrainian ensemble Berezil, had directed two films for VUFKU (the All-Ukrainian Photo-Cinema Administration) during the summer of 1924, the youngsters of the Leningrad-based Factory of the Eccentric Actor (FEKS) were preparing their first short film, while Eisenstein (who had already incorporated a brief movie in his Proletkult production of Ostrovsky's *Enough Simplicity for Every Wise Man*) was completing *The Strike* [Stachka, 1924].

Nor was Granovsky's the only Jewish theatre poised to enter the movies. In the spring of 1925, when his *Jewish Luck* [Evreiskoe schast'e] finally went into production, eighteen members of the Hebrew-language Habima theatre were set to appear in an elaborate adaptation of Sholom Aleichem's *The Deluge*. First serialised in 1907, this was the Yiddish writer's most overtly political work – the story of three Jewish families, all with radical children, caught up in the tumultuous events of 1905. *Jewish Luck*, Granovsky's more modest production, was also adapted from Sholom Aleichem, drawing on the same 'Menakhem Mendl' stories that had inspired one of the skits in *A Sholom Aleichem Evening*, the 1921 production which, designed by Marc Chagall and starring Solomon Mikhoels, had effectively launched his theatre in Moscow.

Hardly restricted to the Yiddish-speaking community, the GOSET's popularity had the aspects of a craze. After Granovsky's 1924 production of Sholom Aleichem's *200,000*, with a modernistic score by the former Bolshoi violinist Lev Pulver, Mikhoels and his co-star Venyamin Zuskin were so famous that they attracted crowds in the street. Muscovites vied with foreign dignitaries to book tickets and, significantly, two-thirds of the audience required Russian-language synopses.[6] This appeal to non-Jews is reminiscent of the slumming parties that visited Harlem during the Jazz Age: like the Cotton Club, the GOSET seemed the cultural expression of an exotic race. Before the Revolution, as the academic B. Gorev observed in a 1922 essay,

> authentic Jewish life remained a book behind seven seals for the Russian intelligentsia, which had neither its Livingstones capable and desirous of penetrating this domestic Africa, nor even its Captain Golovnins, who by accident might have dwelt for a substantial time in this alien world.[7]

*Figure 15 Jewish Luck*: 'semi-documentary in its representation of a dilapidated . . . Berdichev, the Ukraine's archetypal Jewish town', with Mikhoels pointing and Moishe Goldblatt behind.

Understandably, the reaction to the GOSET within the Jewish community was mixed and not only because of the theatre's hard-line anticlericalism. The Yiddish-speaking audience had barely entered the secular realm of art and was scarcely prepared to see its naturalistic precepts inverted. Moreover, Granovsky and his troupe were clearly turning the idiom of the *shtetl* against the *shtetl*. Still, as the Soviet Union's premier Yiddish theatre, the Moscow GOSET exerted considerable influence on Jewish culture. Each summer the company toured the Yiddish heartland of Belorussia and the Ukraine, and it was in that 'domestic Africa' that Granovsky set his first film.

Shot mainly in exterior, *Jewish Luck* is almost semi-documentary in its representation of a dilapidated *shtot* – evidently a tumble-down section of Berdichev, the Ukraine's archetypal Jewish town. Natan Altman's naturalistic production design is virtually ethnographic in its concern for detail; although *Jewish Luck* is pointedly a critique of life before the Revolution, much of it is underscored by a preservationist spirit. Unsentimental but affectionate, the film tempers the savage parody of Granovsky's stage work. Despite Mikhoels's delicately exaggerated performance as the feckless Menakhem Mendl, *Jewish Luck* eschews the grotesque make-up, gymnastic cavorting and percussive tempo that had been the GOSET's hallmark. Yakov Protazanov's *Aelita*, which was partly designed by GOSET associate Isaak Rabinovich, had already brought such theatrical avant-gardism to the Soviet film. Granovsky's strategy was precisely the opposite.

More than any subsequent Soviet film, *Jewish Luck* celebrates the heritage of the *shtetl*. If religious ritual is conspicuously absent, the lengthy open-air wedding that ends the movie is a veritable précis of traditional elements, including a chanting *badkhn* (wedding jester), a band of itinerant *klezmerim* (musicians) and a variety of Hasidic dances. The Jewish folk are rich in culture, poor in opportunity. As an impoverished dreamer, the archetypal *luftmensh* drifting from one failed scheme to the next, Menakhem Mendl was a useful emblem for the Jewish plight under the tsars. In *Jewish Luck*, this hapless optimist is shown as an instrument of the bourgeoisie and a victim of the *ancien regime*. The scenario – credited to Granovsky's assistant director Grigori Gricher-Cherikover, Boris Leonidov (a specialist in action dramas) and the pre-Revolutionary Odessa director I. Teneremo – passes over Menakhem Mendl's misadventures as a speculator to focus on his difficulty in eking out a living of any kind.

*Jewish Luck* opens amidst the chaos of its hero's large and underfed family. Together with his young and equally marginal friend Zalman (Moishe Goldblatt, who later directed Moscow's Gypsy Theatre), Menakhem Mendl leaves Berdichev for Odessa where he hopes to sell corsets. After the comic failure of even this modest enterprise, he stumbles upon a book which contains a list of prospective brides and decides to become a matchmaker: '*Shadkhn* – that's a real profession!' In the film's climax, this new career goes spectacularly awry when the would-be 'king of the *shadkhonim'* inadvertently arranges a match between two girls. Although his blunder ultimately brings together the film's two young lovers, Menakhem Mendl is betrayed by his employer and left to wander off alone.

Bucolic in spite of itself, *Jewish Luck* has marked affinities with the American comedies which successfully infiltrated the Soviet market during the mid-1920s. The diminutive Mikhoels gives Menakhem Mendl a Chaplinesque aura of shabby gentility and scurrilous pathos. Obsequious yet irrepressible, he cuts an endearing figure; unlike Chaplin, however, he is never permitted to triumph – even temporarily – over his social betters. Mikhoels's performance is almost ideogrammatic: whether taking a swim (still in his hat and selling insurance all the while) or simply riding on a train, he moves with fantastic, almost mincing precision. Accused of smuggling by a tsarist policeman, he becomes fawningly coy, offering the official a bribe – with Granovsky lavishing close-ups on his elaborate hand gestures.

In the film's marvellous set piece, Menakhem Mendl dreams that he is a *shadkhn* of international proportions. He meets an elegant prospective bride on the steps of the Odessa harbour, presents her with a bouquet and introduces her to the legendary Jewish philanthropist Baron de Hirsch, who informs him that America is suffering from a shortage of eligible brides. Begged to thus 'save America', Menakhem Mendl mobilises Berdichev. The vision grows increasingly elaborate – its extravagant plenitude of marriage-minded women rivalling the climax of Keaton's contemporary *Seven Chances* – and in hindsight, more than a little sinister, as box-cars filled with Jewish maidens, already dressed in their wedding gowns, arrive in Odessa for export overseas.[8]

Alone among Soviet Yiddish films, *Jewish Luck* had the authority of a folk tradition and the weight of official sanction. In addition to Mikhoels, Altman and Pulver, the project involved another prominent Jewish artist: the humorous, idiomatic intertitles were written by Isaak Babel, whose violent, sardonic stories of the Polish–Soviet war had recently been published to great acclaim. The movie's première was treated as a gala event: Pulver conducted his score with a symphony orchestra at a special preview sponsored by the GEZERD (Society for the Resettlement of Jewish Workers on the Land), a quasi-public agency closely associated with the Yevsektsiya.

*Jewish Luck* appears to have been both a popular and a critical success – as well as being one of the first Soviet films offered for export. (Within fifteen months of its domestic première it was shown in the Baltic states, Hungary and China.)[9] Writing in *Pravda* (15 November 1925), Boris Gusman cautiously termed the movie a 'transitional' work, overly episodic and theatrical – as well as lacking that 'element of propaganda which is essential to the Soviet film' – but nevertheless intelligent, lucid and ingenious: 'Seeing the film, one can think that something worthwhile has been contributed to cinema . . . a good "theatrical" film is better than a slapdash cinematographic "original".'[10]

In fact, *Jewish Luck* is impressively non-theatrical – as anyone who has seen the excellent surviving print can attest. *The Deluge* [Mabul, 1926] presented greater problems. Reports in the American Jewish press suggest that the film was intended to mark the twentieth anniversary of the 1905 Revolution.[11] This seems to have been a relatively lavish production with sequences shot on location in the Jewish quarter of Vinnitsa, Natan Altman's home town, as well as in the nearby *shtetl* of Litin. Habima actor Raikin Ben-Ari, who appeared in the film, maintains that neophyte director Yevgeni Ivanov-Barkov, a former set designer and a non-Jew, showed considerable – even obsessive – concern for Yiddish culture. Despite this, however, he proved unable to finish the movie.

According to Ben-Ari, 'the government official whose job it was to pass on the ideological and political complexion of the film brought in another director. He too was unable to do a satisfactory job.' This was Ivan Pyriev, an assistant on Sovkino's successful *Wings of a Serf* [1926], and later a prominent Ukrainian director. Finally, Boris I. Vershilov, the assimilated Jew who had staged Habima's production of *The Golem*, was pressed into service. Vershilov 'brought some sort of order in the chaos, but for all his efforts the film had little artistic achievement to its credit'.[12]

Even as Granovsky completed *Jewish Luck*, Soviet cinema was accommodating the aspirations of various national groups. In 1924 an amateur film-maker, Vladimir Ballyuzek, made the first Azerbaidzhani movie, *The Legend of the Maiden's Tower* [Legenda o devich'ei bashne]. The following year saw the first Uzbek film, the documentary *The Starving Steppe Revives* [Khlopkovodstvo v Golodnoi stepi], directed by another amateur, N. Shcherbakov, and the first Chuvash effort, *Volga Rebels* [Volzhskie buntary], directed by Pavel Petrov-Bytov. In 1926 the Georgian Amo Bek-Nazarov directed the first Armenian feature, *Honour* [Namus]. By 1927 all these nationalities – as well as Georgians and Belorussians – had their own local production agencies.

Unlike Georgians, Armenians, Belorussians, Uzbeks, Chuvash and Azerbaidzhanis, however, the Soviet Union's 2.6 million Jews had neither republic nor autonomous region, let alone a movie studio. For the most part, the Soviet Jewish homeland was negatively visualised as the *shtetl* and the Jewish cinema was tied to that of the Ukrainians and Belorussians, the two major nationalities with whom Jews shared the pre-Revolutionary Pale of Settlement. Over 1.5 million Jews, more than 60 per cent of the entire Soviet Jewish population, still lived in the Ukraine. During the brief and bloody interlude of Ukrainian independence, Jews had enjoyed a measure of national autonomy and there was even a ministry of Jewish affairs. Although the first few years of Soviet rule were characterised by a negative attitude towards Yiddish (and Ukrainian) cultural activities, restraints relaxed after the Twelfth Party Congress in April 1923.

In 1926, the same year that a Soviet government commission raised the possibility of relocating half a million Jews on Ukrainian and Crimean collective farms, VUFKU itself explored a number of Jewish projects.

Commercial considerations were probably as important as political ones: Jews outnumbered Ukrainians in the urban areas where most cinemas were located and were consequently an important segment of the movie audience. Alexander Dovzhenko developed *The Homeland*, an unrealised (and presumably anti-Zionist) comedy about Jews in Palestine, while Abram Room made *Jews on the Land* [Evrei na zemle, 1927], a 20-minute documentary on Jewish settlements in the Yevpatoria district of the Crimea. (A native of Vilna, Room had headed an amateur Yiddish art theatre there during the First World War.) Lily Brik supervised the production, while Vladimir Mayakovsky and Viktor Shklovsky collaborated on the script.

Exhibiting a certain amount of 'Jewish' irony, *Jews on the Land* opens with scenes of a war-devastated *shtetl* (all that is left of the central market is a single pathetic fish stall), then shows an elderly Jew wandering about an even more desolate wilderness. Soon, however, sod-brick settlements rise and, as irrigation ditches criss-cross the once-barren plain, the now-productivised Jews are equally transformed: a new-born baby is named 'Forget-Your-Sorrows'. Tractor drivers and 'Young Pioneers' are given particular pride of place and the film-makers emphasise that, among other livestock, these new Jewish 'peasants' are raising pigs.

More substantially, VUFKU inherited a pair of projects developed by Isaak Babel: the first, a script based on Babel's tales of the Odessa underworld and its Jewish 'king' Benya Krik, the other taken from Sholom Aleichem's novel *Wandering Stars*. An instant literary celebrity after the publication of *Red Cavalry* in 1924, Babel was much in demand as a scenarist. In December 1924, the Eisenstein group prepared a script based on Babel's stories of the Soviet–Polish war. The project was shelved that April but, during June and July 1925, while Eisenstein was shooting the film eventually released as *The Battleship Potemkin* [Bronenosets Potemkin, 1926], he and Babel worked on an early version of *Benya Krik*. The same summer, after Babel had completed the titles for *Jewish Luck*, he was commissioned by Goskino to adapt *Wandering Stars* as a follow-up production for the Moscow GOSET. Such was Babel's reputation that both the 'film novella' *Benya Krik* and the 'film script' *Wandering Stars* [Bluzhdayushchie zvezdy] were published as pamphlets in 1926, well before either reached the screen.

*Benya Krik*, filmed during the summer of 1926 by the veteran theatre director Vladimir Vilner, arrived first, despite the necessity for several rewrites.[13] The first two-thirds of Babel's script were taken from a pair of published stories, 'The King' (set on the eve of the First World War) and 'How It Was Done in Odessa' (with the action explicitly located during the ineffectual rule of the Provisional Government). The last section, set shortly after the October Revolution, was original – albeit based on the actual demise of Benya's real-life prototype, Mishka Vinitsky – and suggests that Bolsheviks were able to maintain order where tsarist and Menshevik regimes failed. Here, Benya's gang has become a swaggeringly corrupt 'revolutionary' regiment. Ordered to disarm them under any pretext, the local military commissar assigns the gang to 'emergency revictualling patrol'. Benya is lulled by this plum assignment, which consists mainly of requisitioning melons from a ship in Odessa harbour, falls into a trap and is shot down by Red soldiers.

*Benya Krik* was Vilner's first film, his inexperience evident from the haphazard *mise-en-scène* and overly stagey performances. (Although a fair amount of authentic-seeming Odessa street life shows through the creaky plot contrivances, Vilner used Ukrainian actors without even the most cursory attention to type.) The film hews closely to Babel's script, yet only two scenes suggest its vitality, however coarsely. The wedding of Benya's sister – much of it shot against a black backdrop – has a frantic assemblage of ravenous pug-uglies and revelling floozies serenaded by a single, hyperactive *klezmer* musician. In a related travesty of a traditional ritual, Benya and his men commandeer a traditional funeral, sending the mourners scrambling through the imposing monuments of Odessa's Jewish cemetery.

In Eisenstein's hands, *Benya Krik* might have presented (if not preserved) this milieu with the sardonic brio of *The Threepenny Opera*. Even a less mediocre film might have transcended its political deficiencies. As it was, *Benya Krik* presented problems by portraying its flamboyant criminal subject as a victim of the Bolshevik regime – as well as evoking the image of the Jew as criminal and profiteer. (In one scene, the 'king' receives a bribe concealed in a torah scroll.) For all the official campaigns against anti-Semitism, Nepmen had, by the mid-1920s, become synonymous with Jews in the popular imagination. Thus, if the film's final sequence offended Party ideologues, the picture of Odessa's *demi-monde* proved no less disturbing to image-conscious Jews. A letter to *Der emes*, the Yiddish-language Party daily, written by S. Daytsherman in the name of the Sovetishe Yidishe Gezelshaftlebkayt [Organisation of Soviet Jews], decries both the paucity of appropriate Jewish nationality films and those few which are made, 'especially here in the Ukraine', witness *Benya Krik* which suggests that 'thieves, prostitutes and speculators created the Revolution, fought for it, defended it and – took advantage of it. . . . The poison and hatred such a film spreads is obvious to anyone who sees it.'

While *The Deluge* and *Wandering Stars* 'demonstrate that film companies act like vandals with the work of Yiddish authors', Daytsherman was more disturbed by the presence of negative Jewish stereotypes in other VUFKU films, including Gricher-Cherikover's *Sorochinski Fair* [Sorochinskaya yarmarka, 1927]. Here, orthodox-traditional Jews appeared in comic roles, as schemers or cowards. 'This may be a trifle,' Daytsherman concludes, 'but . . . it has a bad smell. Especially now, during the struggle against anti-Semitism, one cannot remain indifferent. It is absolutely necessary that the Yiddish press and Organisation of Soviet Jews use their authority and speak out, so that VUFKU and the like are compelled to consider the Jewish masses.'[14]

Released in January 1927, *Benya Krik* was banned almost immediately by the Ukrainian Office for Political Education.[15] The movie was never shown in Moscow – reputedly 'so poor a film' that Jay Leyda 'never found anyone who could tell [him] about it'.[16] Despite this fiasco, however, Vilner was subsequently entrusted with bringing Fyodor Gladkov's proto-socialist realist classic *Cement* to the screen while, as recommended by Eisenstein, an English translation of Babel's script was published in London in 1935.

The sensitive nature of any Jewish material is reflected in Babel's remarkably apologetic introduction to *Wandering Stars*. 'Sholom Aleichem's novel was absolutely alien to me, filled with bourgeois motifs and uncinematic elements', the author maintains, adding that it took him two months just to forget the book and begin work on the screenplay.[17] The published scenario bears scant resemblance to Sholom Aleichem's good-naturedly barbed portrait of the itinerant Yiddish theatre – Babel emphasises pre-Revolutionary Jewish persecution, in part by transforming the novel's heroine from an actress into an aspiring doctor and eventual political activist: 'One can say of Rachel that her love of science is as great as the love of truth, of Lenin, of Darwin, or of Spinoza.'[18]

In his introduction, Babel maintains that the script was in constant flux as he reworked it to meet the contradictory requirements of the various actors and directors successively involved with the project. (The one constant stipulation, according to the writer, was that the protagonists be forced to flee abroad.) But, however it originated, *Wandering Stars* ultimately wound up at VUFKU, directed by Gricher-Cherikover, who made his own revisions. The finished film omitted the Yiddish theatre troupe altogether – thus erasing 'the last traces of Sholom Aleichem', as Osip Lubomirsky complained in *Der emes* when, optimistically advertised as 'The hit picture of the season!', *Wandering Stars* opened in mid-February 1928 at two centrally located Moscow cinemas.[19]

Babitsky and Rimberg report that, although *Wandering Stars* was 'an original combination of bitter humour and a melodramatic plot of persecution in a Jewish village', critics regarded the film as 'ideologically deficient', as well as 'over-involved with the Jewish past' and 'provincial'.[20] This is hardly surprising: most VUFKU treatments of Ukrainian history and literature were attacked in analogous terms and, along with the Ukrainian Communist Party, the movie studio underwent an anti-nationalist purge during 1927–8. Although *Wandering Stars* travelled to Paris and Berlin as part of an exhibition of recent VUFKU releases,[21] its domestic distribution was further complicated by the Sovkino purge of 1928: in May, *Wandering Stars* was one of eighteen films withdrawn from circulation because, according to the film magazine *Kino*, 'they idealise the pathological and decadent mood of the decaying bourgeoisie, popularise covert prostitution and debauchery'.[22]

The first nationality films tended to deal with the Civil War and pre-Revolutionary traditions. After 1927, emphasis shifted to the new life of the present. Although Sholom Aleichem remained a standard of the state Yiddish stage and a talismanic figure in *Der emes* (as well as the only Jewish culture-hero who has never fallen from Soviet grace), his writings provided material for only one further film, Gricher-Cherikover's *Through Tears* [Skvoz' slezy], also released by VUFKU in 1928.

More self-contained than either of the Babel productions, *Through Tears* elaborates the critique of the pre-1917 *shtetl* initiated with *Jewish Luck*. The film has no single protagonist: Sholom Aleichem's 'The Enchanted Tailor' is interwoven with several tales of the orphaned cantor's son Motl Peyse, to create an overall view of two imaginary towns, Zlodyevke and Kozodo-yevka. For Sholom Aleichem and his commentators, the impish Motl is a figure with a particular resonance: the Jews were sometimes said to be a *faryossemt folk*, an 'orphaned people'. For the film-makers, however, Motl may have offered the most politically safe of Sholom Aleichem adaptations. In its entry on the author, the third edition of *The Great Soviet Encyclopedia*

*Figure 16 Through Tears* [1928], Gricher-Cherikover's second Sholom Aleichem adaptation, showed the *shtetl* as a 'backwater where . . . young people attempt . . foredoomed get-rich-quick schemes'.

singles out the Motl cycle in particular for 'posing the question of the fate of the masses under capitalism'.[23]

As a child of the *shtetl* bound for the Lower East Side, Motl embodies the transitional generation of East European Jews. It is scarcely coincidental that he is introduced as his father, the cantor, lies dying. But if Motl is the most resilient of Sholom Aleichem characters, 'The Enchanted Tailor' is an absurdist nightmare of non-adaptation. The tailor Shimen-Elye buys a she-goat which mysteriously changes sex every time its new owner stops for a drink at the inn between the *shtetl* Kozodoyevka, where he purchased the creature, and the *shtetl* Zlodyevke, where he lives. That the story, one of the author's darkest, has strong intimations of the collapse of the religious world-view doubtless recommended it to the film-makers, who raise the level of class consciousness by having the 'pauper' Shimen-Elye persecuted by the bourgeois adherents of a rabbinical court.

Shot, like *Jewish Luck*, with near-documentary verisimilitude and demonstrating an even more pronounced graphic flare, *Through Tears* is less concerned with folklore than propaganda in depicting the teeming gregariousness and bitter marginality of *shtetl* life. Hardly a place of nostalgia, the Jewish hamlet is a dusty, ramshackle backwater where, no less than Menakhem Mendl, young people attempt a series of foredoomed get-rich-quick schemes. The two movies have virtually identical openings, plunging the viewer into domestic disorder and impoverishment but, here, there are neither community rituals nor fanciful dreams – the plight of the *luftmensh* has been globalised into a universal principle.

Scoring political points wherever possible, however, Gricher-Cherikover and his co-scenarist I. Skvirsky augment the original stories with scenes emphasising Jewish powerlessness in the face of tsarist oppression – choosing, for example, to end the movie with the cruel and arbitrary expulsion of Shimen-Elye and his family from their home. But, if the film-makers render Sholom Aleichem melodramatic and exaggerate his anti-clericalism, they are, for the most part, faithful to his spirit. Even a chaotic sequence set in a *kheyder* (a traditional Jewish primary school) reflects the author's satirical view: the *kheyder* was a target of the nineteenth-century Jewish Enlightenment no less than the twentieth-century Communist Party. Indeed, some characterisations are actually softened in the film, which was criticised by at least one Yiddish critic as sentimental: 'We find here none of the lyrical irony which is the essence of all Sholom Aleichem's writings. . . . The screenwriters have consciously or unconsciously killed his humour.'[24]

In a pattern that would repeat itself elsewhere (and with other national minorities), the harshest critics of the new Yiddish culture were Jewish communists. More self-conscious and less secure than their Russian comrades, these cultural *apparatchiks* did not hesitate to attack those artists who diverged from the official norms of their *Sovetish heymland*. When VUFKU's monthly film journal *Kino* published several articles on Jewish cinema in March 1928, the Ukrainian critic M. Makotinsky praised *Wandering Stars* and, particularly, *Through Tears* (as well as *Jewish Luck* and *The Deluge*) for helping the 'village masses' understand 'the roots of anti-Semitism';[25] the bluntest criticism was offered (in Yiddish, without Ukrainian translation) by the poet and ideologue Itzik Fefer.

As Fefer surveyed 'the realm of Jewish creativity', one field struck him as particularly underdeveloped. This was the motion picture. Fefer scorned the 'pre-Revolutionary way of life' dramatised in the three VUFKU features, *Wandering Stars*, *Through Tears* and *Benya Krik* ('if we can even consider this a Jewish film'). Meanwhile:

> The life of the Jewish working man and working woman, their struggle against the wealthy and 'charitable', against the Jewish bourgeoisie, and the great role they played in all aspects of the Revolutionary movement before and after October have yet to be shown on film.

Sterner than Daytsherman, Fefer formulated the problem in class (rather than national) terms.

> While Ukrainian cinema may boast a number of worthy films on working-class life and revolutionary struggle in the Ukraine, the national minority sector cannot do the same.
>
> And there happens to be much to say. . . .
>
> More than anyone else, we Yiddish writers are in a position to hear the complaints of workers at literary evenings.
>
> The workers ask, 'Why do you only write about *Jewish Luck*? About *Benya Krik* and *Wandering Stars*? Why don't you write about us?'
>
> They ask, 'Is *Benya Krik* more interesting than we are?'
>
> The working class wants to see itself, its struggle and its life in the new art.
>
> The working class is right.[26]

But, even as Fefer advised VUFKU to 'involve itself with the Jewish literary community and, with its help, create the film for which the Jewish worker has waited so long', that community was itself divided. *Prolit*, the official organ of the Yiddish members of the All-Ukrainian Association of Proletarian Writers, attacked a number of prominent Yiddish authors for variously 'cutting themselves off from real life', 'moving towards individualism', indulging in the 'idealisation of gradually disappearing classes', exhibiting 'lack of self-definition', or demonstrating 'a passive attitude towards our reality'.[27] Indeed, during the summer of 1928, a similar attack would be directed against the Soviet movie industry as a whole.

The first film to prefigure the new line, emphasising class struggle and revolutionary heroism on the Jewish street, was Grigori Roshal's *His Excellency* [Ego prevoskhoditel'stvo, 1927], released in the United States as *Seeds of Freedom* and known alternatively in the Soviet Union as *The Jew* [Evrei]. Roshal, who studied with Meyerhold, began his career as a stage manager. In the early 1920s he was associated with Moscow's Theatre of Youth (along with Ilya Ehrenburg) and Habima; in 1926 he made his first film, *The Skotinins* [Gospoda Skotininy], a caricature of the stupid and depraved gentry, loosely based on a comedy by the eighteenth-century satirist Denis Fonvizin and edited by no less an eminence than Anatoli Lunacharsky, the Soviet People's Commissar for Enlightenment.

*His Excellency* was shot the following year at the newly established Belgoskino's Leningrad studio. The cast was distinguished by the presence of Leonid Leonidov, a star of the Moscow Art Theatre, and, in a small part, Nikolai Cherkasov. According to Roshal, his subject-matter was so delicate that Lunacharsky oversaw the production personally.[28] One reason, doubtless, was that *His Excellency* took as its protagonist the Jewish shoemaker Hirsh Lekert, executed in 1902 for his attempted assassination of the Vilna governor-general, Viktor von Wahl. While Lekert was an authentic proletarian hero, he was also the most celebrated martyr of the Jewish Labour Bund, an organisation officially identified with 'petty-bourgeois nationalism'. Expelled from the Russian Social-Democratic Labour Party in 1903 for its insistence on organisational autonomy, the Bund was suppressed altogether after the Revolution. In 1921, its left wing joined the Communist Party, contributing substantially to the leadership of the Yevsektsiya.

There is no mention of the Bund in *His Excellency*. The film, which was co-written by Roshal's sister, Sofiya Roshal, and his wife Vera Stroyeva, shifts Lekert's act forward several years to the period of the 1905 Revolution and sets it in an unspecified city. The protagonist, who here successfully kills the governor, is identified only as 'the Jewish fighter'. Openly anti-clerical, the film implicates a Jewish religious leader in the reactionary status quo. Indeed, to make this completely obvious, Leonidov plays a dual role – governor and rabbi. *His Excellency* is further schematised as a generational melodrama: 'suffocating' under her father's rule, the rabbi's adopted daughter (Tamara Adelheim, the ingénue in *Jewish Luck*) joins a clandestine band of youthful socialists.

Thus, in finally putting forth a Jewish revolutionary hero, the film carefully stresses the solidarity between Jewish and Russian political prisoners, while making a programmatic comparison between honest Jewish workers and cowardly Jewish reactionaries. The latter are stigmatised with a number of politically incorrect, if contradictory, traits: they are not only bourgeois but seemingly Germanised, they meet beneath a portrait of Theodor Herzl and yet are beholden to a traditional-orthodox rabbi. Here, too, the battle lines are clearly drawn. Not only does the rabbi curse his child for her involvement with a 'goy', he excommunicates her Jewish comrades.

Almost in spite of itself, *His Excellency* explicates a Russian Jewish dilemma, existing under the Soviets no less than the tsar. The bourgeois Jews are terrified that they will be blamed for the disturbance created by their proletarian co-religionists – 'We're not revolutionaries, we're Zionists,' one protests in vain – and they send a delegation to the governor to plead for protection from the anticipated pogrom. As feared, these law-abiding Jewish leaders are held accountable and ordered to punish revolutionaries themselves or else face the consequences. 'The law of Israel will be used to crush them,' the rabbi promises, more like Fefer than either he or that communist true believer might ever imagine. (If *His Excellency* attempted to recuperate a Jewish hero for Bolshevism, however, it apparently succeeded. The year after its release, Fefer's ally Aron Kushnirov wrote a verse play on Lekert which premièred in Minsk at the Belorussian GOSET.[29])

The exigencies of the new climate may also be seen in VUFKU's last three Yiddish films. Although more pathetic and less militant than *His Excellency*, Vilner's *Eyes That Saw* [Glaza, kotorye videli, 1928], released in the USA as *A Simple Tailor*, similarly emphasises class struggle on the Jewish street. While the idealistic tailor Motl enlists in the tsar's army, his sister is compelled to wed the odious son of the factory owner Shklyansky. The rich Jews live in luxury; when the army orders all Jews to evacuate the town on trumped-up charges of spying for the Austrians, the capitalist and his property are afforded military protection. Meanwhile, in a paroxysm of victimisation, Motl is killed at the front at precisely the same moment that his wife and child are massacred in a pogrom.

Less apocalyptic but equally class-conscious, *The Land is Calling* [Zemlya zovet, 1928], directed by Vladimir Ballyuzek (who, four years before, had made the first Azerbaidzhani film) from a script by Moisei Zats and Boris Sharansky and co-designed by Natan Altman, was a post-Revolutionary *shtetl* drama set in the Crimea, in which a rabbi's daughter spurns the son of a rich landowner for love of the young blacksmith who has organised an agricultural co-operative to work the kulak's confiscated property.

Writing in *Kino*, M. Makotinsky considered *The Land is Calling* an elaboration on Room's *Jews on the Land* and a sequel to *Through Tears*. Praising its 'bright picture of determined work', he called for a final section of the 'trilogy' which would show the lives of those 'sons and grandsons of Sholom Aleichem' who work in the ports and factories of 'our socialist construction'. Gricher-Cherikover's *Suburban Quarters* [Kvartaly predmest'ya, 1930], from a script by *Kino*'s 25-year-old editor, the Ukrainian Futurist Mykola Bazhan, loosely fits the description. A young Jewish girl flouts her religious parents to marry a gentile Komsomol member, only to encounter the anti-Semitism of *his* family. The film ends happily when a public court criticises the husband's behaviour, his wife defends him, and all recognise the evil of petty-bourgeois religious prejudices.

In May 1928, the Ukrainian Communist Party held a special conference on anti-Semitism. Among the resolutions was one that VUFKU would prepare an 'appropriate moving picture' to deal with the problem; *Suburban Quarters* may well be that film. Around the same time, Sovkino and its successor Soyuzkino produced three films critical of anti-Semitism: Pavel Petrov-Bytov's *Cain and Artyom* [Kain i Artem, 1929], from a story by

Maxim Gorky, A. Galai's *Our Girls* [Nashi devushki, 1930], like *Suburban Quarters* an account of conflict arising from a mixed Jewish–Russian marriage, and I. Mutanov's *Remember Their Faces* [Zapomnite ikh litsa, 1930]. All three emphasised the co-operation between Russian and Jewish workers, the latter two consecrating it under Komsomol auspices.

Roshal followed *His Excellency* with two films at VUFKU. The first, *Two Women* [Dve zhenshchiny, 1929], attacked the now defunct NEP. The second, *A Man from the Shtetl* [Chelovek iz mestechka, 1930], released in the USA, with intertitles by the American proletarian writer Mike Gold, as *A Jew at War*, was another evocation of Jewish revolutionary martyrdom. Venyamin Zuskin, Mikhoels's most celebrated colleague at the Moscow GOSET, played David Gorelik, a poor Jewish youth drafted into the tsar's army. The film offered a uniquely Jewish perception of the First World War, the first conflict that ordinary Jews had experienced both as combatants and antagonists: Gorelik struggles against a German soldier on the battlefield, then realises his adversary is a Galician whom he knew before the war.

Having thus met, the two friends desert their imperial masters and join the Red Army. But friendship and ethnic solidarity go only so far. When the Galician, now a commissar, is convicted of a capital crime, Gorelik is charged with carrying out the sentence. As in *His Excellency*, albeit from a superficially different perspective, Roshal's Jewish characters have the responsibility of disciplining their own. In this sense, the film is an epitaph for the national policies of the 1920s.

Stalin's struggle against 'rightist deviation' with the Party was accompanied by increased centralisation and diminishing national autonomy. As early as 1927, Ukrainian 'nationalists' were removed from prominent positions; two years later, there were similar purges in Belorussia, Armenia and Turkestan, while leading Jewish communists came under fire for 'idealising' the pre-Revolutionary Jewish labour movement. Since the early 1920s, the Party had successfully channelled the Yevsektsiya's anti-bourgeois antagonism, using the Jewish Section to police the Jewish street. Now, the Party would intimidate these same activists by raising the spectre of their Bundist past. The beleaguered Yevsektsiya made plans for its first conference since 1926. In January 1930, however, the leadership of the republics' communist parties met and 'reorganised', dissolving all national sections.[30]

It was at this very moment that the development of sound threatened the universality of the silent film, raising anew the question of national cinemas. Yuli Raizman's *The Earth Thirsts* [Zemlya zhazhdet, 1930] all but allegorised this dilemma. In this late silent, produced by Vostokkino (a studio created in 1928 to make films for the Crimea, North Caucasus and Volga regions, as well as Siberia and Buryat-Mongolia) and re-released in 1931 with a postsynchronous soundtrack, a group of idealistic young engineers (one Russian, one Turkmen, one Jew, one Ukrainian, one Georgian – all communists) band together to overcome local superstitions to construct a canal in a remote Turkmenian village.

Less homogenous in its representation of minority culture, Belgoskino's first sound film, Yuri Tarich's one-reel *Poem of Liberation* [Poema imeni osvobozhdeniya, 1931], featured traditional Belorussian, Polish and Yiddish songs. Unlike the Ukraine, the Belorussian Soviet Socialist Republic was organised as a multinational state, with Yiddish one of four official languages. Many non-Jewish Belorussians spoke some Yiddish which, throughout the 1920s and well into the 1930s, was extensively used on posters, street signs and building façades. (Indeed, an actress who grew up in the heavily Jewish city of Gomel recalls seeing silent movies with Yiddish intertitles.[31])

In 1932, Belgoskino went a step further and produced *The Return of Nathan Becker* [Vozvrashchenie Neitana Bekkera], a feature-length talkie starring Solomon Mikhoels, which exists in both Russian and Yiddish versions. The latter (known as *Nosn Beker Fort Aheym*) may have been for export only; in any case, it is only the incomplete Russian version which survives in Soviet archives while a fragment of the Yiddish version has been recovered in the USA by the National Center for Jewish Film.

Directed by Boris Shpis and Rokhl M. Milman from a scenario by Yiddish poet Peretz Markish, *The Return of Nathan Becker* wedded Yiddish folk culture to that of the first Five Year Plan, not to mention the Factory of the Eccentric Actor. Shpis, who was not Jewish, had served as an assistant director on *The Overcoat* [Shinel', 1926] and *SVD* [1927] by Grigori Kozintsev and Leonid Trauberg. His first feature, *Someone Else's Jacket* [Chuzhoi pidzhak, 1927], a satire on the NEP, was heavily populated by FEKSniks, including Sergei Gerasimov. Milman, married to a prominent economist and related to Osip Brik, served as assistant director on all five of Shpis's features, co-scripting *The Avenger* [Mstitel', 1931], his semi-documentary on the modernisation of the Tungus tribe in Siberia.

*Nathan Becker* gave Jewish national aspiration a similar twist: after twenty-eight years in America 'laying bricks for Rockefeller', Nathan Becker (David Gutman, who had played the department-store owner in Kozintsev and Trauberg's *The New Babylon* [Novyi Vavilon, 1929]) leaves the land of bread-lines and Depression for his Belorussian home town and thence, having been reunited with his aged father Tzale (Mikhoels), the new industrial centre of Magnitogorsk.

Released almost simultaneously, *Nathan Becker* and Dovzhenko's Ukrainian-language *Ivan* were the ethnic components in a cycle of Soviet talkies dealing with social conflict and epic industrialisation. Alexander Macheret's *Men and Jobs* [Dela i lyudi, 1932] pitted a Russian worker against an American engineer during the construction of the Dneprostroi power station; Fridrikh [Friedrich] Ermler and Sergei Yutkevich's *Counterplan* [Vstrechnyi, 1932] showed 'bourgeois specialists' sabotaging Bolshevik work targets at a Leningrad factory; Boris Barnet's *Outskirts* [Okraina,

1933] evoked divided national loyalties in a Russian village during the First World War.

Like *Men and Jobs*, *Nathan Becker* also belongs to a group of early talkies involving foreign visitors to the Stalinist utopia. These include *Tommy* [1931], in which a British soldier is converted to Bolshevism, and Pudovkin's *The Deserter* [Dezertir, 1933], which concerns an exiled German communist. The most ambitious exercise in proletarian internationalism was undoubtedly *Black and White*, conceived in early 1932 to dramatise American racial problems. Set in the steel mills of Birmingham, Alabama, the movie was to be made in English with American actors but was never completed, perhaps a casualty of improved relations between the Soviet Union and the United States.

*Nathan Becker*, too, is distinguished by a certain ambivalence regarding the realm Jewish immigrants called *di goldene medine* (the golden land). America the decadent is briefly (and pragmatically) represented by stock footage of the Manhattan skyline. In a startling *hommage* to the most radical aspects of silent Soviet technique, the image of a boat steaming out from New York harbour is intercut with a stroboscopic montage of cars, cosmetics and can-can dancers – the images, culled mainly from German magazines, held as briefly as two frames. A mock-lyrical shot of garbage floating in the harbour provides a segue to Nathan aboard the ship. 'Well, Mayke, we are going home,' he informs his dubious wife (Yelena Kashnitskaya). The couple are travelling with Nathan's black colleague Jim (Kador Ben-Salim). 'You, also, are going home,' Nathan tells him.

An actor whose mere presence signified American injustice, Ben-Salim had recently appeared in P. Kolomoytsev's *Black Skin* [Chernaya kozha, 1931] a Ukrainfilm production that favourably compared Soviet racial attitudes to those of the United States; his first and most famous role was as the street acrobat Tom Jackson in Georgian director Ivan Perestiani's popular Civil War adventure *Little Red Devils* [Krasnye d'yavolyata, 1923] and its four sequels. Although Ben-Salim is used more as a prop than a performer in *Nathan Becker*, his incongruous appearance in the Belorussian *shtetl* is a subject for mild vaudeville humour. 'Is he a Jew too?' Tzale asks. 'He is a bricklayer,' Nathan replies. The town cantor rushes over to Tzale's hovel, shakes Jim's hand and is suitably impressed: 'This is Nosn? Your Nosn from America? How did he get so blackened . . . like the earth?'

Unlike Jim, the figure of Nathan was not completely exotic. As did the early 1920s, the early 1930s saw a small reverse immigration from the USA back to the Soviet Union. In his memoirs of the period, the journalist Eugene Lyons reports that 'the news that Russia had liquidated unemployment and was in dire need of labour power brought hundreds of foreign job hunters to Moscow'. Most, however, were disappointed. 'Even where they had specific mechanical trades, only one in a hundred managed to cut through the jungles of red-tape around Soviet jobs.' According to Lyons, by

*Figure 17* Solomon Mikhoels in the first Yiddish talkie, *The Return of Nathan Becker* [1932].

the year of *Nathan Becker*'s release, 'these hordes of stranded Americans became a real problem'.[32]

*Nathan Becker* has received scant attention in Soviet film histories although, in a 1935 essay on 'Film Art in Soviet White Russia', the film was singled out for particular praise by Sergei Dinamov. A leading cultural *apparatchik*, the editor of *Literaturnaya gazeta*, Dinamov had set the tone of the January 1935 All-Union Creative Conference on Cinema Affairs, over which he presided, when he defined the basis of the new Soviet cinema as 'optimism, heroism and theatricality'. Dinamov had publicly dismissed Kuleshov, Eisenstein and Pudovkin, but, in describing *Nathan Becker*, he evinces considerable enthusiasm:

> The artist, the producer, and the [camera] operator have shown here with great force the life of a Jewish townlet that preserved its old appearance during the first years after October. Houses that look like dovecots, brick buildings that look worn out by age. The brick does not at all resemble

brick, it looks so rotten and chipped. And the people still breathe the pre-October air.

Years go by. Into the life of the townlet there breaks in the fresh wind from far-away Magnitogorsk, where grand industrial construction is in progress. Old Becker and his son Nathan, just returned from America, go out to work there. . . . Magnitogorsk opens up a new world to both the father and the son, but they conceive it differently. The regenerated townlet after the Revolution has re-educated the old man Becker.

(Re-educated in some respects, that is: as Jay Leyda notes in *Kino*, Mikhoels speaks a markedly purer Yiddish than Gutman, whose command of the *mameloshn* has been corrupted by America.) 'There are beautiful and fascinating passages in this picture,' Dinamov concludes. 'The language is succulent, the words sinewy and precise. The author of the scenario, the well-known Yiddish writer Peretz Markish, has splendidly coped with his task.'[33]

Markish, the only Soviet Yiddish writer to receive the Lenin Prize (awarded to him in 1939, the year Dinamov was arrested and executed), was born in 1895 in a Volhynian *shtetl*, received a traditional *kheyder* education, rebelled at an early age, and ran away from home to become an itinerant child cantor. A flamboyant, Byronic personality, he started writing poetry at 15 and established a precocious reputation as one of the 'Kiev group' of Yiddish modernists. In 1921, he left the Soviet Union for Warsaw where he remained long enough to collaborate with I. J. Singer on an avant-garde anthology, before departing on a whirlwind international tour. The poet had not, however, lost his faith in the Revolution and, after five years abroad, he returned to the Soviet Union.

With no political irregularities in his past for which to atone, the charismatic Markish became a literary hero for radical Jewish youth. His two-volume novel *A Generation Goes, A Generation Arrives*, published in 1929, is proudly anti-traditional. (A wooden synagogue in a Ukrainian *shtetl* is described as looking 'as if it were wearing shingle rags and sinking into the earth . . . its crooked back carrying the women's section with the tiny windows the way you carry a paralytic.'[34] Despite his anti-clerical attitudes, Markish was targeted for criticism. After his novel was published, he was publicly rebuked by *Der emes*'s editor Moyshe Litvakov (himself trying to establish his credentials with the 'proletarian' militants) for exhibiting a 'national apologetic point of view' in making his revolutionary protagonists all Jews and ignoring class divisions in the *shtetl*.

As though consigning the misery of the Diaspora to the dustbin of history, *Nathan Becker* gives less authority to tradition – even as an adversary – than any previous Soviet Yiddish film. The movie opens in a miserable tumble-down *shtetl* populated mainly by old men, stray dogs and ragged urchins. Unlike the Ukrainian settings of *Jewish Luck* or *Through Tears*, this dilapidated Belorussian village is eerily underpopulated, halfway towards a ghost town. The natives seem weak and dispirited; as Dinamov observes, the non-bricks are literally falling out of the houses. (Seen today, the *shtetl*'s haunting sense of emptiness and abandonment carries unintentional associations with the catastrophic, man-made famine that was then decimating the Ukraine.)

The sense of entropy is emphasised by Yevgeni Brusilovsky's mournful score, and the accompanying montage of crooked roofs and empty mud streets. Nathan's arrival draws a motley crowd of urchins, layabouts and beggars. A ragged *klezmer* plays his clarinet and sings a toneless song. Intentionally or not, this opening is a parody of those 16mm home movies produced by successful immigrants of their old world birthplaces: 'In America, you would become rich with this performance,' Nathan expansively tells the musician. But, even as the returning son is greeted by old Becker, the town is honoured with another distinguished visitor. When a pretty young communist appears in an official car to recruit workers to help build Magnitogorsk, an enthusiastic mob abruptly materialises, falling over themselves in their desire to leave the *shtetl* for the steel city beyond the Urals.

Constructed in the first frenzy of the Five Year Plan, Magnitogorsk was its crucible. The same year *Nathan Becker* was released saw Joris Ivens's 50-minute documentary paean *Song of the Heroes*, scored by Hanns Eisler and focusing on the building of a blast furnace by the young workers of the Komsomol. 'A quarter of a million souls – Communists, kulaks, foreigners, Tartars, convicted saboteurs and a mass of blue-eyed Russian peasants – making the biggest steel combinat in Europe in the middle of the barren Ural steppe,' the American welder John Scott wrote in his first-hand account of the city's rise. 'Money was spent like water, men froze, hungered and suffered, but the construction work went on with a disregard for individuals and a mass heroism seldom paralleled in history.'[35]

These new arrivals to south-west Siberia included some 40,000 Jews. Indeed, one of the outstanding figures of Five Year Plan literature – David Margulies, the positive hero of novelist Valentin Katayev's 1932 celebration of Magnitogorsk, *Time, Forward* – is nominally Jewish. Margulies, however, is an engineer; most of the labour was unskilled, with bricklayers such as Nathan and Jim in particular demand at the beginning of 1933.

*Nathan Becker* salutes the city of steel with appropriately heroic music. Here, the *shtetl* Jews are educated in progressive work methods by enthusiastic young communists. Nathan is assigned to the Central Institute of Labour as an instructor, along with a German specialist who has been imported to teach the workers a regimen of movements that combine efficiency, artistry and pleasure. (This unspecified form of Taylorism suggests the theories of the 'Expressionist' critic and director Ippolit Sokolov who, dismissing Meyerhold's Biomechanics as unscientific, believed that actors must be trained like workers to synthesise 'physical culture and the labour process'.[36] 'Are they studying to become actors?' the incredulous Nathan asks. 'The worker plays his work as though it were a piano,' the instructor explains – and the solicitous, optimistic construction leader Mikulich (Boris Babochkin, who would soon become a national hero as the eponymous hero of *Chapayev*) adds that 'the backs of the workers are as important to us as the building of the wall'.

Unconvinced, Comrade Becker petulantly overturns the table on which the bricks have been arranged in rows: 'The piano they play? Why don't you hire musicians then? *Meshugoim!*' The American considers his Soviet colleagues to be lunatics and, unpacking his trowel, proposes an 'American-style' competition. 'I will show them who works better, *Sovetishe klezmer* or American bricklayer.' When the Yiddish version of *Nathan Becker* opened in New York in April 1933, the *Daily Worker* would note that '28 years of intense economic struggle to live have left their mark on Nathan Becker. He has become a machine, an automatic robot. . . . The new type of Soviet worker whom he now meets, a new man with a new outlook on life, is incomprehensible to him.' (The *Worker*, however, missed the nuance. Nathan is not robotic enough. As Katerina Clark points out in her study of socialist realist literature, the industrial utopia envisioned during the Five Year Plan embraced such automation: 'It was often claimed, especially in fiction, that human psychology could be changed by putting people to work at machines: inexorably, the machine's regular, controlled, rational rhythms would impress themselves on the "anarchic" and "primitive" psyches of those who worked them.'[37])

Despite its schematic narrative, *Nathan Becker* is a surprisingly playful film. As the advertisement in New York's Yiddish-language communist daily proclaimed when the film opened in New York in April 1933: 'Jewish worker, this is your holiday!'[38] *Nathan Becker* is at least as full of comic routines – one of them devoted to the old men of the *shtetl* signing up for the 'shock brigade' – as it is steeped in Stalinist propaganda. 'There's a definite strain of the native Jewish sense of humour,' *Variety* observed. 'A Soviet film that has definite laugh situations! That's news in itself.' The reviewer added that 'a lad named S. M. Mikhoels plays the part of a stuttering old Jew with beautiful perfection'.[39]

Indeed, the 42-year-old Mikhoels is delightful. As in *Jewish Luck*, Mikhoels constructs his persona out of stylised bits of business. (In one comic throwaway, he picks up a handy bust of Marx, stares at it, and reflectively strokes his own beard.) His is an overwhelmingly tactile performance, as rigorous in its movements as a ballet dancer's. The fractured language he speaks is virtually his own – interspersed with chuckling, clucking and the continual humming of a *nign* (a traditional prayer chant). If glum David Gutman is a stolid proletarian type with a generic resemblance to William Bendix, looking more like Mikhoels's brother than his son, Yelena Kashnitskaya is also something of a comedienne whose constant confusion as to the date – she is always asking when it will be the sabbath – is a joke on the Soviet 'continuous-production week' (four days of work followed by one day of rest) instituted during the Five Year Plan.

Given the movie's light mood, it seems appropriate that a circus ring should provide the site for the bricklaying competition where, for a seven-hour shift, Nathan will compete against a Soviet worker. (Shpis and Milman here acknowledge their FEKS background although, according to Scott, the circus was Magnitogorsk's most popular form of entertainment.[40]) Old Becker watches the contest intently, as do the other bearded Jews. Inspecting the walls between rounds offers another excuse for clowning. By the seventh hour, Nathan is exhausted: as the unflustered Russian forges ahead, he vainly remembers the class in mechanical movements. Humiliated by his defeat, Nathan decides to return to America. His wife reminds him of the unemployed fighting for soup, but he is determined to leave until Mikulich confronts him: 'You're not in America. We're not going to fire you. We're going to learn from you. But you should learn from us too.' The chief of operations praises Nathan's work – he was working more efficiently but tired sooner than his rival – and suggests combining the systems. The synthesis of American and Soviet techniques will increase production.

This conclusion not only sent a fraternal message to American Jewish communists and fellow-travellers, it also smacks of applied Eccentrism. In their admiration for the dynamism and unpretentious populism of American mass culture, FEKS theorists had issued the ultimatum: 'Either American-isation or the undertaker'.[41] Proletarian poets like Alexei Gastev also imagined adding 'the pulse of America' to 'the hurricane of revolution', and the notion acquired an official pedigree when, in the late 1920s, Stalin spoke of fusing 'American efficiency with Russian revolutionary scope'.[42] Markish's novelisation of the film, published in 1934, is somewhat sterner: Nathan gradually comes to understand that, despite hardships and in-efficiency, the new Soviet way of life is, on the whole, superior to that of America.

Despite the absence of a harsh moral or strong positive hero, however, *The Return of Nathan Becker* fulfils the Zhdanov capsule formula for Socialist Realism ('a combination of the most matter-of-fact, everyday reality with the most heroic prospects'). True to its genre, the movie ends with a hymn to labour. 'We must win. We will win,' the workers' chorus sings. 'Long live the day of victory!' Meanwhile, the camera peers up at happy Nathan perched on the scaffolding beside old Becker and Jim. 'Here the workers work not only with their hands but also with their hearts,' the American rhapsodises. ('And also with their heads,' his father adds.) In a final gag that recalls the exercises of the Institute with its own blend of folk Taylorism, old Becker instructs Jim in the fine points of his ubiquitous *nign*, complete with appropriate hand gestures.

As the Stalinist cultural revolution gathered momentum, the anti-Soviet, petty-bourgeois Jews found in the novels of the 1920s vanished. In Russian as well as Yiddish literature, there remained only two types of Jewish characters: the dispirited 'little' Jews of the *shtetl* and their children, the optimistic, 'productivised' zealots of the Komsomol or kolkhoz.[43]

The lone cinematic example of the latter appears as the indomitable hero of Soyuzkino's *The Rout* [Razgrom, 1931] directed by N. Beresnev from Alexander Fadeyev's much-praised 1926 novel. Other Jewish film protagonists were an ambiguous mixture of the little and the heroic. The same year as *Nathan Becker*, Lev Kuleshov took a similar theme for his first talkie, *Gorizont* [1932], released in the USA as *Horizon, the Wandering Jew*. Drafted into the tsar's army when the First World War breaks out and deserting soon after, Leo Gorizont (Nikolai Batalov, star of *The Path to Life*) makes his way to New York to discover his uncle Isaac and cousin Rose being evicted from their apartment. Gorizont and Rose care for the elderly Isaac; however, after the girl runs off, Isaac commits suicide and Gorizont enlists in the American army. His unit is despatched to Russia to aid the Whites but, deserting once more, Gorizont joins the Bolshevik cause. The film ends, some fifteen years later, with Gorizont a distinguished locomotive engineer contrasted to a former bourgeois who cannot reconcile himself to the Soviet regime.

*The Age of Majority* [Sovershennoletie, 1935], directed by Boris Schreiber for Belgoskino from Johann Seltzer's scenario, is based on a reverse transformation: the Bolshevik hero goes underground as a Jewish factory foreman. In Vladimir Korsh-Sablin's *The First Platoon* [Pervyi vzvod, 1933], another Belgoskino production, David Gutman plays an aged but virtuous Jewish worker. A pair of stereotypical 'little' Jews appear in Ivan Kavaleridze's *By Water and Smoke* [Koliivshchina, 1933], made for Ukrainfilm and released in the USA as *Mass Struggle*, along with Moshko, 'a young Jewish worker in revolt against the ancient submissiveness of his race'.[44] The saga of an eighteenth-century peasant uprising against the Polish aristocracy, the film featured dialogue in Ukrainian, Polish and Yiddish, as well as Russian. (To judge from surviving publicity photos, Kavaleridze's 1935 *Prometheus* [Prometei, 1935] also features traditional Jewish characters.)

In 1933, Ukrainfilm unceremoniously cancelled Vladimir Vilner's partially shot *Shtetl Ladeniu* [Mestechka Ladeniu], adapted from a comedy by the Ukrainian-Jewish writer Leonid Pervomaisky that had been produced by Berezil the previous year.[45] Still, one last Soviet *shtetl* film was released in June 1935, two months before the formal proclamation of the Popular Front.

Lenfilm's *The Border* [Granitsa], was one of several Soviet films made during the transitional 1933–5 period that portray the hostile regimes (but fraternal workers) surrounding the Soviet Union. Thus, the pre-Revolutionary *shtetl* is located in contemporary Poland – only a few miles from the Lenin kolkhoz and the Belorussian SSR, but clearly another world. Here, in old Dudino, the worst of the old ways prevail. The oppressed Jews have made a religion of their despair. A rich factory owner dominates the town's economic life. (Thoroughly cynical and yet not altogether inhuman, this class enemy not only uses the local rabbi as his front, but betrays the innocent young woman who asks his help, 'Jew to Jew, Zionist to Zionist'.) Meanwhile the superstitious villagers try to improve conditions by staging a 'Black Crown', marrying the *shtetl*'s oldest spinster to an eligible widower in the cemetery at midnight. The prospective bridegroom, a poor shoemaker, agrees only because the authorities have duplicitously agreed to release his imprisoned son and daughter, a communist organiser and a Zionist fire-brand respectively. When the wedding is disrupted by Polish soldiers, the bridegroom kills one and has to be smuggled across the Soviet border.

This promised land is never seen, only described: 'We saw camp-fires and people singing around them. The songs were definitely Jewish,' says the returned smuggler, a young clerk played by Venyamin Zuskin. 'There, it is possible to live.' The film ends with Zuskin humming that wordless yet affirmative 'Jewish song' he learned at the kolkhoz. In the final moments, his Belorussian comrade (Nikolai Cherkasov), previously described as one of 'those strange strong people who drink vodka and hate Jews', joins fraternally in the revolutionary *nign*, drawing deeply on his hearty baritone, jaunty cigarette, and proletarian smile.

Written and directed by 36-year-old Mikhail Dubson – who, as a diplo-matic attaché, had made his first movie seven years before in Berlin – *The Border*, which is leavened with much incidental Yiddish, is at once comically anti-clerical and subversively nostalgic. Both attitudes are immediately evident in the lengthy opening scene, set in a wooden synagogue. The cantor chanting throughout, Dubson cuts back and forth between gossiping (or wailing) women and mumbling men. The synagogue, while satirised, exudes vitality even as the cantor's prayer is presented as a virtuoso performance. When the *khazn* glances out of the window and catches a peasant woman's eye, he flirtatiously redoubles his effort. Although ostensibly meant to ridicule, the sequence is as powerfully imagined as a child's first memory.

Deliberately paced, shot mainly in close-up, and accompanied by Lev Pulver's spare, eloquent score (the source of many innovative sound bridges), *The Border* achieves a kind of voluptuous stasis. The compositions are strong; the figures skilfully modelled by light. The stark and misty Black Crown sequence, much of it framed by the Mogen David in the cemetery gate, is a lyrical grotesque worthy of Granovsky. GOSET-like as well is another synagogue scene in which the deaf shoemaker and the rabbi converse in superbly laconic gestures, the latter praying all the while. *Variety*'s Moscow correspondent found *The Border* reminiscent of *Humoresque* but 'more genuine and less sentimental', predicting this 'un-pretentious' picture 'should enjoy a world-wide Jewish nabe market'.[46] (Indeed, there does seem to be a line for the international audience. When one worker wonders why a Jewish kolkhoz has been named for Lenin, another explains that 'for a Jew, he's a Jew. For a Russian, he's Russian. For

Americans . . .') Nevertheless, although listed in Amkino's catalogue, the film seems never to have enjoyed an American theatrical release.

At home, *The Border* was praised in *Kino* as 'an event in our art' and 'a lesson in revolutionary vigilance'.[47] Still, so far as Soviet film-makers were concerned, the *shtetl* was obsolete, if not the issue of Jewish resettlement. In 1926, one year after the first Jewish agricultural colonies were established in the southern Ukraine and the Crimea, the undeveloped, sparsely populated region of Birobidzhan, bordering China in the Soviet Far East, was offered as a national homeland. Despite concerted recruitment, the remoteness of the region – not to mention its primitive conditions – discouraged immigration. By 1933, a year when more settlers left than arrived, there were only 8,000 Jews in the region; the original timetable called for six times as many.

Jews formed less than 20 per cent of the total population when, in May 1934, Birobidzhan was declared a Jewish autonomous oblast with Yiddish its official language. That year, the distinguished Yiddish novelist David Bergelson published his *Birobizhaner*, an idealised account of Jewish settlers who transform the taiga as well as themselves – ex-*luftmenshn* chopping down the primeval forest to build schools and homes. Birobidzhan offered the most radical transformation yet: Ben-Zion Goldberg, an important American Jewish fellow-traveller (as well as the son-in-law of Sholom Aleichem), visited the autonomous oblast in 1934 and reported back that 'instead of being built up by Jews in what we call a typical Jewish manner, Birobidzhan is being reclaimed with that Soviet efficiency which came into play in the construction of Dneprostroi and Magnitogorsk'.[48]

Far more than an extension of the Five Year Plan or a replacement for the Yevsektsiya, the Birobidzhan project was a counter-Zionism (and, in some cases, a crypto-Zionism). The prospects for peaceful settlement, the friendliness of the indigenous population, and the existence of government support were favourably contrasted to the difficult lot of the Jewish settlers in Palestine, caught between Arab hostility on one hand and British imperialism on the other. In April 1935, the Acme Theatre in New York opened *Birobidjan*, a Yiddish-language 'documentary featurette' written and directed by M. Slunsky for Soyuzkino News, with a musical score by Lev Pulver. Introduced by the chairman of the pro-Soviet Association for Jewish Colonization in Russia (IKOR), this half-hour film played on a bill with another Soviet ethnic item, *A Song of Happiness* [Pesnya o schast'e, 1934], directed by Mark Donskoi and Vladimir Legoshin for Vostokkino in the Mari Autonomous Region. (As a follow-up, Donskoi was reportedly 'looking for a scenario on Jewish life'.[49])

As the Nazis consolidated power in Germany, the propaganda offensive gathered momentum. In May 1936, the Soviet ambassador to the United States told a gathering in New York that Birobidzhan was 'the symbol of the struggle against anti-Semitism and against the entire medieval darkness'.[50]

That summer, the Soviet Central Committee announced that, 'for the first time in the history of the Jewish people, its burning desire for the creation of a homeland of its own, for the achievement of its own national statehood, has found fulfilment'.[51] This fulfilment was illustrated by Belgoskino's *Seekers of Happiness* [Iskateli schast'ya] which, well in advance of its appearance, was cited by Boris Shumyatsky as one of the best Soviet movies of 1936 (along with *We from Kronstadt* [My iz Kronshtadta, 1936] and *A Son of Mongolia* [Syn Mongolii, 1936]).[52]

Released in the USA as *A Greater Promise*, *Seekers of Happiness* was co-directed by Vladimir Korsh-Sablin and I. Shapiro, from a script by Johann Seltzer and G. Kobets. Although made in Russian, the film featured a number of Yiddish songs arranged by the enormously popular director of the Leningrad Music Hall, Isaak Dunayevsky, and a star turn by Venyamin Zuskin. As an appeal to Jewish nationalism and a criticism of Jewish life in the Diaspora, the film went well beyond *Nathan Becker*. A poor family of foreign, most likely Polish, Jews – the incorrigible *luftmensh* Pinya Kopman (Zuskin), his long-suffering wife Dvoira (the popular character actress and People's Artist, Mariya Blumenthal-Tamarina), and their daughter Rosa – immigrate to the promised land of Birobidzhan, where Dvoira's relatives have already settled on the *Royte Feld* (Red Field) kolkhoz. (Birobidzhan was officially opened to foreign settlers in 1936; by the end of the year, according to the *Vilner Tog*, newcomers included Jews from Poland, Latvia and Lithuania, as well as America and even Palestine.[53])

Despite the Yiddish poster of heroic Jewish peasants that dominates the Leningrad office where the Kopman family apply for their permits, Pinya imagines Birobidzhan as one *shtetl* get-rich-quick scheme. After nearly dying in his obsessive attempt to find gold, however, he comes to his senses and, encouraged by his Party-identified brother-in-law, learns that 'honest collective work' is worth more than money. Assimilation too is part of the programme. As part of the happy ending, Rosa marries the young Russian hunter who has saved Pinya's life and the film ends with a lengthy wedding scene in which individuals representing a variety of nationalities (including Mongolian, Korean, Siberian, Cossack) present the couple with gifts and serenade them in Yiddish.[54]

*Seekers of Happiness* received an extraordinary amount of publicity in the English-language *Moscow Daily News*. Although Mikhoels – who, earlier that year had sung a Yiddish lullaby in Grigori Alexandrov's *The Circus* [Tsirk, 1936] – was listed as 'acting consultant', Korsh-Sablin took credit for the film's transformations: 'I have straightened up the stooping Jews, shaved off the beards and cut their hair and have shown them as healthy, good-looking people, full of life and energy.'[55] On that hygienic note, the *shtetl* Jew vanished utterly from the Soviet screen.[56]

As befits a national cinema without a national republic, the dozen years of Soviet Jewish movies were dominated by the search for a satisfactory homeland. Compelled by poverty or the tsar to leave their backward *shtetlekh*, protagonists set out upon the 'crooked path of Jewish luck' that led from booming Odessa to decadent Europe and false America back to Magnitogorsk, the Lenin Kolkhoz and beyond – past Siberia to the Chinese border. This was truly the end of the line. In 1937, within a year of the release of *Seekers of Happiness*, the People's Commissariat for Internal Affairs (NKVD) became responsible for transportation of Jewish settlers to Birobidzhan, while the oblast's entire leadership was purged in the Great Terror.

# 8 A fickle man, or portrait of Boris Barnet as a Soviet director

*Bernard Eisenschitz*

Henri Langlois used to show *By the Bluest of Seas* [U samogo sinego morya, 1936] and *The Wrestler and the Clown* [Borets i kloun, 1957] so regularly at the Cinémathèque Française that intrigued audiences ended up actually going to see them.[1] We used to wonder at a plot that had to be followed without any translation, but even more about such an 'American' director amid the acknowledged Soviet classics. Despite this misunderstanding (as it turned out), there could be no mistaking Barnet's immense adaptability in the face of any kind of material, his narrative skill, his freedom and his lack of interest in any kind of 'message'.

It is always irritating not to know more about a film-maker, even though the films themselves should suffice. A short interview by Georges Sadoul seemed to substantiate the discovery – together with Godard's oft-quoted remark about the 'famous Triangle style' of which Barnet was the heir – but only after the director's death.

Sadoul spent the evening of 12 September 1959 with Boris Barnet. Six years later he wrote:

> I should perhaps have asked Barnet more about his work and creative concerns at the end of the 50s. But as a historian preparing a study of Soviet silent cinema I concentrated instead, rather too much perhaps, on the beginning of his career.[2]

Barnet himself, however, ranged a little more widely:

> In thirty-seven years I've managed to direct about twenty films, most of which have not satisfied me at all. My favourite ones are *The Girl with a Hatbox* [Devushka s korobkoi, 1927], *Outskirts* [Okraina, 1933] and *Annuskha* [1959], which I've just finished. I also quite like *The Wrestler and the Clown*, which I completed after the death of Yudin, who had only directed one reel. But I don't care at all for *Bounteous Summer* [Shchedroe leto, 1951], which seems to be admired in France. That's a film which suffered too much from the constraints of a difficult period.
>
> Speaking generally about my attitude towards cinema, I like comedy best of all. I like to insert amusing scenes into dramas and dramatic scenes into comedies, but of course it's all a matter of proportion.

With a few obvious exceptions, all my films, for better or worse, deal with contemporary life and its problems. When I have had the option, I have always chosen contemporary subjects, even though it is not always easy to tackle these.

In this connection, let me tell you one of my favourite stories. A great Japanese painter reviewed his life and work as follows: from twenty to forty he did still lifes and landscapes; between forty and sixty he painted birds; then from sixty to eighty geese, ducks, chickens – all sorts of domestic animals. And it was only at the beginning of his hundredth year that he felt ready to portray humans.

My ambition has also been to show the place of man in contemporary life. I could and would not wait that long before taking my chance. But I wonder now if I will live long enough to provide a true picture of man.

I am not and never was a man with theories. I always found my material in everyday life. However I would like one day to introduce mythological themes in depicting the Krivoi Rog brigades and their dramatic conflicts. But am I ever likely to have the chance to tackle such a big subject?

This interview, not published until six years later, was the only occasion apart from his films when we heard the voice of Barnet. Even if it does not offer much insight, the sound of his voice is there: this is the man himself speaking, not a conventional figure of the period. All the more reason to understand why, and to what extent, he remains the great unknown of Soviet cinema. Barnet's films have not been ignored or unavailable (other than those from the war period and the very last ones): he has been duly recognised by historians of all shades as the founder of Soviet comedy – and *The Girl with a Hatbox* certainly justifies that reputation, as does *The House on Trubnaya* [Dom na Trubnoi, 1928], while *By the Bluest of Seas* remains unclassifiable, and certainly not a comedy even if it provokes laughter. Of course, as with most directors, his range is much greater than that of a single genre.

Yelena Kuzmina demonstrated this refusal to see him in other terms when I interviewed her in Moscow in November 1977. While she spoke with insight about her work with Kozintsev and Trauberg (*The New Babylon*) and with Romm, she had no fond memories of Barnet, despite having been (reluctantly, she claimed) his wife and leading actress at the beginning of the 1930s:

At that time films were like banners, with such epics as *Potemkin* and *Storm Over Asia* [Potomok Chingis-Khana, 1929]. There were also the comedies with Igor Ilyinsky, which seemed much less interesting and were considered things done for money rather than as art. But Barnet risked filming things differently, showing the lives of ordinary, unimport-ant people and their aspirations. He dealt with people instead of statues.

I was in Odessa to make *Gorizont* [1933] with Kuleshov. This was when I got to know Barnet and it was a drama for him: he fell in love with me. I had heard a lot of bad rumours and did not want to work with him. So I signed a contract which stipulated that for *Outskirts* I would devise my own role, but he forced me to become his wife! He was the father of my daughter Natasha and her son resembles him. These family likenesses often show up a generation later, but in fact Barnet and I were physically very like each other and people used to say that we could live together for a century. In fact we spent four years together before I fled. Romm helped me do this.

In personal terms, he treated me badly and it was difficult to work with him. He was a fickle man. And I believe that art is a jealous mistress: it does not permit any infidelity, either with drink or women. So, little by little, Barnet began to decline.

Why did I find it difficult to work with him? I had been trained by the FEKS, by Kozintsev and Trauberg, who had given me scope to be creative. They had shaped me as a thinking actress. This was how Gerasimov became a director and, if I had been gifted in that way, which I wasn't, I could have become a director too.

Barnet did not like this at all. He gave strict direction: it was always 'Do this', 'Do that'. . . . We had furious arguments. But when he really wanted something, nothing stood in his way.

He used to say: 'Everyone must create at least one thing' and this is how he would create *his* thing – he never kept to the original scenario. He would write out each shot painstakingly and stick these pieces of paper one after another to make a long scroll. Then he would unroll this on the ground and get down on his knees to search for the shot he was about to do. And in the end he would shoot something quite different, improvising on the spot. This is the reason for the 'freedom' in his films.

'Proportion' says Barnet, and Kuzmina speaks of 'freedom': these terms seem inescapable when one tries to take stock of his films. From *Miss Mend* [1926] onwards, they use a wide variety of rhythms to give an impression of nonchalance (another term commonly used by critics in relation to Barnet, Ioseliani and their like) in the execution of a very precise project. We are reminded of Renoir speaking about his liking for chaos while directing a film; or of Shklovsky declaring that a book gets written only when the subject allows it by virtue of the attraction between its contents.

In Soviet cinema of the 1930s, the scenario became a sort of fetish, as if it guaranteed the conformity of the product to literary form and to expressed intentions (thus negating the very idea of cinema which had been developed in the 1920s). But for Barnet, the written word was never more than a springboard. Indeed he had been reproached for this even before the 1930s, according to the Soviet book devoted to him: a film magazine published extracts from the script of *The House on Trubnaya* and invited its readers to find any points of similarity with the film.[3] Obviously he could cope with the challenge; instinct went hand in hand with a very sure 'touch'. Barnet is one of those rare film-makers whose narrative forms were not bound by those of the stage (act, scene, etc.).

His films convey more than most the intensity of happiness, the physical pleasure of meeting and contact, the inevitable tragedy of relationships. If a wounded man smiles and says quietly, 'I'm coming,' at the end of *Outskirts*, this is not accompanied by an arching of the back, as in Dovzhenko, but by a wish to avoid the pain of death. 'What goings-on,' he murmurs mildly before the final moment. *Outskirts* interlaces, with the intricacy of a miniaturist and simultaneously an epic feeling, the tale of a Russian gutter-snipe in love with a German prisoner and the course of events which leads to revolution, as seen in a provincial town. These strands are interwoven within each sequence and even each shot. *The Girl with a Hatbox*, which is contemporary with Katayev's play *The Squaring of the Circle* and Ilf and Petrov and Mayakovsky's *The Bed-Bug*, shows, like no other film of the time, the city and the countryside, handicrafts (here the making of hats), overcrowded trains, people asleep on stations, the dizzying impact of city life and of Nepmen – and all these in an exhilarating visual geometry which simul-

*Figure 18* Anna Sten in *The Girl with a Hatbox*, directed by Barnet for Mezhrabpom in 1927.

taneously evokes Griffith, Keaton and Vertov (as does in more controlled fashion *The House on Trubnaya*): the servant of a bourgeois hairdresser assumes an alarming angle on top of a stepladder in order to dust, both parties in a marriage of convenience conduct warfare in an empty room with a pile of books, a hatbox, a pair of boots and a white mouse.[4]

'Nothing stood in his way.' This can be understood literally as well as figuratively when one has learnt to recognise the sturdy silhouette of Barnet, from *Mr West* and *Miss Mend* to his magnificent little scene in *Storm Over Asia* and as the German general in *The Exploits of a Scout* [Podvig razvedchika, 1947] whom he refuses to make odious. The films themselves are athletic, not only in their direction (Otsep, apparently, was too lazy to keep up with the pace of shooting on *Miss Mend* and Kuzmina tells evocatively of the long-awaited storm that broke south of Baku during *By the Bluest of Seas*) but in the very body of the narrative. People run, hurl themselves against the elements or the enemy, against gravity itself (in *The Wrestler and the Clown*). The loss of this vigour is in part the subject of Barnet's last film.

As for the famous 'decline' of which Kuzmina and many others have spoken, an exemplary retrospective organised by the British Film Institute in 1980 finally dispelled this myth, born of historians' indifference to that part of cinema which does not sell itself, promote itself with claims to artistic distinction. For one of these historians (who saw the mediocre *One September Night* [Noch' v sentyabre, 1939] as 'a didactic film about sabotage, but in which the images are carefully composed') the Barnet of the later films 'is only a shadow of his former self'. This is the verdict which prevails among many historians – disciples no doubt of Carlos Anglada, invented by Borges and Bioy Casares, who was working on a 'scientific history of cinematography and preferred to rely for evidence on his infallible artist's memory, avoiding the contamination of any actual viewing which would always be imperfect and misleading'.[5]

After the release of *By the Bluest of Seas* in April 1936, Barnet did not make a film for three years. We know from his biographer, the cautious Kushnirov, that Eisenstein recommended him for a job in a studio linked with the Moscow Art Theatre.[6] The project did not materialise, but the anecdote suggests the esteem in which Eisenstein held Barnet (otherwise expressed only in one of his famous obscene puns referring to Barnet's powers of seduction).

It would be reassuring to interpret Barnet's silences as proof of his moral probity, as a refusal of complicity. After the freedom of *By the Bluest of Seas* (a freedom which in 1936 would have been unthinkable anywhere), one might have expected silence, exile, or internal resistance. For a French writer in *Télérama* the highest praise that can be accorded Barnet is the fact that 'Eventually he committed suicide [in 1965] like Mayakovsky'.[7] In other words, the good Soviet is a Soviet martyr. But the actual consequence of silence is frustration. When he did at last return to production, the resulting *One September Night* was steeped in the atmosphere of the time, reflecting the same sabotage psychosis as other films of the period, such as Macheret's *Engineer Kochin's Mistake* [Oshibka inzhenera Kochina, 1939] and Gerasimov's *Komsomolsk* [1938].

One should not, however, think of Barnet's engagement as purely formal. His last silent film, *The Ice Breaks* [Ledolom; alternative title: Anka, 1931], portrays an intensely political period. Deeply impressed by *The Earth*, he committed himself to a strange reworking of Dovzhenko's film, based on the same situation of a village terrorised by kulaks, in which each frame, action and cut is carefully thought out to express fully the tension of class conflict. *The Ice Breaks* is indeed the only one of his films in which form assumes an autonomy to the extent of becoming a discourse in its own right. In short, a truly Formalist film, which might seem quite natural for Barnet, but in fact was alien to him.

*One September Night*, on the other hand, is not only a badly made film, but in truth hardly seems made at all. Although Alexei Stakhanov's name appears in the credits as an 'adviser', the emphasis is on bomb-planters and kidnappers, a lurid counterpoint to the heroic tone called for by the staging of historical characters (Ordzhonikidze), mass meetings and stentorian music.[8] A girl detained in a clinic and moaning on a bed is unusually framed by the diagonal line of an attic roof, itself balanced by the diagonal pipe, with the light coming from the door: a stronger echo of the world of *Caligari* and *Mabuse* than of anything from Gorky. In this film supposedly dedicated to the rhythm of work, the characters seem to laze about. One scene begins with some older men taking a discreet interest in the food baskets brought by the youngsters and ends with them stuffing themselves, without even waiting for the hero in whose honour they have gathered. All of which counts for little in such a hopeless film, even if one wishes to interpret it ironically.

Barnet's next film, by contrast, could not have been further from topical concerns. In the loosely connected episodes of *The Old Jockey* [Staryi naezdnik, 1940, released 1959], an ageing jockey is defeated, his daughter leaves the village to meet him, they return together, train for a last win, success results and the illusory promise of other victories. It is hard to imagine a less 'American' film. Indeed, it is surely a reaction against Alexandrov's great comedy success, *Volga-Volga* [1938], an Americanised and stereotyped film which the scriptwriters for *The Old Jockey*, Erdman and Volpin, had written a year earlier.[9]

It was an important collaboration for Barnet, who paid tribute to the two writers, stating publicly that it was the best screenplay he had ever filmed and even admitting that he did not feel he had risen to the level of his script. Such a remark would have its consequences, when the author of *The Suicide* was exiled from Moscow. Barnet had already worked with Erdman on *Trubnaya*, which brought together among its six scriptwriters (even though these never met except in twos) the 'Formalist' Shklovsky and two signatories of the 1919 Imaginist Manifesto who were also close to Erdman, Shershenevich and Marienhof. He also employed Erdman's father as an actor (in *Outskirts*) and his brother as a set decorator.[10] This fidelity seems to have been typical, whether he was using an actor like Koval-Samborsky again after an interval of thirty years (during which period, according to Leyda's euphemism, he had 'disappeared for some time'); or helping a dying Protazanov when he himself was in difficulties.[11] We know that Protazanov had encouraged Barnet's first efforts at Mezhrabpom and had even convinced the great Serafima Birman (the future Yevfrosinia in *Ivan the Terrible*) to appear in this 'urchin's' film, *The Girl with a Hatbox*.[12] Birman, in turn, would remain a faithful friend of Barnet to the end.

*The Old Jockey* opens with a close-run trotting race, which the ageing Trofimov loses. Then we move to a restaurant near the race-course, in the company of two punters. Trofimov's rival, Pavel, is trying to have him excluded from the club. From this scene with its unpleasant odour of denunciation, we pass to something totally different. In the country, peasants are making parachute jumps from a tower. News comes of a packet just arrived from Moscow, which turns out to contain a sound recording of

*Figure 19  The Old Jockey*, made in 1940, was not released until 1959.

Marusya's grandfather speaking to her. At the station, she says goodbye to her timid suitor and to the local hairdresser. All we see of the city is the railway station steps, where the girl asks a youngster for directions. Soon she reaches the café where she is to meet her grandfather, and where the two punters make her acquaintance. She consoles the grandfather and they return home together, to a village welcome. Trofimov holds forth in a monologue; he rests. Without telling anyone, he sets off for the race-course. She brings him back. Together they train a horse, which disrupts the daily life of the village. A year later, at the race-course, Trofimov wins, and vanishes. 'We will race again and win again,' he says to his rival, who accepts the challenge, and they shake hands.

No lesson taught, no exemplary characters: a loose sequence of events within a tight structure. From *Miss Mend* onwards, Barnet made his films by setting in motion a variety of characters and events, quite independent of each other, then organising their intersection. The structure is as rigorously planned as in *By the Bluest of Seas*, which ends as it began, with all the narrative relationships, the dynamics of scenes and gags, arranged symmetrically. But within this scrupulous equilibrium, everything is constantly displaced. Once the point of a scene or a shot is established, it is immediately side-stepped, as if being shown through the wrong end of a telescope, or at least not developed. The rules of American (and indeed of Soviet pre-war) cinema – maximum impact and maximum economy, following the shortest line from one point in the story to the next – were not Barnet's, even if he knew how to make use of them.

The main characters are coming along the road: a kid slips under a fence. What is going to happen: a meeting, a gag? In this case, nothing. A dissolve and we move on to something else. The film is prodigal in its offering of inventions and ideas – like the accident-prone female doctor. Every gesture, however minimal in itself, carries an equal weight without also bearing an ideological price ticket. The vivid secondary characters are by no means the least interesting. From the parachute jumping and the letter recorded on a flexible disc, we see how minor incidents can give rise to emotions that are simultaneously grave and gay: ageing, friendly rivalry, patient effort; the city represented by a restaurant in which the race-course grandstands are reflected, while the country is represented by wooden fences in the style of John Ford.

*The Old Jockey* was one of those films which, according to the quaint Soviet expression, 'did not reach the screen': it had to wait until 1959 for release. Alexander Mitta (*Shine, My Star, Shine* [Gori, gori, moya zvezda, 1970]), who later worked with Erdman and Volpin, recalls:

During the war, Barnet had three films banned one after another [the second must have been *The Novgoroders* [Novgorodtsy, 1942]. He used to say of himself that he had become a 'director-colonel'.[13] Erdman and Volpin told me about him. He was definitely not a dissident and knew absolutely nothing about politics. Outside the cinema, he might almost have been thought somewhat silly. He was absolutely and completely an artist. He thought that the people who had been put up there to rule us were great figures, simply because they were there; he listened to their speeches and really wanted to put these themes into films. But he did not know how to make the stereotypes that the bureaucrats gave him: he only knew how to reflect life. He did not attack the stereotypes, but life seeped into them, washed them away, and that made the bureaucrats absolutely mad because it could not be corrected. Life had taken the place of the stereotypes.

After the war, in 1947, the 'director-colonel' played a Nazi officer for the second time in *The Exploits of a Scout*, his most popular film in the USSR and, of those we know, the least personal. The artificial style of its décor recalls the most Expressionist aspects of American wartime cinema, as does the nightmare atmosphere of the ruins where the hero stages the fake execution of a traitor, then later really executes him. The film, however, is not set in some distant country, but in Kiev, where it was actually shot and which is seen only in two short sequences shot outside the studio amid the ruins. One might detect here the kind of theatricality that Noel Burch felt in certain sequences of *By the Bluest of Seas* (and which is probably also present in *Once at Night* [Odnazhdy noch'yu, 1948], which I have not seen). On the other hand, a more likely influence can be traced in the many Anglo-American films available during the war.[14] What Barnet took from these would have fed his desire to construct each film according to a closed, coherent system.

Barnet's characteristic shot structure [*découpage*] and his organisation of space are evident here: there is symmetry rather than directional or temporal continuity, and careful attention to the subdivision of space. In one scene, the hero passes in front of a hairdressing salon in which we see a manicurist; then the same décor appears from the inside, looking through the window, anticipating a meeting which is to take place there. The reception at the Pommers' is set in an elongated room with the Nazi son in the distance, while the camera follows and 'punctuates' on a secondary character, Frau Pommer; and the false Eckert (the secret agent, or 'scout' of the title) occupies a double office where he can in turn observe his employees and visitors, or shield himself behind a curtain. Other scenes take place in front of the cinema, with a path leading to the entrance, a grille on one side where the meeting takes place, a staircase in front of the entrance and the audience entering and leaving. Two car journeys by the resistance fighters are seen going from right to left, then from left to right, and so on. Symmetry, scenes repeated; the first and last kiss between the hero and his fiancée. Trick effects: a photograph of generals in the newspaper – one suddenly comes alive. Montage: as in the previous example, scenes which end with a cue leading directly into the next, or which begin with a close-up, so that the space is progressively discovered by changing the axis or by camera movement.

Such a formal system might explain indirectly the fame of this film, which conventional opinion has attributed to the authenticity of its portrayal of events or to the public's interest in the subject, whereas war themes had almost been abandoned by 1947. In these years of Hitchcockian influence – found in films all over the world, ranging from early Bergman to Shen Fu's *Cutting the Devil's Talons* [China, 1953] – Barnet was one of the few to use film narration itself as a source of emotion, following Hitchcock in treatment as well as imagery, and going against the then predominantly 'realistic' trend.

One should thus look forward, at least with curiosity, to the three films Barnet made during the 'very difficult' period of Stalin's last years. Although he disliked these, some Western spectators have praised them in whole or in part, and we do not have to share the director's own estimate.[15] In 1957, *The Poet* [Poet], filmed in Odessa, recaptured briefly the open-air freshness of *Miss Mend*, for example, in the panic-stricken evacuation of the city when the good citizens abruptly turn into a lynch mob chasing Bolsheviks. Written by a native of Odessa, Valentin Katayev (as had been Barnet's *Pages from a Life* [Stranitsy zhizni, 1948]), this film probably reflects as much the charming writer of *The Squaring of the Circle* [Tsvetik-semitsvetik, 1948] and *Lone White Sail* [Beleet parus odinokii, 1937] as it does Barnet, whose charms are usually more energetic.

The hero is a poet who joins the Revolution, while his best friend, also a poet, joins the Whites. In fact, the film's theme is the usefulness of artists in a revolution, no matter which school they belong to. When several painters working on propaganda pictures start to argue about the styles of Picasso, Matisse and Repin, an old revolutionary (played by a Barnet regular, Kryuchkov) steps in and brings everyone to agreement. Cubist or realist, he urges, the important thing is to give us great works (at a distance of twenty-five years, the scene is a rebuttal of a similar one in Chiaureli's *Out of Our Way* [Khabarda, 1931]). The rhetoric is typical of this period of the Twentieth Congress (also reflected in Donskoi's remake of *The Mother* [Mat', 1956], Alov and Naumov's *Pavel Korchagin* [1957], Raizman's *The Communist* [Kommunist, 1958]; and in the 'unchained camera' demonstrated by Sergei Urusevsky as cinematographer on such films as Chukhrai's *The Forty-First* [1956], Kalatozov's *The Cranes Are Flying* [Letyat zhuravli, 1957] and his later *I Am Cuba* [Ya Kuba, 1963]). Here, shots that last longer than usual and interrupted camera movements evidence a somewhat feeble attempt at lyricism. Barnet is more interested in staging relationships within the frame, and produces striking spatial effects: a courtyard in which the arms of the discontented bourgeoisie are requisitioned, the hovel where the poet lives, a couple of chase sequences. In the poets' soirée at the beginning of the film – where we first meet some of the characters who will appear later, as they perform before a mixed audience of smug bourgeois, vociferous members of the rabble and soldiers, and which a revolutionary patrol further disrupts – Barnet arranges yet another of his meetings of disparate elements from which fiction can develop in all its complexity. Later, the hero is rescued from a firing squad by the girls we saw in the poets' club, now camouflaged as a happy wedding party, playing music and singing before disarming the soldiers.

This is a picaresque view of the Revolution, enhanced by the careful use of colour (in this case, muted shades of blue, grey, pink, ochre) which also distinguishes *The Wrestler and the Clown* – Barnet's best-known film, justifiably, of this period (for which reason I will not discuss it here).[16] The challenge of taking over a film begun by another ultimately made *The Wrestler and the Clown* an almost perfect film. On the other hand, Barnet's most carefully prepared project, *Annushka* [1959], left him strangely cold. Perhaps because his films have less to do with families than with wanderings, and reflect little nostalgia for that type of community, melodrama – and *Annushka*, centring on motherhood and the desire for a home, is that – remains alien to Barnet's film-making.

Better to pass on, for *Alyonka* [Alenka, 1961] and *Whistle-Stop* [Polustanok, 1963], Barnet's two last films, once again display his stronger qualities. The credits of *Alyonka* appear over a long aerial shot of fields both green and gold, which closes in on a road busy with lorries carrying corn. Cut to a close-up of a child watching the lorries. Reverse angle: wide shot of the lorries. The child again. The same wide shot, in which she now comes closer to the unbroken stream of traffic, fascinated, then crosses the road and returns twice. Combine harvesters thunder by. She comes forward, in a lateral tracking shot, and in front of a shower of golden grain, announces: 'I am looking for Daddy.'

After such an opening, what follows could be something of an anticlimax. But we are not disappointed. The little girl sets off on a lorry heading for the Virgin Lands (this is 1955, at the beginning of the mass exodus to open up Kazakhstan). In the steppe, a man and his dog emerge from a cloud of dust. They join the other passengers (it is Vasili Shukshin) and, as they all travel east, each tells his story.[17] The little girl's flashback is done in the style of her telling, using animation and speeded-up action, with the voice of Alyonka alternately synching for that of the adults in her story, and annotating their replies with 'Daddy said' and the like.

The second story is told by the Shukshin character, and it almost seems as if Barnet is adopting the style of the future film-maker (already a published writer and well-known actor by then).[18] The tractor driver Stepan crosses the path of a girl on the escalator of the Moscow metro. He follows her and finds her crying. A few seconds later (in the film), they are kissing passionately . . . then living together. He blows up tyres in their bedroom, while she lies in bed. She reads Chekhov's *The Lady with a little Dog*, then appears with her little dog on the building site where he works. Hoping to sort things out, he buys two railway tickets for the Virgin Lands, where he redoubles his efforts: he improvises a mouse-trap and buys her a handsome picture. But she is unable to stand the boredom and runs off into the steppe. He finds her and throws the dog out. 'Culture, that's what matters!' is Stepan's inconclusive verdict, before the dog finally helps him find his straying wife. All the stories remain open like this: some find what they are looking for, while others don't. The film ends in a railway station, where Alyonka is eating ice-creams with a little Kazakh boy.

When *Alyonka* failed at the box office, which seems to have discouraged Barnet, Mosfilm 'assigned' him to *Whistle-Stop*, based on a scenario by one Radi Pogodin.[19] Close friends advised him not to accept the first job that came along. That he should have insisted on doing the film is a puzzle to Kushnirov, who notes that the film 'aroused no interest'.[20] One might conclude that those who could have appreciated it (including the biographer!) never had a chance to see it, thus keeping intact their image of Barnet as a great man who had none the less given up 'real' film-making.

Those who did see *Whistle-Stop* in London in 1980 took a very different view. I needed no less than seven shorthand notebook pages for a simple inventory, made during the screening, of the physical action and images that fill the screen for some sixty-five minutes of running time. From the amateur piano-playing which contrasts with the Mosfilm statue before the animated credits which falsely celebrate the joy of holidays, we are once again in a typically Barnetian structure, where every pan – and even some rather unhappy zooms – yields a surprise.[21] The cartoon gives way to live action: a man arrives in a village. He first meets a young girl who takes his luggage. A child on a motor cycle watches him. Pan to an old woman, and the kid matter-of-factly sums up the situation: 'Another painter has arrived.' Caught up in the calm rhythm of a village, with its fisherman and single shop, its drinkers and courting couples, the academician who came here on his doctor's advice finds little rest.

What plot there is is atomised, conveyed by single gestures and images. A girl in an office shouts into the telephone that the chairman is in the vicinity. Pan to a young girl who comes into the office with him. The chairman picks up the telephone and starts to shout. The youngster is being scolded. The chairman objects: 'I am trying to telephone.' The child denounces the boy who is courting the girl: 'He is going to see the milkmaids!' She is furious and, after everyone leaves, she kicks the door shut several times. On the third occasion, it hits the academician-Sunday painter, who enters clad in a paint-splashed shirt. Pan: he sits down facing her. The child timidly comes back in. The girl furiously wields a rubber stamp and makes to kick the door shut again, close to tears, while snapping, 'Don't smoke.' The academician leaves and the child brings back the telephone, whispering confidentially to her father, and obviously telling him the story of the kicked door. The kid and her father leave, while the girl stays behind, her hand resting on the papers which the wind is rustling.

Despite the number of doors opened and closed, Barnet remains far from

Lubitsch: his 'touch' consists precisely in defusing the gag before it becomes openly comic. The film's closing is an appropriately modest testament.

The academician receives a telephone call from the city. 'They have found me,' he says resignedly. Even as he prepares to leave, he goes on mending things that the villagers bring him, repeating, 'It's not my speciality.' He leaves his canvas and palette, and a message on the stove for the child who built it without knowing how to. First he writes an invitation, which he rubs out, then a farewell message: 'You will do more and better than me. We have given you all that we have been able to achieve. Don't let us down.' A long shot of the house ends the film.

This character is tired and still suffers from war wounds, but he cannot help tinkering with a sewing machine or a telephone receiver whenever he is asked to repair it. His tiredness is probably akin to that of Barnet himself, who must have known these emotions so well (cf. *The Poet*). There is hardly any bitterness in the portraits drawn by those who knew him late in life, especially fellow film-makers, all of whom would concur with Sadoul's tribute: 'overflowing with life and generosity'. Otar Ioseliani (not an arbitrary choice on my behalf to end this essay) recalled their meeting:

I knew him through his editor, who was also his girlfriend and in her twenties. She was a very lively girl, and I remember her saying: 'Watch what I'm going to do when Barnet comes.' She went up to him and ordered: 'About turn!' This immense figure turned round smartly and she jumped on to his back, calling 'Gee up!' That's how I met him.

He asked me: 'Who are you?' I said: 'A director' (this was when I was making *April* [Aprel', 1962]). 'Soviet,' he corrected, 'you must always say "Soviet director". It is a very special profession.' 'In what way?' I asked. 'Because if you ever manage to become honest, which would surprise me, you can remove the word "Soviet". Now I am a "Soviet director", although I only became one recently.'

Then we had a drink and he told me: 'Above all, don't watch my films twice.' 'Why?' I enquired. 'Because they are made for one viewing and afterwards, when you go for a walk and remember them, they become better. I am not', he told me, 'a chemist like Eisenstein, who poisons slowly.'

I fell in love with him the first time I saw *By the Bluest of Seas*. It was in the editing class given by Felonov, an excellent teacher, who told us: 'There is no logic to this film, none at all, and no measurement, but it is very well filmed.' (He was used to measuring everything and thought that all films were calculated.) 'It is very well made. I am not teaching you the craft in order to follow this example. I noticed how much you liked it' (I had badgered him to let me see it again on the editing table) 'so here it is, but don't take it as an example. Even though it is better made than, say, *Ivan the Terrible*.'

He was a poet at a time when cinema had thrown out all its simple, unmannered poets, in order to implant mannerism. Dovzhenko's poetry is really mannerism, with those apples around the old man dying. . . . Barnet's films like *The Girl with a Hatbox* and *Trubnaya* were very much influenced by their epoch. They were light-hearted and very funny. They were ironic and even carried their propaganda well: 'Things are bad,' they said, 'but they will improve and this will only be temporary.'

Ideologically, he belonged to that company of film-makers, but morally he didn't take part in their games. Why do I say that? Because a director who had gone through it all and been broken by the demands of the time, who had started to make films about the kolkhozes, said of him that he was an enemy. Just like that. Indeed he was distrusted by all his colleagues, for what he had done? What did *By the Bluest of Seas* amount to? In our epoch of construction, with all its serious and weighty problems, what's all this about a wave which sweeps a woman into the cabin of a boat? This really has nothing to do with reality!

I have the impression that professionals, the same ordinary technicians who still work at Mosfilm who had contact with him, adored him as a person. This was in contrast to those directors who exemplified what a film-maker should be. Happy, straightforward, generous, a drinker and a child, all at once. He had no anxiety about being humiliated; he could say, 'I don't know how that's done.'

This is a craft which should be plied happily if at all possible. But you never get good results if, as in France, you try to please the producer. Barnet made a charming, silly film, *Lyana*. He was dead-drunk and surrounded by gypsies singing and dancing through the shoot. He had a wonderful time. Rather than conform, if one has to film something stupid, better not to take part in the shooting. Just opt out.[22]

# 9 Interview with Alexander Medvedkin

*Question*:   How did you start work in cinema and why?

*Medvedkin*:[1]   The story of my start in cinema is somewhat unusual. The positions that I stand for in cinema are upsetting. They differ from those of my colleagues. I'll tell you in my own words the essence of my position in cinema.

I've worked in cinema for nearly sixty years and my positions haven't changed. I've paid very dearly for this, because I've had to overcome enormous obstacles and a great deal of misunderstanding, great resistance, and so perhaps the most valuable thing that you will get from me is the knowledge of what I wanted in cinema. What I wanted, and what I still want, from cinema is that it should be a weapon of attack, an offensive weapon in the battle against evil, wherever it originates and however limited our resources for that battle are.

I'll try and give you a few examples of the limitations and the difficulties that I've encountered in my life. Before I became involved in cinema I played an active part in the Civil War. There was something called Budyonny's cavalry. I was a trooper, a combat commander in battle and a teacher, a political worker, once the war was over. People forget nowadays that around 1921–2 things were quite different from the way they are now. The country was in ruins, people were exhausted and the male population had been decimated in the Civil War. There was no bread, industry had been laid waste, the transport system wasn't functioning. On top of that, because of the First World War, a generation of illiterates had grown up. Russia has always been known for the great tragedy of its peasantry. As a peasant country it has always been illiterate. We had recruits who were illiterate and we taught them to read. We made them into human beings. Roughly 70 per cent of our recruits were illiterate. I'm proud of the fact that I played a part in the process of educating this problem generation, so that by the time of the Great Patriotic War [1941–5] the illiterate soldiers who had come to us in complete ignorance had become the backbone of the command. They were in charge of battalions, tanks, brigades. A very large number rose to the rank of colonel, commanding regiments. Many of them had previously passed through our hands . . . and now I'm getting round to why I started in cinema.

I had my own methods of educating these people. I thought that for a teacher words were very costly. So I declared war immediately on verbosity, repetition and everything that was wasteful. I felt that using words to educate someone like this was very expensive. I felt that there must be a better way to turn a simple illiterate man into a great soldier.

I had my own theatre. I used grotesques, clowning, burlesque. I did all this off my own bat, with no theatre training or experience. But I put this little theatre to work straight away to educate these young people. It was quite unique. We used comedy, circus, *lubok*, farce. The theatre dealt with all the most important questions. I didn't consult the commanders and I had some big battles with them because they had no faith in my methods. But I did all sorts of things that later helped me find my way in cinema. There was one key example, one key production.

In a very remote Cossack village a long way from the nearest railway we put up a notice announcing, 'Today the General Assembly of Horses opens in the club.' We were really treating the theme of horses in the army for the first time and yet, in the cavalry, the horse is half your strength. You start with your horse and the rider merely sits on it. A General Assembly of Horses. The horses had the floor for the very first time.

For this production I made the horses' heads and cloaks out of papier mâché, out of old newspapers – a cloak and a head was enough to make a horse. It wasn't just a comedy, though, and it wasn't just a play because, before I put it on, I gathered all sorts of evidence about the ways in which these young people maltreated their horses. They weren't familiar with horses, so we called the horses together. The curtain opened.

On the stage was the Presidium: they were all horses. There was a rostrum. On the rostrum, instead of a carafe of water, there was a bucket full of water and the horses were drinking from it. The speaker was a horse. What was he speaking about? I'd collected some funny satirical examples of the maltreatment of horses. Poor grooming, wrong feeding and watering, bad treatment – in other words, everything that went on in the squadrons and commands, complete with the names of the men who'd done the horses harm. All this was brought out in the play and the whole regiment had a good laugh.

In the audience there were some 'plants', as we say – in other words, trained actors who would say, 'What?' So then the horse-speaker would begin: 'There's that blacksmith Ivanov who killed a horse, wounded the horse while he was shoeing it. He got angry and hit it with a rasp, and he wasn't even put in detention.' Then our actor in the audience shouted out, 'He's sitting here in the audience.' 'Where? . . . Stand up!' So he stood up: 'I won't do it again. That's the last time.' People laughed so much.

Another horse went to the rostrum. His head was tied up as though he had toothache and he complained that his rider had left him out in the cold wind.

The rider had gone to see his girlfriend and had left his horse outside in the cold wind all night while he made love. 'No,' the commander shouted, 'I didn't.' So it was a very jolly, very impassioned and a very effective method of satire. It worked like a good whip, lashing whatever harm was done to horses, making it unthinkable. They were all afraid that they'd be a target so they had to kiss their horses' heads – or else they'd be exposed on stage. That's how it all began, that's an example.

Often there were no examples to follow, but that was one. We had all sorts of interesting scenes, like a *lubok*. The Russian *lubok* was a kind of painting on a panel, like a cartoon in a newspaper. They pasted up the newspapers, made a panel, and painted a man's face on it. That was a *lubok*. It had a special text and every two or three days we had a very funny special show that served as an experimental laboratory for me, where I learned to master comedy. That was more or less the inspiration that determined my work in cinema. It had enormous consequences too for the rest of the division and ultimately the whole army.

The experiment was written up in the newspapers. I suddenly rose through the ranks, moving higher and higher, and in the end, two years later, I was summoned to Moscow and that's where I came into contact with the cinema organisation Gosvoyenkino, the military studio for military films. I had such a wealth of experience in comedy, in what made people laugh, that it was easy for me to start with comedy. So I started working on comedy films. In 1931 I released five experimental comedies that were just as trenchant as that whip of a play. They were comedies that provoked anger, laughter and anger. . . . They really got up your nose! There was protest and everything else in them. They weren't comedies just to make people laugh. The times were so very difficult: our first Five Year Plan had only just begun.

There are not many of us left who lived through that first Five Year Plan. But it marked a break, a turning-point, a kind of cataclysm when everything was re-examined, everything was rejected, while here and there new shoots appeared unexpectedly. They were still tender, still unsure of themselves, but they did appear. Yet in cinemas you'd still hear the pianist accompanying pictures with titles like *Sadness*, *Be Silent*, *Fireside Blues*, *I Love You* and suchlike.

As a warrior, a soldier in a victorious army and a political activist who was used to dealing with the education of Red Army soldiers, I entered cinema in order to attack this kind of film, to defeat it and to arm cinema with the new, rich political genre of satire. That was my starting-point and I must say that at first not everything worked out, but that's only natural. The tasks that I set myself could scarcely be realised at that time: there was no experience of this kind of film satire either in the Soviet Union or abroad.

So that you will understand what I did, let me explain that I decided to make one-reelers, films with a maximum length of eight or ten minutes. This was forced on me by the fact that you needed a year to make a full-length film on a large-scale theme and I wanted to release one or two films a month.

What were these films about? Their themes were prompted by conditions in the country. It was very difficult for us to embark on the construction of socialism because we had no skilled personnel. There were a large number of foreigners who were more interested in hindering us than in helping. We had no experience of construction and our building materials were not always of good quality. We'd lost our specialists during the Civil War and hadn't yet managed to train new ones.

I'll tell you the plots of two of my films, so that you'll understand what I was doing. Some bricklayers are putting up a new building. They've already put seven floors up and they're putting the eighth up there on top somewhere. A shoe factory has already moved in downstairs. All this is done in a grotesque circus-like manner. A fantastic machine churns out shoes, but the shoes are useless because you can't put them on. Suddenly there's an enormous crack like lightning through all seven floors. All seven have split open. The shoemaker runs out and shouts, 'Hey, what are you up to?' They reply, 'We've got no time. We're shock-workers.' He protests, 'You mustn't do that!' They go on building, but the edifice has been destroyed. Suddenly from somewhere up above an enormous brick sails down until it hits the shoemaker on the head and crumbles to dust. It's a bad brick. The shoemaker picks up a piece of the brick, rubs it between his fingers and, looking the audience in the eye, says, 'Is this really a brick?'

And the second plot: a crowd of people with clubs, sticks and stones are running along a street: 'Stop him!' Stop him!' The intertitle: 'Stop him, he built the house.' It's the same bricklayer.

These were very topical subjects. They couldn't have been more topical. They were received by audiences with great enthusiasm because our first new buildings, and the whole conditions for construction, were not ideal. We didn't know how to build: we had neither the experience, nor the skilled men, nor the materials. The people were well aware of this. But there were still a lot of enemies in our country. There were remnants of the White Guards, small groups of kulaks and our rabid enemies who used, or could have used, these films to discredit us by saying, 'What kind of builders are they? They can't build socialism. They can't even build a simple house, let alone socialism!'

This serious situation provoked a very pointed and wide-ranging discussion in our cinema organisation, which was called the Association of Revolutionary Cinematography, or ARK.[2] We had some very heated discussions there and in the course of them some quite improbable arguments were put forward against my films. People said that the proletariat could do without satire and that it had no need of humour, which was a phenomenon of bourgeois culture. Things were not very pleasant for me at that time because the question arose of stopping my experiments. When things were already bad, and I was no longer allowed to work, Anatoli Vasilevich Lunacharsky got to know about my difficulties.[3] He viewed my films and realised that this was an exceptionally valuable experiment that must be allowed to continue at all costs, but at the same time he criticised me very severely for the carelessness of my aim. He said, 'You knock your own side and others. But you shouldn't knock your own people. You have to knock the others without touching your own people.' But how could I knock the others without touching my own side? If I took such sharp and severe criticism seriously, if I got hold of an idiot, dragged him to the screen and said, 'This is an idiot,' the enemy would still see it [and be able to make capital out of it]. Or perhaps I shouldn't concern myself with these idiots at all? Nevertheless, he said, 'This is a very valuable and necessary lesson. Cinema must employ satire and for this reason we must give Medvedkin every assistance.' So I made five comedies like that, taking no notice of what my colleagues were doing. When these comedies were released, there was an enormous scandal.

People began to criticise me. They tried to drive me out of cinema but Lunacharsky spoke up for me. He took me under his wing and then I made a special pronouncement that cinema is a weapon. Satire is an offensive weapon, not just something that satisfies the aesthetic requirements and interests of the audience, but a weapon that attacks shortcomings, that lashes like a whip, that lashes everything that interferes with life. So you can see that I advocated using cinema in a way that nobody else used it. I think that cinema can be a very real weapon in the battle for construction, in the battle against our enemies, against the people who get in our way.

It was in this light that I decided that I could make films on the film train. I decided to build up a team from scratch, equip three railway carriages and travel on wheels whenever there was something wrong. This was a kind of special fire brigade to put out problem fires. Wherever there was something amiss, like the plan not being fulfilled, wherever there was bad management, there our train went, gathered information and filmed.[4] So much has been written about the train since then but it has all missed the point. It was a kind of public prosecutor's cinema.

Basically we made newsreels from documentary materials. These were unusual films and the shows were quite extraordinary. We rejected the idea of shooting a newsreel and screening it as information with musical accompaniment: something that would have first a fire, then someone killed, next a flood, then someone who'd hanged himself, and so on. We weren't interested in that sort of thing. Nor did we require music, which would have been out of place because this cinema was not there to give the audience aesthetic pleasure. We used the technique and genre of newsreel as the occasion to raise the great issue of construction on the screen in a very relevant manner and in various genres.

It was rather like the prosecutor's speech in a courtroom: it showed what was wrong on screen. It painted a nasty picture, some problem that had not been put right, and this was always accompanied by the title, 'What are *you* doing, dear comrades, what are *you* doing?' This was followed by a fearless presentation of the problems: a 'document', a 'film document', a newsreel. It was like a word spoken in the midst of utter silence and the film ended with a contrast with model examples. Somewhere we'd found a good mine, a good kolkhoz, a good factory and we said, 'Look at them!' Our subjects, the people we were castigating, always made the excuse that this or that was missing, that there was no bread, that there were no people. Nothing, nothing, nothing! So we told them to look at other places. After that there was a sort of production conference where they all put their cards on the table, examined what was wrong and passed a resolution. We didn't leave until, with the aid of our films, the tide had turned and everything that was wrong had been eliminated.

That's how I accumulated my experience of satire: comedy, satire, farce, cabaret, burlesque – everything the screen can use to open the audience's eyes, to surprise them. I've used it all without worrying about appearances. It did a great deal to define my later paths. The film train made seventy-two films in one year: they were shown straight away and were effective. . . . That means around 25,000 metres of film. Seventy-two films. Usually one-reelers, because they weren't just shown but also discussed and resolutions were passed. They were all silent films. In 1932 sound film was only just getting off the ground.

That's the story of the film train. It was the second stage of my work but even on the film train I was busy with satirical comedies. Our train was conceived on a grand scale: we had the capacity to process ourselves 2,000 metres of film every day on the train, whether it was stationary or in motion. We worked round the clock. There were eight cameramen: they did all the shooting for these films. I put them together, approved the script. I was in charge: I was the scriptwriter and the chief director and I had four or five directors under me. There we were all crowded together, terribly crowded, a group of enthusiasts and romantics. If someone came to us who was idle, who didn't like getting up in the middle of the night, he didn't last long. We'd warn him once, twice at most, and then quietly, all smiles and without scolding him, we'd buy him a ticket back to Moscow. We'd shake him by the hand and take him to the station. The others – we had a complement of thirty-two – worked an eighteen-hour day. My job was not to drive them on but to pull them off their jobs when they needed sleep, when they were falling asleep while working in the laboratory or shooting the titles. That was how we worked in those days.

Our eleventh Five Year Plan is now coming to an end. Then it was the *first* Five Year Plan, when the country was living in great poverty, very frugally. There were enormous deprivations, great difficulties. As yet there were no trained cadres, no machinery. One statistic will show you how difficult it was. In Moscow our leaders were struggling to make sure that we produced 9 million tonnes of steel. Now we produce something like 200 million tonnes. 200 million now and 9 million then. The legacy of old Russia was so rotten and stultifying. The country was illiterate, starving, unshod, unclothed . . . torn in half. It was difficult to manage, to move forward. In the course of these eleven Five Year Plans we have created an entirely different world. Just look at the people then. Take just one village, see how it was in 1927. Now everything is quite different: everything has changed and in my view this great work has been worthwhile.

*Question*:   You worked with Nikolai Okhlopkov?[5]

*Answer:*   I joined Gosvoyenkino at the same time as Okhlopkov and began my creative career in cinema as his assistant director. The two of us made a short military training film called *The Searchlight* [Prozhektor, n.d.] and then we made a more interesting film called *The Way of the Enthusiasts* [Put' entuziastov, 1930]. This film was experimental. Without thinking, we experimented and our experiments went beyond the confines of cinema. We sanctioned a whole series of incorrect and questionable political truths. The film was philosophically so confused that it was not released. We'd put our souls into it. There were a large number of creative innovations in it. Both Okhlopkov and I realised that it wasn't really suitable for release. But the great value of the film lay in the fact that we had made it completely by ourselves, discovering for ourselves as a group the most critical and unexpected situations and the most unexpected forms.

Okhlopkov was an unusually interesting actor. He left Meyerhold's theatre but took with him Meyerhold's passion for turning theatrical stereotypes and clichés on their heads. Okhlopkov took Meyerhold's campaign against the old traditional theatre and translated it to cinema.

*Question*:   How did you come to make *Happiness* [Schast'e, 1935]?

*Answer:*   Fiction film had always attracted me. I had a longing for art but this was all black bread, a job for an unskilled worker.[6] It was a reaction not to my own inner spiritual requirements, but to the need to help at a most difficult moment, to use the film camera as a weapon, as a machine gun, an offensive weapon, a weapon of mobilisation. This was, of course, a long way removed from art.

Then I made *Happiness*: it was my greatest achievement. I'd like to tell you something that seems to have escaped the attention of the critics and journalists who've written about the film. I've never managed to ensure that people understood the real meaning of this film, which is as follows. When the first kolkhozes appeared around 1929–30 the country was still impoverished; we hadn't cleared up the devastation and we had a very poor inheritance. The railways had no engines, no wagons. The factories had no machinery, and so on. Things were generally hard. It is through heroic effort that we've completely transformed the country in the past fifty or sixty years.

In the history of our country there is one very significant page. That was when the peasants, exhausted by the war and deprived of the most elementary comforts and material conditions, took the road to socialism. But we couldn't give them what they wanted overnight. Lenin said that we must emerge from misery and poverty by small steps. But the peasant himself – and this is not just true of our country, it's part of the social psychology of mankind in all civilised nations – dreams of ownership. He wants a prosperous life, to set himself apart from his thousands and millions of neighbours; he wants to creep ahead and have his own barn, his own horses, his own grain. In short, he wants to be his own boss.

Of course, for every 1,000, only one will manage it: the other 999 will remain farm-hands and starve, but this dream lives on among the peasants. Just imagine what happened when the vast millions of the peasant mass said yes and rejected the kulak path, and we created a collective economy together! But the peasant joined the kolkhoz dreaming of owning his own barn and his own horse. It was hard for him to cast all that aside: it was very deeply ingrained. Working on the film train, we travelled to different areas, to the Ukraine, to Siberia, along the Kuban River, and everywhere we came across the same thing: people who had joined the kolkhoz thinking they'd get everything they wanted straight away. They didn't. But, you know, it's a very difficult step to give up your horse, to blot out your dream and become

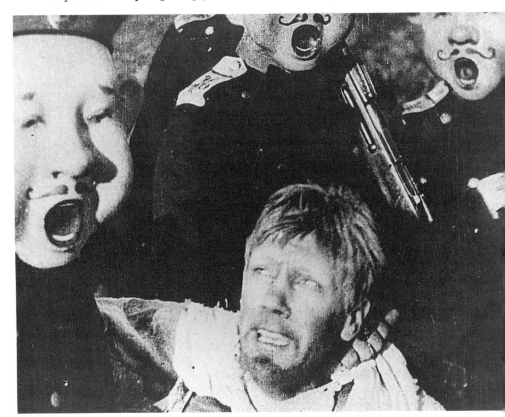

*Figure 20* Medvedkin's *Happiness* [1935], influenced by Lloyd, Keaton and Chaplin.

involved in a completely different way of life when you don't know what's going to happen. So a peasant like Khmyr lived with the dream of his own horse, his own barn, his own grain, his own fence, because his next-door neighbour was eating fruit dumplings while he just licked his lips in anticipation.[7]

So *Happiness* is a satirical picture. I made it as the nail in the coffin of this rosy dream. I ridiculed that dream because it's unrealistic: 999 people out of 1,000 get nothing from a dream like that. One person gets everything and then he crows about it and tramples the others underfoot. That's how *Happiness* was conceived and I think that's how it worked on the peasant audience, by telling them they had a choice. It was inspired by observations of real life and I did not skimp on tricks, hyperbole, farce, burlesque and all the other methods to make sure that it was very funny and at the same time very effective. It meant an end to all the Khmyrs – and Russia was full of them.

That's how it came about and it's still going strong today. It's fifty years since I wrote *Happiness* and it's still in distribution. I've just had a postcard from Paris to say they've extended the distribution contract with our Sovexportfilm for another five or ten years. According to our representatives, it's been shown in a programme with Chaplin's *Modern Times* [USA, 1936]. For me, of course, it's a really marvellous and great reward to be seen alongside Chaplin, to be compared to him. A difficult film has stood the test of time. It is a difficult film in the sense that it was difficult to put two epochs together. It was unconvincing. . . . No, it *was* convincing throughout, both at the beginning when Khmyr was trying to be a kulak and later on when his wife turned him into a real man.

*Question*:   May I ask which Chaplin and Keaton films you had seen then?

*Answer:*   I got to know Chaplin a bit later. It was after Okhlopkov and I had gone our separate ways that I saw Chaplin's *The Kid* [USA, 1921], *The Pilgrim* [USA, 1923], and a few of his early comedies. I've forgotten their names now.

I think that I'd already seen *The Gold Rush* [USA, 1925] by then. When I saw it on the screen I realised straightaway that it's difficult to make a comedy and it's something you have to learn. It's true that I'd gained considerable comic experience in theatre. That's why I was now writing things like the conference of horses or things for other variety acts that we put on in the evenings and that made people laugh a lot. If people laughed, that meant it was good. If they didn't laugh, you had to rework it. This theatre of mine served as a good creative laboratory so that, when I started making films, I knew the secrets of making people laugh. After I'd seen Chaplin and Harold Lloyd I saw Buster Keaton's *The Three Ages* and *Our Hospitality* [both USA, 1923], both of which I liked a great deal.

But it was Harold Lloyd who interested me more than anyone else. This may be because the first American comedy that I ever saw was *Grandma's*

*Boy* [USA, 1922]. I watched it and realised straightaway that directing comedy films was very difficult. Then I decided to learn, to teach myself. I watched this Harold Lloyd picture, went home and spent four days writing out the script because I could remember every shot, what happened where, which stunts were used. Then I began to analyse which gags had provoked the greatest laughter, which had passed without provoking a reaction, what had struck me most forcefully and what had left me unmoved, what hadn't aroused my emotions. As I recall, I worked like this for four days. I'd written out the script, recorded everything. I'd remembered it so clearly.

Then I went and watched the film again. This second viewing revealed the film's secret. I began to realise why particular gags were used. The film is full of gags. Of all American comedies (at least for me, but there's a lot I haven't seen) this Harold Lloyd comedy seemed the richest in its gags. One comic sequence ends and straight away, without a break, you start to laugh at another gag. It went from laugh to laugh without long motivating links, whereas in comedy nowadays people stop laughing. Now the director and the scriptwriter spend such a long time preparing each gag that the audience cools down in between them and has to be warmed up again like a samovar.

It was not so much from Lloyd's films as from Chaplin's that I understood the principle of progression from one laugh to another. It's the basic principle in Chaplin's work, beginning, perhaps, with his very first feeble and immature works. A pie is thrown into someone's face and they laugh. Chaplin doesn't let the audience cool down: he disturbs their equanimity. The audience is wound up because it knows that now it will be kicked, the door will open, the wife will burst in, and so on. Laughter, laughter, laughter. A cascade of laughter, of comic turns, clowning that's close to the circus. This is the great art of Chaplin. I very much regret that he abandoned this kind of comedy and went in for more-or-less serious things like *Monsieur Verdoux* [USA, 1947], *The Countess from Hong Kong* [Great Britain, 1966] and *A King in New York* [Great Britain, 1957].

That's not Chaplin. It was Charlie who gave pleasure to millions of people in every language, on every continent: it was Charlie the king, Charlie the clown, Charlie the unhappy and downtrodden little man who had such a heart, who aroused such enormous sympathy, who enriched people of the most varied nationality and skin colour. It was from Chaplin, from his early works, rather than from Harold Lloyd that I learned how much more it was possible to do: today a pie in the face, tomorrow a cake in the eye – and [it was from Chaplin that] I realised how limited this all was.

I did not know that cinema would develop to such an extent that it would be possible to get away from all this. But I did understand the mechanics of laughter, its technique, so to say, and in my subsequent work I tried to do things so that the laughter was already there and didn't result from a door bursting open or someone being kicked. Because behind this laughter there is often a very important idea. That's why we need laughter in film, that's why we must strive for it.

Eisenstein wrote a very good review of my film *Happiness* in which he compared me to Chaplin.[8] It is worth thinking about because, from an analytical point of view, Eisenstein understood *Happiness* better than I do.

*Question*:   And what did you do after *Happiness*?

*Answer:*   After the success of *Happiness* – and it was very successful: it was well received by everyone from unsophisticated audiences to the intelligentsia – what was I to do? I was interested in developing the theme of the first three reels of *Happiness*: they show Khmyr's life – his misery, his dreams, his unhappy fate, the lack of any prospects in life. I felt limited by length and structure in my depiction of two epochs. You could cram two epochs into a single film in one of those eighteen-part TV serials they make nowadays, but in those days you had to be extremely concise. So after *Happiness* I still had so many ideas and images that I hadn't managed to use in the limited space available. I realised that it would be very valuable to make a film, not about an individual like Khmyr but about the fate of the nation, of the peasantry as a whole. I thought it would be a good idea to make an epic film about the fate of the peasantry, which had been very downtrodden in the old pre-Revolutionary Russia. People were traded like cattle. The landowners and the exploiters were barbaric. The people paid for it: all progress, every step forward has been paid for in their blood. This tragedy seemed insurmountable. So I decided to show that there was no place in Russia for the muzhik, for the peasantry, on the land. It was a satirical paradox: how could there be no place for the lord of the land? But it turned out that there wasn't, and that's how I developed the structure of a new comedy, a new philosophical comedy that I called *The Damned Force* [Okoyannaya sila]. The damned force was the peasantry, a gigantic force . . .

*Question*:   Why didn't you make the film?

*Answer:*   Well, they were difficult times. I didn't persevere very hard. Other more contemporary themes distracted me. I made a comedy about contemporary life: partly to test myself, partly to scotch the rumours that I could portray the old Russia but not the present day. This was *The Miracle Worker* [Chudesnitsa, 1937], a good film, but it wasn't *Happiness*, of course. It was weaker, but it had a very great success and they still have it in Gosfilmofond. Jay Leyda liked *The Miracle Worker* better than *Happiness*.

When I made *The Miracle Worker*, I realised that all these films, the usual sort depicting love, the good life and good positive people, were not for me. I think that a comedy that has some greater philosophical meaning will succeed, but the kind where Vanya loves Tanya or Tanya loves Petya and so there's a triangle – I leave that kind of work to others. I do not believe that it is true to life. That is not my way.

# 10  Making sense of early Soviet sound

*Ian Christie*

It is one of the movies' little ironies that the most important development in film-making – the revolutionary work of the Soviet cinema – should have taken place at the precise moment when the coming of sound made it temporarily invalid; that the one theory which might have saved the silent cinema from destruction arrived just as the silent cinema had drawn its last breath.

C. A. Lejeune[1]

The world-wide impact of early Soviet cinema from 1926 to 1930 was so great that it opened, quite literally, a new chapter in world cinema history, but a chapter that demanded to be written quite differently from all others. The first films of Eisenstein, Pudovkin and Kuleshov to be seen abroad claimed – and won – recognition on the grounds of their essential *difference* from all other films, whether the difference was perceived in stylistic, political, or psychological terms. But, despite this universal acclaim, the reputation of Soviet cinema was soon to prove vulnerable. One theme which emerged in the early 1930s was a reaction against the extreme enthusiasm of the early period of 'discovery', no doubt linked with the political disillusionment of the period. A typical response was that of Grierson, who had been closely involved in launching *Potemkin* in New York in 1926 and urging Soviet techniques as models for the emergent documentary movement in Britain, yet who, by 1935, found it 'remarkable how, after the first flush of exciting cinema, the Russian talent faded'.[2] As the Griersonian 'theory of decline' took hold abroad, a second threat became evident at home: the heroic achievements of the montage period petrified into a conventional monument to the theory and experiment of the early 'pioneers'.

Subsequent developments in both Soviet and non-Soviet cinema historiography have tended to confirm this latter tendency. Bazin's opposition between 'image' and 'reality' in silent cinema has exercised a persuasive influence on several generations, discrediting the 'manipulation' and 'trickery' of montage and Expressionist cinema, and thus further ensuring the relegation of montage to the museum.[3] Soviet cinema historians, on the other hand, have tried to reconcile the evident contradiction between 1920s montage cinema and the approved models of 1930s 'realism', tacitly acknowledging the world-wide reputation of the former at the expense of the latter. Even recent 'revisionist' work – whether supporting Vertov's ultra-radical montage position, or challenging the 'tyranny' of montage – has tended to accept as given the heroic mythology of montage and to ignore the challenge, or the 'catastrophe',[4] of the coming of sound.

Looking at the frozen legacy of early Soviet cinema, inscribed alike in conventional and radical histories, the absence of any sustained treatment of the long transition to sound is striking. It is as if the brute industrial fact of sound, with its attendant aesthetic and ideological implications, constitutes too great a *disturbance* for narrative history, or indeed montage theory. Yet the introduction of sound coincides with, and helps to define, the turning-point in Soviet cinema. It is an example *par excellence* of the generally ignored intersection between the specificity of cinema and the histories – economic, technological, political, ideological – that determine and are determined by it.[5] Soviet sound cinema is effectively a 'new apparatus' by the late 1930s and the investigation of its emergence as a domestic mass medium out of the pluralist 'international' cinema of the late 1920s increasingly seems a priority, in order to 'unblock' the wider study of Soviet cinema and indeed the history of world cinema.

## THE THREAT OF THE TALKIES

The introduction of sound to Soviet cinema had two distinctive, perhaps unique, features. First, because the rapid culmination of sound technology development in Europe and the United States coincided with the end of the New Economic Policy (NEP) and a new drive towards self-sufficiency in the USSR, there was a long phase of rumour and speculation – to which the celebrated 'Statement' by Eisenstein, Pudovkin and Alexandrov belongs – before indigenous sound production finally started in 1930. Second, even when production was under way, sound and silent cinema continued to coexist for nearly six years – a length of transition exceeded only in Japan.[6] Received opinion concludes that these delays were wholly beneficial, allowing Soviet directors to avoid the 'mistakes made elsewhere' and to tackle sound production with confidence.[7] But a closer reading of even the few documents available suggests other considerations. This extract from the memoirs of the veteran screenwriter Yevgeni Gabrilovich usefully summarises the concerns of the wider community of Soviet film-makers on the eve of sound and vividly evokes their response:

> What subjects there were to discuss in those far-off days! How should one depict the positive hero – simply positive, or with some human flaw? May the heroine of a film be pretty, or is that a concession to bourgeois taste? What is optimism and what pessimism? In what lies decadence and in what heroism? How to vanquish formalism? How should satire be made

an affirmation of life? How should one react to the evident lack of political culture of certain young masters of cinema who take themselves much too seriously? Does the worker class need fiction films or documentaries? With or without a story? With or without a personal drama? What best accentuates the heroism of the masses – everyday heroism or monumental romanticism?

But the essential question, which brought bitterness, passion, despair to these discussions, was the problem of sound films. Those who only know sound cinema cannot imagine the panic which struck writers, directors, actors, cameramen and editors the moment when, quite unexpectedly, the cinema screen gave forth sounds. Documents in the archives, the stenograms and articles of the period are only a pale and fleeting reflection of all the emotion, the worry, the panic. For it was all the poetry of film art, believed to be of its essence mute, that was in the balance and threatened with extinction.[8]

The industrial upheaval recalled here is already familiar from the American experience; and equally familiar is the apparently genuine *fear* that sound would in some way destroy the 'essence' of film art.

What was the reason for this evidently widespread fear? Most aesthetic discussions of sound in the 1930s come down to the unhelpful assertion that, since film is *essentially* visual and *therefore* silent, sound will inevitably distract from its artistry. But a more interesting perspective is outlined by Theodor Adorno and Hanns Eisler in their book on film music, where they trace the origin of accompanying music for films to a need to still the unconscious fear of silent moving images that disturbed early cinema audiences.[9] From this premiss they argue that music has an equally important function in sound cinema, since the 'immateriality' of quasi-realistic speech is equally disturbing in relation to the two-dimensional images. Thus, dialogue in the talkie is the direct successor to the silent cinema's intertitles and both of these instances of language offend against the basic 'discovery' of cinema, which is the representation of movement. The fundamental divergence between speech and image is noted unconsciously by the spectator, hence the need for music in sound films to 'set in motion' and 'justify' the essential dimension of movement, which speech would otherwise inhibit, and to preserve the 'fragile' representation of the external world offered by the sound film.[10] Adorno and Eisler's theory suggests a possible explanation for the deep-seated fear of sound that went beyond immediate industrial consequences: it identifies the threat of de-stabilisation of the institution which had grown up during the silent period, in which the mere presence of music played a crucial *binding* (rather than expressive) role.

But there was another consideration that may have seemed more pressing to the Soviet montage school. The late 1920s had seen a remarkable convergence of theoretical and practical work around the concept of montage, which went beyond such film-maker theorists as Eisenstein, Pudovkin and Kuleshov (each with his own version of montage) to include writers, literary theorists, visual artists, theatre workers and others.[11] Montage had become a key concept in many fields after its initial development as a theory of the specificity of film: and with it was linked another key concept, that of 'inner speech'. The origins of this notion may have been in Stanislavsky's interest in 'inner monologue' or in Piaget's study of language acquisition,[12] but by the mid-1920s it had become a central feature of 'Formalist' critical theory and played an important part in Eikhenbaum's seminal essay on the poetics of cinema, 'Problems of Film Stylistics'.[13] For Eikhenbaum, montage is the rationalisation of the basic laws of film construction, controlling the viewers' 'sense of time'; and montage relies upon – and to some extent produces – a constant subjective 'accompaniment' to the experience of film viewing:

> For the study of the laws of film (especially of montage) it is most important to admit that perception and understanding of a motion picture are inextricably bound up with the development of internal speech, which makes the connection between separate shots. Outside this process only the 'trans-sense' elements of film can be perceived.[14]

If 'inner speech' provides the guarantee of film intelligibility, it is also the basis on which filmic metaphor and other rhetorical structures depend. According to Eikhenbaum. 'film metaphor is entirely dependent on verbal metaphor'.[15] Clearly such speculation was of prime importance to Eisenstein in the development of his conception of 'intellectual cinema' and many of the montage 'tropes' of *October* [Oktyabr', 1927] and *The General Line* [General'naya liniya, 1929] can only be interpreted according to the 'inner speech' hypothesis. By 1932, he was reminded of

> The 'last word' on montage form in general that I foresaw theoretically long ago, of the fact that montage form as structure is a reconstruction of the laws of the thought process.[16]

Leaving aside Eisenstein's hopes for sound as a 'new montage element', if the whole edifice of montage was believed to rely upon the institutionalised activation of inner speech, then the 'outer speech' of the talkie posed obvious danger. Not in terms of a 'visual' art threatened by language, but of the plasticity and allusiveness of inner speech suppressed by the standardisation of everyday audible speech. What Eikhenbaum had termed 'the intimate process of forming internal speech',[17] interrupted hitherto only by the demands of reading intertitles, was to be replaced by a pre-formed, externalised address *from* the screen which would make the spectator little more than a passive eavesdropper. What was at stake in the sound revolution, for the montage school, was nothing less than the underlying principle of montage itself, the poetic interplay of inner speech and montage figures, the participation of the spectator as actor.

## CRISIS AND COUNTERPOINT: ANTICIPATING SOUND

The 'Statement on Sound', signed by Eisenstein, Pudovkin and Alexandrov,[18] needs to be read against the background of anxious speculation that preceded actual experience of sound in the Soviet Union, if only because it is a deeply ambivalent text. Although generally regarded as a cautious acceptance of sound, it can equally be read as an ingenious rejection of the basic *un*acceptable discovery of the talkie, synchronised speech – which, it should be remembered, was not Hollywood's original aim in developing sound reproduction. More precisely, the overall strategy of the 'Statement' is to mount a tactical defence of montage by conceding certain criticisms, while seeking to relocate the inner speech/montage relationship within the new ensemble of sound cinema.

The 'Statement' claims that montage is 'the indisputable axiom upon which world cinema culture rests'. From this point of view:

> Sound is a double-edged invention and its most probable application will be along the line of least resistance, i.e. in the field of the *satisfaction of simple curiosity.*[19]

As a result of such innocent demonstrations of the ' "illusion" of people talking, objects making a noise, etc.' there is the likelihood of an institutionalised theatrical phase, characterised by 'dramas of high culture'. At first sight, this prediction seems close to what actually happened as Hollywood turned to Broadway for its actors and ready-made scripts, but in fact it had a particular and rather different meaning in the Soviet context. Ever since the pre-Revolutionary period there had been an intense struggle between partisans of theatre and cinema over the autonomy and specificity of the latter.[20] After the Revolution the debate continued and became even more complex, with Meyerhold, who had proclaimed the 'cinefication of the theatre', and former theatre experimentalists such as Eisenstein and the FEKS group, ranged against the Moscow Art Theatre and supporters of non-montage and 'theatrical' cinema.[21] But the main thrust of the argument is that sound used naturalistically would, quite simply, 'destroy the culture of montage' by substituting a linear, narrative syntax for the dialectical and disjunctive syntax of montage.

Then the proposal:

> *Only the contrapuntal use* of sound vis-à-vis the visual fragment of montage will open up new possibilities for the development and perfection of montage.
>
> *The first experiments in sound must aim at a sharp discord with the visual images.* Only such a 'hammer and tongs' approach will produce the necessary sensation that will result consequently in the creation of a new *orchestral counterpoint* of visual and sound images.

How elementary work on disjunctive sound/image relationships might develop to the stage of 'orchestral counterpoint' is not explained and has received little attention until recently, doubtless because there was so little evidence of it in early Soviet sound cinema. However, Kristin Thompson has surveyed a group of early sound films for instances of counterpoint and, perhaps not surprisingly, found more traces than might have been expected from a reading of conventional histories.[22] The potential value of this survey is, however, somewhat limited by its narrow, Formalist terms of reference. Taking the proposal of the 'Statement' at face value, 'counterpoint' is projected into the sound period in a classic example of what Paul Willemen has termed the 'audio-visual phantasy', whereby 'all relations between the two blocks [sound and vision] become entirely external, formal, optional and ultimately dispensable'.[23] Thus Thompson does not attempt to correlate the political and wider cultural upheaval of the transition period with that in cinema, while unfortunately categorising such otherwise innovative films as *The Great Consoler* [Velikii uteshitel'] and *Three Songs of Lenin* [Tri pesni o Lenine, 1934] as 'close to Hollywood' or 'playing safe', because they do not rely on *ostentatiously* disjunctive sound-image relations. She finds Kozintsev and Trauberg's *Alone* [Odna, 1931] the most interesting specimen, though does not mention that it was in fact shot as a silent film and experimentally post-synchronised, no doubt under the influence of the 'Statement'.[24] Above all, the problem of *spoken language* – symptomatically treated in the 'Statement' as a limitation – is not directly addressed. Such limitations in what was none the less a pioneering study merely underline the problems that still persist in studies of Soviet cinema which venture outside the canonic periods and personnel.

Given the lack of any significant sequel to the 'Statement's' call for counterpoint, it seems possible that this was little more than a tentative, theoretical move in defence of montage – an estimate supported by Pudovkin's collaborator, Anatoli Golovnya, who attributed it to 'imperfect knowledge of sound films'. Golovnya's claim that, when Pudovkin 'had been able to digest the technique and prospects of sound, it was quite clear that the ideas expounded [in the 'Statement'] had no lasting significance for him', is less plausible.[25] This ignores Pudovkin's almost unique experiments in counterpoint and 'asynchrony', both in his delayed first sound film *The Deserter* [1933] and in its predecessor *A Simple Case* [Prostoi sluchai, 1932], originally planned as a sound film, although released silent, and still showing signs of his somewhat doctrinaire attempt to use sound, evoking 'definite and exact associations', as a basis for a non-diegetic 'visual impression'.[26] Eisenstein, on the other hand, appears to have moved on rapidly from the 'Statement' programme, with its avoidance of speech, to a characteristically ingenious (if implausible) position, influenced by his meeting with Joyce in Paris and based directly upon 'the syntax of inner speech as distinct from outer speech':

And how obvious it is that the raw material of sound film is not *dialogue*. The true material of sound film is, of course, monologue.[27]

The following section of the 'Statement' has received less attention, although it amounts to an admission that montage has reached an impasse. Sound used contrapuntally is seen as 'an organic escape for cinema's cultural avant-garde from a whole series of blind alleys which have appeared inescapable'. Two specific examples are given: the intractable problem of integrating intertitles into montage structures and the disruptive need for explanatory sequences, such as long shots,[28] in montage sequences consisting for the most part of rapidly edited close-ups. The latter problem was perhaps more Pudovkin's than Eisenstein's. Noël Burch has drawn attention to the ultimate paradox in Pudovkin's method of analysis into the simplest and most expressive montage elements, i.e. by close-ups:

> Wishing to carry to its extreme consequences the logic of linearisation through editing, Pudovkin comes up against the same obstacle encountered by the pioneers when they were casting about for methods capable of overcoming the unfortunate 'dissociative' effect which the first interpolated close-ups had upon the unity of films that still depended almost exclusively on the lay-out of the primitive tableau. In both cases this disintegration, as it were, was the price that had to be paid for an increase in 'expressiveness'. . . . Striving to remain within the bounds of fundamental linearity and to strengthen that linearity, Pudovkin fails to see that the enunciation characteristic of the system is not simply a succession of signs, as decomposed as possible, but that it is founded on a dialectic between such 'stripped down' images and a more complex spatiality offering complementary guarantees.[29]

Burch's general argument is that early Soviet cinema owed its pluralism and originality to the 'unfinished' representational system which it inherited. The 'Statement' suggests that this phase had run its course, at least for the director who had just finished *October* and returned to work on *The General Line*:

> Every day the problems of theme and plot grow more complex; attempts to solve them by methods of purely 'visual' montage either lead to insoluble problems or involve the director in the field of fantastic montage constructions, provoking a fear of abstruseness and reactionary decadence.[30]

It is well known that Eisenstein was already looking forward to sound as a 'new montage element' while working on *The General Line*, which he also considered turning into a sound film with music by Meisel,[31] but the 'Statement' here suggests a crisis in confidence in the 'intellectual cinema' towards which *October* pointed.

The 'Statement' ends with a further, prophetic, argument against the talkies. Only contrapuntal sound films will escape the inevitable restriction of naturalistic sound films to their own language communities. The authors of the 'Statement' foresaw what was soon to happen as the 'internationalism' of silent cinema – which made the United States as open to European[32] and even Soviet[33] films as Europe and the USSR were to American films[34] – turned to one-way traffic from the United States to the rest of the world. After a brief phase of dual and multi-language production in Europe, foreign-language films met with increasing resistance in the United States, while American films continued to increase their penetration of foreign markets, generally in dubbed versions. For the still-young Soviet cinema, which had achieved an extraordinary international prestige and corresponding domestic privilege in the late 1920s, this was perhaps the most serious long-term threat posed by sound. As the debate around 'Socialism in one country' was resolved in Stalin's favour, so the international propaganda role of Soviet cinema dwindled in importance to the point where, by the time of Eisenstein's return from the United States in 1932, foreign travel and contacts were beginning to be regarded as dangerous cosmopolitanism.

## VERTOV: ENTHUSIASM FOR SOUND

Before considering the profound upheaval in Soviet life which was the background to the introduction of sound, the views of Vertov on sound are worth noting, especially since they directly challenged those of the 'Statement' and in fact closely – if briefly – matched the new mood of the 'construction' period. In 1925 Vertov had already anticipated the potential of sound reproduction as a mass medium with his film *Radio-Cine-Pravda* [Radiokinopravda] and manifesto '*Cine-Pravda* and *Radio-Pravda*'.[35] As early as 1923 he foresaw 'radio newsreels' linked with film newsreels[36] and, with his background in Futurist 'noise music' experiments, he experimented more fully than any of his contemporaries with 'implied' sound through sequences of sound-related images in, for example, *Forward, Soviet!* [Shagai, sovet!, 1926]. In 1930, when he was making one of the earliest full-length Soviet 'direct-sound' films, *Enthusiasm* [Entuziazm, a.k.a. *The Donbass Symphony* [Sinfoniya Donbassa]], he commented obliquely on the 'Statement' in a question-and-answer article for the journal *Kino-Front*:

> Declarations on the need for non-correspondence between the visible and the audible, like declarations on the need to make only natural sound or talking films, are, as they say, not worth tuppence. In sound, as in silent, cinema we draw a clear distinction between only two types of film: documentaries (with authentic dialogue and sound, etc.) and played films (with artificial dialogue and sound, etc., specially created during the shooting).
>
> Neither *correspondence* nor *non-correspondence* between the visible and the audible is by any means obligatory for either documentaries or played films. Sound and silent shots are both edited according to identical principles: the montage may make them correspond or not, or interweave in whatever combination is required. The important thing is to end the

absurd confusion caused by categorising films as talking, noise or sound films.[37]

Vertov's statement, of course, was made after the period of anticipation and at the beginning of actual sound production and it challenges not only the 'Statement on Sound' but other widely held views of the period. In a later article, after the release of *Enthusiasm*, he described the film as a 'negation of the negation' proposed by the critic Ippolit Sokolov, who had claimed that neither nature nor everyday life were 'sonogenic' and that efforts to record natural sounds would result in a 'concert of caterwauling'.

For Vertov and his group what is of most interest is a 'many-sided' analysis of the film, not as a 'thing in itself', but as a part of 'all our work in switching rails from the silent to the sound cinema, in this branch of our socialist film industry'.[38] While Vertov boldly seized the opportunity to link his polemic for documentary with the new technology, Eisenstein chose to travel abroad – ostensibly to study sound film techniques – and other film-makers, less famous or more fearful, devised long-term projects to help them weather the coming storm.[39]

## INDUSTRIAL AND CULTURAL REVOLUTION

Recent studies of the introduction of sound in Hollywood have stressed the economic imperatives at work in what had hitherto been regarded as a technological and aesthetic process. In the Soviet case, an even greater range of processes is implicated in assessing the transition to sound, as I have argued elsewhere: the following main elements may be sketched.[40]

The essential dynamic of the late 1920s in the USSR was the accelerating development of a 'command economy' which would eventually bring all areas of Soviet work and life under centralised authority, eliminating independent initiatives and concentrating resources behind imposed policies. This dynamic took the form of preparation for and implementation of the first Five Year Plan in 1928–9,[41] with its central theme of industrialisation and, superimposed upon this without warning, Stalin's forced collectivisation of agriculture. A 'cultural revolution' was planned to accompany the Five Year Plan and preparations for this ran in parallel through 1927–8 with work on the Plan. Richard Taylor has already charted in detail the intense debate that surrounded the First All-Union Party Conference on Cinema in March 1928: the essential issues at stake were close Party control of cinema and the development of cinema as an efficient mass medium.[42] When the Party finally succeeded in establishing controls in 1930, with the reorganisation of all cinema affairs under Soyuzkino, headed by Boris Shumyatsky, Soviet film-makers and administrators had, for the first time, an authoritative – if ultimately contradictory – brief:

> In the period of socialist construction cinema must, first and foremost, be the most powerful instrument for deepening the class consciousness of the

workers, for the political re-education of the non-proletarian strata of the population and the peasantry.[43]

Ivor Montagu has suggested that the centralisation and rigidity of the Five Year Plan may in fact have delayed the introduction of sound to cinema,[44] but a crucial link was forged in 1930 between the new technology and the new themes of the 'cultural revolution'. The first sound films all dealt with aspects of construction: whether industrialisation in Abram Room's *The Plan for Great Works* [Plan velikikh rabot, 1930] and Vertov's *Enthusiasm*; regional development in Yuli Raizman's *The Earth Thirsts* [1930] and Kozintsev and Trauberg's *Alone*; or social problems in Nikolai Ekk's *The Path to Life* [Putevka v zhizn', in 1931]. Special emphases of the Plan strategy were also reflected in films with a precision unparalleled in the 1920s: the training of peasants as construction workers in Dovzhenko's *Ivan* [1932]; the goal of 'catching up with and surpassing America' in Alexander Macheret's *Men and Jobs* [1932]. And in a little-known film by Esfir Shub, *KShE (Komsomol: Patron of Electrification)* [KShE (Komsomol – Shef elektrifikatsii), 1932], the technology of sound recording is actually shown as a prelude to the study of an electrification project.

The fervent debates on the political and artistic role of cinema which had been a feature of the 1920s were subordinated to the new demand that films should be 'intelligible to the masses'.[45] Thus the actual structure of early

*Figure 21* Shub's *Komsomol – Patron of Electrification* [1932] echoed the Constructivist *faktura*, with its self-referential demonstration of the new sound-film technique.

sound films becomes more schematic, while the strong vein of social criticism
– of bureaucratic inefficiency, managerial privilege, youthful immorality –
so marked in late 1920s films, disappears. Under Shumyatsky's regime,
many of these tendencies, which were already evident, were encouraged and
welded into a distinctive new policy of developing exemplary and repro-
ducible *models* for Shumyatsky's 'cinema for the millions'.[46] Shumyatsky
did not discount the importance of international prestige, but it was not to be
won at the expense of the growing domestic market by making avant-garde
films for the international intelligentsia. Instead *The Path to Life* was
successfully shown at the Venice Festival and *Chapayev* [Chapaev, 1934]
proudly inaugurated the fifteenth anniversary year of Soviet cinema, which
included the first Moscow Film Festival in 1935. As an indication of the
complicated linkage between the investment demands of sound as a new
technology, the new direction in film policy and the increasing involvement
of the state, Shumyatsky claimed that the three sound features completed in
1931 – *The Path to Life*, *Alone* and Sergei Yutkevich's *The Golden Mountains* [Zlatye gory] – were seen by Stalin, who decided as a result to devote
additional resources to the development of sound.[47] Up to this point, the
Plan imperative to end dependence on imported film stock and equipment
had taken precedence over conversion to sound. But Shumyatsky's evident
success in curbing 'Formalist excesses' and bringing forth exemplary works
such as *The Path to Life* and *Ivan* was to gain new political prestige for
cinema.

Burch has suggested that the introduction of sound may itself have
precipitated a new level of political interference in films:

> political cadres suddenly found themselves confronted with a medium
> which involved spoken discourse, i.e., the very substance of their political
> practice. Their competence to intervene far more directly than before was
> suddenly legitimised.[48]

Given that closer political attention was already being paid to cinema (and to
all the arts) by 1930, it may have been a foregone conclusion that the
substance of the 'talkies' would attract close scrutiny. But it may be
significant that local state censorship also made its first appearance in the
United States shortly after the arrival of the talkies. The immediacy of
spoken discourse clearly invited a detailed 'textual' censorship which was
unknown in the American silent period. Sound cinema also clearly invited
closer scrutiny at the script stage, since the finished film was considerably less
easy to alter 'invisibly' than the flexible silent film with intertitles. In the
USSR this relative 'rigidity' of the sound film appears to have reacted back
on the planning stage, lengthening and bureaucratising the production
process. This tendency, together with the concern for 'exemplary' works,
led to a drastic slowing-down of production in the 1930s, to the point where
only twenty-nine films were finished in 1933, compared with the high point of
112 in 1928.[49]

These are the essential features of the transitional period which need to be set alongside the conventional emphasis on Socialist Realism as the new guiding doctrine for all Soviet art in the 1930s. Undoubtedly the assimilation of sound played an important part in the construction of Socialist Realist cinema but the immediate priority here is to pursue the legacy of the silent period into the early years of sound.

## FIRST STEPS IN SOUND

The long period of anticipation was followed by an equally long and gradual transition to 'full sound'. The first public cinema to be re-equipped for sound, the Khudozhestvennyi [Artistic] in Moscow, opened in March 1930 and the rate of conversion continued to be slow, especially in the country-side. While the need for silent production remained, sound production was correspondingly limited.[50] Three more or less distinct, though overlapping, phases can be distinguished within the first period, 1930–2:

(a) *Demonstration pieces* – in addition to the earliest short items which were grouped into three *Compilation Sound Programmes* [Zvukovye sbornye programmy], demonstration films included a direct-sound report on a political trial, *Thirteen Days*, and a documentary on a collective farm, *One of Many*, complete with animal sounds!
(b) *Post-synchronisation* – the practice of dubbing already-completed silent films with 'artificial' soundtracks began early with *The Earth Thirsts* and *Alone* and continued with the refurbishment of primitive soundtracks.
(c) *Full sound production* – *The Plan for Great Works*, Room's compilation on aspects of the Five Year Plan, and *The Path to Life* are generally regarded as the first 'full sound' features intended for general release, closely followed by *Enthusiasm*, *The Golden Mountains* and *Ivan*.

Alongside these phases there are traces of 'sound' thinking and construction in a number of silent productions dating from 1928–9 to their final disappearance in 1935–6.

From a preliminary survey[51] of some of the lesser-known films of this transitional period, what is striking is not the sporadic evidence of sound/image counterpoint, but of the deeper 'structuring impact of the verbal'[52] and of a wide range of responses to the challenge of 'outer speech'. These are manifested in a number of thematic devices and rhetorical strategies which focus attention on the *novelty* of sound and specifically on the new dimension of audible speech. Below are five examples of this 'thematisation': two of 'parapraxis', in Freud's sense of a symptomatic error or bungled action; two of the 'delay' occasioned by translation between languages functioning as a cognitive metaphor; and one of 'miscueing' used to create complex extra-narrative associations.[53]

**Parapraxes**

*1*

Macheret's *Men and Jobs* [1932] deals with the Five Year Plan policy of bringing in foreign 'experts' to supervise major technological projects and train Soviet technologists. In this film, the American construction expert, Mr Klin, is first seen arriving by train with his portable gramophone and jazz records. His relationship – at first antagonistic, eventually friendly – with an archetypal Soviet shock-worker, played by Nikolai Okhlopkov,[54] forms the central body of the film. The theme is the need to learn from foreign experts and the potential for converting them. What is remarkable, however, is the device on which the final sequence turns: Klin is writing home to his wife, explaining his change of heart on the Bolsheviks and that he intends to stay longer, when a record playing on his gramophone suddenly sticks in a groove and the word 'darling' begins to repeat. This is gradually transformed on the soundtrack into the Russian word '*udarnik*' [shock-worker] as Klin goes to the window and looks out proudly over the construction site. His moment of commitment is signalled by a 'symptomatic' interruption in routine and 'slippage' between languages.

*2*

Alexander Fainzimmer's *Lieutenant Kizhe* [Poruchik Kizhe, 1934] is an unexpectedly stylised comedy, with Prokofiev's independently famous music closely integrated into its structure. The story and script were by the Formalist critic Yuri Tynyanov,[55] and, apart from its many intriguing visual devices – such as the use of obvious model soldiers and optically duplicated images – the mainspring of the plot is a slip between the written and the spoken word. Disturbed sound-image relations are present from the beginning as two furtive lovers make contact by exchanging cat and dog sounds, until the silence of the tsar's sleep is shattered by an alarm call shouted from guard to guard in a rising crescendo. The central slip is of course the invention of Kizhe, who owes his birth to a clerk's error in drawing up an army promotion list. An ink blot is inadvertently converted into the name Kizhe – which imaginary officer is promptly blamed for the original disturbance and starts his career by being sent into exile in Siberia. Later, as he rises through the ranks and is married, his bride punningly explains to the wedding guests that Kizhe has no 'presence', to account for his invisibility during the ceremony. *Lieutenant Kizhe* is in fact a remarkable working model of Formalist literary theory, couched in the form of a fable on the generative power of language.

These and, doubtless, other examples point to an awareness of the potential for renewing perception, as Formalist theory would have it, and exploring the new terrain of *talking* cinema by introducing speech-specific devices. It would be interesting in this respect to discover how the early sound film that featured a gramophone as its 'central character', *The Mechanical Traitor*, made use of this novel 'thematisation' of mechanically reproduced sound.[56]

## Translation

The need for translation between languages was, on one level, an inevitable realistic consequence of sound films involving speakers of different nationalities. But this new problem of communication could also serve as a means of 'defamiliarising' by delaying what would otherwise be naturalistic dialogue. Again, I give two instances.

### 3

*The Deserter* [1933] is the story of how a German workers' leader, Renn, is selected to go on an exchange visit to the USSR after his comrades have

*Figure 22  The Deserter* [1933]; Pudovkin's first, experimental sound film.

experienced a severe political defeat. Renn seizes the opportunity to escape from a difficult situation and stays on after the others return, becoming a valuable member of a factory shock-brigade. At a mass meeting to celebrate the brigade's achievements, his conscience forces him to decline the invitation to join the factory committee and instead he declares publicly – and haltingly through a translator, since he has learned little Russian – that he must return to take his place 'at this decisive moment of the class struggle'. Pudovkin has described his approach to the sequence in psychological terms:

> At the beginning of this scene we see and hear shots longish in duration, first of the speaking hero, then of the translator. In the process of development of the episode, the image of the translator becomes shorter and the majority of his words accompany the images of the hero, according as the interest of the audience automatically fixes on the latter's psychological position.[57]

Here the 'delay' of translation, coming after the linguistic isolation of Renn's stay in the USSR, produces a graphic representation of his alienation, which is ended by a 'correct' decision that restores to him the effective power of speech. (A similar sequence involving translation and the symbolic exchange of halting words in the other language occurs in *Men and Jobs*.)

*4*

In *Tommy* [1931], Yakov Protazanov's first sound film, based on Vsevolod Ivanov's celebrated 1920s play *Armoured Train 14–69*, an English soldier serving with the intervention forces is captured by Red partisans. In a brilliant 'subjective' trope the lone soldier on duty day-dreams of the foundry where he works at home and imagines that a crane knocks him over – just as the partisans surprise him! The partisan leader, unable to speak English, desperately tries to explain to the soldier what they stand for: he shouts 'Lenin' and gets a glimmer of response; then he seizes an icon of Abraham and Isaac and with vigorous gestures 'interprets' it as an allegory of the bourgeoisie attacking the proletariat, with the angel standing for imperialist intervention by Britain and the USA. Tommy finally 'gets the picture' and joins forces with the partisans, while elsewhere his captain chats with White Russian officers and explains that he learned his fluent Russian looking after British industrial interests before the Revolution. Here the triumph of non-verbal communication between 'natural' class allies is set against the easy but empty exchanges of the officer classes and, as so often in Protazanov's unjustly neglected work, schematic confrontation is fleshed out in dialectical and satirical detail.

**Miscueing**

5

Several possibilities opened up by a limited form of 'local' asynchrony are explored in Boris Barnet's masterly first sound film, *Outskirts* [1933]. This opens with what appears to be an explicit homage to the 'talking horse' of Dovzhenko's *The Arsenal* [1929], which alerts the spectator to a whole *metaphoric* level of sound use throughout the film. Twice the sound of gunfire – the film is set during the First World War in a small town – is transposed from its diegetic source to another, purposefully ironic, source. Thus the sound of troops shooting to disperse crowds gathered in the town square on the eve of war is laid over the image of a boy with a rattle; while the machines installed in the town's boot factory, to step up production after the 1917 February Revolution, also make a sound like gunfire, signifying the continuation of the war by the Provisional Government. More than any other film of this era, *Outskirts* showed how sound had indeed become, in Jakobson's term, the new 'dominant' or 'focusing component' of Soviet cinema's expressive apparatus.[58]

## FROM 'INNER SPEECH' TO 'OUTER SPEECH'

Instead of looking for evidence of the survival of montage procedures, such as counterpoint or radical 'asynchronism' in the early sound period, it may in fact be more productive to see this long transition as one of negotiation between two distinct regimes of discourse. The montage regime, with its origins in the early post-Revolutionary *agitki* and the analytical experiments of Kuleshov, Vertov and Shub, had become increasingly formalised and intellectualised as an artistic system. By contrast, the emergent Soviet 'popular' cinema remained highly eclectic and pragmatic, drawing from a wide range of foreign examples and shamelessly imitating them. 'Inner speech' was proposed first as the theoretical 'guarantee' of montage's coherence and was later taken up, notably by Eisenstein, as a model for the further elaboration of the montage system.

The threat of the new sound regime lay in its apparent alliance with a series of established 'public discourses' – theoretical, literary, political – and the danger of the cinema losing its hard-won specificity, identified with montage, by collapsing into one or other of these. Outer speech appeared to threaten the sophisticated inner speech model with banalisation and, in-deed, with forms of censorship and repression unknown in the silent period. But this is not to suggest that 'inner speech' no longer played a part in the construction of sound cinema: on the contrary, its role was to be redefined as spectators adjusted to the new address of the talkies. The new situation can be characterised by reference to another strand in Formalist theory,

Voloshinov's paper (from the Bakhtin school) on 'Reported Speech', in which he defines the problem posed by dialogue:

> How, in fact, is another speaker's speech received? What is the mode of existence of another's utterance in the actual, inner speech-consciousness of the recipient? How is it manipulated there, and what process of orientation will the subsequent speech of the recipient have undergone in regard to it?[59]

Soviet film-makers of the early sound period were faced with a bewildering range of problems in the technical, political and aesthetic spheres. With sound as the new 'dominant' of the transitional period, they tackled the problem with an originality that has largely remained unacknowledged and unexamined. Not until the interpretative myths of the later 1930s and the Cold War have been peeled back and the texts and films made widely available, will any full assessment of the achievements of this crucial period be possible.[60]

# 11  Ideology as mass entertainment: Boris Shumyatsky and Soviet cinema in the 1930s

*Richard Taylor*

> A film and its success are directly linked to the degree of entertainment in
> the plot . . . that is why we are obliged to require our masters to produce
> works that have strong plots and are organised around a story-line.
>
> Boris Shumyatsky, 1933[1]

The conventional approach to Soviet cinema looks at the films produced almost exclusively in terms of the men who directed them: Eisenstein, Pudovkin, Vertov head a long, and lengthening, list of what film critics and historians would, borrowing from their French counterparts, nowadays call *auteurs*. Yet our approach to Hollywood, which is both more familiar to us, and more influential over us, is rather different: the *auteur* theory persists in the discussion of such important individual directors as Alfred Hitchcock or John Ford but we are much more prepared to concede that a film is the result of a variety of influences, perhaps even of a collective effort – at best a collective work of art, at worst a mere industrial commodity destined for mass consumption. In the Hollywood context, therefore, we talk of a studio style or of the influence of a producer like David O. Selznick. We group American films according to their scriptwriter (Jules Furthman or Clifford Odets), their genre (the western, the musical, the war film) or their star (Marlene Dietrich, Marilyn Monroe, James Dean). But we never apply these criteria to Soviet cinema.

There are, of course, good historical (and ideological) reasons for this: one of the principal reasons is quite simply lack of adequate information. But, if we do not ask different questions, we shall never get different answers or, indeed, much new information at all. In concentrating exclusively on directors, our approach to Soviet cinema lacks an important dimension. We ignore the different styles that emanate from different studios and we ignore the role of a man like Adrian Piotrovsky, head of the script department of the Leningrad studios in the early 1930s, in creating a studio style. We ignore the threads of continuity in the work of a scriptwriter like Mikhail Bleiman, whose first script was filmed in 1924 and who was still active in the 1970s, or Nina Agadzhanova-Shutko, who scripted films for both Eisenstein (*The Battleship Potemkin*, 1926) and Pudovkin (*The Deserter*, 1933). We ignore the importance of Soviet actors like the comedian Igor Ilyinsky or the more serious Nikolai Cherkasov or massively popular stars like Lyubov Orlova or Tamara Makarova. And we ignore the significance in Soviet cinema of genres like musical comedy (*The Happy Guys* [Veselye rebyata, 1934], *The Circus* [1936], *Volga-Volga* [1938] or *The Tractor Drivers* [Traktoristy, 1939]), Civil War films (*Chapayev* [1934], *We from Kronstadt* [1936], *Shchors* [1939]), or 'historical-revolutionary' films (the Maxim trilogy [1934–8], *A Great Citizen* [Velikii grazhdanin, 1937–9], *Lenin in October*, 1937] etc.). As a result our view of Soviet cinema has been both distorted and impoverished.

But perhaps the most surprising omission of all is our constant underestimation of the importance of those who actually ran the film industry at the highest political level, those who took the major policy decisions and who held the ultimate responsibility. This underestimation is a limitation we share with Soviet cinema historians, although the ideological origin of their blind spot is rather different from that of ours. In this chapter I want to look at the role of the man who dominated Soviet cinema for seven years from 1930 until the end of 1937: he was neither a film director nor a scriptwriter, neither an actor nor a cameraman, but a Party activist and an administrator and his influence on Soviet cinema can still be felt today. His name was Boris Shumyatsky.

Boris Zakharovich Shumyatsky was born on 4 November 1886 (old style) to an artisan family near Lake Baikal, joined the Party in 1903, played a leading part in the disturbances in Krasnoyarsk and Vladivostok in 1905–7 and, after 1917, held a number of important position in the Soviet governmental and Party apparatus in Siberia. From 1923 to 1925 he was Soviet plenipotentiary in Iran and on his return he became rector of the Communist University of Workers of the East and a member of the Central Asian Bureau of the Party Central Committee. This might seem an unlikely background for his next appointment, which is the one that concerns us here: in December 1930 he was made the chairman of the new centralised Soviet film organisation, Soyuzkino. But it was precisely this background as Old Bolshevik, Party activist and administrator that did qualify him, in the authorities' eyes, for the task in hand.[2]

There had been two previous attempts to organise Soviet cinema along centralised lines since the film industry had been nationalised in August 1919. In December 1922 Goskino had been established to put Soviet cinema on a secure footing: it had failed, partly because it was underfunded and partly because it had to compete with numerous other organisations, some of which were privately funded. Learning from these mistakes, Narkompros established Sovkino in December 1924 to perform a fundamentally similar task. But even Sovkino did not have the resources to compete adequately with the private sector and Soviet cinema audiences still flocked to see either imported films like *Broken Blossoms* [USA, 1919], *The Mark of Zorro* [USA, 1920], *Robin Hood* [USA, 1922] or Soviet films that imitated imported models. An excellent example of this last category is the film

*The Bear's Wedding* [1926],[3] made by Konstantin Eggert in 1925 for Mezhrabpom-Rus, the joint-stock company in which he had a large share-holding, from a story by Prosper Mérimée adapted for the screen by Anatoli Lunacharsky, the People's Commissar for Enlightenment, with Lunacharsky's wife, Nataliya Rozenel, playing the female lead. The story is set in the forests of Lithuania and contains the stock horror-film elements of murky castles, human beasts, hereditary insanity, storms and dungeons. It was unashamedly a commercial film aimed at attracting audiences through entertainment and diversion rather than through edification, agitation or propaganda. Showing in Moscow at the same time as the state film organis-ation's *The Battleship Potemkin*, it attracted more than twice as large an audience and was advertised as 'the first hit of 1926'.[4] Later in the year 'public demand' led to *Potemkin* being replaced by Douglas Fairbanks in *Robin Hood*.[5]

Since Soviet cinema was expected to stand on its own two feet financially, Sovkino had to make films that were commercially rather than ideologically orientated. What surplus, if any, was left from the production and distrib-ution of *kassovye* (cash) films was to be used to finance *klassovye* (class) films. Sovkino was bitterly attacked from all sides for its heavy-handed attitudes and for its failure to make any real attempt to combine ideological rectitude with box-office success. Mayakovsky, echoing Lenin's remarks to Clara Zetkin, commented in an October 1927 debate on 'The Paths and Policy of Sovkino':

> We're merely saying that the masses who pay to see films are not the upper stratum of NEP or the more-or-less well-to-do strata but the many tens of millions of the mass of those same textile-workers and students who pay kopeks but produce millions. And, however much you might try and try, however much profit you make from the public by catering for their tastes, you are doing something foul and nasty.[6]

Adrian Piotrovsky, the critic and scriptwriter who was later to become the head of the script department of the Leningrad film studios, argued that Sovkino should tackle its problems not by a rigid division between the commercial and the ideological, not by a slavish imitation of 'bourgeois' cinema but by a more efficient concentration on low-budget films offering a quick return on capital expenditure:

> Our businessmen would probably agree that they need a quick return on their capital expenditure, a quick return even on small amounts. It is only average-cost topical contemporary films that can provide this. In their own way these films are the cruisers of our cinema fleet and it is certainly no accident that in our current naval fleet it is the fast and light cruisers that are replacing the expensive armoured hulks. A stake in the average-cost Soviet film should be the basis of our production. This should become clear from distribution too and that will then put an end to the complaints

that not enough is done to make Soviet films popular: these complaints are after all caused by the distributors' secret distrust of the commercial possibilities of Soviet 'ideological' films.[7]

Sovkino's continuing problems came under closer scrutiny at the First All-Union Party Conference on Cinema in March 1928. The resolutions passed by this conference reflected the same kind of Party balancing act that can be seen in earlier resolutions on literature and theatre. The Party was unwilling to endorse any particular group or school but offered a framework for the guidance of Soviet film-makers:

> In questions of artistic form the Party cannot support one particular current, tendency or grouping: it permits competition between differing formal and artistic tendencies and the opportunity for experimentation so that the most perfect possible film in artistic terms can be achieved.
>
> The main criterion for evaluating the formal and artistic qualities of films is the requirement that cinema furnish a 'form that is intelligible to the millions'.[8]

But the Party's endorsement of the importance of 'entertainment quality . . . proximity to the worker and peasant audience and a form that corresponds to the requirements of the broad mass audience'[9] left the door open to the more vociferous critics of Sovkino in the hierarchy of ARRK,[10] the film-makers' equivalent of RAPP, to insist on the supremacy of their own positions.

The widespread criticism of Eisenstein's *October* [Oktyabr', 1927] for obscurantism and self-indulgence[11] was symptomatic of an emerging attempt to establish a so-called 'proletarian hegemony' in Soviet cinema, such as RAPP was trying to establish in literature. It was no use making films on contemporary themes set in a working-class milieu if those films were made by effete intellectuals whose contact with that milieu was tenuous in the extreme. The faults of Soviet cinema were thus laid at the door of an intelligentsia severed from the proletariat and an avant-garde portrayed as making films largely for its own benefit. Because the films that they produced were divorced from the masses and therefore from reality (or so the argument went), their achievement was an empty and a purely formal one. Thus the avant-garde intellectuals were tarred with the brushes of aestheticism and Formalism as well.

One of the leading exponents of the proletarian hegemony was the scriptwriter and director Pavel Petrov-Bytov. In April 1929 he wrote:

> When people talk about Soviet cinema they brandish a banner on which is written: *The Strike, The Battleship Potemkin, October, The Mother, The End of St Petersburg* [Konets Sankt-Peterburga, 1927] and they add the recent *New Babylon* [1929], *Zvenigora* [1929] and *The Arsenal* [1929]. *Do 120 million workers and peasants march beneath this banner? I quite categorically state that they do not.* And never have done.

. . . the people who make up Soviet cinema are 95% alien, aesthetes or unprincipled. Generally speaking, none of them has any experience of life. Can these people, who are capable of understanding abstract problems but not life, serve the masses? Yes, they can if they are born again or regenerated. If their hearts beat in unison with the masses. If the joys and sorrows of these masses are as dear and close to them . . . .

If they are regenerated in this way, there will be honour and a role for them in Soviet cinema. If not, the workers and peasants will show them their proper place. So far they have not been regenerated but they shout from the house-tops: 'We shall lead the masses behind us.' *I am sorry, but you will not lead with 'Octobers' and 'New Babylons' if only because people do not want to watch these films. Before you lead the masses behind you, you must know them. For this you must either be from the masses yourself or have studied them thoroughly, and not just studied but also experienced what these masses themselves experience.*[12]

Petrov-Bytov's solution to the problem he had diagnosed was somewhat extreme:

The public-spirited artist who works on the masses and leads them must, before being an artist, spend a couple of years in the worker's 'school of life' and two years in the peasant's, or he must come from this milieu.[13]

But he was echoing the solution favoured by the Party leadership which in January 1929 had issued a decree 'On the Strengthening of Cinema Cadres':

The task of the Party is to use all measures to strengthen its leadership of the work of the cinema organisations and, by preserving the ideological consistency of the films produced, to combat decisively the attempt to bring Soviet cinema nearer to the ideology of the non-proletarian strata.[14]

The Party viewed the problems of cinema at least in part as a result of its rapid growth. In 1914 there had been only 1,412 cinemas, 133 of them in rural areas: by 1928 the figures had grown to a total of 7,331, with 2,389 in rural areas and cinema was serving an annual audience of 200 million people.[15] In 1922/3 only twelve feature films had been released: in 1926/7 the figure was more than ten times higher.[16] In 1924 thirty-four directors had been working in Soviet cinema but by 1928 this had risen to ninety-five.[17] But the artists' trade union Rabis estimated that only 13.5 per cent of these ninety-five were Party members[18] and Party statistics suggested that 97.3 per cent were of non-proletarian origin.[19] That such figures were taken seriously is itself an illustration of the obsessive nature of the debate. None the less, the intelligentsia were clearly dominant and, equally clearly, they were not enamoured of Petrov-Bytov's proposed solutions. But his diagnosis that Soviet cinema was producing films that were either unpopular with mass audiences or popular but ideologically unsuitable was a diagnosis that most contemporaries would have agreed with. Our conventional approach to

Soviet cinema has tended to obscure that argument by overlooking the wider political context.

We have largely ignored the implications of Lunacharsky's observation that in the Soviet Union too 'cinema is an industry and, what is more, a profitable industry'[20] and his subsequent conclusion that:

> Many of our people do not understand that our film production must whet the public appetite, that, if the public is not interested in a picture that we produce, it will become boring agitation and we shall become boring agitators. But it is well known that boring agitation is counter-agitation. We must choose and find a line that ensures that *the film is both artistic and ideologically consistent and contains romantic experience of an intimate and psychological character.*[21]

The lessons of Lunacharsky's remarks may have been lost on 'many of our people' but they were not lost on Boris Shumyatsky.

Shumyatsky was appointed head of Soyuzkino when the 'proletarian hegemony' was at its height. Many leading directors had turned to making films on contemporary themes drawn from the everyday experience of the Soviet worker or peasant. Ermler was making *Counterplan* [Vstrechnyi, 1932], Ekk *The Path to Life* [1931] and Yutkevich *The Golden Mountains* [1931], while the Kozintsev and Trauberg film *Alone* [1931] was greeted warmly by Sutyrin, the editor of the monthly journal *Proletarskoe Kino*, in a review significantly entitled 'From Intelligentsia Illusions to Actual Reality'.[22] (Despite its name, *Proletarskoe kino* was not quite the forcing ground for proletarianisation that it might have seemed, or wanted to seem, to be: its editorial board, in addition to Sutyrin, included the directors Pudovkin and Ermler while Petrov-Bytov became editor of the mass-circulation Leningrad film magazine, *Kadr*.) Shumyatsky himself paid little more than lip service to the campaign, preferring to concentrate on the broader problems of Soviet cinema, which were enormous, and as much industrial as political.

In the year 1927/8 box office receipts from Soviet films had exceeded those from imports for the first time,[23] but this did not mean that Soviet films were intrinsically more popular. It meant that a shortage of foreign currency had led to a severe reduction in the number of films imported while the Soviet films that filled the gap were on the whole imitative of Western models. The rapid expansion of the cinema network during the first Five Year Plan period accentuated the problem and the spread of cinemas to the countryside created a new audience for Soviet films.

While we cannot talk in conventional Western terms of supply and demand, we can say that those responsible for Soviet cinema, from Lunacharsky and Shumyatsky downwards, realised that the industry was not producing enough films, or enough of the right films to meet the demand that they perceived. Hence the emphases on attracting established authors into writing scripts, on adapting the established classics and on tackling themes

*Figure 23* Soundproofing the first Soviet sound studio with 'torfoleum', a derivative of peat.

and developing genres that were immediately relevant to the ever-widening audience. The shortage of foreign currency meant that Soviet cinema also had to try to achieve self-sufficiency in the production of film stock, projectors and other equipment and to achieve this as quickly as possible.

Lastly, the Soviet Union had, like other countries, to come to terms with the advent of sound film. This meant 'the agitation, the anxieties and the alarm' that the scriptwriter Yevgeni Gabrilovich detected among 'scriptwriters, directors, actors, cameramen and editors when the screen suddenly, surprisingly and quite unexpectedly began producing sounds'.[24] It also meant a further massive investment in re-equipment and yet another headache for Shumyatsky.

Initially Shumyatsky had then to devote his attention to the immediate day-to-day problems of running Soviet cinema. Symptomatic is the battle he was forced to fight for sound cinema equipment, the battle he describes in his first published article, 'Alarm Signal' in *Proletarskoe kino*, May/June 1931.[25] In October 1930 Soyuzkino had ordered a thousand sound projectors but the producing organisations would agree only to a target of 700, which they further reduced in December 1930 to 500. In February 1931 production ceased altogether for a month and it was only under pressure from Vesenkha, the Supreme Council for the National Economy, that they agreed to a revised target of 400 projectors by the end of 1931. In April a further reduction to 275–95 projectors and a unit price increase from 9,000 roubles to 27,000 roubles were announced. Given Soyuzkino's budgetary limits, this threefold price increase meant that the cinema organisation had funds only for 100 projectors, a tenth of the target six months earlier. By May 1931 only one projector instead of the projected 47 had been delivered so that there was only one cinema in the entire Soviet Union equipped to show the emerging queue of sound films: in six months the original target figure had been reduced a thousandfold. This in turn meant that, because there was nowhere to show the sound films, silent versions of these sound films had also to be released, diverting funds that could more profitably have been deployed in the making of new films. During this period of transition Soyuzkino was therefore simultaneously producing: (1) silent films; (2) sound versions of silent films; (3) sound films; (4) silent versions of sound films. This clear duplication of resources and effort led Shumyatsky to introduce more stringent overall planning controls. The nucleus of Party and Komsomol members in the film industry was to be strengthened and better management techniques introduced but the linchpin of the reforms was to be the further development of the annual 'thematic plan' [templan] for film production to overcome the 'backwardness' that so many of its critics lamented.[26] Annual thematic plans had been introduced by Sovkino in the mid-1920s but these plans were drawn up *in vacuo* by the administrative heads of studios. Under Shumyatsky the impetus for discussion was to come from the film-makers themselves who were to be consulted and represented at annual thematic planning conferences, such as that held in December 1933.[27]

But Shumyatsky's problems were not always internal to the industry: in June 1932, while he was on extended leave in Sochi, the People's Commissariat of Light Industry, Narkomlegprom, tried to take over Soyuzkino, apparently without any Party or government orders and allegedly without even the knowledge, not just of Shumyatsky but also of the People's Commissar for Light Industry, Lyubimov, himself.[28] In an impassioned speech on 2 July 1932 Shumyatsky attacked what he called 'a sad misunderstanding' and argued that a 'People's Commissariat' was an inappropriate form of organisation for an industry like cinema that was also an art form. Shumyatsky was particularly appalled at the way in which his subordinates had meekly accepted the proposed reorganisation:

Where have they been in the last month and a half while the storm of liquidation has been raging about Soyuzkino? Why did they remain silent and not protest? Surely even a blind man could have seen that the proposed reorganisation was wrong and that it was being carried out in the absence of the responsible authority. They remained silent and were passive. Their behaviour is a cause for regret.[29]

He proposed a rapid return to normal work and an overhaul of methods and procedures – 'It's back to how it was at the end of 1930, more like a bivouac than an institution'[30] – but he did remark prophetically: 'We live in the Soviet Union and we shall be reorganised more than once.'[31] It was on 11 February 1933 that Soyuzkino became the Principal Directorate for the Cinema and Photographic Industry (GUKF), headed still by Shumyatsky, but with powers similar to those of a People's Commissariat and directly subordinated to Sovnarkom, the Council of People's Commissars.[32] Thus was Shumyatsky's position strengthened and apparently secured. He could now devote his time to thought as well as action.

Shumyatsky's ideas were developed in two books published in 1934 and 1935.[33] By then he had the time and the experience to consider the longer-term aims and achievements of Soviet cinema: he was no longer dealing with a period of acute crisis. Like others before him, he asked where Soviet cinema had gone wrong. For him the answer lay not with a predominance of non-proletarian strata (although he made the by now standard reference to sabotage by class enemies and their exposure by OGPU)[34] but with the primacy of montage in Soviet film theory in the 1930s:

> The overvaluation of montage represents the primacy of form over content, the isolation of aesthetics from politics.[35]

The prime object of Shumyatsky's critique was not, as is usually supposed, Eisenstein but Lev Kuleshov whose early concentration on montage he denounced as 'typically bourgeois' because Kuleshov had emphasised form and ignored content. He was therefore a Formalist, one who had no sense of the coherence of life, one for whom 'life is a collection of individual phenomena, incidents and anecdotes'. Kuleshov's early films, such as *The Extraordinary Adventures of Mr West in the Land of the Bolsheviks* [1924], could, in Shumyatsky's view, have been produced in the West: there was nothing specifically Soviet about them, while his most recent film, *The Happy Canary* [*Veselaya kanareika*, 1929], was 'objectively hostile to Soviet art'.[36]

Kuleshov attracted Shumyatsky's venom because it was he who had first developed the theory of montage as the essence of cinema specificity. Early film theorists had sought to justify cinema as an independent art form and they had in particular to delineate its independence from theatre. In 1917 Kuleshov was the first to argue that the distinctive feature of cinema was montage:

> The essence of cinema art in the work of both director and art director is based entirely on composition. In order to make a film the director must compose the separate, unordered and unconnected film shots into a single whole and juxtapose separate moments into a more meaningful, coherent

and rhythmical sequence just as a child creates a whole word or phrase from different scattered letter blocks.[37]

In March 1918 he went further:

Montage is to cinema what the composition of colours is to painting or a harmonic sequence of sounds is to music.[38]

In a series of film experiments he demonstrated what is now known as the 'Kuleshov effect'. He took a still shot of the actor Ivan Mosjoukine staring expressionless straight ahead of him and cut that shot into three different sequences: the context in which the shot was placed turned Mosjoukine's expressionlessness into expression – into sadness, laughter, anger, hunger.[39] It is from these experiments that the whole notion of the fundamental importance of montage develops. Vsevolod Pudovkin and other members of Kuleshov's Workshop later remarked: 'We make films but Kuleshov made cinema.'[40]

For a newer and younger generation of artists, inspired by the ideals of the October Revolution and dedicated to the construction of a new society and a new way of life, cinema was seen as *the* art form with which to shape the new man. One critic remarked: 'Theatre is a game: cinema is life',[41] another defined it as 'the new philosophy',[42] while a third argued:

There can be no doubt that cinema, this new art form, is the rightful heir for our time, for its melodiousness, its rhythm, refinement and its machine culture, and it therefore represents the central art form of the current epoch.[43]

Even Lenin stated, 'Of all the arts, for us cinema is the most important.'[44] It therefore mattered uniquely if Soviet cinema was not playing, or was thought not to be playing, a central role in the transformation of Soviet society and this 'backwardness' became a particularly acute embarrassment at the time of the 'cultural revolution' that was to accompany the first Five Year Plan. But, as we have seen, this was not a new problem, rather a more acute manifestation of an old problem.

Shumyatsky argued that the inaccessibility or unintelligibility ascribed to some of the major triumphs of Soviet silent film (Eisenstein's *The Strike* or *October*, the Kozintsev and Trauberg *New Babylon* or almost any of Vertov's documentaries) resulted from an emphasis on the primacy of montage at the expense of other elements such as the script or the acting. This emphasis on montage paralleled a similar emphasis on the director at the expense of the scriptwriter or the actor. People behaved 'as if the director was empowered to do with a film whatever he *and he alone* wanted'.[45] The underestimation of the role of the scriptwriter had, in Shumyatsky's view, made it very difficult to attract good writers to the screen and this had resulted in recurring 'script crises', acute shortages of material that was suitable for filming, and Soviet cinema had suffered from an almost continuous series of such 'crises' since its inception. Although there were some notable exceptions (Mayakovsky and Shklovsky are obvious examples) the majority of writers regarded scriptwriting as a somewhat inferior and even unworthy activity; this was a view they shared with their colleagues in other countries. Repeated efforts to encourage writers to play a more active part in cinema culminated in a Central Committee decree in the spring of 1933 designed to stimulate such participation on a more regular and organised basis. Gorky was quoted as regarding film scripts not just as a worthwhile activity in themselves but as 'the most complex dramaturgical work'.[46] For Shumyatsky the principal task facing Soviet cinema in the mid-1930s was 'the battle for high-quality scripts'.[47]

Montage had, as I have indicated, played a central part in attempts to distinguish theoretically between silent cinema and theatre: it was prominent in the writings of Soviet film-makers of different schools, from 'fiction' film-makers like Eisenstein, Kuleshov and Pudovkin to documentarists like Shub and Vertov. In silent cinema the absence of sound gave the visual image an inevitable primacy over the word. This had certain political advantages: it could simplify a film's narrative structure, thus broadening its appeal. But it also had certain political disadvantages: it could encourage an experimental search for non-narrative structures of exposition, emphasising visual continuity or discontinuity through montage leading in some instances to an abandonment of conventional plot and story-line altogether. Eisenstein's 'montage of attractions' in which each attraction 'collides' with another is one example that confused worker audiences and Dziga Vertov's Cine-Eye 'factory of facts' and 'life caught unawares' is another. Both represented attempts to replace what were perceived as bourgeois narrative forms imitative of Hollywood with new forms of exposition deemed more appropriate to a revolutionary art form.

But the abandonment of conventional narrative structures and the notion that a film might in some way be 'plotless' were a particular *bête noire* for Shumyatsky:

> The plot of a work represents the constructive expression of its idea. A plotless form for a work of art is powerless to express an idea of any significance. That is why we require of our films a plot as the basic condition for the expression of ideas, of their direction, as the condition for their mass character, i.e. of the audience's interest in them. Certainly, among our masters you will find people who say: 'I am working on the plotless, storyless level.'
> People who maintain that position are profoundly deluded.[48]

Accusing them of 'creative atavism', Shumyatsky maintained that 'they have not yet got used to the discipline of the concrete tasks that our mass audience is setting them'.[49] Without a plot, no film could be entertaining:

A film and its success are directly linked to the degree of entertainment in the plot, in the appropriately constructed and realistic artistic motivations for its development.

That is why we are obliged to require our masters to produce works that have strong plots and are organised around a story-line. Otherwise they [the works] cannot be entertaining, they can have no mass character, otherwise the Soviet screen will not need them.[50]

In Shumyatsky's view then it was the hegemony of montage and the primacy accorded by montage to the director that represented the root cause of the dalliance with 'plotlessness' that he deplored. Montage lay in complete antithesis to the entertainment film that he considered so important. Montage represented 'creative atavism': plot represented 'the discipline of the concrete tasks that our mass audience is setting'. Plot necessitated script and an effective script had to be worked out carefully, in detail and in advance: 'At the basis of every feature film lies a work of drama, a play for cinema, a script.'[51] The notion that a script was 'a play for cinema' represented a complete reversal of the general desire that we have seen among film-makers to distinguish cinema from theatre. It represented in particular a realisation of the worst fears expressed by Eisenstein, Alexandrov and Pudovkin in their seminal 'Statement on Sound', published in August 1928:

Contemporary cinema, operating through visual images, has a powerful effect on the individual and rightfully occupies one of the leading positions in the ranks of the arts.

It is well known that the principal (and sole) method which has led cinema to a position of such great influence is *montage*. The confirmation of montage as the principal means of influence has become the indisputable axiom upon which world cinema culture rests.

The success of Soviet pictures on world markets is to a significant extent the result of a number of those concepts of montage which they first revealed and asserted.

And so for the further development of cinema the significant features appear to be those that strengthen and broaden the montage methods of influencing the audience.[52]

Those significant features included the development of colour and stereoscopic film but the most important feature of all was the advent of sound:

Sound is a double-edged invention and its most probable application will be along the line of least resistance, i.e. in the field of the *satisfaction of simple curiosity*. . . .

The first period of sensations will not harm the development of the new art; the danger comes with the second period, accompanied by the loss of innocence and purity of the initial concept of cinema's new textural possibilities, which can only intensify its unimaginative use for 'dramas of high culture' and other photographed representations of a theatrical order.[53]

It is significant that the shortage of suitable scripts led Shumyatsky to encourage film-makers to turn their attention to adaptations of the classics[54] thus producing precisely those 'dramas of high culture' that the 1928 'Statement' was denouncing. It is also significant that the advent of the doctrine of Socialist Realism and the proclaimed need to produce films that were 'intelligible to the millions' led to an increase in 'photographed representations of a theatrical order', and a reinstatement of more familiar conventional narrative structures so that Eisenstein could write in the spring of 1938, a few months after Shumyatsky's fall from grace, that:

> There was a period in our cinema when montage was declared 'every-thing'. Now we are coming to the end of a period when montage is thought of as 'nothing'.[55]

But for the time being the primacy of montage and the hegemony of the director were blamed by Shumyatsky for the shortage of suitable scripts.

Similarly the downgrading of the actor's role had in his view led to a deterioration in the standard of film acting. This had even been formalised by some directors. Eisenstein had renounced professional actors for his first four films (*The Strike*, *The Battleship Potemkin*, *October* and *The Old and the New* [Staroe i novoe, 1929, a.k.a. *The General Line*]) and resorted to 'typage', where non-actors were selected who simply looked right for the part, who were in some way 'typical' of the mass: this process culminated in the use of worker Nikandrov as Lenin in *October*.[56] Kuleshov had also renounced a conventional theatrical style of acting and deployed the quasi-Meyerholdian *naturshchik* or model, a specialised cinema actor highly trained in specific external movements and gestures that would replicate his internal state of mind. As two recent Soviet critics have observed:

> What was required above all else from the *naturshchik* was the appropri-ate external trappings – speed of reaction, accuracy and precision of movement – that is, external qualities more reminiscent of the require-ments of sport than of the criteria of art.[57]

In Shumyatsky's view the use of both the *naturshchik* and typage had led to a breakdown in communication with the audience who had no one in the film real enough for them to identify with. The cardboard effigies on the screen were not the psychologically real 'living men' that RAPP and ARRK had demanded: they were not convincing.

To some extent of course this lack of realism and exaggerated dependence on mimetic gesture was an inherent attribute of silent film: in the absence, or virtual absence, of words there was no alternative means of communication. But the dependence on the external trappings of mimetic gesture vitiated against a psychologically convincing development of characters and led to an underestimation of the actor's full potential. The film actor's role was a two-dimensional one: small wonder then that, just as creative writers had proved reluctant to furnish scripts, so theatre actors had also proved reluctant to act on film. This, Shumyatsky agreed, was also partly because of the loss of live contact with the audience but mainly because cinema did not use the actor efficiently. He cited the particular instance of the actor Naum Rogozhin who, in the period January–September 1935, worked for only six full days.[58] Rationalisation of acting commitments was another problem to be dealt with by the annual thematic plan, for the actor's role was in fact quite central:

> The Soviet actor creates the popularity of our art. The creative success of cinema is to a significant extent based on the success of our acting resources.[59]

The role of the actor is yet another aspect of Soviet cinema that we in the West have tended to overlook.

If, as Shumyatsky thought, the problem of Soviet cinema lay with the predominance of the director at the particular expense of the scriptwriter and the actor, the obvious question then arose as to how the imbalance could be rectified. Shumyatsky's answer lay in a collective approach in which the plot outline, then the script and then the rushes would be discussed by all concerned to eliminate errors and infelicities at the earliest possible stage; significantly that collective approach was to include the management of the film industry and by clear implication and known practice also direct representatives of the Party – for each film there was to be in effect *a thematic plan in microcosm*. Shumyatsky's argument ran like this:

> The creation of a film is a *collective process* because a film unites the creative potential of many of its participants, from the scriptwriter and the director to the actor, the composer, the designer, the cameraman – and beginning and ending with the management. . . . The time has come at last to speak unequivocally of the *direct creative* participation of the management in a film because it is the management that accepts the script and the general plan (and often even the plot outline), the management that criticises and makes suggestions and corrections, views the filmed material and asks for changes if those changes are necessary, it is the management that accepts films and so on and, it must be admitted, it is the management that often authors (without copyright!) both the plan and the details of a work.[60]

It was the management that would direct film-makers, as indeed Shumyatsky directed Eisenstein. In 1934 he praised him for his return to the notions of plot and acting and for his renewed theatrical activity.[61] But in March 1937 he ordered him to stop work on *Bezhin Meadow* [Bezhin lug] because he had wasted 2 million roubles, indulged in 'harmful Formalistic exercises', and produced work that was 'anti-artistic and politically quite unsound'.[62]

Shumyatsky admitted 'that I bear the responsibility for all this as head of GUK [Gosudarstvennoe upravlenie kinematografii, State Cinema Enterprise][63] and reiterated that, 'It was inadmissible to allow a film to go into production without establishing beforehand a definite script and dialogues'.[64] The ban on *Bezhin Meadow* was not an isolated incident and certainly not the result solely of any antipathy between Shumyatsky and Eisenstein. The tone of the argument in this instance was characterised as much by sorrow for a master gone astray as by anger. In the spring of 1934 there had been a much greater public furore over Abram Room's failure to shoot more than 5 per cent of the footage for his projected film comedy *Once One Summer* [Odnazhdy letom] after spending more than half a million roubles. On that occasion both Pudovkin and Dovzhenko had joined the chorus of denunciation.[65] None the less, by stopping the production of *Bezhin Meadow*, Shumyatsky claimed, 'the Party has shown once again the Bolshevik way of resolving the problems of art'.[66]

This 'Bolshevik way of resolving the problems of art', this enhanced role for management, was in fact of course a way of resolving the political problems of art. When the Central Committee had turned its attention to the strengthening of film cadres in January 1929[67] its concern had been to improve the political rather than the artistic performance of Soviet cinema. Similarly, Shumyatsky's emphasis on a prepared and detailed script facilitated the elimination at an early stage of undesirable elements from the completed film, whose undesirability derived from ideological as well as aesthetic considerations. Nevertheless he claimed:

> This organisation frees creativity and promotes the creative independence of each participant in the film.[68]

We have seen the main thrust of Shumyatsky's critique of Soviet cinema: primacy of montage and the hegemony of the director had led to a series of 'script crises' and to the production of films that were all too often 'unintelligible to the millions'. But we need to consider also the kind of films that Shumyatsky wanted to put in their place. The negative critique was balanced by the positive exhortation. How then was this 'creative independence' to be used?

The Conference of Film-Makers held in the wake of the August 1934 Writers' Congress in Moscow in January 1935 under the slogan 'For a Great Cinema Art'[69] revealed, as Shumyatsky himself admitted, that:

> We have no common view on such fundamental and decisive problems of our art as the inter-relationship between form and content, as plot, as the pace and rhythm of a film, the role of the script, the techniques of cinema and so on.[70]

The first tasks therefore were: (1) to create a common language of cinema, in which sound was to play a vital role and (2) to train suitable masters to use that language.[71] Just as the management leadership of the film industry was to intervene to revise the relationship between the director and other participants in a film, so in the wider context the political leadership was to inspire and, if necessary, intervene:

> The leader of our Party and our country, the leader of the World Revolution, Comrade Stalin, devotes a great deal of attention to art and finds the time to watch our best films, to correct their errors, to talk to our masters and indicate the direction that each of them should take.[72]

The principal source of inspiration for Soviet film-makers was to be the collected observations of Stalin on cinema:

> If only we were to collect all the theoretical riches of Joseph Vissarionovich's remarks on cinema, what a critical weapon we should have for the further development not just of cinema but of the whole front of Soviet arts.[73]

It is somewhat difficult to take this at least of Shumyatsky's statements seriously. When in 1939 the historian Nikolai Lebedev edited a collection entitled *The Party on Cinema* he managed to fill only 4 of its 142 pages with quotations from Stalin and most of them can be traced back either to Lenin or, more particularly, to Trotsky.[74] One such seminal contribution to Soviet film theory is usually attributed to Stalin's remark at the Fifteenth Party Congress in December 1927:

> I think that it might be possible to begin the gradual abolition of vodka by introducing instead of vodka such sources of revenue as radio and cinema.[75]

But the idea undoubtedly derives from an article by Trotsky which appeared in *Pravda* on 12 July 1923 under the heading 'Vodka, the Church and Cinema'.[76] However, although this notion might conceivably have inspired some artists to creative endeavour, it hardly provided any clear indication of precisely what was required. For this film-makers had to look to Shumyatsky rather than Stalin.

Shumyatsky was particularly concerned to provide Soviet cinema audiences with a greater degree of variety in their staple diet:

> We need genres that are infused with optimism, with the mobilising emotions, with cheerfulness, joie-de-vivre and laughter. Genres that provide us with the maximum opportunity to demonstrate the best Bolshevik traditions: an implacable attitude to opportunism, with tenacity, initiative, skill and a Bolshevik scale of work.[77]

He urged a concentration on three genres: drama, comedy and, perhaps somewhat surprisingly, fairy tales. He was especially interested in developing these last two. Of comedy he wrote, in a chapter entitled 'The Battle for New Genres':

In a country where socialism is being constructed, where there is no private property and exploitation, where the classes hostile to the proletariat have been liquidated, where the workers are united by their conscious participation in the construction of a socialist society and where the great task of liquidating the remnants of the capitalist past is being successfully accomplished by the Party even in the consciousness of the people – in this country comedy, apart from its task of exposure, has another, more important and responsible task: the creation of a good, joyful spectacle.[78]

In this instance he argued for the satisfaction of audience demand:

The victorious class wants to laugh with joy. That is its right and Soviet cinema must provide its audiences with this joyful Soviet laughter.[79]

The two films that Shumyatsky held up as examples were Alexander Medvedkin's satire *Happiness* [1935] and Grigori Alexandrov's jazz musical comedy *The Happy Guys* [1934] which he described as 'a good *start to a new genre*, the Soviet film comedy'.[80] Shumyatsky was particularly incensed by the criticisms levelled at *The Happy Guys* at the Writers' Congress in August

*Figure 24 The Happy Guys* [1934]; 'A good start to a new genre, the Soviet film comedy' (Shumyatsky).

1934: he compared its detractors to preachers from the Salvation Army and retorted:

> Neither the Revolution nor the defence of the socialist fatherland is a tragedy for the proletariat. We have always gone and in future we shall still go into battle singing and laughing.[81]

In Shumyatsky's view, a variety of genres was the spice of socialist cinema art.[82]

Shumyatsky used a similar defence for the fairy-tale film:

> There is a new genre that we are now trying to introduce into our plan: it is the fairy-tale film that treats the raw material of scientific fantasy. Here too any notion that there is a limit to what is permissible is dangerous. Here everything is permissible, provided only that it is imbued with definite progressive ideas.[83]

But, lest anyone should imagine that Shumyatsky's blueprint should mean that Soviet cinema concentrate entirely on comic and fairy-tale escapism, he emphasised that Soviet science fiction should be based on reality rather than utopia. Whereas for the scientist, he argued, unfinished experiments

> are merely a job half done, it is another matter for the artist. For him the world of as yet unfinished scientific experiments is a Klondike of creative ideas and story-lines.[84]

Perhaps the best example of the kind of film that Shumyatsky had in mind is Yuri Zhelyabuzhsky's *Cosmic Flight* [Kosmicheskii reis], a Soviet parallel to *Things to Come* [Great Britain, 1936], released in 1935,[85] although the film can hardly be said to contain a 'Klondike of creative ideas'!

Soviet films were to be firmly tied to reality, or at least to the socialist realist perception of it, by their subject-matter which was to be relevant, topical and realistic. Shumyatsky designated five principal themes for film-makers to pursue. The most important of these was the process of the collectivisation of agriculture. The reasons for this are obvious: it was a policy that had encountered more widespread opposition than any other and a greater propaganda effort had therefore to be directed towards making it more palatable, if not to the expanding audiences for cinema in the countryside, who were after all those most closely affected, then at least to audiences in the towns and cities. A large number of films can be counted in this category, from Medvedkin's already mentioned *Happiness* and other earlier efforts such as Ermler's *Peasants* [Krest'yane, 1934] through Eisenstein's abortive *Bezhin Meadow* to the series of what are best described as 'kolkhoz musicals', such as Savchenko and Schneider's *The Accordion* [Garmon, 1934] and Pyriev's extraordinary *The Tractor Drivers* [1939].

Of almost equal importance are films depicting the socialist construction of industry such as Macheret's *Men and Jobs* [1932], Dovzhenko's *Ivan* [1932] or Ermler's *Counterplan* [1932]. This theme was closely related to another: the depiction of the Revolution through the portrayal of its effect on an individual who, while being a fully developed character in his own right (unlike Eisenstein's 'types' or Kuleshov's *naturshchiki*), also represented the mass. The Kozintsev and Trauberg Maxim trilogy is perhaps the best example of this, although their *Alone*, Ekk's *The Path to Life*, Yutkevich's *The Golden Mountains*, Pudovkin's *The Deserter* or Raizman's *The Pilots* [Letchiki, 1935] would also suffice. This theme was again intertwined with what Shumyatsky termed 'the everyday life of the new man'.[86] One of the most intriguing films in this field, Abram Room's *A Severe Young Man*, from a script by Yuri Olesha, was in fact banned because it confronted in a politically unacceptable way the question of inequalities in Soviet life and both director and scriptwriter were disgraced. It is worth noting, however, that, despite the thorough discussion of the film at all stages of its production, it was actually completed[87] – unlike *Bezhin Meadow*, and unlike Room's earlier project, *Once One Summer*. Quite how it was completed, given the controversial nature of its subject-matter, is one of the many questions that still await an answer.

The last theme that Shumyatsky urged upon Soviet film-makers was that of defence. Again it is difficult to consign particular films to any one thematic division but, if we are to include the defence of the Revolution, then the list is almost endless: Soviet cinema has from its inception produced a steady flow of 'historical revolutionary' films. We could again include the Maxim trilogy, *The Deserter* and, for different reasons, *The Pilots* and *The Tractor Drivers* but we should also recall Barnet's *Outskirts* [1933], Dovzhenko's *Aerograd* [1935], Dzigan's *We from Kronstadt*, the Zarkhi and Heifits *The Baltic Deputy* [Deputat Baltiki, 1936] and, of course, Eisenstein's one completed 1930s film, *Alexander Nevsky* [1938]. Lastly, we might also include films about the rise of anti-Semitism and fascism in the West: Pyriev's *The Conveyor-Belt of Death* (Konveier smerti, 1933], Kuleshov's *Gorizont* [1932], Roshal's *The Oppenheim Family* [Sem'ya Oppengeim, 1938] or the Minkin and Rappaport film *Professor Mamlock* [1938].

But one of the most important themes for Soviet film-makers in the 1930s was the Civil War of 1918–21. Its role for Soviet cinema was comparable to that of the western for Hollywood and it had many of the same ingredients: action and excitement, clearly defined 'goodies' and 'baddies' (Reds and Whites instead of cowboys and Indians), and the security of a known '*kheppi-end*' that established and then confirmed a myth and in this instance helped to legitimise the Revolution and the sacrifices in the eyes of the cinema-going public.

The great model for the Civil War film was of course *Chapayev*, made by the Vasiliev 'brothers' in 1934, which, perhaps not surprisingly, won the Grand Prix at the 1st Moscow International Film Festival in 1935. No other Soviet film, not even *The Battleship Potemkin*, has ever been accorded such widespread official sanction so quickly and so repeatedly. Shumyatsky wrote:

In 1934 the best film produced by Soviet cinema in the whole period of its existence was released: it was *Chapayev*, a film that represents the genuine summit of Soviet film art.[88]

The strength of *Chapayev* lay in its action rather than its 'psychologising' and in its simultaneous portrayal of the positive and negative sides of the Red Army in the Civil War period. The hero of the film was portrayed realistically, warts and all, while the Whites were depicted as a powerful enemy that could only be defeated by a considerable effort, an enemy worth defeating:

> In *Chapayev* the heroism of the movement of the masses is depicted alongside the fate of individual heroes and it is in and through them that the mass is graphically and colourfully revealed. . . . The film *Chapayev* has proved that in a dramatic work it is the *characters*, the intensity of the tempo, the ideological breadth that are decisive.[89]

The relative subtlety of the characterisation, the clouding of the absolute distinctions between black and white (at least in comparison with films like *The Battleship Potemkin* or *October*), involved the audience more closely in the film and its developing story-line:

*Figure 25* '*Chapayev*, a film that represents the genuine summit of Soviet film art' (Shumyatsky).

Chapayev's development does not take place *on the actual screen (as in many of our films) but in the audience's own eyes.* Chapayev is not finished and ready made, as all too often happens: he becomes a type through the plot, through dramatic changes. There is no head-on confrontation here, no exaggerated tendentiousness: the tendentiousness derives from the very essence of the action, from the deeds of the characters themselves.[90]

*Chapayev* then was *the model film.* In his message of congratulation to Soviet film-makers on the fifteenth anniversary of Soviet cinema in January 1935, Stalin said:

Soviet power expects from you new successes, new films that, like *Chapayev*, portray the greatness of the historic cause of the struggle for power of the workers and peasants of the Soviet Union, that mobilise us to perform new tasks and remind us both of the achievements and of the difficulties of socialist construction.[91]

It was also Stalin who personally suggested to Dovzhenko that he should make 'a Ukrainian *Chapayev*', a project realised in 1939 in the film *Shchors*.[92]

Shumyatsky angrily rejected the view, expressed by the writer and former RAPP activist Vladimir Kirshon among others, that Soviet art was developing in an irregular pattern and that the emergence of *Chapayev* was in some way accidental.[93] Soviet cinema was, he claimed, 'the most organised of all the arts in our country'[94] but it should be raised to the level of the best:

The *whole* Soviet cinema can work better. The *whole* of Soviet cinema, by aligning itself with the best films, can and must achieve better results.[95]

In order to do this, Soviet cinema had to undergo a radical reorganisation and overcome its 'backwardness'. Shumyatsky was keen for Soviet cinema to learn from the West, just as other spheres of Soviet industry were encouraged in the 1930s to 'catch up and overtake' the West by deploying foreign advisers.[96] In the summer of 1935 Shumyatsky headed an eight-man commission that visited the West to study film production methods in the larger studios. Shumyatsky, the Leningrad director Fridrikh Ermler and the cameraman Vladimir Nilsen visited Paris, New York, the Eastman Kodak plant in Rochester, NY, Hollywood (where they were welcomed by Frank Capra, entertained by Rouben Mamoulian and met, *inter alia*, Marlene Dietrich, Gary Cooper, Adolphe Menjou – that later scourge of 'un-American' activities, Cecil B. DeMille, G. W. Pabst and Erich von Stroheim, and watched Charles Laughton filming for *Mutiny on the Bounty*)[97] and London. Ermler and Nilsen then went on to Berlin, where they toured the UFA studios, but Shumyatsky, for reasons of prudence, returned directly to Moscow.[98]

The Shumyatsky Commission concluded that 'The entire Soviet cinema is today producing fewer films than one Hollywood studio'.[99] The reason for this was, in their view, quite simple:

When they make a film our directors are achieving a synthesis of various authors (the dramatist, the composer, the designer, etc.) but they are overburdened with administrative and organisational functions and this turns them into 'Jacks of all trades' without proper conditions and qualifications. This situation hinders the creative development of the director and similarly obstructs the development of the other co-authors of the film, subjugating them in administrative terms to the director.[100]

As we have seen, this was the opposite of what Shumyatsky wanted. Drastic measures were called for:

Setting ourselves the task of producing in the first instance 300 films a year, with a subsequent expansion to 800, we conclude that there is an inescapable need to build a single cinema centre in the southern and sunniest part of the Soviet Union, near the sea and the mountains.[101]

This project became popularly known as *sovetskii Gollivud* – the 'Soviet Hollywood' – and officially known as *Kinogorod* or 'Cine-City'.[102]

The full details of the 'Soviet Hollywood' are properly the subject for another essay. Suffice it to say here that the Shumyatsky Commission was impressed by the efficiency of Hollywood's production methods and recommended their adoption by and adaptation to Soviet cinema.[103] Above all, they were impressed by the facilities afforded to American film-makers by the climate and location of Hollywood. The decisive factor in favour of the eventual choice for a 'Soviet Hollywood' – the south-western corner of the Crimea – against competition from what we might nowadays describe as the rest of the USSR's 'sunbelt' was that it provided the closest approximation to conditions in the original Hollywood and the surroundings of Los Angeles.[104]

The relatively balmy climate of the Crimea would make location shooting possible throughout the year and liberate Soviet cinema from the rigours of the northern winter, which limited outdoor work to four or five months a year.[105] The location, the wide variety of the surrounding scenery and the opportunity to construct permanent sets that could be used over and over again for different films would obviate the need for costly filming expeditions to remoter parts of the Soviet Union and lead to an overall reduction in production costs.[106]

Cine-City was only one part of the Shumyatsky Commission's plan to revitalise Soviet cinema but it was the focal point. While the production from existing studios was to be increased to 120–50 films a year through reorganisation, reconstruction and modernisation,[107] the bulk of the expansion in production was to be concentrated in the Crimea. Cine-City was to provide the necessary capacity to produce 200 films a year.[108] Its internal organisation was supposed to adapt the best of American practice and serve as a model for the other smaller studios.

Cine-City was to consist of four studios, each sharing certain common facilities and employing, by December 1940, around 10,000 people.[109] Each of the four studios was to be composed of ten artistic production units (Kh. P. O. or *khudozhestvenno-proizvoidstvennye ob"edineniya*) and each of these units was to comprise five filming groups (*s"emochnye gruppy*). Each unit was to be headed by a producer (or *prodyusser* – even the word was imported from Hollywood), whose function was to relieve the director and his creative workforce of the administrative and organisational burdens that had apparently 'hindered his creative development':[110]

> The producer must know everything that is going on in his filming groups, he must organise them and direct them towards their work, he must free the director from the functions that are not properly his and must render him every possible assistance in realising his creative potential. . . . The producer has an enormous responsibility: he must represent the interests of the entire studio.[111]

There is an echo of the artistic production units in the creative units present in Soviet studios today through which veteran directors transmit their experience and expertise to the younger generation. A base for the filming expeditions that Shumyatsky so deprecated was constructed on the Crimean site but the rest of the project for a 'Soviet Hollywood' never progressed beyond the planning stage.

One reason for this was undoubtedly the enormous expense: the plans envisaged that construction costs would reach almost 400 million roubles for the period 1936–40.[112] Another reason was that Shumyatsky, like so many others at the time, was slipping gradually from Stalin's favour and his 'Soviet Hollywood' became an albatross around his neck.[113] Actions spoke louder than words and Shumyatsky had in the final analysis failed to produce the goods or, more precisely in this instance, the films. The production statistics were not refuted:[114]

|  | Planned | Completed |
|------|---------|-----------|
| 1935 | 130 | 45 |
| 1936 | 165 | 46 |
| 1937 | 62 | 24[115] |

The financial, technical and political difficulties of Soviet cinema, many of which were beyond Shumyatsky's control, were disregarded, the enormous burden of conversion to sound ignored. All Shumyatsky's exhortations had been in vain, all the rewards for film-makers in the shape of prizes,[116] of fast cars and luxurious dachas on the Hollywood model,[117] had failed to produce their intended results.

A Soviet anecdote relates that at some time in the course of 1937, when he was already under attack in the press, Shumyatsky complained to Stalin that Soviet film-makers would not co-operate with his plans. Stalin is said to have replied, 'But they are the only film-makers we have.'[118] Shumyatsky was not, however, the only administrator at Stalin's disposal. He was arrested on 8 January 1938 and denounced in *Pravda* the following day,[119] reviled as a 'captive of the saboteurs' in *Kino* on 11 January[120] and as a 'fascist cur' and a member of the 'Trotskyite-Bukharinite-Rykovite fascist band' in the film monthly *Iskusstvo kino* in February.[121] Sent into internal exile, he was executed on 29 July 1938,[122] his reputation in ruins and his name mentionable in public only as a term of abuse. But 1938 was not a very good year for reputations.

Shumyatsky's replacement, Semyon Dukelsky, was appointed on 23 March 1938[123] but sacked on 4 June 1939.[124] He was in turn replaced by Ivan Bolshakov (of whom Leonid Trauberg has said that 'He had as much connection with cinema as a policeman on point-duty'[125]), who was to survive the war to become the first USSR Minister of Cinematography in March 1946.[126]

Shumyatsky's achievement, even if not realised or fully appreciated in his own curtailed lifetime, was to have laid the foundations for a popular Soviet cinema, one that entertained, amused and attracted audiences as well as providing the agitation and propaganda that the political authorities required. He recognised that film-makers needed a certain freedom to experiment and that they needed protection both from administrative burdens and from outside financial pressures: *pace* Eisenstein, Shumyatsky is remembered now by veteran Soviet film-makers as the man who understood their needs and *let them get on with the job*.[127] He was a complex man in a complex position. But he recognised above all that cinema was a popular art form or it was nothing. A film without an audience was useless, even to the director who made it, and what a socialist film industry had to produce was encapsulated in the title of Shumyatsky's most important book: a 'cinema for the millions'.

# Notes

In these endnotes works cited frequently or by several authors are abbreviated as follows:

| | |
|---|---|
| Babitsky and Rimberg | P. Babitsky and J. Rimberg, *The Soviet Film Industry* (New York: 1955) |
| *ESW 1* | S. M. Eisenstein, *Selected Works* (ed. and trans. R. Taylor) vol. 1: *Writings, 1922–34* (London and Bloomington, Ind.: 1988) |
| *FF* | R. Taylor and I. Christie (eds), *The Film Factory: Russian and Soviet Cinema in Documents, 1896–1939* (London and Cambridge, Mass.: 1988) |
| *Film Form* | S. M. Eisenstein, *Film Form: Essays in Film Theory* (ed. and trans. J. Leyda) (New York: 1949) |
| Ginzburg | S. S. Ginzburg, *Kinematografiya dorevolyutsionnoi Rossii* [The Cinema of Pre-Revolutionary Russia] (Moscow: 1963) |
| Levaco | R. Levaco (ed. and trans.), *Kuleshov on Film* (Berkeley, Calif.: 1974) |
| Leyda | J. Leyda, *Kino. A History of the Russian and Soviet Film* (London: 1960) |
| *LVK* | *L. V. Kuleshov, Stat'i. Materialy* [L. V. Kuleshov, Articles. Materials] (Moscow: 1979) |
| Marchand and Weinstein | R. Marchand and P. Weinstein, *L'Art dans la Russie Nouvelle: Le Cinéma* [Art in the New Russia: Cinema] (Paris: 1927) |
| Pudovkin | V. I. Pudovkin, *Film Technique and Film Acting* (ed. and trans. I. Montagu) (London: 1954) |
| *SKhF* | A. V. Macheret *et al.* (eds), *Sovetskie khudozhestvennye fil'my. Annotirovannyi katalog* [Soviet Fiction Films. An Annotated Catalogue] (continuing series, Moscow: 1961 onwards) |
| Taylor | R. Taylor, *The Politics of the Soviet Cinema 1917–1929* (Cambridge: 1979) |
| Youngblood | D. J. Youngblood, *Soviet Cinema in the Silent Era, 1918–1935* (Ann Arbor, Mich.: 1985) |

## INTRODUCTION

1 *FF*, p. 1.
2 Yuri Tsivian *et al.* (eds), *Testimoni silenziosi. Film russi 1908–1919/Silent Witnesses. Russian Films, 1908–1919* (Pordenone and London: 1989).

3 L. Schnitzer, J. Schnitzer and M. Martin (eds), *Le Cinéma soviétique par ceux qui l'ont fait* (Paris: 1966), translated and edited by D. Robinson as: *Cinema in Revolution* (London: 1973).

1   **EARLY RUSSIAN CINEMA: SOME OBSERVATIONS**
    *Yuri Tsivian*

1 *The Moving Picture World*, vol. 35, no. 5 (1918), p. 640.
2 *Kino-gazeta*, no. 15 (1918), p. 5.
3 S. Goslavskaya, *Zapiski kinoaktrisy* [Notes of a Cinema Actress] (Moscow: 1974), p. 116; for *lubok*, see p. 167 this volume.
4 Transcript of a conversation with Giatsintova. T. Ponomareva Archive.
5 G. A. Pratt, *Spellbound in Darkness* (Greenwich, Conn.: New York Graphic Society, 1973), p. 126.
6 For Aleinikov, see pp. 84–6, 102 this volume.
7 The word for cinema in Russian, as in English, was neither static nor consistent at this time: *kino, kinematograf, kinema, sinema, sinematograf, kinotvorchestvo* and *svetopis'* were among the more common terms deployed. I have used 'cinema', except where 'cinematograph' seemed obviously more appropriate. Stainslavsky consistently used *sinematograf* to describe his stage concept. (Translator's note)
8 *Ezhegodnik MKhT. 1944*, vol. 1 (Moscow: 1946), p. 120.
9 M. Aleinikov, 'Zapiski kinematografista. Vospominaniya' [Notes of a Cinematographer. Memoirs], TsGALI (Central State Archive of Literature and Art), 2734/1/19, p. 33.
10 Valeri Bryuov (1873–1924), leading Russian Symbolist poet.
11 Aleinikov, p. 34.
12 M. A. [Moisei Aleinikov], 'Khudozhestvennaya postanovka i sinematograf' [Artistic Production and the Cinematograph], *Cine-Phono*, no. 3 (1907), p. 1.
13 Khanzhonkov and Pathé were the two leading film companies in Russia at that time.
14 N. I. Orlov, 'Pervye kinos''emki v Rossii' [The First Filming in Russia], Central Film Museum Archive, Moscow.
15 *Peterburzhskaya gazeta* [The Petersburg Gazette], no. 161, 15 June 1907.
16 Orlov, p. 6.
17 ibid., pp. 7–8.
18 ibid., p. 7.
19 ibid., p. 8.
20 ibid.
21 Aleinikov, p. 45.
22 F. Otsep, *Kinematograf* [Cinema] (Plan for a book), TsGALI, 2734/1/72.
23 I. Petrovskii, 'Kinodrama ili kinopovest'?' [Film Drama or Film Story?], *Proektor*, no. 20 (1916), p. 3.
24 *Proektor*, no. 19 (1916), p. 11.
25 *Proektor*, no. 9 (1916), p. 15.
26 Petrovskii, p. 3.
27 V. R. Gardin, *Vospominaniya* [Memoirs], vol. 1: *1912–21* (Moscow: 1949), p. 151.
28 V. Gaidarov, *V teatre i kino* [In Theatre and Cinema] (Moscow: 1966), pp. 101–2.
29 I. Mozzhukhin [Mosjoukine], 'V chem defekt?' [Where Lies the Defect?], *Teatral'naya gazeta*, no. 30 (1915), p. 13.
30 *Teatral'naya gazeta*, no. 19 (1914), p. 11.
31 *Teatral'naya gazeta*, no. 43 (1915), p. 16.
32 A. Levinson, 'O nekotorykh chertakh russkoi kinematografii' [Some Character-

istics of Russian Cinema], *Poslednie novosti* [The Latest News] (Paris), no. 1512, 29 March 1925.

33 Petrovskii, p. 3.

34 Moscow Art Theatre Museum, 5323/1250.

35 Petrovskii, p. 3.

36 *Proektor*, no. 17 (1916), p. 3.

37 A. Voznesenskii, 'Kinodetstvo' [Cinema Childhood], *Iskusstvo kino* [The Art of Cinema], no. 11 (November 1985), p. 93.

38 V. Meierkhol'd [Meyerhold], 'Portret Doriana Greya' [The Picture of Dorian Gray], in *Iz istorii kino 6* (Moscow: 1965), p. 24.

39 'Mister Ray', 'Leonid Andreyev u Tolstogo' [Leonid Andreyev at Tolstoy's], *Utro Rossii* [The Morning of Russia], no. 134 (29 April 1910), p. 2.

40 I have used the term 'speaking picture' for the Russian '*kinogovoryashchaya kartina*' to distinguish it from the rather different 'talking picture' [govoryashchaya kartina] which emerged in the late 1920s. (Translator's note)

41 Ya. Zhdanov, 'Po Rossii s kinogovoryashchimi kartinami' [Through Russia with Speaking Films], Central Cinema Museum Archive, pp. 2–3. The film to which Zhdanov referred was the early Lumière short *L'Arrivée d'un train en gare de La Ciotat* [The Arrival of a Train at La Ciotat Station, France, 1895], which formed part of the first cinematograph programmes.

42 K. Novitskaya, 'Vospominaniya o stareishem rezhissere Petre Ivanoviche Chardynine' [Memoirs of the Senior Director Pyotr Ivanovich Chardynin], Central Cinema Museum Archive, no page nos.

43 Zhdanov, p. 3.

44 L. Forest'e [Forestier], *Velikii nemoi* [The Great Silent] (Moscow: 1945), p. 55.

45 Zhdanov, p. 5.

46 Novitskaya.

47 *Cine-Phono*, no. 3 (1913), p. 26.

48 M. Daniel', *Pervyi raz v kino* [First Time at the Cinema] (Moscow/Leningrad: 1940), p. 13.

49 Zhdanov, p. 11.

50 Novitskaya.

51 M. Malthête-Méliès, *Méliès l'enchanteur* [Méliès the Enchanter] (Paris: 1973), pp. 398–9.

52 'Agasfer', 'Maks Linder v Peterburge' [Max Linder in St Petersburg], *Kino-kur'er* [Cine-Courier], no. 1 (1913), p. 15.

53 P. Konradi, 'Teatr i kinematograf' [Theatre and Cinema], *Kinematograficheskii teatr* [Cinema Theatre], no. 15 (1911), p. 6.

54 *Artist i stsena* [The Artist and the Stage], no. 10 (1911), p. 22.

55 'Impressionist' [B. Bentovin], 'Samooborona' [Self-Defence], *Teatr i iskusstvo* [Theatre and Art], no. 40 (1911), p. 740.

56 E. Beskin, 'Karamazovy na stsene' [*Karamazov* on Stage], *Rannee utro* [Early Morning], 15 October 1910.

57 V. I. Nemirovich-Danchenko, *Izbrannye pis'ma* [Selected Letters] (Moscow: 1979), vol. 2, p. 42.

58 ibid., p. 43.

59 'Impressionist', p. 740.

60 *Teatral'naya gazeta*, no. 12 (1913), p. 11.

61 Gardin, pp. 79–80.

62 E. Beskin, 'Ne tovarishch' [Not a Comrade], *Teatral'naya gazeta*, no. 47 (1914), p. 3.

63 P. Orlenev, *Zhizn' i tvorchestvo russkogo aktera Pavla Orleneva, opisannye im samim* [The Life and Work of the Russian Actor Pavel Orlenev as Described by Himself] (Leningrad/Moscow: 1961), pp. 251–2.

64 *Teatr*, no. 1684 (1915), p. 3.
65 ibid.

## 2 KULESHOV'S EXPERIMENTS AND THE NEW ANTHROPOLOGY OF THE ACTOR
*Mikhail Yampolsky*

1 Yu. A. Ozarovskii, 'Sushchnost' mimicheskogo ucheniya Del'sarta' [The Essence of Delsarte's Teaching on Mime], *Golos i rech'* [Voice and Speech], no. 1 (January 1913), p. 5.
2 J. d'Udine [Zh. D'Udin], *Iskusstvo i zhest* [Art and Gesture] (St Petersburg: 1912), p. 73.
3 ibid., p. 95.
4 ibid., p. 22.
5 ibid., p. 100.
6 ibid., p. 220.
7 S. Volkonskii, *Chelovek na stsene* [Man on Stage] (St Petersburg: 1912), p. 150.
8 ibid. p. 127.
9 S. Volkonskii, *Vyrazitel'nyi chelovek. Stsenicheskoe vospitanie zhesta (po Del'sartu)* [Expressive Man. Stage Gesture Training (after Delsarte)] (St Petersburg: 1913), p. 79.
10 Cited in: S. Volkonskii, *Otkliki teatra* [Theatre's Responses] (Petrograd: 1914), p. 123.
11 ibid., p. 152.
12 ibid., p. 169.
13 ibid., p. 178.
14 Volkonskii, *Vyrazitel'nyi chelovek*, p. 132.
15 V. R. Gardin, *Vospominaniya* [Memoirs], vol. 1: *1912–21* (Moscow: 1949), p. 143.
16 ibid., p. 139.
17 ibid., p. 170.
18 ibid., p. 178.
19 L. V. Kuleshov and A. S. Khokhlova, *50 let v kino* [50 Years in Cinema] (Moscow: 1975), p. 74.
20 See: E. Gromov, *L. V. Kuleshov* (Moscow: 1984), p. 103.
21 The Film School became GTK in 1925–30 and then GIK in 1930–4, since when it has been called VGIK.
22 Kuleshov and Khokhlova, pp. 74–5.
23 Gardin, p. 52.
24 ibid., p. 134.
25 ibid., p. 120.
26 ibid., p. 138.
27 ibid., p. 192.
28 ibid.
29 ibid., p. 203.
30 *Golos i rech'*, no. 3 (March 1913), p. 26.
31 V. Turkin, 'Litsedei i naturshchiki' [Simulators and Models], *Kino-gazeta*, no. 29 (July 1918).
32 A. Lee, 'Ekran i ritm' [The Screen and Rhythm], ibid.
33 ibid.
34 ibid.
35 L. V. Kuleshov, 'Iskusstvo svetotvorchestva' [The Art of Cinema] (*svetotvorchestvo*, literally 'light creation', was one of the early Russian words for cinema), *Kino-gazeta*, no. 12 (March 1918); *FF*, pp. 45–6.

36 L. V. Kuleshov, 'Znamya kinematografii' [The Banner of Cinema], first published in: *LVK*, p. 90.
37 Strzhigotskii (pseudonym of V. Turkin), 'Spor o printsipakh ili bor'ba za stil'? [An Argument about Principles or a Battle for Style?], *Kino* (Moscow), no. 1 (20 October 1922), p. 11.
38 Gardin, p. 174.
39 ibid., p. 195.
40 L. V. Kuleshov, 'Chto nado delat' v kinematograficheskikh shkolakh' [What Must Be Done in Film Schools], probably written in 1921 and first published in: *LVK*, p. 158.
41 ibid.
42 ibid., p. 159.
43 ibid., p. 160.
44 ibid.
45 Cited in: ibid., p. 134.
46 Kuleshov and Khokhlova, pp. 68–9.
47 V. T. [V. Tikhonovich], 'Zakonomernyi teatr' [Regulated Theatre], *Vestnik iskusstv* [Herald of the Arts], no. 1 (1922), pp. 12–13.
48 B. Ferdinandov, 'Teatr segodnya' [Theatre Today] in the book *O teatre* [On Theatre] (Tver: 1922), p. 47.
49 ibid., p. 44.
50 ibid., p. 46.
51 N. L'vov, 'Analiticheskii teatr' [Analytical Theatre], *Vestnik iskusstv*, no. 2 (1922), pp. 5–6.
52 I. Sokolov, 'Metro-ritm Ferdinandova' [Ferdinandov's Metro-Rhythm], *Vestnik iskusstv*, no. 3/4 (1922), p. 15.
53 L. V. Kuleshov, 'Kinematograf kak fiksatsiya teatral'nogo deistviya' [Cinema as the Fixing of Theatrical Action], *Ermitazh*, no. 13 (8–13 August 1922), p. 15; reprinted in *LVK*, p. 116; translated in: *FF*, pp. 66–7.
54 'Plan rabot eksperimental'noi kinolaboratorii na 1923/24 god', first published in: *LVK*, p. 199.
55 Volkonskii, *Otkliki*, p. 188.
56 N. M., 'Ballet i kinematografiya' [Ballet and Cinematography], *Ekran*, no. 22 (21–28 February 1922), p. 4.
57 V. Turkin, *Kino-akter* [The Cinema Actor] (Moscow: 1925), pp. 9–10.
58 ibid., p. 10.
59 A. Belenson, *Kino segodnya. Ocherki sovetskogo kino-iskusstva (Kuleshov–Vertov–Eizenshtein)* [Cinema Today. Essays in Soviet Cinema Art (Kuleshov–Vertov–Eisenstein)] (Moscow: 1925), p. 23.
60 L. V. Kuleshov, *Iskusstvo kino* [The Art of Cinema] (Moscow: 1929), pp. 24–7; translated in: Levaco, p. 51.
61 I. Sokolov, 'Industrializatsiya zhesta' [The Industrialisation of Gesture], *Ermitazh*, no. 10 (July 1922), p. 6.
62 ibid., p. 7.
63 O. Bir, 'Chelovek i mashina. Kino i teatr' [Man and Machine, Cinema and Theatre], *Vestnik iskusstv*, no. 3–4 (1922), p. 14.
64 ibid.
65 A. Gan, 'Kino-tekhnikum' [The Cine-Technicum], *Ermitazh*, no. 10 (July 1922), p. 11.
66 'Istoriya gosudarstvennogo Instituta Kinematografii', *Kino-Fot*, no. 3 (19–25 September 1922), pp. 8–9.
67 A. Voznesenskii, *Iskusstvo ekrana. Rukovodstvo dlya kino-aktërov i rezhissërov* [The Art of the Screen. A Guide for Film Actors and Directors] (Kiev: 1924), pp. 121–2.

**3 *INTOLERANCE* AND THE SOVIETS: A HISTORICAL INVESTIGATION**
*Vance Kepley, Jr*

1  S. M. Eisenstein [Eizenshtein] 'Dickens, Griffith and the Film Today', in: *Film Form*, pp. 195–255; Pudovkin, pp. 47 *et passim*; L. V. Kuleshov, 'David Griffith and Charlie Chaplin', in: Levaco, pp. 144–5. For other Soviet acknowledgements see: S. I. Yutkevich, 'Griffit i ego aktëry' [Griffith and His Actors'], in *O kinoiskusstve* [On Cinema Art] (Moscow: 1962), pp. 154–72; and Leonid Trauberg's letter to Griffith, 7 September 1936, in the Griffith Collection at the Museum of Modern Art, New York.

2  See: I. Barry, *D. W. Griffith: American Film Master* (New York: 1965), p. 26; and S. Stern, 'The Soviet Directors' Debt to D. W. Griffith', *Films in Review*, vol. 7, no. 5 (May 1956), pp. 203–9. In the standard English-language history of Soviet cinema, Jay Leyda (Leyda, p. 143) even goes so far as to claim that, in the wake of the introduction of *Intolerance* into the Soviet Union, no important film made in the USSR for the next decade 'was to be completely outside *Intolerance*'s sphere of influence'.

3  See: D. Bordwell, 'The Idea of Montage in Soviet Art and Cinema', *Cinema Journal*, vol. 11, no. 2 (Spring 1972), pp. 9–17; and G. Huaco, *The Sociology of Film Art* (New York: 1965), pp. 347–9.

4  'Amerikanshchina', *Kino-Fot*, no. 1 (25–31 August 1922), pp. 14–15; 'Americanitis' in Levaco, p. 128; 'Americanism', *FF*, pp. 72–3. For a detailed discussion of the *detektiv* and its evolution in the hands of the Soviets, see: V. Revich, 'Soratniki Zorge' ['Sorge's Advisers'], in: M. Dolinskii and S. Chertok (eds), *Ekran 1968–1969* (Moscow: 1969), pp. 139–44; and S. Yutkevich *et al.* (eds), *Kinoslovar' v dvukh tomakh* [Cinema Dictionary in 2 vols] (Moscow: 1966), vol. 1, cols 447–8.

5  Pudovkin interview with Jeanne Gauzner, cited in Leyda, p. 150.

6  Marchand and Weinstein, p. 42.

7  Conflicting accounts of this survive. Leyda (p. 142, n. 2) reports that distributor Jacques Cibrario was commissioned to persuade Griffith to work in the USSR. Journalist George MacAdam claims that a Soviet emissary named Joseph Malkin extended the invitation ('Our New Art for Export', *New York Times*, 13 April 1924, sec. 4, p. 2).

8  S. P. Hill, 'Kuleshov – Prophet Without Honor?', *Film Culture*, no. 44 (Spring 1967), pp. 8, 21. See above, ch. 2, n. 35.

9  D. Vertov, *Stat'i. Dnevniki. Zamysli* [Articles. Diaries. Projects] (ed.: S. V. Drobashenko) (Moscow: 1966), p. 116; A. Michelson (ed.), *Kino-Eye: The Writings of Dziga Vertov* (trans. K. O'Brien) (Berkeley, Calif.: 1984), p. 94.

10  S. Ginzburg, *Kinematografiya dorevolyutsionnoi Rossii* [The Cinema of Pre-Revolutionary Russia] (Moscow: 1963), pp. 273–4. Cf. the discussion by Yuri Tsivian, p. 7 this volume.

11  For examples of widely read histories that repeat the legend, see: Leyda, p. 142; and G. Mast, *A Short History of the Movies* (New York: 1971), p. 190.

12  Ginzburg, p. 212.

13  ibid., p. 213, n. 1. Cibrario was to become an infamous figure in the annals of Soviet film when he later swindled the Soviets on an equipment deal.

14  V. Listov (ed.), 'Prolog k *Neterpimosti*' [The prologue to *Intolerance*], *Iz istorii kino 9* (Moscow: 1974). p. 189.

15  ibid.

16  *Izvestiya*, 27 May 1919. p. 4.

17  E. Kartseva (ed.), 'Amerikanskie nemye fil'my v sovetskom prokate' [American Silent Films in Soviet Distribution], *Kino i vremya 1* (Moscow: 1960), p. 193.

18  The appearance of *Intolerance* in the Soviet Union marked the beginning of a

period in which foreign films dominated Soviet screens. For catalogues of foreign films appearing in the USSR in the 1920s, see: Kartseva, pp. 193–225; Yu. Greidung (ed.), 'Frantsuzskie nemye fil'my v sovetskom prokate' [French Silent Films in Soviet Distribution], *Kino i vremya 4* (Moscow: 1965), pp. 348–79; and N. Egorova (ed.), 'Nemetskie nemye fil'my v sovetskom prokate' [German Silent Films in Soviet Distribution], ibid., pp. 380–476.

19  Listov, p. 189.

20  ibid., p. 191.

21  *Pravda*, 29 May 1921, p. 4.

22  The screening was even delayed to allow the Cinema Committee to prepare multi-language texts of the prologue for the delegates (Listov, p. 191). This was all in keeping with the policies of internationalism of the pre-Stalinist Soviet Union. In the same vein as the *Intolerance* prologue, for instance, Glebov Putilovsky and his Petrograd Cinema Committee published a photographic history of the October Revolution for workers and radicals in Western Europe and America. The book was supposed to demonstrate the utility of the 'new international language of picture facts' (*Fotoocherk po istorii Velikoi oktyabr-'skoi revolyutsii, 1917–1920* [A Photographic Essay on the History of the Great October Revolution, 1917–20] (Petrograd: n.d.)).

23  Listov, pp. 189–90.

24  ibid., p. 190.

25  ibid.

26  ibid.

27  ibid.

28  ibid., p. 191.

29  Playbill for *Intolerance*, from the Griffith Collection, Museum of Modern Art, New York.

30  *Film Form*, p. 243.

31  I am indebted to Professor Steven P. Hill of the University of Illinois and to Professor Russell Merritt of the University of Wisconsin for their advice and assistance.

32  This translation by Richard Taylor is based on a draft by Betty and Vance Kepley of: N. N. Glebov-Putilovskii, *Prolog k kinospektaklyu 'Neterpimost'*' [Prologue to the Film Show *Intolerance*] (Petrograd: 1921), reproduced in Listov, pp. 189–91.

33  This anachronism is in the original Russian text.


**4   THE ORIGINS OF SOVIET CINEMA: A STUDY IN INDUSTRY
DEVELOPMENT**
*Vance Kepley, Jr*

1  See: E. Schmulévitch, 'Le Décret de nationalisation du cinéma russe', *Positif*, no. 178 (February 1976), pp. 34–40; ibid., no. 179 (March 1976), pp. 55–62; ibid., no. 180 (April 1976), pp. 55–61.

2  See the figures provided in S. P. Hill. 'A Quantitative View of Soviet Cinema', *Cinema Journal*, vol. 12, no. 2 (1972), p. 21.

3  See, for example: G. Mast, *A Short History of the Movies* (3rd edn, Indianapolis, Ind.: 1981), ch. 8; and A. Knight, *The Liveliest Art* (rev. edn, New York: 1979), pp. 65–85.

4  Leyda (3rd edn, Princeton, NJ: 1983), p. 7.

5  Babitsky and Rimberg, ch. 1; Taylor, chs 3–7.

6  The following outline of developmental principles and their application to the Soviet economy, encompassing the next several paragraphs of text, draws from several sources. On developmental principles generally, see: C. R. McConnell,

*Economics: Principles, Problems, and Policies* (7th edn, New York: 1978), ch. 21. On their applications to the Soviet system, see: N. Spulber, *Soviet Strategy for Economic Growth* (Bloomington, Ind.: 1964); D. A. Dyker, *The Soviet Economy* (New York: 1976), ch. 1; R. W. Campbell, *The Soviet-Type Economies* (3rd edn, Boston, Mass.: 1974), chs 1, 4 and 6; E. Zaleski, *Planning for Economic Growth in the Soviet Union, 1919–1932* (Chapel Hill, NC: 1971), chs 1–2. On the history of the Soviet economy, especially the transition from War Communism to the New Economic Policy, see: A. Nove, *An Economic History of the USSR* (Harmondsworth: 1969), chs 3–4; M. Dobb, *Soviet Economic Development since 1917* (rev. edn, New York: 1966), chs 4–8.

7 Nove, pp. 46–69.
8 ibid., p. 47; Dobb, pp. 84–8.
9 I. S. Smirnova (ed.), *Samoe vazhnoe iz vsekh iskusstv: Lenin o kino* [The Most Important of All the Arts: Lenin on Cinema] (Moscow: 1973), pp. 116–17; Marchand and Weinstein, pp. 14–15; I. N. Vladimirtseva and A. M. Sandler (eds), *Istoriya sovetskogo kino 1917–1967* [The History of Soviet Cinema 1917–1967] (4 vols, Moscow: 1969–76), vol. 1, p. 14.
10 L. Aksel'rod, 'Dokumenty po istorii natsionalizatsii russkoi kinematografii' [Documents on the History of the Nationalisation of Russian Cinema], *Iz istorii kino 1* (Moscow: 1958), pp. 25–7; Vladimirtseva and Sandler, vol. 1, p. 19.
11 Aksel'rod, pp. 26–8; Marchand and Weinstein, pp. 17–19; Vladimirtseva and Sandler, vol. 1, pp. 15–18.
12 Marchand and Weinstein, pp. 33–4; Aksel'rod, p. 31.
13 Aksel'rod, pp. 29–34.
14 ibid., pp. 32–4; Vladimirtseva and Sandler, vol. 1, p. 19; N. F. Preobrazhenskii, 'Vospominaniya o rabote VFKO' [Reminiscences of the Work of VFKO], *Iz istorii kino 1* (Moscow: 1958), pp. 85–90.
15 Smirnova, p. 51.
16 Vladimirtseva and Sandler, vol. 1, pp. 22–3; Preobrazhenskii, pp. 88–9.
17 Vladimirtseva and Sandler, vol. 1, p. 22.
18 ibid., p. 21; Aksel'rod, pp. 35–6.
19 These figures are derived from production catalogues in *SKhF*, vol. 1, pp. 5–31 and vol. 3, pp. 249–306. Roughly one-third of the private production activity took place in outlying areas, most commonly on the Black Sea coast.
20 On exhibition arrangements, see: *Economic Review of the Soviet Union*, 15 March 1932, p. 142; Vladimirtseva and Sandler, vol. 1, pp. 16–17; Aksel'rod, p. 31; Preobrazhenskii, p. 90. On precedents for the portable cinemas, see: M. L. Sanders, 'British Film Propaganda in Russia, 1916–1918', *Historical Journal of Film, Radio & Television*, vol. 3, no. 2 (1983), pp. 117–29; Taylor, p. 9. On the intensive utilisation of the rail system, see: Campbell, pp. 150–1.
21 Nove, pp. 83–90.
22 Dobb, pp. 132–8.
23 Vladimirtseva and Sandler, vol. 1, p. 23; Marchand and Weinstein, pp. 45–57; S. Bratolyubov, *Na zare sovetskoi kinematografii* [At the Dawn of Soviet Cinema] (Leningrad: 1976), p. 13.
24 A. M. Gak, 'K istorii sozdaniya Sovkino' [Towards a History of the Creation of Sovkino], *Iz istorii kino 5* (Moscow: 1962), p. 131; A. V. Ryazanova *et al.* (eds), *Lunacharskii o kino* [Lunacharsky on Cinema] (Moscow: 1965), pp. 29–35; Vladimirtseva and Sandler, vol. 1, p. 23; Babitsky and Rimberg, pp. 270–1. The value of the rouble fluctuated during the 1920s, but the exchange rate of gold-backed currency averaged about two roubles to the US dollar.
25 Gak, pp. 134–5; Ryazanova, pp. 22–4, 28–35.
26 Nove, p. 89; E. H. Carr, *A History of Soviet Russia* (14 vols, London: 1954–78), vol. 5, pp. 454–5.

27 Gak, pp. 134–5; Vladimirtseva and Sandler, vol. 1, p. 30; Ryazanova, p. 264; Smirnova, pp. 105–7, 169–70.

28 Y. A. L'vunin, 'Organizatsiya Mezhdunarodnaya Rabochaya Pomoshch' i sovetskoe kino' [The Workers' International Relief Organisation and Soviet Cinema], *Vestnik Moskovskogo universiteta*, 9th series, no. 4 (1971), pp. 21–6; Yu. A. L'vunin and I. Polyanskii, 'Blagodarya lichnomu sodeistviyu V. I. Lenina' [Thanks to Lenin's Personal Assistance], *Iskusstvo Kino* (January 1978), pp. 7–8.

29 L'vunin and Polyanskii, pp. 6–8; L'vunin, pp. 27–33; W. Münzenberg, *Solidarität: Zehn Jahre Internationale Arbeiterhilfe, 1921–1931* (Berlin: 1931), pp. 519–20.

30 L'vunin and Polyanskii, p. 8; Münzenberg, pp. 510–13.

31 Vladimirtseva and Sandler, vol. 1, pp. 24–6, 30; Gak, p. 132; *New York Times*, 5 August 1932, sec. 2, p. 1.

32 Ryazanova, p. 262; Smirnova, p. 42; the Lenin quotation is translated in: *FF*, p. 57.

33 Nove, p. 89; Carr, vol. 5, pp. 441–4, and vol. 10, p. 708.

34 On the government's foreign trade monopoly, see: A. Nove, *The Soviet Economic System* (London: 1977), pp. 267–87; on the USSR's general procedures for importing foreign films, see: B. Kepley and V. Kepley, 'Foreign Films on Soviet Screens, 1922–1931', *Quarterly Review of Film Studies*, vol. 4, no. 4 (1979), pp. 429–42.

35 Gak, p. 136; V. Golovskoi (ed.), *Kino i zritel'* [Cinema and the Audience] (Moscow: 1968), p. 14. See above, ch. 3, n. 18.

36 Gak, pp. 133–8; Vladimirtseva and Sandler, vol. 1, pp. 27–9.

37 Nove, *Economic History*, p. 103; Dobb, pp. 142–3.

38 Vladimirtseva and Sandler, vol. 1, pp. 28–9; Gak, pp. 139–41.

39 The number of operating commercial theatres dropped to 20 per cent of the 1917 level in Ural-Siberia, for example, 20 per cent in Samarkand, 50 per cent in Tashkent, and 40 per cent in Rostov: Gak, p. 136.

40 Gak, pp. 139–44.

41 ibid., pp. 141–4; Vladimirtseva and Sandler, vol. 1, pp. 30–1.

42 M. D. Kann (ed.), *Film Daily Yearbook – 1927* (New York: 1928), pp. 949–50; idem, *Film Daily Yearbook – 1930* (New York: 1931), p. 1043; *Economic Review of the Soviet Union*, 1 January 1930, p. 8; A. V. Troyanovskii and R. I. Eliyazarov, *Izuchenie kino-zritelya* [The Study of the Cinema Audience] (Moscow: 1928), pp. 39–43.

43 The figures are from E. Lemberg, *Kinopromyshlennost' SSSR* [The Cinema Industry of the USSR] (Moscow: 1930), appendix 4, n.p.

44 ibid., p. 71.

45 *Economic Review of the Soviet Union*, 15 March 1932, p. 142; ibid., January 1935, p. 8.

46 *New York Times*, 31 July 1927, sec. 7, p. 2; N. Lebedev (ed.), *Lenin, Stalin, partiya o kino* [Lenin, Stalin, the Party on Cinema] (Moscow: 1939), p. 56.

47 *Economic Review of the Soviet Union*, January 1930, p. 8.

48 Hill, p. 21; Lemberg, p. 47.

49 Vladimirtseva and Sandler, vol. 1, p. 32; *Economic Review of the Soviet Union*, 1 January 1929, p. 17; ibid., 15 March 1932, p. 143; Carr, vol. 10, pp. 705–16.

50 Hill, p. 21.

51 I wish to thank Betty Kepley for her advice and assistance.

**5 DOWN TO EARTH: *AELITA* RELOCATED**
*Ian Christie*

1 'O literature, revolyutsii, entropii i prochem' [On Literature, Revolution,

Entropy and Other Matters], in: *Pisateli ob iskussive i o sebe* [Writers on Art and on Themselves] (Moscow: 1924), translated in M. Ginsburg (ed. and trans.), *A Soviet Heretic: Essays by Yevgeny Zamyatin* (Chicago: 1970), p. 109.

2 *High Treason* [Great Britain, 1929], directed by Maurice Elvey, and *Things to Come* [Great Britain, 1936], directed by William Cameron Menzies, are typical of the many science-fiction and fantasy films widely reputed – in the absence of frequent screenings – to be less impressive in dramatic terms than their striking publicity stills. Another instance, closer to the case of *Aelita*, is Harry Lachman's *Dante's Inferno* [USA, 1935] from which only stills of the final 'Hell' sequence, uncharacteristic of the film as a whole, are ever reproduced.

3 See, for example, C. Lodder, *Russian Constructivism* (New Haven, Conn.: 1983), p. 292, and J. Milner, *Russian Revolutionary Art* (London: 1979), p. 64. Both of these use a number of *Aelita* stills and reach different verdicts on the 'Martian' decor, but fail to make clear that it features as a dream. Similarly D. Albrecht, *Designing Dreams: Modern Architecture in the Movies* (London: 1987), describes the film as 'a science-fiction fantasy set mainly on Mars' (p. 52); and D. Elliott, *New Worlds: Russian Art and Society, 1900–1937* (London: 1986), refers to 'a Soviet expedition to Mars' in a section headed 'Visions of the future' (p. 99). Typical of the synoptic surveys that describe the film as an expedition to Mars is D. Menville and R. Reginald, *Things to Come: An Illustrated History of the Science-Fiction Film* (New York: 1977), p. 29. One of the few general cinema histories to describe *Aelita* accurately and discuss it sympathetically is E. Rhode, *A History of the Cinema from its Origins to 1970* (London: 1976), pp. 115–16.

4 The most famous contemporary attacks were by Kuleshov, himself a former art director in the pre-Revolutionary cinema. For instance, 'Pryamoi put'. (Diskussionno)' [A Straight Path (Ideas for Discussion)], *Kino-gazeta*, no. 48 (25 September 1924); in Ye. Khokhlova (ed.), *Lev Kuleshov: Fifty Years in Films* (Moscow: 1987), pp. 60–1. For other dismissive mentions, see also: V. Blyum, 'Against the "Theatre of Fools" – For Cinema', *FF*, p. 117; A. Goldobin, 'Our Cinema and its Audience', *FF*, p. 125.

5 *The Extraordinary Adventures of Mr West in the Land of the Bolsheviks* [Neobychainye priklyucheniya Mistera Vesta v strane bol'shevikov, 1924] consists of a series of tricks played by conmen on the innocent Mr West, ending with a tour of the 'real Moscow' after his rescue. *The Great Consoler* [Velikii uteshitel', 1933] sets a fantastic tale of the Wild West within a framing story of the author O. Henry's imprisonment.

6 The New Economic Policy came into force during 1921, as it became clear to Lenin that full-scale nationalisation and centralisation of the Soviet economy were not working. In a series of measures, private trading was re-legalised, co-operatives were encouraged, the state monopoly on trade was abolished and the right to organise small business enterprises was granted. Heavy industry, banking and foreign trade remained state monopolies. The entrepreneurs of the NEP were known as 'Nepmen', who soon became popular targets of rumour and satire. For many Bolsheviks, NEP represented a retreat, though Lenin defended it as a return to the policies of 1918, before these had been distorted by the exigencies of 'War Communism'. However, his failing health from 1922 limited his contribution to the debate over NEP, which reached its peak in 1923–4. The policy theoretically continued until the start of the first Five Year Plan in 1929. See A. Nove, *An Economic History of the USSR* (Harmondsworth: 1969), chs 4 and 5. See also pp. 67–79 this volume.

7 Nikolai Tsereteli (Los/Spiridonov) and Konstantin Eggert were leading actors at the Moscow Kamerny [Chamber] Theatre; Igor Ilyinsky (Kravtsev) belonged to Meyerhold's company from 1920; Yuliya Solntseva (Aelita) had no previous stage or screen experience. All were making their film début – and Eggert was so

impressed that he left the theatre permanently for cinema, according to M. Arlazorov, *Protazanov* (Moscow: 1973), pp. 120–1. Other actors were drawn from cinema and theatre, making the production famous for its diversity of acting talent. (I am grateful to Richard Taylor for this and other translations from Arlazorov.)

8 For contemporaneous accounts, see: H. Carter, *The New Theatre and Cinema of Soviet Russia* (London: 1924); O. Sayler, *Inside the Moscow Art Theatre* (New York: 1925); R. Fülöp-Miller and J. Gregor, *The Russian Theatre* (trans. P. England) (London: 1930). The Kamerny Theatre toured Western Europe in 1923.

9 See Sayler, pp. 96 ff. for a description of Rabinovich's set, consisting of grouped classical columns connected by curving pediments, for *Lysistrata*; also an interview with this prolific designer, who also worked for the Kamerny and Habima theatres.

10 Arlazorov, p. 122.

11 *Pravda*, 1 October 1924 (thanks are due to Jeffrey Brooks for this reference); *Kino-gazeta*, no. 48 (23 September 1924), quoted in Arlazorov, p. 123, which is also the source for other information about the film's première.

12 A copy of this is preserved in the Central Film Museum at the Moscow Film Centre and was kindly made available by Rashit Yangirov.

13 No actual figures are available, but these should emerge from the empirical work on Soviet popular cinema currently being done by Maya Turovskaya and Yekaterina Khokhlova. All sources, however, point to *Aelita* as probably the biggest box-office success before *The Bear's Wedding*.

14 *The Bear's Wedding* was scripted by Lunacharsky, whose wife appeared in it. Konstantin Eggert played the lead and co-directed with the experienced Vladimir Gardin. Leonid Trauberg recalled, in conversation, Eggert's popularity with women after his portrayal of the vampire count.

15 *Pravda*, 1 October 1924.

16 *Izvestiya* quoted in: J.-L. Passek (ed.), *Le Cinéma russe et soviétique* (Paris: 1981), p. 183; Lunacharsky quoted by L. Pliushch in a note on *Aelita*, in: *La Victoire sur le soleil: Russe 1905–1935*, documentation accompanying an exhibition and film programme at the Cinémathèque de Toulouse, 1984.

17 T. Dickinson and C. De la Roche, *Soviet Cinema* (London: 1948), p. 20. Although there are references to a print of *Aelita* in London in the 1920s, it appears never to have been shown publicly.

18 Bryher [pseud. of W. Ellerman], *Film Problems of Soviet Russia* (Territet, Switzerland: 1929), pp. 113–14.

19 ibid.

20 P. Rotha, *The Film Till Now* (London: 1929; expanded edn 1960), p. 98.

21 This short account of Mezhrabpom-Rus and its links with Germany owes much to Vance Kepley's valuable article, 'The Workers' International Relief and the Cinema of the Left 1921–1935', *Cinema Journal*, vol. 23, no. 1 (Autumn 1983), pp. 7–23. 'Left' in the Soviet context of this time meant formally experimental or avant-garde, while elsewhere it tended to mean socialist or sympathetic to the USSR. See also pp. 70–1 this volume.

22 Leyda, p. 146.

23 ibid., p. 147.

24 Kepley, 'The Workers' International Relief . . .', p. 12.

25 *FF*, p. 97.

26 *Four and Five* was announced as opening at the Ars Cinema on 19 September 1924 and reviewed in *Pravda* on 24 September.

27 A. V. Lunacharskii, 'Revolyutsionnaya ideologiya i kino – tezisy', *Kinonedelya*, no. 24 (1924); *FF*, p. 109.

28 On Protazanov's career in France, see: L. Borger, 'From Moscow to Montreuil: The Russian Emigrés in France 1920–1929' and K. Thompson, 'The Ermolieff Group in Paris: Exile, Impressionism, Internationalism', *Griffithiana* (Pordenone, Italy), no. 35–6 (October 1989), pp. 28–39, 50–7. On the terms of Protazanov's invitation, see Leyda, p. 186n. Arlazorov refers to an 'Ivan the Terrible' project he had interrupted and did not return to (p. 128).

29 Arlazorov, p. 119.

30 Letter to Nikolai Chaikovsky quoted in M. Slonim, *Modern Russian Literature* (Oxford: 1957), p. 370.

31 Surveyed in D. Suvin, 'The Utopian Tradition of Russian Science Fiction', *Modern Language Review*, no. 66 (1971), pp. 145–51.

32 All references to the translation by Leland Fetzer, *Aelita, or the Decline of Mars* (Ann Arbor, Mich.: 1985).

33 Ye. Zamyatin, 'Novaya russkaya proza' [The New Russian Prose], *Russkoe iskusstvo*, nos 2–3 (1923); translated in Ginsburg, p. 102.

34 Arlazorov, pp. 118–19, quotes an interview with Tolstoi in *Literaturnyi Leningrad* (n.d., but probably 1937).

35 Dates taken from English-language titles on an American distribution print (Films Inc.) of unknown provenance. Bryher cites the period as 1919–23, but had not seen the film.

36 V. Alexandrova, *A History of Soviet Literature 1917–64* (New York: 1964), pp. 239–40.

37 Yu. Tsivian *et al.* (eds), *Silent Witnesses: Russian Films 1908–1919* (Pordenone and London: 1989), pp. 160–2.

38 ibid., pp. 422–6; see also: Denise J. Youngblood, p. 107 this volume.

39 Arlazorov, p. 117.

40 ibid., p. 119.

41 See: I. Christie, 'Making sense of early Soviet sound', p. 190 this volume.

42 On the 'boundary situation', or entry from the real into the fantastic world, see M. Mendelson, 'Opening Moves: The Entry into the Other World', *Extrapolation*, vol. 25, no. 2 (Summer 1984), pp. 171–9.

43 H. Carter, *The New Spirit in the Cinema* (London: 1930), p. 251n.

44 P. Jensen, *The Cinema of Fritz Lang* (New York and London: 1969), p. 62.

45 Thompson, pp. 51–4; Albrecht, *Designing Dreams*, pp. 43 ff.

46 S. Lawder, *The Cubist Cinema* (New York: 1975), pp. 200–2.

47 P. de Francia, *Fernand Léger* (New York and London: 1983), p. 62.

48 ibid., p. 94.

49 R. Cohen, 'Alexandra Exter's Designs for the Theatre', *ArtForum* (Summer 1986), pp. 46–9.

50 ibid., p. 47.

51 R. Williams, *Artists in Revolution: Portraits of the Russian Avant-Garde 1905–25* (London: 1978), pp. 87, 95.

52 S. Makovskii, 'Golubaya roza', *Zolotoe runo* [The Golden Fleece], no. 5 (1907); quoted in C. Gray, *The Russian Experiment in Art 1863–1922* (London: rev. edn 1986, p. 75 and ch. 5.

53 A. Nakov, *Avant-Garde Russe* (Paris and London: 1986), p. 62. The translations from this source are by Ian Christie.

54 J. Bowlt, Catalogue: *Stage Designs and the Russian Avant-Garde 1911–29* (Washington DC: 1976), pp. 8–9.

55 Nakov, p. 62.

56 See: H. Marshall, *The Pictorial History of the Russian Theatre* (London: 1977), p. 113, for striking photographs of the Kamerny *Romeo and Juliet*.

57 Lodder, p. 155.

58 Bowlt, pp. 8–9.

59 ibid.
60 ibid.
61 Arlazorov, p. 119. Simov and Kozlovsky worked together on Starewicz's *Cagliostro* [Kaliostro, 1918] and on *Masons* [Masony, 1918], begun by Starewicz but finished by Chargonin.
62 A. A. Bogdanov, *Krasnaya zvezda* (St Petersburg, 1908) and a sequel, *Engineer Menni* [Inzhener Menni, Moscow, 1913], both included in: L. Graham and R. Stites (eds), *Red Star: The First Bolshevik Utopia* (trans. Charles Rougle) (Bloomington, Ind.: 1984).
63 L. Heller, *De la Science-fiction soviétique* (translated from Russian: Lausanne: 1979), p. 39.
64 On Shaginyan's inspiration from pre-Revolutionary material, see: J. Brooks, *When Russia Learned to Read* (Princeton, NJ: 1985), p. 153.
65 See, for example, the FEKS manifesto with its reference to 'Music-Hall Cinematographovich Pinkertonov', *Ekstsentrism* (Petrograd: 1922); translated in: *FF*, pp. 58–64.
66 K. Lewis and H. Weber, 'Zamyatin's *We*, the Proletarian Poets, and Bogdanov's *Red Star*', in *Russian Literature Triquarterly*, no. 12 (1975), pp. 252–78.
67 L. Trotsky, *Literature and Revolution* (Ann Arbor, Mich.: 1960), p. 210.
68 Heller, pp. 40–1; Williams, pp. 129–30.
69 Pliushch, see above, n. 16.
70 Published in 1877.
71 Suvin, p. 143.
72 C. Pike, 'Dostoevsky's "Dream of a Ridiculous Man": Seeing is Believing', in: J. Andrew (ed.), *The Structural Analysis of Russian Narrative Fiction* (Keele: n.d.), pp. 26–53. Bakhtin's analysis of the story is in: M. M. Bakhtin, *Problemy poetiki Dostoevskogo* (2nd edn, Moscow: 1963); translated by R. W. Rotsel as *Problems of Dostoevsky's Poetics* (Ann Arbor, Mich.: 1973), pp. 122–3.
73 Pliushch, see above, n. 16.
74 See, for example, R. Yurenev, quoted in: Passek, p. 113; I. Vorontsov and I. Rachuk, *The Phenomenon of Soviet Cinema* (Moscow: 1980), p. 60.
75 Bakhtin, pp. 94–7.
76 ibid., p. 100.
77 Leyda, p. 274.
78 I am indebted to Rashit Yangirov for information about the Foregger script.
79 Leyda, p. 186.
80 Erlich, the returning crook, 'takes pleasure in his new role as a Soviet official', but continues to cheat and steal. The NEP was widely believed to be an excuse for such activities.
81 The Serapion Brotherhood (named after a story by Hoffmann) was a group of young Petrograd writers who experimented enthusiastically with language, narrative and genre in the early 1920s, under the patronage of Shklovsky, Zamyatin and Gorky. One of the founders, Lev Lunts, envisaged 'a brotherhood of the plot' who would study Western popular writing in order to inject its dynamism and variety into traditional Russian literature. See: G. Kern and C. Collins (eds), *The Serapion Brothers: A Critical Anthology* (Ann Arbor, Mich.: 1975). Yevgeni Zamyatin (1884–1937), author of the celebrated dystopia and parody of Bogdanov, *We* [My], a versatile novelist, playwright, essayist and eventually film scenarist, was driven into exile after a campaign to silence him in the late 1920s. Yuri Olesha (1899–1960) wrote some remarkable satirical fantasies in the 1920s, *The Three Fat Men* [Tri tolstyaka] and *Envy* [Zavist'], as well as journalism; but in 1934 was severely reprimanded for scripting Room's long-banned *A Severe Young Man* [Strogii yunosha, 1934].
82 *Chess Fever* was co-directed by Nikolai Shpikovsky and Pudovkin, and includes

in its eclectic cast members of the Kuleshov group, Vladimir Fogel and Ivan Koval-Samborsky, the future star of several of Protazanov's films, Anatoli Ktorov, the chess master José Capablanca (as himself), and Protazanov with his then assistant, the long-serving director Yuli Raizman. As well as demonstrating many of Kuleshov's tropes in action, it incorporates American-style sight gags along very similar lines to Kravtsev's role in *Aelita*.

83　*A Severe Young Man* has remained banned until recent years. It includes degrees of stylisation and outright fantasy that were unique in Soviet cinema of the time, outside Alexandrov's musicals.

84　*Lady in the Dark* [USA, 1944], directed by Mitchell Leisen, analyses its heroine by means of her lurid dreams; *Spellbound* [USA, 1945], directed by Alfred Hitchcock, features a dream sequence designed by Salvador Dali; *Dead of Night* [Great Britain, 1945] is a compendium of ghost stories; *A Matter of Life and Death* [Great Britain, 1946], directed by Michael Powell and Emeric Pressburger, pits the subjective fantasy of a heavenly trial against its hero's medical treatment, and his love of a woman against love of country; *Orphée* [France, 1950], directed by Jean Cocteau, takes its poet-hero through the looking-glass into a highly charged netherworld of symbols and portents.

85　Protazanov will be the subject of a future retrospective, to include all his extant films, jointly organised by the Pacific Film Archive in Berkeley and the British Film Institute in London, which will provide scope for testing the claims made here and elsewhere by Denise J. Youngblood and others. Thanks are due to Richard Taylor, Julian Graffy and Jeffrey Brooks for advice and help with research for this essay, which was begun while teaching in Spring 1989 in the Art Department of the University of South Florida, Tampa. I am grateful to Bradley Nickels and other colleagues, the USF Library and my students studying Russian art for their encouragement and enthusiasm.

## 6　THE RETURN OF THE NATIVE: YAKOV PROTAZANOV AND SOVIET CINEMA
*Denise J. Youngblood*

1　The research for this essay was supported in part by a grant from the International Research and Exchanges Board. My thanks to Anna Lawton for her careful reading of an earlier version and to the Pacific Film Archive, Berkeley, and the All-Union State Institute of Cinematography [VGIK], Moscow, where I viewed the films.

   For descriptions of Protazanov's pre-Revolutionary work, see: Leyda, pp. 63, 80, 88; Ginzburg; M. N. Aleinikov (ed.), *Yakov Protazanov. O tvorcheskom puti rezhissera* [Yakov Protazanov: On the Director's Creative Path] (2nd edn, Moscow: 1957), hereafter cited as *YaP*; M. S. Arlazarov, *Protazanov* (Moscow: 1973). See also Tsivian, pp. 15–16 this volume.

   On Protazanov's French films, see: R. Abel, *French Cinema: The First Wave, 1915–1929* (Princeton, NJ: 1984), pp. 19–20; Abel, who uses the French spelling of the director's name, Jakob Protazanoff, does not mention his important role in either Russian or Soviet cinema.

2　Aleinikov, 'Zasluzhennyi master sovetskogo kino' [An Honoured Master of Soviet Cinema], *YaP*, p. 27. Aleinikov says that Protazanov was homesick, but adds no supporting detail.

3　N. M. Zorkaya, 'Protazanov', in: *Kino. Entsiklopedicheskii slovar'* [Cinema. An Encyclopaedic Dictionary] (Moscow: 1986), p. 337. Zorkaya has also written an insightful analysis of the director, 'Ya. Protazanov', in her collection of essays *Portrety* [Portraits] (Moscow: 1965), pp. 140–75, in which she persuasively stakes a claim for Protazanov as one of the key figures in Soviet cinema. It should be added that some latter-day support for Protazanov may arise from aesthetic conservatism, in that it is 'anti-montage' rather than pro-Protazanov.

4 Of course, some of the younger directors, like Eisenstein and Vertov, *courted* controversy at first and were only troubled by it later.

5 Given that Protazanov's pre-Revolutionary estate [soslovie] was merchant [kupechestvo] and that he was a native of Moscow, it is almost certainly not coincidental that an editorial in *Kino-Front* [Cine-Front], denouncing the state of cinema affairs, referred in several places to an unnamed 'little Moscow merchant': 'Za ratsionalizatsiyu proizvodstva' [For the Rationalisation of Production], *Kino-Front*, no. 7/8 (July/August 1926), pp. 9–13.

6 Protazanov's long-time friend and colleague Aleinikov confirms this and reports that Protazanov was fond of saying 'My pictures speak for me' – as of course were other directors who had no taste for aesthetic controversies, like Boris Barnet, Ivan Perestiani and Fridrikh Ermler; Aleinikov, 'Zasluzhennyi master', *YaP*, p. 27.

7 Vladimir Gardin and Alexander Ivanovsky were in the same position.

8 Unless otherwise noted, biographical details are drawn from Arlazorov, pp. 5–30, and from 'Protazanov o sebe' [Protazanov on Himself], *YaP*, pp. 287–309. Arlazorov's book, the most comprehensive account of Protazanov's life and work, is unfortunately somewhat 'novelised' and completely undocumented. Arlazorov did, however, have extensive conversations with Protazanov's youngest sister, N. A. Andzhanaridze, and details in this early section of the book ring true. 'Protazanov o sebe', pieced together by Aleinikov from various jottings by the director, is a disjointed account that ends with the Revolution.

9 'Protazanov o sebe', *YaP*, p. 287. Aleinikov, in 'Zasluzhennyi master', *YaP*, p. 6, says Protazanov mainly attended the Moscow Art and Maly theatres, noted for their realism.

10 'Protazanov o sebe', *YaP*, p. 288.

11 This is the *image* of Protazanov that emerged from his biographers, but it is based on inference, rather than on any statement that he made.

12 Arlazorov, pp. 22–3; O. L. Leonidov, 'Yakov Aleksandrovich Protazanov', *YaP*, p. 345, says Protazanov's family was 'horrified'. On money matters, see 'Protazanov o sebe', *YaP*, p. 297.

13 Arlazorov, p. 29, implicitly contradicts Protazanov's account by saying that Gloria was *purchased* by Thiemann & Reinhardt. The studio's name was actually 'Gloria', spelled with Roman letters, and not its Russian equivalent, *slava*.

14 'Protazanov o sebe', *YaP*, p. 297.

15 Protazanov attributed his success with actors to the high regard he felt for them; see: 'Protazanov o sebe', *YaP*, pp. 307–8.

16 Preobrazhenskaya went on to become Russia's first woman director and an important director in the Soviet period, too.

17 Aleinikov, 'Zasluzhennyi master', *YaP*, p. 20.

18 See Leyda's description of the reception of this film, p. 63; unfortunately Leyda does not credit his source but it was probably: B. S. Likhachev, *Kino v Rossii (1896–1926)* [Cinema in Russia (1896–1926)] (Leningrad: 1927). See also: Arlazorov, who reports that the box-office receipts were 'insane', pp. 47–8; and 'Protazanov o sebe', *YaP*, p. 299. Aleinikov rather obviously disapproves of the film and stresses that Protazanov adapted classics as well; see 'Zasluzhennyi master', *YaP*, p. 16.

19 See: J. Brooks, *When Russia Learned to Read* (Princeton, NJ: 1985), e.g. his comments on Verbitskaya's readership, pp. 158–60.

20 *Satan Triumphant*, described by Leyda, p. 88, does not fit the image that Soviet scholars have painstakingly crafted of Protazanov as maker of healthy

entertainment pictures. The movie is, however, included in the apparently complete filmography which appears in *YaP*, pp. 387–412.

21  Aleinikov, 'Zasluzhennyi master', *YaP*, p. 17, and Arlazorov, p. 60.

22  The information comes from Arlazorov, pp. 72–3.

23  Aleinikov calls *Father Sergius* a pre-Revolutionary film, giving its date of release as 1917, although the filmography contradicts this. This can probably be explained by confusion between *production* and *release* dates. See: 'Zasluzhennyi master', *YaP*, p. 26.

24  Arlazorov, pp. 80–2, making reference to Frida Protazanova's diaries. No date is given for the departure from Moscow, nor have I been able to find it in any other source. Protazanov himself is completely silent on this subject.

25  The reason for Protazanov's sudden move to Berlin remains a mystery; even Arlazorov refuses to speculate, p. 90.

26  As Lev Kuleshov's ruined career only too convincingly demonstrates, however, efficiency was not necessarily a saving grace.

27  Thiemann & Reinhardt's 'Golden Series', to which Protazanov had been the chief contributor (as everyone well knew), was frequently used as an epithet in the 1920s. See, e.g.: I. Fal'bert, 'Zolotaya seriya (*Medvezh'ya svad'ba*)' [The Golden Series (*The Bear's Wedding*)], *Kino*, no. 6 (1926), p. 2.

28  These aesthetic controversies are discussed in detail in Youngblood, pp. 63–80 and 133–44.

29  V. Kepley, Jr and B. Kepley, 'Foreign Films on Soviet Screens, 1922–31', *Quarterly Review of Film Studies*, vol. 4, no. 4 (Fall 1979), pp. 429–50.

30  The Petrov-Bytov/Piotrovsky debate of 1929 summarises this issue well; *FF*, pp. 259–64.

31  Movies scripted by Lunacharsky or based on his plays include: *The Locksmith and the Chancellor* [Slesar' i kantsler, 1924], *The Bear's Wedding* [1925], *Poison* [Yad, 1927] and *The Salamander* [Salamandra, 1928]. He also wrote *Kino na zapade i u nas* [Cinema in the West and at Home] (Leningrad: 1928).

32  V. Kepley, Jr, 'The Workers' International Relief and the Cinema of the Left, 1921–1935', *Cinema Journal*, vol. 23, no. 1 (Fall 1983), pp. 7–23. 'Mezhrabpom' was the Russian acronym for the WIR.

33  *Aelita. Kino-lenta na temu romana A. N. Tolstogo* [Aelita. A Film Based on A. N. Tolstoi's Novel] (1924), p. 45.

34  Information on casts and crews for all films discussed is drawn from *SKhF*, vol. 1; *Kinoslovar'* [Cinema Dictionary] (2 vols, Moscow: 1966–70); and *Kino. Entsiklopedicheskii slovar'*, cited in n. 3 above. I have seen all ten of Protazanov's Soviet silents, plus *Father Sergius* and *Without a Dowry*; information on content comes from my viewing notes, unless otherwise indicated.

35  'Po SSSR' [Around the USSR], *Kinonedelya* [Cine-Week], no. 1 (1925), p. 25.

36  P. Rotha, *The Film Till Now* (London: 1930; reprinted 1967), p. 228. For Soviet reactions, see especially 'N. L.' [probably Nikolai Lebedev], '*Aelita*', *Kinogazeta*, no. 39 (1924), p. 2, and 'Poputchiki ili prosoedinish'sya' [Fellow-Travellers or Ralliés], ibid., no. 43, p. 1. These sentiments did not, however, constrain *Kino-gazeta* from running advertisements for *Aelita* (money talked in the early days); see: no. 43, p. 7. The term 'ralliés' was introduced into Soviet cultural politics by Trotsky: 'ralliés' were 'the pacified Philistines of art', lesser creatures than fellow-travellers; L. Trotsky, *Literature and Revolution* (Ann Arbor, Mich.: 1960), p. 37.

37  A. V. Goldobin, 'Blizhaishie zadachi kino' [The Immediate Tasks of Cinema], *Proletarskoe kino* [Proletarian Cinema], no. 1 (1925), pp. 4–5; G. Lelevich, 'Proletarskaya literatura i kino' [Proletarian Literature and Cinema], *Kinonedelya*, no. 3 (1925), p. 5; A. Syrkin, 'Mezhdu tekhnikoi i ideologii (O kinopoputchikakh i partiinom rukovodstve)' [Between Technique and Ideology

(On Cinema's Fellow-Travellers and the Party Leadership)], *Kinonedelya*, no. 37 (1924). (This *Proletarskoe kino* should not be confused with the journal of the same name published during the Cultural Revolution.)

38 These viewers were assuredly carefully selected, although *Kinonedelya* implied that they were 'typical': 'Chto govoryat ob *Aelite*' [What They Say about *Aelita*], *Kinonedelya*, no. 37 (1924), p. 6.

39 For Kuleshov's remarks see 'Ob *Aelite*' [On *Aelita*], *Kinonedelya*, no. 47 (1924), p. 3. For Sokolov's see: I. Sokolov, *Kinostsenarii: Teoriya i tekhnika* [The Film Scenario: Theory and Technique] (Moscow: 1926), p. 64; idem, 'Material i forma' [Material and Form], *Kinozhurnal ARK* [ARK Film Journal], no. 9–10 (1926), p. 15; idem, 'Kuda idet sovetskoe kino' [Where Is Soviet Cinema Heading], *Sovetskii ekran* [Soviet Screen], no. 37 (1926, p. 3.

40 *Aelita* is listed among films scathingly labelled 'first class Russian cigarettes' [papirosy vysshego sorta] in *Novyi Lef* [New LEF], no. 2 (1928), p. 28.

41 E. Kuznetsov, 'Kak vy zhivete?' [How Are You?), *Kino* [Cinema], no. 45 (1932). Others cited as living well were Vsevolod Pudovkin, Oleg Leonidov, Osip Brik and Natan Zarkhi – an odd assemblage.

42 'Nasha kino-anketa' [Our Cinema Questionnaire], *Na literaturnom postu* [On Literary Guard], no. 1 (1928), pp. 71–6, and no. 2 (1928), pp. 50–4. Protazanov's response, bringing up the rear, appears on p. 54. Ilyinsky's anecdote can be found in I. V. Il'inskii, 'Bogatoe nasledstvo' [A Rich Legacy], *YaP*, p. 203.

43 A. Dubrovskii, 'Opyt izucheniya zritelya (Anketa ARK)' [An Attempt to Study the Audience (An ARK Questionnaire)], *Kinozhurnal ARK* no. 8 (1925), p. 8.

44 See: A. Kurs, 'O kino-obshchestvennosti, o zritele i nekotorykh nepriyatnykh veshchakh' [On the Cinema Public, the Audience and Some Unpleasant Things], *Kinozhurnal ARK*, no. 3 (1925), pp. 3–4; Sokolov, 'Material i forma', p. 17; B. Mal'kin, 'Mezhrabpom-Rus'', *Sovetskoe kino* [Soviet Cinema], no. 8 (1926), p. 9; and G. Boltyanskii, 'Kino v derevne' [Cinema in the Countryside], in: I. N. Bursak (ed.), *Kino* [Cinema] (Moscow: 1925), p. 41. Khrisanf Khersonskii complained somewhat half-heartedly that *His Call* lacked detail about workers' lives and the mass movement in '*Ego prizyv*' [His Call], *Kinozhurnal ARK*, no. 3 (1925), pp. 31–2.

45 A. V. Troyanovskii and R. I. Eliazarov, *Izuchenie kinozritelya (Po materialam issledovatel'skoi teatral'noi masterskoi* [The Study of the Cinema Audience (From Materials of the Theatre Research Workshop)] (Moscow: 1928), p. 31.

46 See: O. Beskin, 'Neigrovaya fil'ma' [Non-Played Film], *Sovetskoe kino*, no. 7 (1927), p. 10, for a somewhat back-handed compliment. In *Kino* for 1927 see: 'Na temu Grazhdanskoi voiny (O *Sorok pervom*)' [On the Civil War Theme (On *The Forty-First*)], no. 11, p. 4; and Khersonskii, '*Sorok pervyi*' [*The Forty-First*], no. 12, p. 3.

47 Arsen, '*Sorok pervyi*' [*The Forty-First*], *Kino-Front*, no. 6 (1927), pp. 15–19. I have not been able to learn Arsen's real name.

48 According to legend anyway; I have yet to find this piece in *Pravda*. See: L. V., 'O sovetskoi komedii: Disput v Dome pechati' [On Soviet Comedy: A Debate in the House of the Press], *Kino*, no. 19 (1928), p. 6.

49 On the problems of comedy as a genre, see: Youngblood, especially pp. 137 and 177–80; R. Taylor, 'A "Cinema for the Millions": Soviet Socialist Realism and the Problem of Film Comedy', *Journal of Contemporary History*, vol. 18, no. 3 (July 1983), pp. 439–61. For reviews of *Don Diego* see: 'Rezolyutsiya po kartine *Don Diego i Pelageya*' [A Resolution on the Film *Don Diego and Pelageya*], *Kino-front*, no. 2 (1928), p. 6; A. Aravskii, '*Don Diego i Pelageya*', ibid., pp. 20–1; as well as L. V., op. cit.; B. Gusman, 'Po teatram i kino' [Round the Theatres and Cinemas], *Revolyutsiya i kul'tura* [Revolution and Culture], no. 3/4

(1928), pp. 13–14; and M. Bystritskii, 'Shag vpered (*Don Diego i Pelageya*)' [A Step Forward (*Don Diego and Pelageya*)], *Kino*, no. 3 (1928), p. 3.

There is an interesting discussion of the film preserved in TsGALI, Moscow, in the ARK files, 2494/1/99: 'Stenogramma sobraniya chlenov ARK po obsuzhdeniyu kino-fil'my *Don Diego i Pelageya Demina*' [Minutes of a Meeting of ARK Members to Discuss the Film *Don Diego and Pelageya Demina*], dated 1 December 1927. In addition to the fear cited above that the film might be misused by enemies of the Soviet Union, there was a heated debate about the recent 'excesses' and abuses of film critics.

50 I. Sokolov, 'NOT v kino-proizvodstve' [The Scientific Organisation of Labour in Film Production], *Kino-Front*, no. 7–8 (1926), p. 11. S. Gekht, 'Kino-parad' [Film Parade], *Sovetskii ekran*, no. 30 (1926), p. 3, says that viewers liked it because it was well shot, had good actors, and a plot with romantic interest.

51 Kh. Khersonskii, 'Komicheskaya i komedii' [The Comic and Comedies], *Kinozhurnal ARK*, no. 11–12 (1925), pp. 27–8.

52 On the Fairbanks/Pickford visit, see: 'Ferbenks i Pikford v SSSR!' [Fairbanks and Pickford in the USSR!], *Kino*, no. 30 (1926), pp. 1 and 3.

53 Troyanovksii and Eliazarov, p. 32; and TsGALI in the Glaviskusstvo files, 645/1/389, 'Svodki anketnogo materiala po izucheniyu vpechatlenii zritelei kino-kartin' [The Results of Surveys of Audience Reaction to Films], pp. 3–4.

54 E. Arnoldi, *Avantyurnyi zhanr v kino* [The Adventure Genre in Cinema] (Leningrad: 1926), p. 68; A. Kurs, *Samoe mogushchestvennoe* [The Most Powerful] (Moscow: 1927), p. 59; and M. Zagorskii, 'Tapioka – Il'inskii – teatr – kino' [Tapioca, Ilyinsky, Theatre, Cinema], *Sovetskii ekran*, no. 38 (1926), p. 5. Kurs noted resignedly:

> *The Three Millions Trial* is a successful picture. I do not want to argue with the viewer. The viewer is always right.
>
> In general one should not argue with the viewer. One needs to study him.

55 S. Eizenshtein, 'Za "rabochii boevik"', *Revolyutsiya i kul'tura*, no. 3/4 (1928), p. 54; *ESW 1*, p. 110.

56 For an in-depth discussion of these issues, see: Youngblood, chs 5–6.

57 As examples of the extremely negative reviews of this film, see in *Kino* (1927): P. Neznamov, 'Chekhov – Krupnym planom' [Chekhov in Close-Up], no. 34, p. 4; M. Shneider, 'Po tu storonu 17-go goda: *Chelovek iz restorana*' [Beyond 1917: *The Man from the Restaurant*], no. 36, p. 3; R. Pikel', 'Ideologiya i kommertsiya' [Ideology and Commerce], no. 41, p. 2. See also: K. Fel'dman, 'Itogi goda v Mezhrabpom-fil'me' [The Year's Results at Mezhrabpom-Film], *Sovetskii ekran*, no. 42 (1928), and V. Kirshon, *Na kino-postu* [On Cinema Guard] (Moscow: 1928), p. 12.

58 See: 'Lef i kino: Stenogramma soveshchaniya' [LEF and Cinema: Minutes of a Conference], *Novyi Lef*, no. 11–12 (1927), p. 54, for Tretyakov's remarks. These were echoed by Osip Brik, pp. 63–4. Vladimir Korolevich had earlier defined *Khanzhonkovshchina* as 'boyar style and the good old days' in: 'Dlya Ars i Arsikov [For Ars and Arsists], *Sovetskii ekran*, no. 5–6 (1927), p. 11.

59 D. MacDonald, 'Eisenstein, Pudovkin and Others', *Miscellany* (March 1931), pp. 145–6.

60 See: P. A. Blyakhin, 'K itogam kino-sezona 1927–28 goda' [On the Results of the 1927–8 Season], *Kino i kul'tura* [Cinema & Culture], no. 2 (1929), p. 10; A. Piotrovskii, *Khudozhestvennye techeniya v sovetskom kino* [Artistic Currents in Soviet Cinema] (Leningrad: 1930), p. 14; I. Sokolov, 'Prichiny poslednikh neudach' [The Causes of the Latest Failures], *Kino*, no. 46 (1928), pp. 4–5; L. Averbakh, 'Eshche o reshitel'nom' [Once More on What is Decisive], *Kino*, no. 45 (1928), p. 3. With the exception of Averbakh, who headed RAPP, these

men were well-established critics. Blyakhin and Sokolov liked 'entertainment' films, while Piotrovsky thought of film as 'art' and was attacked as a 'Formalist'.

61 See, for instance: Prim, 'General'naya liniya Mezhrabpomfil'ma' [Mezhrab-pomfilm's General Line], *Sovetskii ekran*, no. 20 (1929), p. 6; and 'Kino' [Cinema], *Na literaturnom postu*, no. 2 (1930), p. 65.

62 *Sovetskoe kino* and *Kino-Front* were liquidated at the end of 1928. *Sovetskii ekran* was purged and retitled *Kino i zhizn'* [Cinema and Life]. *Kino* also underwent 'restructuring' at this time.

63 See: Youngblood, ch. 8; and P. Kenez, 'The Cultural Revolution in Cinema', *Slavic Review*, vol. 47, no. 2 (Fall 1988), pp. 414–33.

64 Kh. Khersonskii, '*Chiny i lyudi*' [*Ranks and People*], *Kino*, no. 40 (1929), p. 5; A. V., '*Prazdnik sv. Iorgena*' [*The Feast of St Jorgen*], *Kino*, no. 51 (1930), p. 4.

65 At the time of writing little is known about audience reactions and box-office receipts in the late 1920s; research currently under way in the USSR may alter this picture substantially.

66 B. Alpers, '*Prazdnik sv. Iorgena*' [*The Feast of St Jorgen*], *Kino i zhizn'*, no. 25 (1930), pp. 7–8.

67 V. B. Shklovskii, *Za sorok let* [For Forty Years] (Moscow: 1965), p. 94, from *Ikh nastoyashchee* [Their Reality] (1927); A. Piotrovskii, *Teatr, kino, zhizn'* [Theatre, Cinema, Life] (Leningrad: 1969), p. 236, from *Khudozhestvennye techeniya v sovetskom kino* (1930); A. V. Lunacharskii, p. 76.

68 G. V. Aleksandrov, 'Protazanov – komediograf' [Protazanov, Comic Film-Maker], in: *YaP*, pp. 162–94.

69 On Ermler, see: D. J. Youngblood, 'Cinema as Social Criticism: The Early Films of Fridrikh Ermler', in: A. Lawton (ed.), *Red Screen* (Washingon, DC: 1990). For the reminiscences of actors who worked with Protazanov, see, for example, in *YaP*: O. V. Gzovskaya, 'Rezhisser – drug aktera' [The Director, the Actor's Friend], pp. 324–39, and A. I. Voitsik, 'Kak uchil menya Protazanov' [How Protazanov Taught Me], pp. 375–82. Laudatory tone aside, both Gzovskaya and Voitsik speak with convincing detail of his calm personality and unflagging professionalism.

70 TsGALI, in the ARK files: 2494/1/99, '*Don Diego i Pelageya*' [*Don Diego and Pelageya*], pp. 3–4. On Vertov's problems with *One-Sixth of the World*, see: Youngblood, pp. 139–41.

71 For example, *Istoriya sovetskogo kino*, vol. 1, *1917–1931* (Moscow: 1969), p. 373, rates him sixth after 'the Five': Kuleshov, Eisenstein, Vertov, Pudovkin and Dovzhenko.

72 Zorkaya, *Portrety*, p. 175. It is worth emphasising that these favourable re-evaluations of Protazanov come from the 'old guard' of present-day Soviet film historians, that is, those who established themselves long before Gorbachev and *glasnost*.

## 7 A FACE TO THE *SHTETL*: SOVIET YIDDISH CINEMA, 1924–36
### J. Hoberman

1 I. Babel, *Lyubka the Cossack and Other Stories* (New York: 1963), p. 131.

2 The most substantial survey in English is: E. A. Goldman, 'The Soviet Yiddish Film, 1925–1933', *Soviet Jewish Affairs* (London), vol. 10, no. 3 (1980), pp. 13–27. A shorter version appears in: idem, *Visions, Images and Dreams: Yiddish Film Present and Past* (Ann Arbor, Mich.: 1983).

3 Z. Gitelman, *A Century of Ambivalence: The Jews of Russia and the Soviet Union, 1881 to the Present* (New York: 1988), pp. 123–4. The destruction of the *shtetl* was so overwhelming, Gitelman notes, that between 1918 and 1921 some

three-quarters of the Russian Jewish population was without regular income (p. 122).

4  A. Yarmolinsky, *The Jews and Other Minor Nationalities under the Soviets* (New York: 1928), p. 131.

5  A. Granovsky, letter to Mendel Elkin, 19 September 1924, cited by F. Burko, 'The Soviet Yiddish Theater in the Twenties' (unpublished PhD dissertation, Southern Illinois University at Carbondale: 1978), p. 148.

6  M. Gordon, 'Granovsky's Tragical Carnival: *Night in the Old Market*', *The Drama Review* (New York), no. 108 (Winter 1985), p. 92.

7  B. Gorev, 'Russian Literature and the Jews', in: V. Lvov-Rogachevsky, *A History of Russian Jewish Literature* (ed. and trans. A. Levin) (Ann Arbor, Mich.: 1979), p. 16. Vasili Golovnin (1776–1831) was a navigator in the Russian navy who was held captive by the Japanese in 1811–13 and subsequently published an account of the experience.

8  This sequence, singled out for particular praise by Soviet critics, is nearly a full reel. The location – not to mention the crediting of Sergei Eisenstein's cameraman Eduard Tisse as one of *Jewish Luck's* three cameramen – has fuelled speculation that it inspired Eisenstein's own use of the Odessa Steps in *The Battleship Potemkin*, which was also shot during the spring and sumer of 1925. In his 'Five Essays About Eisenstein', Viktor Shklovsky compares 'Eisenstein's flight of steps and the steps in Granovsky's film' to show that Eisenstein, and not Tisse, is the visual intelligence behind *Potemkin*: 'The flight of steps is the same, and the cameraman is the same. The goods are different.'

9  Leyda, p. 218.

10  Cited in J.-L. Passek (ed.), *Le Cinéma russe et soviétique* (Paris: 1981), pp. 122–3.

11  *Jewish Theatrical News* (New York), 16 February 1926, p. 2.

12  R. Ben-Ari, *Habima* (trans. A. H. Gross and I. Soref) (New York: 1957), p. 144.

13  Babitsky and Rimberg, p. 135.

14  S. Daytsherman, 'About Jewish Films (A Letter to the Editor)', *Der emes* [The Truth, cf. *Pravda*] (Moscow), 15 March 1928, p. 5. In fact, Mishka Vinitsky remained an Odessa folk hero throughout the 1920s because his gang had protected the city's Jews against White pogroms.

15  ibid.

16  Leyda, p. 230.

17  I. Babel', *Bluzhdayushchie zvezdy. Kino-stsenarii* [Wandering Stars: A Film-Script] (Moscow: 1926), p. 3.

18  I. Babel, 'Wandering Stars: A Film Story', *The Forgotten Prose* (ed. and trans. N. Stroud) (Ann Arbor, Mich.: 1978), p. 111.

19  'Theatre and Film: Wandering Stars', *Der emes*, 19 February 1928, p. 4. Although this review has been cited as part of the political attack on the film, the actual thrust is far less ideological than aesthetic. Dismissing *Wandering Stars* as an inept American-style melodrama ('empty and heavy-handed', 'a puzzle whose pieces do not fit together'), Lubomirsky blames Gricher-Cherikover for failing to realise Babel's 'brilliant, cinematographically rich' scenario.

20  Babitsky and Rimberg, pp. 134–5. See also: Goldman, p. 18.

21  'Motion Pictures', in: V. Kubijovyc (ed.), *Ukraine: A Concise Encyclopedia* (Toronto: 1971), vol. 2, p. 664.

22  *Kino* (Moscow), no. 20 (1928), quoted by Youngblood, p. 162.

23  *The Great Soviet Encyclopedia* (New York: 1982), vol. 29, p. 531a.

24  I. Fefer, 'Through Tears', *Kino* (Kiev), no. 3/39 (1928), p. 3.

25  M. Makotinskii, 'Trilogy', *Kino* (Kiev), no. 39 (March 1928), pp. 8–9.

26  I. Fefer, 'For a National-Minority Film: Regarding a Jewish Cinema', *Kino* (Kiev), no. 3/39 (1928), p. 2, quoted by Goldman, pp. 21–2.

27  A. Abshtuk, 'On Alien Paths', *Prolit* [acronym for 'Proletarian Literature'] (Kharkov), no. 8/9 (1928), p. 78, quoted by Ch. Shmeruk, 'Yiddish Literature in the USSR' in: L. Kochan (ed.), *The Jews in Soviet Russia* (Oxford: 1978), p. 259.

28  Goldman, p. 23.

29  Although Kushnirov's play was anti-Bundist, it did not wholly escape ideological error. In the January 1934 issue of *The International Theatre Bulletin* Osip Lubomirsky wrote:

> Kushnirov sees in Lekert a personification of the passionate urge of the working masses to revolutionary action against the evasive tactics of the conciliatory leadership of the Bund. Kushnirov's political orientation is communistic, but by his lending justification to certain opinions expressed by Lekert with regard to the Party programme, which bear a strong flavour of anarchism, Kushnirov stumbles into a grave political error.

30  N. Levin, *The Jews in the Soviet Union since 1917: Paradox of Survival* (New York: 1988), pp. 278 ff.

31  N. Sirotina, transcribed interview (1980), p. 19, William E. Wiener Oral History Library, American Jewish Committee, New York.

32  E. Lyons, *Assignment in Utopia* (New York: 1937), pp. 520–1.

33  S. Dinamov, 'Film Art in Soviet White Russia', in: A. Arossev (ed.), *Soviet Cinema* (Moscow: 1935), p. 115.

34  P. Markish, 'Generations', in: J. Neugroschel (ed. and trans.), *The Shtetl: A Creative Anthology of Jewish Life in Eastern Europe* (New York: 1979), p. 462.

35  J. Scott, *Behind the Urals: An American Worker in Russia's City of Steel* (Cambridge, Mass.: 1942), pp. 91–2.

36  M. Gordon, 'Program of the Minor Leftists in the Soviet Theater, 1919–1924' (unpublished PhD dissertation, New York University: 1982), p. 205.

37  K. Clark, *The Soviet Novel: History as Ritual* (Chicago: 1981), p. 94.

38  *Morgn freyheyt* [Morning Freedom] (New York), 14 April 1933, p. 7.

39  *Variety* (New York), 25 April 1933, n.p.

40  Scott, p. 240.

41  *Ekstsentrizm* (Petrograd: 1922); *FF*, p. 58.

42  M. Heller and A. M. Nekrich, *Utopia in Power: The History of the Soviet Union from 1917 to the Present* (New York: 1986), p. 217. The hero of N. Smirnov's popular novel *Jack Vosmerkin the American*, also cited by Heller and Nekrich, anticipated Nathan Becker in returning from America to his native village in order to serve the Revolution with New World know-how.

43  B. J. Choseed, 'Jews in Soviet Literature', in: E. J. Simmons (ed.), *Through the Glass of Soviet Literature* (New York: 1961), p. 132.

44  '*Mass Struggle*', New York State Board of Censors file, New York State Archives, Albany.

45  B. Berest, *History of the Ukrainian Cinema* (New York: 1962), p. 233.

46  *Variety* (New York), 23 October 1935, n.p.

47  D. Maryan, *Kino*, 4 June 1935; M. Grinberg, *Kino*, 10 June 1935, quoted in notes prepared by Naum Kleiman for the 'Unknown Soviet Cinema' screenings at the Pacific Film Archives, Berkeley, Calif., November 1989.

48  'Russia's Daniel Boones: Jewish Pioneers Who Are Blazing a New Trail in Biro-Bidjan', 1934 mimeographed text, cited in: Z. Szajkowski, *The Mirage of American Jewish Aid in Soviet Russia 1917–1939* (New York: 1977), p. 163.

49  J. Leyda, 'New Soviet Movies: Films of the National Minorities', *New Theatre* (New York), vol. 2, no. 1 (January 1935), p. 20.

50  M. Epstein, *The Jew and Communism* (New York: 1959), p. 313.

51  S. Schwartz, *The Jews in the Soviet Union* (Syracuse, NY: 1951), p. 181.

52  B. Shumyatskii, 'Za sovershenstvo masterstva', *Iskusstvo kino*, no. 7 (July 1936), pp. 6, 8; 'Perfecting Our Mastery', *FF*, p. 374.
53  Quoted by Lvov-Rogachevsky, p. 300. According to figures given by Szajkowski (p. 167), between 1931 and 1936 fewer than 1,400 Jews immigrated to Birobidzhan from abroad.
54  As in *Nathan Becker* agitprop was leavened with entertainment value. The film was revived in Moscow in the 1960s because of its appeal as ethnic comedy.
55  *Moscow Daily News*, 11 October 1935, n.p.
56  The lone exception is, of course, Alexander Askoldov's *The Commissar* [Komissar, 1967/87], which was completed in 1967 and shelved for twenty years thereafter. *The Commissar* not only includes a sympathetic, indeed positive, image of a 'little' Jew but also several lines of spoken Yiddish – the first heard in any Soviet film since the Second World War.

## 8  A FICKLE MAN, OR PORTRAIT OF BORIS BARNET AS A SOVIET DIRECTOR
*Bernard Eisenschitz*

1  Henri Langlois (1914–77), co-founder and first director of the Cinémathèque Française from 1936, was well known for his eccentric working methods and his imaginative programming.
2  G. Sadoul, 'Rencontre avec Boris Barnett' [*sic*], *Cahiers du Cinéma*, no. 169 (August 1965).
3  For extracts from this critique of *The House on Trubnaya* and other valuable contextual material, see: F. Albera and R. Cosandey (eds), *Boris Barnet: Ecrits. Documents. Etudes. Filmographie* (Locarno: 1985), where this essay first appeared.
4  Valentin P. Katayev (b. 1897) published important works in every decade from the 1920s to the 1970s, beginning with a satirical novel of the NEP, *The Embezzlers* in 1927. His 'industrial' novel, *Time, Forward!* (1932), applied cinematic techniques to the description of a vast building project; and later works experimented further with literary 'montage'. Yevgeni P. Katayev (1903–42) was the brother of Valentin and half of the 'Ilf and Petrov' partnership, with Ilya A. Ilf (1897–1937). These popular satirists are best remembered for *The Twelve Chairs* and *The Golden Calf*, both about NEP themes, including the stereotypical rich 'Nepmen', although they also wrote film scripts and travel books. When Vladimir Mayakovsky committed suicide in 1930, he left behind him two devastating comedies satirising the betrayal of communist ideals under NEP: one was *The Bed Bug*, the other *The Bathhouse*.
5  J. L. Borges and A. Bioy Casares, *Six Problems for Don Isidro* (trans. N. Thomas di Giovanni) (London: 1980), p. 83. Carlos Anglada is a fictitious author of vast erudition encountered by the incarcerated detective-hero of this book.
6  M. Kushnirov, *Zhizn' i fil'my Borisa Barneta* [The Life and Films of Boris Barnet] (Moscow: 1977), p. 153.
7  *Télérama*, 8 February 1984.
8  The film officially purports to be a thinly fictionalised account of the origins of the Stakhanovite movement, set in the Donbass in 1935, but there is little in the story-line to substantiate this claim. However, several film historians claim to have found anti-Semitic touches in the depiction of the criminal doctors.
9  Kushnirov, pp. 157–61. Nikolai R. Erdman (1902–70) was a playwright and author of numerous screenplays from 1927 until his death; see *Comédie-Française*, no. 129–30 (May–June 1984), with texts on Erdman by Jean-Pierre Vincent, Beatrice Picon-Vallin, Jean Ellenstein, Michel Vinaver and Bernard Eisenschitz on Erdman and film. Mikhail D. Volpin (b. 1902) was a poet who

worked with Mayakovsky during the Civil War on the ROSTA posters – *Volga-Volga* was his first screenplay.

10 Leyda, p. 271.

11 ibid., p. 388.

12 'Dramaturgiya i masterstvo aktera', *Iskusstvo kino*, no. 6 (June 1952), p. 101.

13 The term often used in Russian for a film director is '*rezhisser-postanovshchik*'. The term coined by Barnet, '*rezhisser-polkovnik*', is thus a play on words, referring partly to his films having been shelved ('*polka*' means 'shelf') and partly to his autocratic style of direction ('*polkovnik*' means 'colonel').

14 An indication of the scale of this opportunity is provided by Eisenstein's diary for 1945, quoted in: J. Leyda and Z. Voynow, *Eisenstein at Work* (New York: 1982), p. 148. Here Eisenstein records having seen in the space of two and a half months more than thirty films, including *The Human Comedy*, *Bathing Beauty*, *Laura*, *Stormy Weather*, *Gaslight*, *Phantom of the Opera*, *Five Graves to Cairo*, *Shadow of a Doubt*, *Star-Spangled Rhythm*, *My Friend Flicka*, various war documentaries and *Henry V* ('three black marks').

15 John Gillett recounts the first five minutes of *Lyana* [1955], which 'shows a village band gathering from various scattered parts of the village'. But it was *Bounteous Summer* which prompted Jacques Rivette to write: 'Eisenstein apart, Boris Barnet must be considered the best Soviet film-maker' (*Cahiers du Cinéma*, no. 30 (February 1953)). Even if this was a provocation launched on the spur of the moment, time has confirmed its prescience, especially in linking these two names. Reading Tarkovsky's *The Mirror* as situated in the tension between Eisenstein and Barnet certainly is not overly interpretative. As to Rivette's remarks on the film itself, however inaccurate these may sound, they are none the less to the point (for Barnet's talent lay in reanimating the most petrified forms):

> Barnet's outlook on the world and on the Soviet universe is one of innocence, but not that of an innocent. He knows that most demanding purity and guards it jealously as his most precious yardstick, the surest protection against a cruel universe which he instinctively mistrusts.
>
> From one film to the next, Barnet's universe is peopled by the same shy and modest characters, who prove unexpectedly impulsive, and whom their humour or heroism does little to protect, although here they have invented a new form of modesty, 'Stakhanovism'.

16 See, for example: J.-L. Godard, 'Boris Barnet', *Cahiers du Cinéma*, no. 94 (April 1959) (trans. T. Milne) in: J. Narboni (ed.), *Godard on Godard* (London: 1972), pp. 139–40. It is in the course of this admiring notice that Godard invokes 'the famous Triangle style' apropos Barnet.

17 Vasili M. Shukshin (1929–74) was a major writer of fiction and scenarios, a leading director from 1964 until his early death, and a popular actor in the films of other directors.

18 On Shukshin's career, see: I. Christie, 'Shukshin: Holidays for the Soul', *Sight and Sound*, vol. 55, no. 4 (Autumn 1986), pp. 261–2.

19 Radi P. Pogodin (b. 1925), the screenplay writer for *Whistle-Stop*, is not to be confused with Nikolai F. Pogodin (1900–62), the better-known playwright and author of *The Man with a Gun* and *Kremlin Chimes*.

20 Kushnirov, p. 206.

21 The studio logo which appears at the beginning of all Mosfilm productions is a production of the vast rhetorical statue by Vera I. Mukhina (1889–1953) of 'A Worker and a Collective-Farm Woman', sculpted originally in 1937 for the Soviet Pavilion at the Paris International Exhibition and now at the main gate of the Exhibition of Economic Achievements in Moscow. To Western eyes, the now

widespread use of zoom-lens shots in Soviet cinema, which was just beginning at the time of *Whistle-Stop*, often seems clumsy and inexpressive.

22 Interview with Otar Ioseliani, Paris, August 1983. Thanks are due to Valérie Pozner and Irène Ténèze for guiding me safely through the book by Kushnirov.

## 9 INTERVIEW WITH ALEXANDER MEDVEDKIN

1 Alexander Medvedkin (1900–89) was something of an *enfant terrible* in Soviet cinema. Best known in the West for his satirical feature *Happiness* [Schast'e, 1935], he was also responsible for the film train that focused on, and tried to solve, industrial problems during the first Five Year Plan in the early 1930s.

2 ARK [Assotsiatsiya revolyutsionnoi kinematografii] had been set up in May 1924 by Eisenstein and others as a revolutionary film workers' organisation. In May 1929 it became the proletarian-orientated Association of Workers of Revolutionary Cinematography [ARRK, Assotsiatsiya rabotnikov revolyutsionnoi kinematografii]. Like the Russian Association of Proletarian Writers [RAPP, Rossiiskaya assotsiatsiya proletarskikh pisatelei], ARRK was dissolved by Central Committee decree in April 1932. Medvedkin must here be referring to ARRK. See also ch. 11, pp. 196, 205 this volume.

3 Lunacharsky was People's Commissar for Enlightenment until 1929 and as such had overall political responsibility for the film industry. His speech defending Medvedkin was delivered to the Moscow branch of ARRK on 12 July 1931 after his retirement and published as 'Kinematograficheskaya komediya i satira' [Film Comedy and Satire], *Proletarskoe kino*, no. 9 (September 1931), pp. 4–15.

4 Chris Marker made a documentary *Le Train en marche* [The Train Rolls On] in 1971 to accompany the release in France of *Happiness*. This included a long interview with Medvedkin in which he talked about the film train.

5 Nikolai Okhlopkov (1900–67) was an actor in the Meyerhold Theatre from 1923, the director of the Realist Theatre in Moscow from 1930 till 1937 and director of the Mayakovsky Theatre from 1943 until 1966. He also acted in a number of films, including Macheret's *Men and Jobs* [1932], Romm's *Lenin in October* [Lenin v oktyabre, 1937] and *Lenin in 1918* [Lenin v 1918g., 1938], Eisenstein's *Alexander Nevsky* [1938] and Pudovkin's *Kutuzov* [1943]. *The Way of the Enthusiasts* was the only feature film that he directed.

6 The reference to 'black bread' goes back to Lenin's conversation in 1920 with Clara Zetkin on the role of art in revolutionary culture. See: *FF*, p. 51.

7 Khmyr is the name of the principal character in *Happiness*.

8 Eisenstein's review, entitled '*The Possessors*' [Styazhateli] (the working title of the film, a reference to the seventeenth-century debate about monastic land-owning), was written in February 1935 but remained unpublished until it appeared in the fifth volume of his posthumous *Izbrannye proizvedeniya* [Selected Works] (Moscow: 1968), pp. 231–5.

## 10 MAKING SENSE OF EARLY SOVIET SOUND
*Ian Christie*

1 C. A. Lejeune, *Cinema* (London: 1931), p. 167.

2 J. Grierson, 'Summary and Survey: 1935', in: F. Hardy (ed.), *Grierson on Documentary* (London: 1966), p. 182. The ambiguities of Grierson's position on Soviet cinema (as on much else) remain to be fully explored. Both in this article and elsewhere he slips between admiration for 'exciting cinema' and contempt for the 'airs and ribbons of art' that have distracted Soviet film-makers from 'coming to grips' with the issues around them.

3 A. Bazin, 'The Evolution of the Language of Cinema', (1955) in: *What Is Cinema?* (Berkeley, Calif.: 1967), pp. 23–6.

4 As Peter Wollen termed it in the discussion following his paper 'Cinema and Technology: A Historical Overview', in: T. de Lauretis and S. Heath (eds), *The Cinematic Apparatus* (London: 1980), p. 24.

5 G. Nowell-Smith, 'On the Writing of the History of Cinema: Some Problems', *Edinburgh '77 Magazine*, p. 11.

6 See: N. Burch, *To the Distant Observer* (London: 1979), ch. 14. Burch makes a case for regarding the five years after the commercial introduction of sound in 1927 as a 'Golden Age' for European cinema.

7 See, for instance: D. Robinson, *World Cinema: A Short History* (London: 1973), p. 175. Other 'short histories', such as G. Mast, *A Short History of the Movies* (New York: 1971), omit even this cursory remark on the introduction of sound.

8 Ye. Gabrilovich, 'Adventures and Encounters of a Scenarist', in: L. Schnitzer, J. Schnitzer and M. Martin (eds), *Cinema in Revolution* (trans. and ed. D. Robinson) (French edn, Paris: 1966) (London: 1973), pp. 168–9.

9 First published in translation as *Composing for the Films* (New York: 1947), and attributed to Eisler alone. The revised 'original' version, attributed to both authors, appeared in West Germany in 1969; I have used the French translation of this: *Musique du cinéma* (trans. J.-P. Hammer) (Paris: 1972), ch. 5.

10 Adorno and Eisler, pp. 85–6.

11 There is evidence of an interdisciplinary group which met in the early 1930s to discuss topics such as 'inner speech'; see: H. Deakin, 'Linguistic Models in Early Soviet Cinema', *Cinema Journal*, vol. 17, no. 1 (Fall 1977), n. 11, referring to research by Annette Michelson.

12 Paul Willemen extended his original discussion of 'inner speech', 'Reflections on Eikhenbaum's Concept of Internal Speech in the Cinema', *Screen*, vol. 15, no. 4 (Winter 1974–5), pp. 57–79, in: 'Cinematic Discourse – The Problem of Inner Speech', *Screen*, vol. 22, no. 3 (1981), pp. 63–93.

13 B. Eikhenbaum, 'Problems of Film Stylistics' (trans. T. Aman), *Screen*, vol. 15, no. 3 (Autumn 1974), pp. 7–32; originally published as 'Problemy kinostilistiki', with contributions by other Formalist critics, in the collection *Poetika kino* (Moscow/Leningrad: 1927). A complete translation of this collection is now available as *The Poetics of Cinema* (Russian Poetics in Translation 9, Oxford: 1982).

14 Eikhenbaum, p. 14.

15 ibid., p. 30.

16 'Help Yourself!', *ESW 1*, p. 236; also translated as 'A Course in Treatment', *Film Form*, p. 106.

17 Eikhenbaum, p. 16.

18 *FF*, pp. 234–5; *ESW 1*, pp. 113–14.

19 *FF*, p. 234; *ESW 1*, p. 113.

20 See, for example, texts by Andreyev, Mayakovsky and Meyerhold in: *FF*, pp. 27–39.

21 *FF*, pp. 271–5.

22 K. Thompson, 'Early Sound Counterpoint', *Yale French Studies*, no. 60 (1980), pp. 115–40.

23 Willemen, 'Cinematic Discourse', p. 66.

24 Thompson, 'Early Sound Counterpoint', pp. 119–27; Leonid Trauberg, co-director of *Alone*, confirmed in an interview with the author, Moscow 1987, that the film was fully post-synchronised.

25 A. Golovnya, 'Broken Cudgels', Schnitzer *et al.*, p. 139.

26 V. I. Pudovkin, 'On the Problem of the Sound Principle in Film', *FF*, p. 265.

27 *ESW 1*, p. 236.

28 Taylor's translation corrects several errors in the previously available version: here 'long shots' [*obshchie plany*] in place of Leyda's 'close-ups'.

29 N. Burch, 'Film's Institutional Mode of Representation and the Soviet Response', *October*, no. 11 (Winter 1979), pp. 87–8.

30 *FF*, p. 235; *ESW 1*, p. 114.

31 According to Y. Barna, *Eisenstein* (London: 1973), p. 134.

32 Alexander Walker records in *The Shattered Silents* (London: 1978), p. 198, the high proportion of European films and actors playing in New York at the beginning of the sound era. By 1930 almost all foreign films had disappeared from mainstream American cinemas.

33 Vladimir Petrić has analysed in detail the pattern of Soviet films entering US distribution from 1926 to 1935. The total imported by 1936 was 184 titles, of which 91 were silent and 93 sound. Petrić records the verdict of their US importer, Amkino, on its liquidation in 1940: 'Soviet talkies have always been less popular than Soviet silent films'; 'Soviet Revolutionary Films in America' (unpublished PhD thesis, New York University: 1973).

34 For details of Soviet dependence on imported American films in the mid-1920s, see: Taylor, pp. 94–6. See also above, ch. 3, nn. 17 and 18.

35 *FF*, pp. 129–31.

36 'The Cine-Eyes. A Revolution', *FF*, p. 93; also translated as 'Kinoks. A Revolution', in: A. Michelson (ed.), *Kino-Eye. The Writings of Dziga Vertov* (trans. K. O'Brien) (Berkeley, Calif.: 1984), p. 5.

37 'Otvety na voprosy' [Replies to Questions], here translated by Richard Taylor and Ian Christie from: S. Drobashenko (ed.), *Dziga Vertov. Stat'i. Dnevniki. Zamysli* [Dziga Vertov: Articles, Diaries, Projects] (Moscow: 1966), p. 129; cf. Michelson, p. 106.

38 'Pervye shagi' [First Steps], Michelson, p. 114. The Sokolov article, 'Vozmozhnosti zvukovogo kino' [The Possibilities of Sound Cinema] had appeared in *Kino*, no. 45 (1929).

39 I. Montagu, *With Eisenstein in Hollywood* (Berlin, GDR: 1968), pp. 27–8.

40 See my introduction, 'Soviet Cinema: A Heritage and Its History', *FF*, pp. 1–17.

41 A. Nove, *An Economic History of the USSR* (Harmondsworth: 1969 and 1976), pp. 144–8, stresses the massive and unprecedented task of *preparing* the Five Year Plan, with minimal planning techniques or statistics; hence the Plan was submitted for approval in April 1929, over six months after it was supposed to have begun.

42 Taylor, ch. 6.

43 *FF*, p. 208.

44 Montagu, p. 27.

45 The phrase was used in the Party Conference resolutions in March 1928 and became a slogan, later taken up by Shumyatsky; *FF*, p. 212.

46 The title of one of Shumyatsky's books, *Kinematografiya millionov* (Moscow: 1935).

47 Shumyatsky, p. 117.

48 Burch, *To the Distant Observer*, p. 147.

49 *FF*, p. 424. Similar figures are quoted in Steven P. Hill's valuable analysis of Soviet pre-war production, 'A Quantitative View of Soviet Cinema', *Cinema Journal*, vol. 11, no. 2 (Spring 1972), p. 21.

50 See pp. 199–200 this volume.

51 Undertaken, like Kristin Thompson's, at the Cinémathèque Royale de Belgique, Brussels, with the kind assistance of the late Jacques Ledoux and at his staff, and at VNIIK, Moscow.

52 See Willemen, 'Cinematic Discourse', pp. 64 ff.

53 S. Freud, *The Psychopathology of Everyday Life* (Harmondsworth: 1975), esp. chs 5, 8 and 9.

54 See above, ch. 9, n. 5.

55 Yuri N. Tynyanov (1894–1943), Soviet author, critic, theorist and scriptwriter, whose earlier scripts included the FEKS films *The Overcoat* [1926], based on Gogol, and *SVD* [1927].

56 Little is known about this film, which was directed by Alexander Andreyevsky, mentioned briefly by Leyda, pp. 283n and 363.

57 V. I. Pudovkin, *Pudovkin on Film Technique* (trans. I. Montagu) (London: 1958), p. 189.

58 R. Jakobson, 'The Dominant', (1935) in: L. Mateika and K. Pomorska (eds), *Readings in Russian Poetics* (Michigan Slavic Contributions 8, Ann Arbor, Mich.: 1978), p. 82. cf. Eisenstein's 'The Fourth Dimension in Cinema', in: *ESW 1*, pp. 181–94.

59 V. N. Voloshinov [M. M. Bakhtin], 'Reported Speech', (1930) in: Mateika and Pomorska, p. 158.

60 Even under *glasnost*, taboos remain which have prevented until recently extensive analysis of Soviet films of the later 1930s. The colloquium organised by FIPRESCI, the USSR Association of Film-makers and VNIIK on 'Cinema in the Totalitarian Epoch', in Moscow in July 1989, provided a rare opportunity to pursue this exploration by making comparisons between rhetorical strategies in German and Soviet films of this period.

## 11 IDEOLOGY AS MASS ENTERTAINMENT: BORIS SHUMYATSKY AND SOVIET CINEMA IN THE 1930s
*Richard Taylor*

1 B. Z. Shumyatskii, 'Tvorcheskie zadachi templana' [The Creative Tasks of the Thematic Plan], *Sovetskoe kino*, no. 12 (December 1933), pp. 1–15.

2 *Bol'shaya sovetskaya entsiklopediya* [The Great Soviet Encyclopaedia] (3rd edn, Moscow: 1970–81), vol. 28, col. 1548.

3 See: *SKhF*, vol. 1, pp. 82–3.

4 *Pravda*, 2 February and 16 February 1926; *Kino-gazeta*, 16 February 1926.

5 *Pravda*, 6 July 1926.

6 V. V. Mayakovskii, *Polnoe sobranie sochinenii* (Moscow: 1959), vol. 12, pp. 353–9.

7 A. Piotrovskii, 'Ob "ideologii" i "kommertsii"' [On 'Ideology' and 'Commerce'], *Zhizn' iskusstva*, 27 December 1927, p. 5; *FF*, pp. 188–90.

8 B. S. Ol'khovyi (ed.), *Puti kino. Vsesoyuznoe partiinoe soveshchanie po kinematografii* (Moscow: 1929), pp. 429–44.

9 ibid.

10 See above, ch. 9, n. 2.

11 See: *FF*, pp. 216–17, 219–20, 225–32.

12 P. Petrov-Bytov, 'U nas net sovetskoi kinematografii' [We Have no Soviet Cinema], *Zhizn' iskusstva*, 21 April 1929, p. 8; *FF*, pp. 259–62.

13 ibid.

14 Quoted in N. A. Lebedev (ed.), *Partiya o kino* [The Party on Cinema] (Moscow: 1939), pp. 82–5. This is *not* the same as the book quoted above in ch. 4, n. 46.

15 A. I. Rubailo, *Partiinoe rukovodstvo razvitiem kinoiskusstva (1928–1937gg.)* [Party Guidance of the Development of Cinema Art (1928–37)] (Moscow: 1976), p. 22.

16 *Kinospravochnik* [Cinema Handbook] (Moscow: 1929), p. 25.

17 Rubailo, p. 20.

18  Ol'khovyi, p. 38.
19  Rubailo, p. 23.
20  A. V. Lunacharskii, 'O kino' [On Cinema], *Komsomol'skaya pravda*, 26 August 1925.
21  Reported in *Zhizn' iskusstva*, 24 January 1928.
22  V. Sutyrin, 'Ot intelligentskikh illyuzii k real'noi deistvitel'nosti' [From Intelligentsia Illusions to Actual Reality], *Proletarskoe kino*, no. 5/6 (May/June 1931), pp. 14–24.
23  E. Lemberg, *Kinopromyshlennost' SSSR* [The Cinema Industry of the USSR] (Moscow: 1930), p. 71.
24  E. Gabrilovich, *O tom, chto proshlo* [About What Happened] (Moscow: 1967), p. 12. See also above ch. 10, n. 8.
25  B. Z. Shumyatskii, 'Signal trevogi' [Warning Signal], *Proletarskoe kino*, no. 5/6 (May/June 1931), pp. 5–7.
26  See, for instance: B. Z. Shumyatskii, 'Zadachi templana 1934 goda' [The Tasks of the 1934 Thematic Plan], *Sovetskoe kino*, no. 11 (November 1933), pp. 1–4; and idem, 'Tvorcheskie zadachi templana', op. cit.
27  Reported in *Kino*, 28 December 1933, pp. 3–4.
28  TsGALI (Central State Archive for Literature and the Arts), 2497/1/64, minute no. 32, dated 27 June 1932, pp. 184–7.
29  The speech is in TsGALI, 2497/1/64, minute no. 33, dated 2 July 1932, pp. 188–95. The quotation is from p. 190.
30  ibid., p. 191.
31  ibid.
32  *Izvestiya*, 12 February 1933.
33  B. Z. Shumyatskii, *Sovetskii fil'm na mezhdunarodnoi kinovystavke* [Soviet Cinema at the International Cinema Exhibition] (Moscow: 1934) and *Kinematografiy millionov* [A Cinema for the Millions] (Moscow: 1935).
34  Shumyatskii, 'Signal . . .', pp. 6–7.
35  Shumyatskii, *Kinematografiya millionov*, p. 52.
36  ibid., p. 53.
37  L. V. Kuleshov, 'O zadachakh khudozhnika v kinematografe' [The Tasks of the Artist in Cinema], *Vestnik kinematografii*, no. 126 (1917), p. 15; *FF*, pp. 41–2.
38  L. V. Kuleshov, 'Iskusstvo svetotvorchestva'; *FF*, pp. 45–6.
39  Pudovkin, p. 140.
40  Preface to L. V. Kuleshov, *Iskusstvo kino* (Moscow: 1929), p. 4; Levaco, p. 41; *FF*, p. 270.
41  K. Samarin, 'Kino ne teatr' [Cinema Is Not Theatre], *Sovetskoe kino*, no. 2 (February 1927).
42  I. Sokolov, 'Skrizhal' veka' [The Table of the Century], *Kino-Fot*, 25–31 August 1922, p. 3.
43  G. M. Boltyanskii, 'Iskusstvo budushchego' [The Art of the Future], *Kino*, no. 1/2 (1922), p. 7.
44  G. M. Boltyanskii, *Lenin i kino* [Lenin and Cinema] (Moscow: 1925), pp. 16–17; *FF*, p. 57.
45  B. Z. Shumyatskii, 'Rezhisser i akter v kino' [The Director and the Actor in Cinema], *Iskusstvo kino*, no. 2 (February 1936), pp. 8–9.
46  B. Z. Shumyatskii, 'Dramaturgiya kino' [The Dramaturgy of Cinema], *Sovetskoe kino*, no. 7 (July 1934), p. 4.
47  B. Z. Shumyatskii, 'K chemu obyazyvaet nas yubilei' [What the Anniversary Obliges Us to Do], *Sovetskoe kino*, no. 11/12 (November/December 1934), p. 13.
48  Shumyatskii, 'Tvorcheskie zadachi templana', p. 6.
49  ibid.

50 ibid., p. 7.
51 Shumyatskii, 'Dramaturgiya kino', p. 3.
52 S. M. Eizenshtein, V. I. Pudovkin and G. V. Aleksandrov, 'Zayavka', *Zhizn' iskusstva*, 5 August 1928, pp. 4–5; translated as 'Statement on Sound' in: *FF*, pp. 234–5 and in: *ESW 1*, 113–14.
53 ibid.
54 Shumyatskii, *Sovetskii fil'm*, p. 84.
55 S. M. Eizenshtein, 'Montazh 1938', *Iskusstvo kino*, no. 1 (January 1939), p. 37.
56 Denounced by Mayakovsky among others in a speech during a debate on 'The Paths and Policy of Sovkino' on 15 October 1927; *FF*, pp. 171–4.
57 I. V. Vaisfel'd and G. R. Maslovskii, 'Formirovanie sovetskoi teorii kino' [The Formation of Soviet Film Theory] in: V. V. Vanslov and L. F. Denisova (eds), *Iz istorii sovetskogo iskusstvovedeniya i esteticheskoi mysli 1930kh godov* [The History of Soviet Art History and Aesthetic Thought in the 1930s] (Moscow: 1977), p. 336.
58 Shumyatskii, 'Rezhisser i akter', p. 8.
59 Shumyatskii, 'K chemu . . .', p. 14.
60 Shumyatskii, 'Rezhisser i akter', p. 8.
61 Shumyatskii, *Sovetskii fil'm* . . ., p. 81.
62 B. Z. Shumyatskii, 'O fil'me *Bezhin Lug*' [On the Film *Bezhin Meadow*], *Pravda*, 19 March 1937, p. 3; *FF*, pp. 378–81.
63 ibid.
64 ibid.
65 *Kino*, 22 March 1934, p. 1; 28 March, p. 1; 4 April, pp. 1–2; 10 April, p. 1.
66 Shumyatskii, 'O fil'me . . .', p. 3.
67 See above, n. 14.
68 Shumyatskii, 'Rezhisser i akter', p. 8.
69 The minutes were published as *Za bol'shoe kinoiskusstvo* [For A Great Cinema Art] (Moscow: 1935).
70 Shumyatskii, *Kinematografiya millionov*, p. 8.
71 ibid., p. 31.
72 ibid., pp. 33–4.
73 ibid., p. 8. cf. p. 34.
74 Lebedev, pp. 41–5.
75 *Pyatnadtsatyi s″ezd V.K. P.(b). Stenograficheskii otchet* [Fifteenth Party Congress. Stenographic Report] (Moscow: 1928), p. 60.
76 L. D. Trotskii, 'Vodka, tserkov' i kinematograf' [Vodka, the Church and Cinema], *Pravda*, 12 July 1923; *FF*, pp. 94–7.
77 Shumyatskii, 'Zadachi templana', p. 1.
78 Shumyatskii, *Kinematografiya millionov*, p. 247.
79 ibid., p. 249.
80 ibid., p. 236.
81 ibid., p. 240.
82 ibid., p. 242.
83 Shumyatskii, 'Tvorcheskie zadachi . . .', p. 11.
84 ibid.
85 *SKhF*, vol. 2, p. 67.
86 Shumyatskii, 'Zadachi templana', p. 2.
87 There is an interesting discussion of this film in I. Grashchenkova, *Abram Room* (Moscow: 1977), pp. 134–75.
88 Shumyatskii, *Kinematografiya millionov*, p. 148.
89 ibid., p. 154.
90 ibid., p. 152.
91 Cited in ibid., p. 7.

92 A. P. Dovzhenko, 'Uchitel' i drug khudozhnika' [The Artist's Teacher and Friend], *Iskusstvo kino*, no. 10 (October 1937), pp. 15–16; *FF*, pp. 383–5.
93 Shumyatskii, *Kinematografiya millionov*, p. 36.
94 ibid., p. 38.
95 ibid., p. 18.
96 Macheret's film *Men and Jobs* [1932] dealt with this theme.
97 Reports in *Kino*, 17 July 1933, p. 1, and 23 July 1933, p. 1.
98 *Doklad komissii B. Z. Shumyatskogo po izucheniyu tekhniki i organizatsii amerikanskoi i evropeiskoi kinematografii* [Report of the Shumyatsky Commission to Examine the Technology and Organisation of American and European Cinema] (Moscow: 1935), pp. 5–6. It was only after 1945 that some three dozen German films from the Nazi period went into Soviet distribution. These included the following anti-British propaganda films: *Der Fuchs von Glenarvon* [The Fox of Glenarvon, 1940; Soviet release title: *Vozmezdie* (Retribution), 1949]; *Das Herz der Königin* [The Heart of the Queen, 1940; Soviet release title: *Doroga na eshafot* (The Path to the Scaffold), 1948]; *Mein Leben für Irland* [My Life for Ireland, 1941; Soviet release title: *Shkola nenavisti* (School for Hatred), 1949]; *Ohm Krüger* [Uncle Kruger, 1941; Soviet release title: *Transvaal' v ogne* (The Transvaal in Flames), 1948]; *Titanic* [1943 but never released in Nazi Germany; Soviet release title: *Gibel' Titanika* (The Sinking of the *Titanic*), 1949]. See: M. Turovskaya (ed.), *Kino totalitarnoi epokhi 1933–1945/Filme der Totalitären Epoche 1933–1945* (Moscow: 1989), pp. 45–6.
99 Doklad, p. 148.
100 ibid., p. 57.
101 ibid., p. 150.
102 Rome's *Cine-Città* was also cited with approval: *Yuzhnaya baza sovetskoi kinematografii (Kinogorod)* [The Southern Base for Soviet Cinema (Cine-City)] (Moscow: 1936), p. 18.
103 ibid., p. 16.
104 *Osnovnye polozheniya planovogo zadaniya po yuzhnoi baze sovetskoi kinematografii (Kinogorod)*, [The Basic Propositions of the Planned Project for a Southern Base for Soviet Cinema (Cine-City)] (Moscow: 1936), p. 3.
105 ibid., pp. 9–10.
106 *Yuzhnaya baza*, pp. 20–6.
107 *Osnovnye polozheniya*, p. 11.
108 ibid.
109 ibid., pp. 12, 58.
110 See above, n. 99.
111 B. Z. Shumyatskii, *Sovetskaya kinematografiya segodnya i zavtra* [Soviet Cinema Today and Tomorrow] (Moscow: 1936), p. 50. This is the published text of the report delivered by Shumyatsky to the Seventh All-Union Production and Thematic Conference on 13 December 1935.
112 *Osnovnye polozheniya*, pp. 96–7.
113 As can be seen from the increasing hostility and mockery in newspaper reports appearing throughout 1937 in *Kino* and *Sovetskoe iskusstvo*, e.g.: D. Alekseev, 'Zadachi sovetskogo kino' [The Tasks of Soviet Cinema], *Sovetskoe iskusstvo*, 5 July 1933, p. 3; idem, 'Nemoshchnyi opekun' ['The Powerless Guardian', i.e. Shumyatsky], *Sovetskoe iskusstvo*, 23 July 1937, p. 3; idem, 'Vygodnaya professiya' [A Profitable Profession], *Sovetskoe iskusstvo*, 23 September 1937, p. 5, or the comments made at the First All-Union Congress of the Union of Film Workers at the end of September: see 'Na s''ezde rabotnikov kino' [At the Film Workers' Congress], *Sovetskoe iskusstvo*, 29 September 1937, p. 5. *Kino* was less outspoken, probably because Shumyatsky, as head of the State Directorate for the Cinema and Photographic Industry (GUKF), still had

nominal control over its contents. See the reports of the congress in *Kino*, 17 September 1937, p. 2; 24 September 1937, p. 2; 29 September 1937, pp. 2–3.

114 G. Ermolaev, 'Chto tormozit razvitie sovetskogo kino?' [What Is Holding Up the Development of Soviet Cinema?], *Pravda*, 9 January 1938, p. 4; *FF*, pp. 386–7.

115 To make matters worse, this figure included a number of films carried over from previous years.

116 For details of the prizes awarded in January 1935, see: *Iskusstvo kino*, no. 1 (January 1935).

117 Leonid Trauberg: interview with the author, March 1983.

118 Related to the author by a Soviet cinema historian who wished to remain anonymous, March 1983.

119 *FF*, pp. 386–7.

120 In an editorial entitled 'K novomu pod''emu' [Towards a New Advance], *Kino*, 11 January 1938, p. 1.

121 'Fashistskaya gadina unichtozhena' [The Fascist Cur Eradicated], *Iskusstvo kino*, no. 2 (February 1938), pp. 5–6; *FF*, pp. 387–9.

122 See above, n. 2. Ironically, his old enemy from the days of the 'proletarian hegemony', Vladimir Kirshon, was shot the previous day. Both have been posthumously rehabilitated but the only biography of Shumyatsky was published in Siberia: B. Bagaev, *Boris Shumyatskii. Ocherk zhizni i deyatel'nosti* [Boris Shumyatsky. A Sketch of His life and Activity] (Krasnoyarsk: 1974).

123 V. E. Vishnevskii and P. V. Fionov, *Sovetskoe kino v datakh i faktakh* [Soviet Cinema in Dates and Facts] (Moscow: 1973), p. 116.

124 ibid., p. 123.

125 Interview with the author, April 1985.

126 Vishnevskii and Fionov, p. 170.

127 Leonid Trauberg, one of the directors closest to Shumyatsky, and Yuli Raizman in separate interviews with the author, March 1985.

# Index

In this index film titles are given in English translation. To assist identification, each title is followed by the name of the director and the year of production and/or release.

*Accordion, The* (Savchenko, 1934) 210
acting in cinema 31–50, 103, 118, 143–4, 180, 205–6, 211; the model actor (*naturshchik*) 31–50, 205, 211; Protazanov and stage actors 111
Adorno, Theodor 178
*Aelita* (Protazanov, 1924) 70, 80–102, 103, 109, 111–12, 113, 122, 127
*Aerograd* (Dovzhenko, 1935) 211
Agadzhanova-Shutko, Nina 193
*Age of Majority, The* (Schreiber, 1935) 146
agitation and cinema 51, 54, 84, 191
*Agonising Adventure, The* (Protazanov, 1923) 91
Aleichem *see* Sholom Aleichem
Aleinikov, Moisei 5, 9–10, 84–6, 91, 103, 108–9, 122
*Alexander Nevsky* (Eisenstein, 1938) 211
Alexandrov, Grigori 122, 149, 156, 177, 180, 204, 209
*Alone* (Kozintsev and Trauberg, 1931) 181, 185, 187, 198, 211
Altman, Natan 127–9, 137
*Alyonka* (Barnet, 1961) 161–2
American cinema, and Soviet cinema 140, 145, 151, 158–60, 173–4, 178, 182–3, 213–15; and *Aelita* 92, 96–7, 104; and the avant-garde 51–9; and popular Soviet cinema 72, 104, 117; *see also* Hollywood; Russian endings
*Andrei Kozhukhov* (Protazanov, 1917) 108
Andreyev, Leonid 19–20, 118

*Anka see The Ice Breaks*
Annensky, Innokenti 93
*Annushka* (Barnet, 1959) 151, 161
anti-religious films 109–10
anti-Semitism 97–8, 137, 148, 211
Appia, Adolphe 93
ARK/ARRK 168, 196, 205, 240 n.2
Ars cinema 82
*Arsenal, The* (Dovzhenko, 1929) 191, 196
*Artist i stsena* (newspaper) 26
*Avenger, The* (Shpis, 1931) 139

Babel, Isaak 124, 128, 130–5
Babitsky, Paul 61, 132
Babochkin, Boris 144
Bakhtin, Mikhail 81, 99, 100–1, 192
*Ballet mécanique, Le* (Léger and Murphy, 1924) 48
Ballyuzek, Vladimir 129, 137
*Baltic Deputy, The* (Zarkhi and Kheifits, 1936) 211
Barnet, Boris 2–3, 50, 139, 151–64, 211
Batalov, Nikolai 95, 100, 111, 146
*Battle of Tsaritsyn, The* (Vertov, 1919–20) 52
*Battleship Potemkin, The* (Eisenstein, 1925) 81, 130, 176, 193, 195–6, 205, 211–12
Bauer, Yevgeni 15–17, 106, 111
Bazin, André 176
*Bear's Wedding, The* (Eggert, 1925) 70–1, 82, 195
*Bed and Sofa* (Room, 1927) 121

Bedny, Demyan 54
Bek-Nazarov, Amo 129
Belenson, Alexander 48
Belgoskino 136, 139, 146, 149
Ben-Ari, Raikin 129
Ben-Salim, Kador 140
*Benya Krik* (Vilner, 1927) 130–1, 135
Berlin 65, 69, 70, 79, 84, 87, 103, 109, 132, 213
*Bezhin Meadow* (Eisenstein project, 1935–7) 206–7, 210–11
Birman, Serafima 157
Birobidzhan 148–9
*Black and White* (project 1932) 140
*Black Skin* (Kolomoytsev, 1931) 140
Bleiman, Mikhail 193
Blumenthal-Tamarina, Mariya 113–14, 149
Bogdanov, Alexander 96–7
Bolshakov, Ivan 216
*Border, The* (Dubson, 1935) 146–8
*Boris and Gleb* (Bauer, 1915) 17
*Boris Godunov* (Drankov, 1907) 8–13; (Drankov, 1911) 21–3; and the Moscow Art Theatre 10, 26
*Bounteous Summer* (Barnet, 1951) 151
Bowlt, John 94
Brik, Lily 130
Brik, Osip 139
*Brothers Karamazov, The* and the Moscow Art Theatre 26–9
Brusilovsky, Yevgeni 143
Bryher (Winifred Ellerman) 83
Bryusov, Valeri 10
Burch, Noël 159, 182, 186
*By the Bluest of Seas* (Barnet, 1936) 151–2, 155, 158–9, 163–4
*By Her Mother's Hand* (Protazanov, 1913) 8
*By the Law* (Kuleshov, 1926) 121
*By Water and Smoke* (Kavaleridze, 1933) 146
Bykov, Anatoli 114

*Cabinet of Dr Caligari, The* (Wiene, 1919) 81, 84, 86, 92, 156
*Cabiria* (Pastrone, 1914) 53
*Cain and Artyom* (Petrov-Bytov, 1929) 137–8
Carter, Huntley 92
*Cement* (Vilner, 1927) 132
Chagall, Marc 125

*Chapayev* (Vasilievs, 1934) 144, 186, 194, 211–13
Chaplin, Charles 30, 128, 172–5
Chardynin, Pyotr 15, 20, 21, 23, 106
Chekhov, Anton 9, 17, 21, 26, 119, 161
Chekhov, Mikhail 117–18
Cherkasov, Nikolai 136, 147, 194
Chernyshevsky, Nikolai 97, 99
*Chess Fever* (Pudovkin and Shpikovsky, 1925) 101
Chiaureli, Mikhail 160
Christie, Ian xi, xiii, xiv, 1–5, 80–100, 176–92
Chukhrai, Grigori 160
Cibrario, Jacques 53, 65
*Cine-Phono* (journal) 10, 84
*Circus, The* (Alexandrov, 1936) 149, 194
Civil War, as theme 132, 211–13; Medvedkin and 165–8
Clair, René 25
Clark, Katerina 144
comedy, as genre 116, 122, 194, 208–10; as weapon 166–7, 169–70, 177–8
Commissariat for Internal Affairs *see* NKVD
Commissariat for Light Industry 200
Commissariat for Popular Enlightenment *see* Narkompros
Commissariat of Foreign Trade 71–5, 79
*Communist, The* (Raizman, 1958) 160
*Compilation Sound Programmes* 187
Constructivism 35, 49, 54, 81–2, 84, 94–7, 111, 185
*Conveyor Belt of Death, The* (Pyriev, 1933) 211
*Convict's Song, A* (Protazanov, 1911) 106
*Cosmic Flight* (Zhelyabuzhsky, 1935) 210
*Counterplan* (Ermler and Yutkevich, 1932) 139, 198, 210
Craig, Edward Gordon 33, 93
*Cranes Are Flying, The* (Chukhrai, 1957) 160
*Crime and Punishment* (Dostoyevsky) 28–9
Cubism 84, 93
Cubo-Futurism 81, 93
Cultural Revolution 118–19, 120, 145, 184–7

Dalcroze, Jacque 31–50
dance, and cinema 31–50
Daytsherman, S. 131, 135
*Dead Souls* (Chardynin, 1909) 23
Delluc, Louis 92
Delsarte, F. A. 31–50
*Deluge, The* (Ivanov-Barkov, 1926) 129, 131, 135
*Deserter, The* (Pudovkin, 1933) 140, 181, 189, 193, 211
*detektiv* 52, 96–8, 101
Dickinson, Thorold 83
Dinamov, Sergei 141–3
*Doctor Mabuse* (Lang, 1922) 156
*Don Diego and Pelageya* (Protazanov, 1928) 109, 113–16, 120, 122–3
*Donbass Symphony, The* (Vertov, 1930) 183–5, 187
Donskoi, Mark 148, 160
Dostoyevsky, Fyodor 26–9, 98–9, 100
Dovzhenko, Alexander 103, 130, 139, 154, 156, 185, 191, 207, 211, 213
*Drama by Telephone* (Protazanov, 1914) 7, 52
Drankov, Alexander 8–13, 15, 21–3
Dubson, Mikhail 147
D'Udine, Jean 32
Dukelsky, Semyon 216
Dunayevsky, Isaak 149
Duncan, Isadora 36
*Dura Lex see By the Law*
Dzigan, Yefim 211

*Earth, The* (Dovzhenko, 1930) 156
*Earth Thirsts, The* (Raizman, 1930) 138, 185, 187
Eccentrism 97; *see also* FEKS
Edison 12, 24, 29
Efros, Nikolai 84
Eggert, Konstantin 71, 78, 111, 195
Ehrenburg, Ilya 136
Eikhenbaum, Boris 179
Eisenschitz, Bernard xii, xiii, 151–64
Eisenstein, Sergei 4, 25, 42, 51, 57–8, 60, 79, 86, 101, 103–4, 112, 117, 125, 130–2, 141, 155, 163, 175–84, 191, 193, 196, 201–7, 210–11, 216
Eisler, Hanns 143, 178
Ekk, Nikolai 185, 198, 211
*emes, Der* (newspaper) 131–3, 142
*End of St Petersburg, The* (Pudovkin, 1927) 196

*Engineer Kochin's Mistake* (Macheret, 1939) 156
*Engineer Prite's Project* (Kuleshov, 1918) 49
*Enough Simplicity for Every Wise Man* (Eisenstein stage production, 1923) 25, 125
*Enthusiasm see The Donbass Symphony*
Erdman, Robert 156–8
Ermler, Fridrikh 101, 104, 122, 139, 198, 210, 213
*Ermolieff see* Yermoliev
*Exploits of a Scout, The* (Barnet, 1947) 155, 159
Expressionism 90, 92, 143, 159, 176
Exter, Alexandra 81, 84, 92–5, 111
*Extraordinary Adventures of Mr West in the Land of the Bolsheviks, The* (Kuleshov, 1924) 81, 155, 201
*Eyes That Saw* (Vilner, 1928) 137

Fadeyev, Alexander 146
Faiko, Alexei 82, 90–1, 98–9
Fainzimmer, Alexander 188
Fairbanks, Douglas 116, 120
*Fantômas* (Feuillade, 1913–14) 97
*Father Sergius* (Protazanov, 1918) 108
*Feast of St Jorgen, The* (Protazanov, 1930) 103, 113, 119–21
Fefer, Itzik 135, 137
FEKS 4, 30, 125, 139, 145, 153, 180; *see also* Eccentrism
Ferdinandov, Boris 37, 46–7, 50
film projection speed 13–18
film recitation 19–24
film school (including GIK, GTK, VGIK) 37–40, 42, 44, 49, 51, 83, 114
film train 169–71
*First Platoon, The* (Korsh-Sablin, 1933) 146
Five Year Plan 139, 143–5, 148, 167, 170–1, 184–8, 198, 202
Ford, John 158, 193
Foregger, Nikolai 37, 101
Forestier, Louis 21–2
Formalism 111, 119, 156, 177, 179, 181, 188–9, 191, 196, 201, 206
*Forty-First, The* (Protazanov, 1927) 109, 113–14, 120, 123; (Chukhrai, 1956) 160
*Forward, Soviet!* (Vertov, 1926) 183

*Four and Five* (Gardin, 1924) 85
*Fragment of Empire, A* (Ermler, 1929) 101
*fremde Mädchen, Das* (Hofmannsthal script, 1913) 18
Fuchs, Georg 93
Futurism 81, 93
Fyodorov, Nikolai 97

Gabo, Naum 96
Gabrilovich, Yevgeni 177–8, 199
Gan, Alexei 49
Gardin, Vladimir 16, 28, 36–42, 44, 47, 49–50, 107, 122
Gaumont 24
*Gay Canary, The see The Happy Canary*
*General Line, The* (Eisenstein, 1929) 179, 182, 205
Gerasimov, Sergei 139, 153, 156
*Girl with a Hatbox, The* (Barnet, 1927) 151–2, 154, 157, 164
Gladkov, Fyodor 132
Glavpolitprosvet 110
Glebov-Putilovsky, Nikolai 54
Godard, Jean-Luc 151
Gogol, Nikolai 23
*Gold Rush, The* (Chaplin, 1925) 173
Goldblatt, Moishe 126–7
*Golden Mountains, The* (Yutkevich, 1931) 186–7, 198, 211
Golovnya, Anatoli 181
Goncharova, Nataliya 93
*Gorizont* (Kuleshov, 1932) 146, 152, 211
Gorky, Maxim 138, 156, 203
GOSET (State Yiddish Theatre) 125–7, 130, 138, 147
Goskino 68–70, 73–5, 130, 194
Goslavskaya, Sofiya 8
Gosvoyenkino 167, 171
*Grandma's Boy* (Lloyd, 1922) 173–4
Granovsky, Alexander 125–9, 147
*Great Citizen, A* (Ermler, 1937–9) 194
*Great Consoler, The* (Kuleshov, 1933) 81, 181
*Great Man Passes On, The* (Protazanov, 1912) 90
*Greater Promise, A see Seekers of Happiness*
Gricher-Cherikover, Grigori 127, 131–4, 137

Grierson, John 176
Griffith, D. W. 7, 50–9, 155
GUK/GUKF 201, 207
Gusman, Boris 128
Gutman, David 139, 142, 144, 146
Gzovskaya, Olga 15, 106

Habima Theatre 125, 129, 136
Hansen, Kai 8
*Happiness* (Medvedkin, 1935) 171–5, 209–10
*Happy Canary, The* (Kuleshov, 1929) 201
*Happy Guys, The* (Alexandrov, 1934) 194, 209
*His Call* (Protazanov, 1925) 109, 113–15, 120
*His Excellency* (Roshal, 1927) 135–8
*His Eyes* (Viskovsky and Volkov, 1916) 13, 18
Hitchcock, Alfred 160, 193
Hoberman, J. xii, xiii, 124–50
Hofmannsthal, Hugo von 18–19
Hollywood 69, 180–1, 193, 203, 213–15; 'Soviet Hollywood' 213–15; *see also* American cinema
*Homeland, The* (Dovzhenko project) 130
*Honour* (Bek-Nazarov, 1926) 129
*Horizon, the Wandering Jew see Gorizont*
*House on Trubnaya, The* (Barnet, 1928) 152–3, 156, 164

*I Am Cuba* (Chukhrai, 1963) 160
Ibsen, Henrik 28–9
*Ice Breaks, The* (Barnet, 1931) 156
Ilf, Ilya and Petrov, Yevgeni 154, 238 n.4
Ilyin, Vasili 36–7
Ilyinsky, Igor 95, 97, 100, 111, 113, 115–17, 119, 152, 193
inner speech 179–81, 191–2
intellectual cinema 182
*Interplanetary Revolution* (1924) 101
intertitles, role in early Russian cinema 18–19
*Intolerance* (Griffith, 1916) 50–9; Soviet prologue 58–9
Ioseliani, Otar 163–4
*Iskusstvo kino* (journal) 216
*Ivan* (Dovzhenko, 1932) 139, 185–7, 211

*Ivan the Terrible* (Protazanov project)
  86; (Eisenstein, 1943–7)  157, 163
Ivanov, Vsevolod  190
Ivanov-Barkov, Yevgeni  129
Ivanovksy, Alexander  122
Ivens, Joris  84, 143
*Izvestiya* (newspaper)  53–4, 83

*Jenny the Maid* (Protazanov, 1918)  16
*Jew at War, A see A Man from the
  Shtetl*
*Jewish Luck* (Granovsky, 1925)
  125–30, 132, 134–6, 142, 144
*Jews on the Land* (Room, 1927)  130,
  137
*Jolly Fellows see The Happy Guys*
Joyce, James  181

*K. Sh. E. see Komsomol: Patron of
  Electrification*
Kachalov, V.  118
Kamerny Theatre  81, 93–4, 96
Karalli, Vera  106
Kashnitskaya, Yelena  140, 144
Katayev, Valentin  143, 154, 160, 238
  n.4
Kavaleridze, Ivan  146
Keaton, Buster  128, 155, 172–3
Kepley, Vance  xi, xiii, 51–79
*Keys to Happiness, The* (Gardin and
  Protazanov, 1913)  16, 37, 103, 107,
  109, 111
Khanzhonkov  10, 21–2, 109;
  '*Khanzhonkovshchina*'  118
Khersonsky, Khrisanf  116
Kholodnaya, Vera  17
*Kino* (Kiev newspaper)  134, 137, 148
*Kino* (Moscow newspaper)  132, 216
*Kino-Fot* (journal)  49
*Kino-Front* (journal)  183–4
*Kino-gazeta* (newspaper)  7, 40, 82–3,
  112
*Kinonedelya* (newspaper)  112
Kirshon, Vladimir  213
*Koliivshchina see By Water and Smoke*
Komarov, Sergei  50
Kommissarzhevsky Theatre  117
Komsomol (organisation)  114, 138,
  143
*Komsomol: Patron of Electrification*
  (Shub, 1932)  185
*Komsomolsk* (Gerasimov, 1938)  156
Korsh-Sablin, Vladimir  146

Koval-Samborsky, Ivan  114, 157
Kozintsev, Grigori  103, 139, 152–3,
  181, 185, 198, 202, 211
Kozlovsky, Viktor  96
*Krasnaya nov'* (journal)  87
Kruchinin, Valentin  82
Ktorov, Anatoli  113, 117, 119
Kuindzhi, Valentina  111
Kuleshov, Lev  2, 31–50, 51–2, 80–1,
  84, 97, 101, 103, 112, 141, 152, 176,
  178–9, 191, 201–3, 205, 211;
  'Kuleshov effect'  42, 52, 202;
  experiments  41–8, 52; Workshop
  43, 202
Kurbas, Les  125
Kushnirov, Aron  137
Kuzmina, Yelena  152–3, 155
Kuznetsov, Pavel  93

*Lady Liza* (Sanin project, 1918)  18
*Lake Lyul* (Faiko play)  98
*Lame Gentleman, The* (Eggert, 1928)
  78
*Land Is Calling, The* (Ballyuzek,
  1928)  137
Lang, Fritz  91–2
Langlois, Henri  151, 238 n.1
*Last Laugh, The* (Murnau, 1924)  117
Lavrenev, Boris  109, 114
Lee, Anna  40–1, 46
LEF  37, 86–7, 101
*Legend of the Maiden's Tower, The*
  (Ballyuzek, 1924)  129
Léger, Fernand  48, 92
Legoshin, Vladimir  148
Lejeune, C. A.  176
Lenfilm  146
Lenin, Vladimir  60, 62–3, 65–7, 69,
  71–2, 79, 81, 96–7, 124, 132, 147,
  171, 190, 195, 202, 205
*Lenin in October* (Romm, 1937)  194
Leonidov, Boris  127
Leonidov, Leonid  136
Levinson, André  17–18
Leyda, Jay  2, 61, 101, 132, 142, 157,
  175
L'Herbier, Marcel  92
*Lieutenant Kizhe* (Fainzimmer, 1934)
  188
Linder, Max  25
*Literaturnaya gazeta* (newspaper)  141
*Little Red Devils, The* (Perestiani,
  1923)  140

Lloyd, Harold 172–4
Lodder, Christina 94
*Lone White Sail* (Legoshin, 1937) 160
*Lonely Villa, The* (Griffith, 1909) 7, 52
*lubok* 166–7
Lumière, Louis 20
Lunacharsky, Anatoli 4–5, 53, 60, 67–72, 75, 84–6, 110–11, 122, 136, 168–9, 195, 198
*Lyana* (Barnet, 1955) 164

MacDonald, Dwight 118
Macheret, Alexander 139, 156, 185, 188, 210
Maeterlinck, Maurice 19
Magnitogorsk 143, 145, 148, 150
Makarova, Tamara 194
Malinovskaya, Vera 117
*Man from the Restaurant, The* (Protazanov, 1927) 109, 113, 117–20
*Man from the Shtetl, A* (Roshal, 1930) 138
Maretskaya, Vera 116
Markish, Peretz 139, 142
Marx, Karl 56–7, 144
*Mass Struggle see By Water and Smoke*
Maxim trilogy (Kozintsev and Trauberg, 1934–8) 194, 211
Maximov, Vladimir 15, 30, 106
Mayakovsky, Vladimir 99, 112, 130, 154–5, 195, 203
Medvedkin, Alexander xii, xiii, 3, 164–75, 209–10, 240 n.1
Meisel, Edmund 182
Méliès, Georges 20, 24–5
*Men and Jobs* (Macheret, 1932) 139–40, 185, 188, 190, 210
*Metropolis* (Lang, 1926) 92
Meyerhold, Vsevolod 19, 46, 54, 93, 97–8, 135, 143, 171, 180, 205
Meyerhold Theatre 114
Mezhrabpom, Mezhrabpom-Rus, Mezhrabpomfilm 70, 82, 84–6, 90, 96–7, 101, 103, 111, 118, 154, 157, 195
Mikhoels, Solomon 125–8, 138–9, 141–2, 144, 149
Milman, Rokhl 139, 145
Minkin, Alexander 211
*Miracle Worker, The* (Medvedkin, 1937) 175
*Miss Mend* (Otsep, 1926) 97, 153, 155, 158, 160

Mix, Tom 17
montage 31, 38, 41–5, 47–8, 50–1, 57, 159–60, 176–80, 201–5
Montagu, Ivor 185
Moscow Art Theatre 9–10, 13, 15, 26–9, 31, 82, 84, 117, 136, 155, 180
Mosfilm 162, 164
Mosjoukine, Ivan 15–16, 42, 44–6, 106, 108, 202
Moskvin, Ivan 119
*Mother, The* (Pudovkin, 1926) 196; (Donskoi, 1956) 160
*Mother's Letter, A* (1912) 23
*Moving-Picture World* (newspaper) 7
Mozzhukin, Ivan *see* Mosjoukine, Ivan
Murnau, F. W. 117
music and film 178, 182
musicals 194, 210
*Mystery Bouffe* (Mayakovsky play) 99

*Na literaturnom postu* (journal) 112
Narkompros 36, 60, 64–6, 68, 74–5, 194
nationalisation of cinema 84
*naturshchik see* acting
Nemirovich-Danchenko, Vladimir 9, 27
New Economic Policy (NEP) 62, 67–79, 81–7, 90–1, 96, 98–9, 101, 125, 138–9, 154–5, 177, 226 n.6
*New Babylon, The* (Kozintsev and Trauberg, 1929) 139, 152, 196–7, 202
newsreel 42, 169–70
Nilsen, Vladimir 213
NKVD 150; *see also* OGPU
Notari, Umberto 109
*Novgoroders, The* (Barnet, 1942) 158
Novitskaya, K. 20–4
*Novyi Lef* (journal) 112

*October* (Eisenstein, 1927) 179, 182, 196–7, 202, 205, 212
OGPU 201; *see also* NKVD
Okhlopkov, Nikolai 171, 173, 188, 240 n.5
*Okraina see Outskirts*
*Old and the New, The see The General Line*
*Old Jockey, The* (Barnet, 1940–59) 156–8
Olesha, Yuri 101, 211, 229 n.81

*Once at Night* (Barnet, 1948) 159
*Once One Summer* (Room project)
207, 211
*One September Night* (Barnet, 1939)
155–6
*One-Sixth of the World see A Sixth Part
of the World*
*Oppenheim Family, The* (Roshal,
1938) 211
Ordzhonikidze, Sergo 156
Orlenev, Pavel 24, 28–9
Orlov, Nikolai 9–10, 12
Orlova, Lyubov 194
Orlova, Vera 111
Otsep, Fyodor 13, 82, 84, 98–9, 111,
155
*Our Girls* (Galai, 1930) 138
*Out of Our Way* (Chiaureli, 1931) 160
*Outskirts* (Barnet, 1933) 139–40, 151,
153–4, 157, 191, 211
*Overcoat, The* (Kozintsev and
Trauberg, 1926) 139
Ozarovsky, Yuri 32, 35

*Pages from a Life* (Barnet, 1948) 160
Pale of Settlement 23, 124
Paris 103, 105, 132
Party 61, 86, 129, 132, 136, 197, 200,
206–9
Party Conference, March 1928 118,
184, 196; Ukrainian anti-Semitism
137; January 1935 141, 207–8
*Path to Life, The* (Ekk, 1931) 146,
185–7, 198, 211
Pathé 10–11, 105
*Pavel Korchagin* (Alov and Naumov,
1957) 160
*Peasants* (Ermler, 1934) 210
Perestiani, Ivan 140
Pervomaisky, Leonid 146
Petrov-Bytov, Pavel 129, 137, 196–8
Pickford, Mary 117, 120
*Pilots, The* (Raizman, 1935) 211
Piotrovsky, Adrian 5, 121, 193, 195–6
Piscator, Erwin 84
*Plan for Great Works, The* (Room,
1930) 185, 187
plot 182, 203–4, 206
*Poem of Liberation* (Tarich, 1931)
139
*Poet, The* (Barnet, 1957) 160, 163
*Polikushka* (Sanin, 1918–19) 84
Polonsky, Vitold 15, 17

Popova, Lyubov 94
Popova, Vera 113
*Poslednie novosti* (émigré newspaper)
17–18
*Pravda* (Party newspaper) 82, 85, 90,
128, 216
Preobrazhenskaya, Olga 42, 107
*Proektor* (journal) 15, 16
*Professor Mamlock* (Minkin and
Rappaport, 1938) 21
Prokofiev, Sergei 188
*Proletarskoe kino* (newspaper), on
*Aelita* 112; (journal) 198, 199
Proletkult 25, 97, 125
*Prometheus* (Kavaleridze, 1935) 146
Protazanov, Yakov 3, 15–16, 52–3,
70, 80–123, 127, 157, 190
Pudovkin, Vsevolod 40, 50–2, 79, 84,
103–4, 140–1, 152, 176–82, 189, 193,
198, 202–4, 207, 211
Pulver, Lev 126, 128, 147
Pushkin, Alexander 9–11, 22, 86, 112
Pyriev, Ivan 129, 210–11

*Queen of Spades, The* (Protazanov,
1916) 84, 98, 107

Rabinovich, Isaak 81, 93–6, 111, 127
*Radio-Cine-Pravda* (Vertov, 1925) 183
Raizman, Yuli 138–9, 160, 185, 211
*Ranks and People* (Protazanov, 1929)
109, 113, 119
*Rannee utro* (newspaper) 27
Rappaport, Herbert 211
*Remember Their Faces* (Mutanov,
1930) 138
Renoir, Jean 153
*Return of Nathan Becker, The* (Shpis
and Milman, 1932) 139–46, 149
rhythm and cinema 31–50, 201–2
Rimberg, John 61, 132
*Road to Life, The see The Path to
Life*
Rodchenko, Alexander 97
Rogozhin, Naum 206
Romm, Mikhail 152–3
Room, Abram 98, 102, 130, 137, 185,
207, 211
Roshal, Grigori 135, 138, 211
Rotha, Paul 84, 92, 112
*Rout, The* (Beresnev, 1931) 146
Rus, Russfilm *see* Mezhrabpom
Russian endings 1–2, 7–8

Sabinsky, Cheslav 122
Sadoul, Georges 151–2
Sanin, Alexander 18, 84
*Satan Triumphant* (Protazanov, 1917)
  90, 103, 107–9
Savchenko, Igor 210
Schneider, Evgeni 210
Schreiber, Boris 146
science-fiction 96–8, 109, 111, 210
script competition 85
script crises 202–3, 205
*Seeds of Freedom see His Excellency*
*Seekers of Happiness* (Korsh-Sablin
  and Shapiro, 1936) 149–50
Seltzer, Johann 146, 149
Serapion Brotherhood 101, 229 n.81
*Seven Chances* (Keaton, 1925) 128
*Severe Young Man, A* (Room, 1934)
  101, 211
Sevzapkino 68, 73
Shaginyan, Marietta 97
Shakespeare, William 93–4
*Shchors* (Dovzhenko, 1939) 194, 213
Shipulinsky, Fyodor 40
Shklovsky, Viktor 97, 121, 130, 153,
  156, 203
Shmeliev, Ivan 109, 118
Sholom Aleichem 125–6, 130, 132–4,
  137, 148
Shpis, Boris 139, 145
*Shtetl Ladeniu* (Vilner project, 1933)
  146
Shub, Esfir 185, 191, 203
Shumyatsky, Boris 148, 184–6,
  193–216; Shumyatsky Commission
  213–15
*Silent Witnesses* (Bauer, 1914) 17
*Simple Case, A* (Pudovkin, 1932) 181
*Simple Tailor, A see Eyes That Saw*
*Sixth Part of the World, A* (Vertov,
  1926) 122
*Skotinins, The* (Roshal, 1926) 136
Socialist Realism 120, 145, 187, 205
Sokolov, Ippolit 47, 49, 112, 143,
  184
Solntseva, Yuliya 88, 111
Sologub, Fyodor 18
*Someone Else's Jacket* (Shpis, 1927)
  139
*Son of Mongolia, A* (Ilya Trauberg,
  1936) 149
*Song of Happiness, A* (Donskoi and
  Legoshin, 1934) 148

*Sorochinski Fair* (Gricher-Cherikover,
  1927) 131
sound cinema 176–92, 199–200,
  204–5; shortage of sound projectors
  199–200
Sovkino 75–7, 111, 118, 129, 194–5,
  200
Soyuzkino 137, 146, 148, 184, 194,
  198–201
speaking pictures 19–24
Spengler, Oswald 98
*Squaring of the Circle, The* (Katayev
  play) 154; (Katayev script) 160
Stakhanov, Alexei 156
Stalin, Joseph 54, 62, 79, 138, 160,
  183–4, 186, 208, 213, 215–16
Stanislavsky, Konstantin 9–11, 27, 31,
  179
Starewicz, Władysław 96
*Starving Steppe Revives, The*
  (Shcherbakov, 1925) 129
Sten, Anna 118, 154
*Stenka Razin* (Drankov, 1908) 9, 12, 14
Stepanova, Varvara 94
*Storm Over Asia* (Pudovkin, 1929)
  152, 155
Strelkova, Mariya 119
*Strike, The* (Eisenstein, 1924) 125,
  196, 202, 205
*Submarine Shipwreck* (1911) 26–8
*Suburban Quarters*
  (Griger-Cherikover, 1930) 137
Suprematism 81
*SVD* (Kozintsev and Trauberg, 1927)
  139
Symbolism 91, 93, 96, 98

*Tailor from Torzhok, The* (Protazanov,
  1925) 109, 113, 115–20
Tairov, Alexander 46, 81, 93
*Tanya Skvortsova the Student* (Turkin,
  1916) 18
*Taras Bulba* (Protazanov project) 86
Tarich, Yuri 139
tax on cinema 74–5
Taylor, Richard xi, xiv, 1–5, 61, 184,
  193–216
Taylorism 49, 143, 145
*Tears* (1914) 19
*Teatral'naya gazeta* (newspaper) 16
theatre and cinema 1–50, 180, 201–2
Thiemann and Reinhardt 8, 106–7
Thompson, Kristin 181

*Three Millions Trial, The* (Protazanov, 1926) 70, 109, 113, 116–20
*Three Songs of Lenin* (Vertov, 1934) 18
*Through Tears* (Griger-Cherikover, 1928) 133–5, 137, 142
Tisse, Eduard 42
Tolstoi, Alexei 28, 81–3, 86–91, 97–100, 109
Tolstoy, Lev 19–20, 85, 87, 90, 108
*Tommy* (Protazanov, 1931) 91, 140, 190
*Tractor Drivers, The* (Pyriev, 1939) 194, 210–11
Trauberg, Leonid 30, 103, 139, 152–3, 181, 185, 198, 202, 211, 216
Tretyakov, Sergei 118
Tretyakova, Olga 111
Trotsky, Lev 97, 208
*Tsar Fyodor Ioannovich* (1914) 28
Tsereteli, Nikolai 88, 94, 111
Tsiolkovsky, Konstantin 97
Tsivian, Yuri xi, xiii, 7–30
Turkin, Valentin 37, 40–2, 47–8
*Two Women* (Roshal, 1929) 138
Tynyanov, Yuri 188

Ukraine 93, 105, 125, 127, 129–32, 135, 137–9, 142–3, 148, 159, 172, 213
Ukrainfilm 146; *see also* VUFKU

Vakhtangov Theatre 113
VAPP 110
Vasiliev 'brothers' 211
velvet screens, Gardin's use of 39
Verbitskaya, Anastasiya 107
Vershilov, Boris 129
Vertov, Dziga 79, 84, 86, 101, 103, 122, 155, 177, 183–4, 191, 193, 202–3
*Vestnik kinematografii* (newspaper) 41
VFKO 36, 66, 68–9
*Victory Over the Sun* (1913 opera production) 94
Vilner, Vladimir 130–2, 137, 146
Vishnevsky, Venyamin 5
Viskovsky, Vyacheslav 15
Voitsik, Ada 114
*Volga Rebels* (Petrov-Bytov, 1925) 129
*Volga-Volga* (Alexandrov, 1938) 156, 194
Volkonsky, Prince Sergei 32–3, 35–7, 39–41, 43–5, 47, 49–50
Volkov, Alexander 37

Volpin, Mikhail 156–8
Voznesensky, Alexander 19, 50
Vostokkino 138, 148
VUFKU 125, 129–35, 137–8; *see also* Ukrainfilm

*Wandering Stars* (Gricher-Cherikover, 1928) 130–5
*War and Peace* (Protazanov and Gardin, 1915) 107
War Communism 62–7
*Way of the Enthusiasts, The* (Okhlopkov and Medvedkin, 1930) 171
*We Don't Need Blood* (Protazanov, 1917) 108
*We from Kronstadt* (Dzigan, 1936) 149, 194, 211
Wells, H. G. 96–8
*Whistle-Stop* (Barnet, 1963) 161–3
*White Eagle, The* (Protazanov, 1928) 109, 113, 117–20, 122
Wilde, Oscar 93
Willemen, Paul 181
*Wings of a Serf, The* (Tarich, 1926) 121, 129
*Without a Dowry* (Protazanov, 1937) 121–2
*Woman in the Window* (Lang, 1944) 91
Workers' International Relief 70–1, 84–6
*Wrestler and the Clown, The* (Barnet, 1957) 151, 155, 161

Yampolsky, Mikhail xi, xiii, 31–50
Yarmolinsky, Avram 125
Yermoliev (studio) 84, 92, 107–9
Yevsektsiya 125, 128, 136, 138, 148
Yiddish cinema 3, 23, 124–50
Youngblood, Denise xii, xiii, 103–23
Yutkevich, Sergei 104, 139, 186, 198, 211

Zamyatin, Yevgeni 80, 88, 101, 229 n.81
Zhdanov, Andrei 54, 145
Zhdanov, Yakov 20–1
Zhelyabuzhsky, Yuri 84, 111, 210
Zhizneva, Olga 117
Zorich, Bella 114
Zorkaya, Neya 123
Zuskin, Venyamin 126, 138, 147, 149
*Zvenigora* (Dovzhenko, 1929) 196